A Boy CALLED *Kid*

Thelma Inman

ISBN 978-1-64416-671-0 (paperback)
ISBN 978-1-64416-672-7 (digital)

Copyright © 2018 by Thelma Inman

All rights reserved. No part of this publication may be reproduced, distributed, or transmitted in any form or by any means, including photocopying, recording, or other electronic or mechanical methods without the prior written permission of the publisher. For permission requests, solicit the publisher via the address below.

Christian Faith Publishing, Inc.
832 Park Avenue
Meadville, PA 16335
www.christianfaithpublishing.com

Printed in the United States of America

Acknowledgment

I WOULD LIKE TO THANK all the people that gave me the encouragement to continue writing my father's stories. Without them, I wouldn't have finished it.

Introduction

A BOY CALLED KID COULD have been written by five different people. Each of Tom's children could have written it, and each would have written it in their own way and how they remembered him. Even though all five stories would be different, all five stories would have been true. Also, it would have been more accurate and true if the first three had written it because they lived through it while Ethel and I only heard the stories.

There were no televisions back then and very few people had radios. Also, no one had air-conditioning. In the summer months, the house would be too hot to stay inside until the sun went down and it began to cool off. So we would sit out on the front porch, and Daddy would tell us stories about his life when he was growing up. Just remember, all the stories are based on stories told to a little girl from the time she was around six or seven or so until she was a teenager. I couldn't swear they are the gospel truth. They are stories written by a ninety-one-year-old woman looking back on her childhood and trying to remember all the stories that her daddy told to her.

Tom wasn't a perfect man by no means. He had his faults just like any other person, but in the eyes of a six-or seven-year-old who looked on him always as her hero and her friend, his good points seemed to always outweigh his bad points in her eyes.

The way the story is written is through the eyes of a six-or seven-year-old and how she remembered it. Tom didn't always finish all the stories completely, so she had to use her imagination, from what he did tell her to how she thought it would have ended. I am sure in knowing how she felt about her daddy, that they would always finish to his advantage.

Also Tom wasn't a well-educated man. He was homeschooled. It probably would have been somewhere between a second, third, or fourth grade education in our standards today. Also after he started working on the ranch full time, he had very little time to use what he had learned. What he did use he remembered well, and no one could cheat him on how much they owed him in wages or in a trade. He would always know what they owed him before they could write it down and had it added up. His English was not always perfect, but that many years ago not too many people's were.

In reading the book, just remember this, these stories are based on what was told to a little girl about her daddy's life and the way he told them. I can't swear to the years, dates, times, and places. It wasn't important to her but just listening to him tell them. I can just hear him say, "Well, sister, you can't always please everyone. Just let them read the book and draw their own conclusion. Whether they are true, partly true, or you and your daddy are two mighty good storytellers or the biggest liars in Texas."

Thelma (Brisco) Inman
In memory of her beloved daddy

Chapter 1

THOMAS JOSHUA WAS BORN TO Kathryn Louisa (Ensey) and James Harrison Brisco. He was the oldest child of five children—Mary Ann, John Washington II, Sallie Elizabeth, and Becky. His mama died when he was eight years old. His dad had gone to town for supplies. She was pregnant with her sixth child. His dad told Tom he was putting him in charge while he was gone. He told him, "Be sure you have the water in and the wood before night. Also, be sure to put all the chickens in the henhouse, the eggs gathered up, and the cow milked."

Tom's mama hadn't felt good all day. He had watched the kids, done the outside work, and fixed dinner and supper for them. Then he had tried to get his mama to eat something, but she said she wasn't hungry. It was around six when he heard his mama call for him. Tom said, as long as he lived, he would never forget that night. Mama told him she was real sick and she wanted him to go get Grandpaw. He lived about a mile away. He remembered her saying, "Now, Tom, I know it's a long way to have to send you, but I don't have anyone else to send. You hurry as fast as you can and tell Paw I need him and to hurry."

Tom ran as fast as he could. He felt like his legs wouldn't take another step. He would stop and get his breath and run again. As soon as the house came into sight, Tom started hollering as loud as he could and waving his arms. Grandpaw and his hired hand was sitting on the front porch. As soon as they saw him, Grandpaw told the hired hand, "Something's wrong at Kathryn's house" and for him to hitch the horse to the buggy as fast as he could. He met Tom before he got to the house.

As Tom crawled into the buggy, he hollered, "Mama is real sick. She said come as fast as you can." Tom said later he didn't think he had ever rode that fast in a buggy, before or after. Grandpaw cracked the whip over the horse's head and hollered all the way. When they got there, he told Tom to take care of the horse and he was gone. As soon as Tom had cooled the horse down and put her in the lot, Tom rushed into his mama's room. Grandpaw was holding her hand. Tom heard her say, "God bless Harrison and the children." And then she was gone. Some way, they got in touch with Papa. Tom felt like he had let his papa down because he had left him in charge. Aunt Lou, Kathryn's sister, came; and somehow they got through the next few days and the funeral. They buried her with the baby boy that caused her to die in the same coffin.

Although their lives had fallen apart, Papa said, "We must go on. Mama wouldn't want us to grieve so." So the next week they started life as usual. On a farm there are always things that have to be done. Papa had the plowing to get done for the coming crop. He took all five of the children to the field. He took one of Kathryn's quilts and made a pallet at the end of the row so he could check on them when he made each round. John was supposed to help Tom watch the girls. At first it worked out all right. The girls were sleepy, and they slept almost all morning. After that they wanted to play, and the pallet wasn't big enough for too much playing.

Harrison plowed from sunup to sundown. It was the second or third week that little Becky took sick. She was running a high fever by that afternoon. Harrison told the kids that Becky had taken pneumonia, and by morning she was dead. Papa buried her beside Mama. Aunt Lou came for the funeral. She stayed two days and helped Papa with the work. Tom heard his papa tell her the house was a mess but he had to get the fields ready to plant. They have got to come first. After he got home each night, he still had the cow to milk. Tom and John gathered up the eggs and got in the water, but he still had supper to fix and the girls to bathe and put to bed.

"Lou," Tom heard him say, "I just don't know what I am going to do. Tom and John helps, but they are just boys, and there is just so much they can do."

After two days Aunt Lou went home. She was having troubles of her own. Her husband had died a few months before, leaving her with five small children and a farm to run.

The next day after she went home, Harrison didn't go to the field. He just sat around most of the day, like he was in deep thought. The next morning he got up early and fixed breakfast, and as soon as they got all the chores done, he called John and Tom together. He told them he was going to be gone all day. "Now you and John watch after the girls." He told them he would be back before dark.

Tom didn't know what was going on, and he didn't find out until he was grown, and that was years later. But that night when he came home, Aunt Lou and all her kids came with him. Papa just told all of them that he and Aunt Lou had just gotten married and she and her kids would be living with them from now on. She started fixing supper as if she owned the place, Tom thought. Harrison and Tom went out to do the night work, and Aunt Lou's kids began to unload the buggy. Just before they went out, Harrison told Lou tomorrow they would take the wagon and go get the rest of her things.

While Papa and Tom were in the barn, Tom tried to tell him that they could have made it without Aunt Lou and all her kids. Papa looked real hurt and told him, "Now, Tom, I am going to tell you this just one time, and I expect it not to be brought up again. I lost Becky by trying to do it all by our self, and I am not taking any chances of losing any more of my children. Tom, don't you see, you kids are all of Kathryn I have left."

Later years, after Tom came home again, Harrison told him that day and night was the longest night and day he had ever spent in his whole life. He said he had prayed most all that whole day and night that God would show him a way that he could raise his children. Grandpa had come over that day and told him that the bank was going to foreclose on Lou's farm. He said, "They didn't know what they were going to do. Guess they will have to move in with me." God had showed him a way.

He told Tom if he remembers that morning. He had left early. He was never so scared. He had gone over to Lou's house. When she came to the door, he told her, "Lou, I have to talk to you," and walked in. She gave him a cup of coffee, and they sat down at the kitchen table. He laughed and told her again that he had to talk to her but he just didn't know how to begin.

She looked at him real funny, then told him, "Well, Harrison, just start talking and I will listen."

He knew she would help him any way she could. He told her, "Lou, you know, I can't work the farm, take care of the kids, the house, and everything by myself. The kids try to help all they can, but they are just kids." Harrison told her, Paw told him she was about to lose her farm because she couldn't work it and take care of her kids. He told her he had a proposition to put to her. That he could make them all a good living if she would agree to take care of both his and her children and the house.

She told him she had prayed ever since the man from the bank told her they were going to have to take the farm or have some money on the note. She told him she had prayed that God would show her a way that she could take care of her children.

"Well, Harrison," she told him, "I guess God had answered both our prayers. It won't be easy, but if it's God's will, we could make it." They went to the preacher's house, got married, got her children, and came home.

It wasn't easy with nine children in a house. Aunt Lou took care of all the children, cooked the meals, kept the house, and did the washing and ironing. Each day, while she and the girls got supper, all the larger boys did the outside chores. They tried to have most of it done before Papa got home. He would work until dusty dark and be back in the field at daylight. Then he would work until dinner and come home. Aunt Lou would always have dinner ready. They would eat, and Papa would change horses and go back to work. In the afternoon Aunt Lou would put the small kids down for a nap while she cleaned the kitchen. In the middle of the afternoon, she would take turns sending some of the boys to the field with a fresh jug of ice-cold water from the well. For two families of children in a house, eleven in all, things went along fairly well. They had their amount of fights and fusses, especially the larger boys. The girls and smaller kids seemed to get along better.

Tom resented Aunt Lou and her kids. He didn't like all of them being there in their house, and he didn't like her staying in his mama's room and especially sleeping in his mama's bed. He was really just mad because she was alive and his mama was dead. It appeared to him that his papa was letting her take his mama's place, and he didn't like it. It kept boiling up until one day it just had to explode.

Sallie and Eva Jewel were playing together, and Sallie took a toy away from Eva Jewel. Aunt Lou made her give it back. Aunt Lou told her, "Eva Jewel had it first, and you need to learn to share." Sallie began to hit Eva Jewel, kicking and screaming. Aunt Lou caught her by the shoulders and barely shook her, saying, "No, no, you can't have it." The more she tried to stop her, the more she screamed and cried. Aunt Lou told her, "Little girl, you can't get by throwing a fit like this." And she turned her over and began to spank her.

Tom resented her already, and when she began to spank his little sister that was just too much. He was setting at the table, and he picked up a butcher knife and threw it at Aunt Lou. As soon as he did it, he regretted it. Aunt Lou looked real shocked and hurt. She told him, "You won't get by with that either, young man," and started toward him. He turned and ran out the kitchen door. She ran to the door and hollered, "You just wait until tonight when your papa gets home." Tom knew he was in serious trouble. He started crying and running. He didn't know where he was going, only one thing he knew, he couldn't go back. He knew his papa wouldn't let him get by with that either. He ran and cried until he came to their church building. It was also their school building during school time.

Tom was hot, tired, and thirsty. He sat down in the shade of the building. He had never been so alone in his whole life. He had lost his mama, and now he was losing his papa and the rest of his family. He didn't know what he was going to do. Only one thing he knew, he just couldn't go back. By then it was getting late in the afternoon. He crawled under the building and started crying again. He must have cried himself to sleep because the next thing he heard was some men calling his name.

Then he heard his papa say, "Just wait until I get a hold of that kid." He was going to beat him half to death. Tom lay real still until he couldn't hear them anymore. He was still afraid they might be close by, so he waited what seemed like hours to him. It was pitch-dark by then, and he was so scared he didn't know what to do. Every noise he heard he thought it was a bugger coming after him. He would hold his breath and crawl a little farther back under the building and lay there.

The night wore on, and he began to see eyes staring at him everywhere. He couldn't stay under that building another minute, so he crawled out and started running. Every step he took, Tom just knew something was going to grab him. He cried and ran all night.

Just at daylight he came to this place where they were unloading cattle out of some long boxcars. Tom had never seen a train, but his papa had told him about them, and he knew this was one. He stood there looking at it and all the cattle they was unloading. He was a sorry-looking little tike. He had run and cried all night on a dirt road with no shoes or shirt on; and his overalls was dirty, sweaty, and had patches over them. His face had tear streaks mingled with dirt all over it, and his auburn hair was tangled and blown everywhere. He looked up to see a man coming toward him. He had a star on his shirt. Tom knew he had to be the law. He wanted to run, but he was afraid to. So he just stood there and waited for him. He came up beside him and said, "Howdy, son." Tom spoke back, and then the man said, "Son, have you ran away from home? What is your name?" Tom knew better than to give his real name, so he said Tom Allen.

About that time this real nice-dressed man came up. He had on real nice-looking pair of pants, a cowboy shirt, and a big black hat. Later on, Tom learned it was a Stetson. He spoke to the lawman. Then he put his arm around Tom's shoulder and told him, "No, he is with me."

The man with the star on his shirt asked him how many cattle did he bring this time and a lot of other stuff that Tom didn't understand. Tom stood there just about scared out of his wits, and that star hadn't made him feel any better.

The lawman said, "Well, guess I had better make my rounds," and turned to leave.

The other man, whose name Tom learned later was Mr. Heart, said, "Hold up and I'll walk a piece with you." Mr. Heart turned to Tom and said, "Son, wait right here and I'll be right back." They walked a little ways off and stood there talking. Tom said later if he had any smart he would have known Mr. Heart was telling the policeman that he was probably a runaway and that the policeman would know where Tom was if anything came up. Mr. Heart took Tom down to a store and told the man he needed some new clothes for this lad. He also bought Tom a hat like his and some new boots. That's when Tom found out that the hat was a Stetson. Mr. Heart said the sun got mighty hot on the ranch where they were going and he would need it. Tom had never had a hat, a cap, but never a hat. And, boy, did he think he was something else. He told Mr. Heart thank you. Then Tom realized he didn't have any money to pay for all these things, and he told Mr. Heart so. He told him not to worry, that he would take it out of his pay when they get to the ranch and he started working.

Mr. Heart took Tom over to the hotel and told them that this lad needs a bath. They took them up to a room and brought in a tub and plenty of hot water. Then Mr. Heart told Tom to hurry and get bathed and dress so they could eat before the train left. Tom had never been in a hotel, let alone eat in one. Mr. Heart waited for him until he bathed and dressed, and when he came down with all his new clothes on, Mr. Heart told him, "Boy, don't you look like a little buckaroo." He had him turn around so he could see them. Tom strutted like a little bantam rooster. He had never in all his life had a full set of clothes before and never anything that looked like these. He had never seen any cowboy boots and hat, let alone wearing them.

They went down to eat breakfast. A woman came over and led them over to a table, and they sat down. She asked Mr.

Heart what he would like to have. He looked at Tom and said, "Kid, are you hungry?" Tom just realized he hadn't had anything to eat since dinner the day before. He told him, you betcha he was. So Mr. Heart said he would order for them. Tom had never seen such a plate of food, but he was hungry and ate ever bit of it. Then Mr. Heart asked him if he could eat a piece of pie. He told him it would be tomorrow before they got a chance to eat a meal again. They finished their pie and went over to catch the train. Anyway, when he left on the train, Tom left with him with a whole set of new clothes, a hat, and some boots.

The conductor was hollering, "All aboard" before they got there, so they just had time to get on and go right to their seats. Mr. Heart asked Tom if he would like to sit by the window, and what boy wouldn't. Tom. Just today has seen his first train, and now he was riding on one. He was so excited he could hardly stay still.

The train finally started. Tom watched out the window as the country started going by at first slow, then faster and faster. Mr. Heart had finally lain back and was sound asleep. There was so much to see Tom thought he would never sleep, but before long he began to get drowsy, and the next thing he knew it was daylight and Mr. Heart woke up about that time.

He said, "Good morning, did you sleep good?"

Tom told him, "I guess so. I don't know what time I went to sleep but am just now waking up."

Mr. Heart laughed and said he guess he did to as he was just now waking up also. He told Tom they would be at their stopping place sometime around five or six o'clock, if they were lucky. He asked Tom if he was hungry, and he pulled out a cloth with four biscuits with bacon and scrambled eggs on them that they had fixed for him at the hotel. They were cold, but they sure were good anyway. They ate in silence as they watched the country going by. Mr. Heart told him that they would come to the end of the train track and then some of his men would meet them with horses and the chuck wagon.

Tom didn't know what a chuck wagon was and asked him. He told him it was a covered wagon with food in it and a cook to fix their meals while they traveled on to the ranch. He said it would take three or four days according to how good of time they made. All of a sudden, as if he had just thought of it, he asked, "Tom, have you ever rode a horse?"

Tom thought a minute and said, "Well, not with a saddle on, but I use to ride bareback when we brought the cows from the pasture."

Mr. Heart noticed he hesitated before he answered him. He didn't want to make the kid lie, so he didn't ask any more questions. Tom took a big sigh of relief because he didn't know what he would have told him if he had asked him anything else.

Sure enough, late that afternoon the train began to whistle. Mr. Heart told him they were at the end of the track. They gathered up their things and were ready to get off by the time the train stopped. Some men begin to back a wagon up to one of the boxcar doors. A man opened it, and they begin to unload the boxcar. Mr. Heart hollered at the men. They all hollered back and asked him about his trip. He and Tom got off the train, and Mr. Heart told them, "Boys, I would like you all to meet a new hired hand I hired while I was gone. This is Tom Allen, boys." He told them he expected them to make him welcome also show him the ropes until he learns his way around. He told Tom, "You wouldn't remember all their names right now if I told you." Then he told them, "I'm hungry. Let's get this job over with so we can go eat. Are you camped in the usual place?" One of the men shook his head yes. Mr. Heart hollered at the man that was standing inside the boxcar and told him, "Bob, Tom can ride with you."

He told them as soon as they got the other wagons loaded he would meet them at the camp ground, and he was gone. They had finished loading one wagon, and another man they called John was pulling his wagon up to the door to be loaded.

The man they called Bob was standing inside the boxcar with several papers in his hands. He would call out, "Flour, twenty sacks. Sugar, ten sacks. Coffee, ten …," until everything on the list was called out and was loaded. Then he would holler, "Next," and the wagon would pull out and another one would pull up. Tom stood looking at them. He had never seen that many wagons being loaded and especially not that fast.

Jim, the man driving the next wagon, hollered, "Hey, kid, so you are going to be a rooten-tooten cowboy."

Tom saw he was kidding him so, he hollered back, "I don't know about the rooten-tooten part, but with all of your help, I hope to make a dog gone good cowboy."

They all laughed, and Jim said, "Well, guess our work is cut out for us. Guess we just as well began now. Come on over here, kid, and crawl up on the wagon and hold these horses while they load 'em up."

Tom ran over feeling six feet tall and climbed up on the seat next to him.

Jim laughed and asked him, "You do know how to hold them, don't you, kid?"

Tom saw he was still kidding, so he reached over and took the reins and told him, "Now, Jim, you just take care of your loading job and leave the horses to me."

They all laughed again, and Bob told them, "Well, boys, I can see we have got a cocky little rooster on our hands to tame."

They all shook their heads and said they shore have and boy was they going to have fun doing it. In the next months to come Tom was to find out they were going to keep their word.

They had several wagons to load, and as soon as one was loaded, a man would climb up and take the reins. Before he pulled the loaded wagon out of the way, Tom would jump off and be waiting for the next wagon to pull up, then he would jump on and finish pulling it up to the door, then the driver would jump off and help load it. He did this until all the wagons were loaded and Bob hollered, "That's all, boys." He climbed upon the wagon where Tom was and said, "Kid, you did a good job." Boy, did that make Tom's head swell. He was as proud as punch. Bob waved his arm and hollered, "Let's roll 'em, the food's getting cold." The men that had horses climbed upon them, and the wagons started rolling. They drove down a dirt street through town, but it wasn't much of a town (a few stores and a corral with some horses in it).

About half a mile out of town Tom saw a covered wagon in a grove of trees. Bob told Tom that was where they were going. They all got down and began to eat, and boy was it good. One of the boys said, "Kid, do you drink coffee," Tom didn't, but he wasn't about to let them know it. So he poured him a cup, and Tom sat there drinking it just as big as the rest of them. It was so bitter he could hardly drink it.

Mr. Heart wasn't there yet, but it wasn't long until he came in. He must have taken a shortcut because he came from behind the chuck wagon. After they all had finished eating, they sat around the fire sipping on another cup of coffee. Finally, Mr. Heart got up and went around the chuck wagon. No one paid much attention to him until he came back leading the prettiest little mare Tom had ever seen. It was a beautiful roan with two white stockings on its back legs and a white heart between its eyes.

Mr. Heart finally said, "Well, kid, are you going to just stand there, or are you going to come over here and take her." He told Tom he thought if he was going to make a cowboy he would need something to ride. He didn't have to tell Tom twice. He was over there before Mr. Heart could say another word. "Now, Tom," Mr. Heart told him, "she is yours as long as you stay at the ranch and as long as you take good care of her. But if I catch you neglecting her, I will take her away so fast it will make your head spin." He went on to tell him that he was to take care of her and that means brushing, feeding, watering, and seeing to all her needs. He would be responsible for her training. "Remember, a man is just as good as his horse."

Tom told him he would take good care of her, that Mr. Heart wouldn't have to worry about that. Tom had never seen a horse as pretty as this one. "What's her name?" he asked Mr. Heart.

"Well, Tom," Mr. Heart told him, "I thought, if she is to be your horse, that you would like to name her."

Tom told him, "The white heart in her forehead stands out so much. How about calling her Hart."

Mr. Heart said, "Well, that's okay with me, if it suits you. It's your horse, kid." Tom told him it suited him just fine. So Mr. Heart said it was settled. His new horse would be called Hart.

They were up early the next morning. Pete had breakfast going—biscuits, scrambled eggs, dry salt meat, gravy, and plenty of coffee. Mr. Heart told Tom to grab a biscuit or two with meat and eggs on it. They wouldn't stop for a hot meal until suppertime. They got the teams hitched, their own horses saddled, and were ready to go in no time flat.

Mr. Heart showed Tom how to put the saddle on and how to get it tight enough so it would stay. Tom got on, and Mr. Heart adjusted the stirrups, short enough for him. Boy, did Tom think he was really something, with his brand-new clothes on, a new Stetson hat, and sitting on his very own horse. Mr. Heart told Tom to ride next to him.

The riding was rough. They stopped when they found a creek to let the horses drink. Mr. Heart told him, "Now, Tom, always see to your horse first. Let her cool down, then make sure you water her good. Remember when you are out like this, you have to depend on your horse to take you where you are going and that you wouldn't last a day in this heat without her."

About noon they found a creek with a nice shade and plenty of green grass. They unsaddled their horses, and Mr. Heart showed Tom how to hobble his horse so she wouldn't wander too far off, and they all rested while the horses grazed. They all put their saddles in the shade, and no one had to tell Tom to lie down and rest. Tom had never been this tired in all his life. He must have dozed off immediately.

The next thing he heard was someone calling, "Kid, you better get up and get your water container filled and eat your biscuit. We are almost ready to pull out." Everyone was sitting around eating their biscuit and drinking coffee that Jake had made. Tom found out that each time they stopped to let the horses rest, Jake always made a pot of coffee. They only had their cold biscuit, but they always had a cup of hot coffee to go along with it. It sure tasted good. They sat around talking and kidding Tom while they ate.

After the first day all the men started calling him Kid. It stuck, and from then on, they all called him Kid.

Jim hollered, "Hey, Kid, do you think you will make it until suppertime without falling off your horse."

Tom knew he was kidding him again, so he straightened his shoulders and told them, "I will still be on my horse when you all fall off yours."

They all laughed, and Mr. Heart said, "Well, little buckaroo, it's time to get our horses saddled and get going." Mr. Heart told him make sure he had plenty of water in his canteen and for him to empty and fill it with fresh cold water each time they stopped, that they never knew how far it would be to the next water hole and "Believe me, good cold water will taste real good along the way."

They rode all evening. Mr. Heart asked him once if he wanted to ride awhile in the wagon with the cook. It was sure tempting, but he wasn't going to let the boys think he couldn't take it. He had bragged that he would still be in his saddle when the last one of them fell off and by George he would be even if it killed him.

The afternoon was long and hard, but late in the evening they came to a real shady meadow with a river running through it. Mr. Heart said, "Well, Kid, this is where we spend the night. It's time to get down and water your horse and brush her down real good." Mr. Heart showed Tom how to brush her down and hobble her again. If they were lucky, Old Jake would have supper ready by then. Well, he didn't, but all the men were headed toward the river with a bar of soap and a towel in their hands. So Tom grabbed his and headed along. He was so dirty from eating dust all day, and he didn't think he had ever had a bath that felt so good. Everyone was too tired to do much kidding. But Bob did say, "Kid, you sure surprised us." They didn't think he would last that long. Tom grinned and told him that he had told them he would be in his saddle as long as the rest of them. They all laughed at him again, and one told him, "Well, Kid, you sure did." Tom was tired, but that made him feel like he was six feet tall again. He felt like he was just as big as any of them.

They all ate their supper, checked their horses one more time, and found them a good comfortable place to pitch their bedroll; and using their saddle for a pillow, they went to bed. Tom was so tired and sore. Every bone in his body seemed to be hurting. He thought he would never go to sleep, but he must have gone to sleep shortly after his head hit the saddle. It was daylight before he knew it, and the cook was hollering breakfast time. Again, they had biscuits, eggs, gravy, and dry salt meat. They all ate and fixed them some biscuits, eggs, and meat to put in their saddlebags for dinner. They all were fixing two, so Tom fixed two also. After they had eaten, they hitched the horses up to all the wagons. Then they saddled their horses and began their second day.

Bob hollered and asked him, "Hey, Kid, how are you doing?"

Well, right then Tom would have gladly traded that horse and saddle for a good soft bed. He was so sore he had trouble getting on the horse, but he wasn't about to let them know it. So he hollered back, "Doing just fine."

Mr. Heart said, "Kid, it will be easier today, and before long you will be riding like you've rode all your life. If you should get tired, you can go ride in the wagon with Bob. That would rest you, and besides, Bob will be glad to have someone to talk to."

About midmorning Mr. Heart told him, "Now, Kid, Hart is getting tired. I'm going to tie her to the back of Bob's wagon, and you go ride with him for a while. The horse is not used to long rides either, and she needs a rest."

Boy, was Tom glad that Hart needed a rest. He was so tired he was about to fall out of his saddle. He asked Mr. Heart how much longer did they have to go. He said if they were lucky they would have about two more days.

Tom made that day a lot better, but he knew Mr. Heart was thinking of him a lot more than he was of Hart. It was about one o'clock or after when they finally found a shady place by a creek with plenty of grass for the horses. They stopped and watered the horses and hobbled them. Tom rubbed Hart down good and went over to lie in the shade and eat his biscuits with the rest of them. Pete as usual had made a pot of coffee to go along with their cold biscuits. They all lay in the shade and rested while the horses rested and grazed. Every day after that Mr. Hart would insist that he ride in the wagon so Hart could have some rest. By then Tom knew for sure he was thinking about him getting some rest more than Hart, but he didn't let on.

Sure enough, on the fourth day, about two o'clock, give or take some, they came to a gate on the right side of the road. The gate had two large post, one on each side of the road that led away from the main road. It had a big wide board from one post to the other, and on each side of the board it had a big heart. In the center, in great big letters, it read, "Our Home."

Mr. Heart told Tom, "Well, Kid, this is it. This will be your new home." He asked Tom if he could see that house away off in the distance. Tom could just barely see it. Mr. Heart told him that was their home and would be his as long as he wanted it. It seemed to Tom that they traveled about two hours or more before they finely got there. Tom noticed, ever since they came through the gate, that all along some wagon would turn off and wave to them. This went on until there were only three left. The house set back from the road a good piece and quite a distance behind it were several barns. The house was made of logs, and Tom never saw anything so big. It had a porch all around the house and at the front and back. It had several wooden rockers with small wooden tables sitting between them. John stopped at the back of the house, and some of the boys began to unload his wagon.

Bob and the other drivers drove their wagons on down to one of the buildings. It set off from the rest of them and had a porch all across the front with rockers setting all along it. Also, it had several shade trees around it. Later, Tom found out it was the bunkhouse where the men lived. It had two rooms with beds in it and several rockers setting around the room. In the kitchen it had the biggest table Tom had ever seen. Bob pulled up to it, and the other boys began to unload his wagon. Mr.

Heart and Tom road their horses down to another barn and unsaddled them. There was a wooden rail along each side in the barn. It ran the whole length of it. Mr. Heart told him it was where they hung their saddles. They put their saddles up and brushed their horses good, then turned them loose in a big fenced pasture.

They walked to the house. It was a pretty good little walk, but it sure felt good to walk after all the riding they had been doing. A little white-headed woman stood on the back porch waving at them. She met them at the steps and hugged Mr. Heart and asked him if they had a good trip. He told her it was a real good trip and the cattle brought a real good price.

Then he turned to Tom and said, "Mama, this is Tom Allen, a new man I've hired while I was gone."

She came over and shook his hand real friendly like and said, "Tom Allen, I am real proud to meet you." The way she acted you would have thought that she was use to her son bringing in stray boys every time he went off.

Mr. Heart told her, "Tom will be staying at the house, and he will help you when we don't need him."

They talked awhile about the trip, then she said she would go in and get supper while they stayed out there and rested. Tom asked her if he could help her, and she said no, but she appreciated him asking.

Mr. Heart told Tom that tomorrow he wanted him to start training Hart. He told Tom when he was out like this, it is real important for his horse to learn to obey him, that he would teach her to come when he called her and stay where he left her, that he must talk to her until she knew the sound of his voice, and to never be mean to her or speak real cross to her. Let her gain his trust, and when she does, she will do anything for him, even risk her own life for him. Let her know he loved her, and she will love him in return. "Remember, your horse will be as good as you train her to be."

About that time Granny heart called supper was ready and they went in. She had fried chicken, cream potatoes, gravy, green beans, and hot biscuits. Mr. Heart commented on how good it tasted after chuck wagon food. Then she brought out a big peach cobbler.

After that they all cleaned the kitchen and as soon as they got through, Mr. Heart said, "Well, Tom, I don't know how you feel, but a bed sure sounds good to me. After all those nights of sleeping on the ground, I think I will turn in."

Tom was ready too. So they got his clothes from the porch where Bob had left them, and Granny Heart showed him where he was to sleep. Tom had never seen a room so big. She told him to put his clothes on a chair, and they would put them away tomorrow. Tom went to sleep as soon as his head hit the pillow. The next thing he heard was Granny Heart calling him for breakfast. They ate and Mr. Heart told him he would stay at the house and help Granny and when she got through with him, he could go down and began to train Hart. He told him to stay around the barn with her and for him not to ride her off anywhere. This is a big place, and he didn't want Tom getting lost. Mr. Heart told him later on they would let him go with them and learn how to get around, but for now he was not to leave here for anything.

Tom helped Granny Heart until noon. They gathered peaches, and he helped her peel them. She canned them while he took the peelings out and got her some wood. After that they ate dinner, and she told him as soon as he got through, he could go down and start training Hart.

Tom was so excited he could hardly eat. He didn't know just how to start to train her. So he called to her. At first he called, "Come here, Hart." But she acted like she didn't even hear him. Then he called "Come here, girl," and still, she didn't pay him no mind. After a while he took the bridle and went down and got her. He led her to the gate and took her up to the backyard. He rubbed her neck and told her how pretty she was. She seemed to like for him to pet her. He put the saddle on her and rode her around the yard for a while. He finally got off and tried to get her to come to him, but she acted like she didn't even hear him again. Tom would walk off a ways from her and tell her to stay, and she would turn and go the other way. Tom was about ready to give up when Granny Heart called him to come in.

When he got there, she was sitting on the back porch with some paper and pencils in her lap. She had a cold glass of milk waiting for him and asked him how it went. Tom told her he didn't know, that Hart didn't seem to understand anything he said. She told him not to get so discouraged, that it would take time. That he would have to work with her every day until she understood what he said.

Then she picked up the pencil and paper and said, "Tom, have you had any schooling at all?"

Tom told her, "I had finished the first grade and had started the second this year."

She didn't ask any more questions, and Tom was glad because he didn't know what to tell her if she had. She said Mr. Heart told her they needed to begin his schooling, so about this time would be a good time with her if it suited him. Tom told her it suited him just fine, that he had liked school.

She said, "Now I don't know how far you have gotten with your numbers and your ABC'S. So we will start at the beginning and will go from there." She had written all the alphabets on a tablet and handed it to him and asked him to read as many as he could. Tom did, but he couldn't read them all. She told him they would go over what he knew for a while, then they would begin to add more until he knew them all. After that she gave him another tablet and told him she wanted him to print the ones he knew on that tablet. He did, and she seemed to be pleased with his printing. She did the same thing with his numbers, and when he had said as many as he could, they stopped there and she had him to print them as far as he knew them. Next she turned the page in his tablet. She had written some problems for him to add from 1+1 up to 10+10. She also, on the next page, had added three more alphabet letters for Tom to make. She gave him the tablet and said she wanted him to make the letters five times and do all the arithmetic problems that he could while she went in and fixed supper and she would go over them with him tomorrow.

Tom did as many as he could and had barely finished when he saw Mr. Heart walking toward the house. Mr. Heart laughed and told Tom, "Guess Granny Heart has kept you busy with your schooling. I hope she hadn't worked you too hard." Tom told him no, that he enjoyed school. Then he asked him if he had time to work with Hart. Tom told him he did, but he couldn't get her to do anything for him, that she acted like she didn't know what he wanted her to do. Mr. Heart told him, like Granny Heart had, not to get discouraged that it would take time, that he couldn't expect her to learn just overnight. He told Tom that before he went down tomorrow, for him to get two or three apples off the tree in the orchard and cut them in pieces. He said to lead Hart to one side of the yard and talk to her and, while he was talking, pet her and give her a piece of apple and then leave her there and walk to the other side and hold out a piece of the apple and call her. He told Tom that this may take time but to keep doing it until she figured out what he wanted her to do, that she would finally come to him but it won't happen overnight.

About then Granny Heart called them to come in for supper. They ate and cleaned up the kitchen. Then they went into to the parlor and talked awhile. Mr. Heart had brought some newspapers to Granny Heart when they came in. So each night she read to them about all the news and everything that was going on in other places. After a while they went to bed, and Tom lay there thinking of his horse and wishing morning would hurry and come so he could work with her some more. The next morning Granny Heart kept him busy until noon. Then they ate their dinner and cleaned up the kitchen. Tom was so anxious to get out to Hart, but he tried not to show it.

Finally, Granny Heart told Tom she guessed they had done all they had to do today so he could go work with Hart if he wanted to. Tom said, "Yes, ma'am," that he sure did and shot out of the house. Then he remembered the apples and went back and asked her if he could have some to use to train Hart to come to him. She told him it was all right and to bring them to the house and she would cut them up for him. She gave him a pan and told him not to get over three or four. Tom ran out with his pan to the orchard and was back in no time flat. Granny Heart cut them up for him and put them back in the pan. Tom thanked her and ran out of the house again.

He ran all the way to the barn and got a rope to lead Hart with. First, he called to her to come to him, but again she acted like she didn't hear him. So Tom went down into the pasture and got her. She wasn't hard to catch, so he led her out like Mr. Heart told him to do, then petted her and talked to her. Then he gave her a piece of the apple. At first she didn't seem too interested in it, so Tom held it up to her nose. When she got a smell of it, she took it, licked his hand, and wanted more. He petted her some more and talked to her, then walked to the other side and left her.

She didn't offer to follow him but just stood there and looked at him as if to say, "Well, what are you doing that for?" Tom called to her and called to her, but she didn't pay any attention to him at all. He finally went back and petted her some more and told her what a pretty horse she was. Then he gave her another piece of apple. He did this over and over until he ran out of apple. Tom was beginning to get aggravated with her, and then he remembered what Mr. Heart said about not getting discouraged with her, that it would take time. So he talked to her and petted her some more. Granny Heart called, so he put her in the pasture and went in to do his lessons. He didn't even ride her. Granny Heart asked him how she did, and he told her of all the trouble he had, and again she told him it would take time.

Every day it was the same routine. He would help Granny Heart until noon, then they would eat. After that he would go out and work with Hart. Tom guessed he used most of the apples on one tree and was beginning to believe she would never learn what he was trying to teach her.

They would work on his lessons for about three hours each day. Granny Heart would correct the pages that she had him do the day before and then show him the ones he had missed. Then she would give him new pages. After that she would go in and get supper. Tom would work on them until Mr. Heart came in for supper. He would always ask him, "How'd it go today?" Tom would tell him, and he would say, "Kid, it will take time, but I know you can do it." Tom didn't know what he would have done without both of them encouraging him. Their faith in him kept him trying each day. If they said he could, then by George he would keep trying until he did it.

Then one day he went down to the pasture and as usual called to her, not really expecting her to respond. When she heard him calling, she raised her head and here she came. Tom was so shocked he nearly fell off the fence. He gave her a piece of apple and then put the rope around her neck and led her to the yard. He was so tickled and proud of her that he gave her another piece of apple. Then he took her to the far end of the yard and told her to stay, but when he started to walk off, she followed. Again, Tom took her back and told her to stay again. She was expecting a piece of apple, but he didn't give her one. He walked off again, and again she followed him. Tom thought he had done this fifty times or more, trying to teach her what he wanted her to do.

Finally, when they both were getting aggravated at each other, and he guessed Hart thought she had better do what he wanted her to do or she would never get any more apple because when Tom took her back and told her to stay, she stood there looking at him and never took a step. He was so proud of her, he gave her several pieces of apple and petted her and told her what a smart horse she was. Again, Tom led her back to the other end of the yard and told her to stay. Again, he walked back to the other end. She didn't move until he hollered for her to come, and here she came running like crazy. Again, he gave her some apples and petted her all the time, telling her what a smart horse she was and how proud he was of her. Then again, he walked back to the other end and again told her to stay. She acted like they was playing a game. She didn't move until Tom reached the other end and hollered, "Come to me, girl." Then here she came again. Tom was so proud of her. He could hardly wait to get to the house to tell Granny Heart. The rest of the evening they just played around. Tom said he would tell her to stay, and he would run to the other end, and the minute he hollered, "Come here, girl," here she came. She never missed a trick. Tom ran out of apple, but she didn't seem to mind.

Finally, Granny Heart called and he took Hart to the pasture. Tom's feet didn't touch the ground all the way to the house. As soon as he was in shouting distance, he began to holler,

"Granny Heart, Granny Heart, she did it. Hart did it." Granny Heart came out the door and saw Tom running toward her, shouting, "She stayed when I told her to." Granny Heart came running to him. She grabbed him, and they danced around the yard like she was his age, both laughing. When they could catch their breath, she said, "See, Tom, I told you she would. Tom, it only takes patience and love. The rest will be easy."

They went to the house to get his lessons, but he was so excited he couldn't keep his mind on his homework. He kept wanting to talk about all the things Hart had done. Finally, Granny Heart told him, "Let's skip the lessons for today, and you can tell me all about it." They talked the rest of his two hours, and Granny Heart listened like it was the most important thing in the whole world.

Then she said, "Tom, don't you think just plain Granny will be enough?"

Tom told her, "It sounds real good to me."

She said, "It does to me too."

So from then on, she became his granny. She told him to put his books away and to come on in. They could talk while they fixed supper. Tom put his books up and rushed to the kitchen. Granny Heart let Tom help her, and when it was ready she told him, he could set the table. He had just finished when Mr. Heart came in. Immediately he saw something was going on. They had to tell him, and that was all they talked about all through supper. He told Tom, like Granny had, "See, Tom, what love and patience can do. With enough love and patience, you can do anything you set your head to do." Mr. Heart told him he knew he could do it.

They finally went to bed, but Tom was so excited he couldn't sleep. He kept thinking of all the things he wanted to teach Hart. He could hardly wait until tomorrow so he could go back to her. Sometime after midnight he went to sleep, and the next thing Granny was hollering, "Tom, it's time for breakfast." He helped Granny in the house all morning. They talked about Hart all the time they were working. Tom thought dinnertime would never come.

Finally, Granny said, "Tom, let's get us some dinner, and then you can go out and work with Hart."

He laughed and told her, "That's what I've been waiting for all morning."

She smiled and started kidding him that she knew his mind wasn't on what he had been doing. She said it was all right, that she was anxious to see what Hart would do today also. They ate dinner, and Tom helped clean up their mess, and then Granny told him he could go. Tom grabbed the apples that Granny had fixed for him, his hat, and was out the door in no time flat.

He ran all the way to the pasture, grabbed his rope, and ran to the gate. As soon as he opened the gate and hollered for her, here she came. He was afraid she wouldn't remember what she had learned the day before, but she acted as if she was waiting for him to come and get her. Tom petted her and gave her a piece of apple. Then he put the rope around her neck and led her through the gate. He closed the gate and took the rope off her neck. He petted her again and then turned toward the yard. He told her "Come, girl," and she began to follow him. Tom walked to the yard with her right behind him. When they got there, he turned to her and gave her another piece of apple. Then he petted her and told her what a smart horse she was. She acted like she really understood what he was saying. They played around for a good while, first getting her to come to him, then follow him, then stay, until he called her. They went back to the barn, and Tom saddled her. He rode her to the porch to ask Granny if he could ride her up the road a piece. They rode the rest of the day. From then on it was easy to train her. She seemed to think everything they did was a game.

Chapter 2

ALL THE TIME TOM HAD been on the ranch Mr. Heart had never let him go with him and the boys to work. Tom had always wanted to go, but every time he has said anything about it, Mr. Heart had always told him later on he would but right now Granny needs him most. Then one night when Mr. Heart came in, he told Tom they were going to start branding the next day, that it was about time to teach Hart how to work with the cattle—that is, if he wanted to. Did he want to? He was so excited he could hardly sleep all that night. He thought morning would never come.

They got up before daylight and went down to the bunkhouse, and all the men were there waiting for them. They were all real proud to see Tom and started hoorawing him. They all wanted to know if he was going to help brand. Tom went along with them because he knew it was all in fun. He told them he didn't know how, but if they would show him how, given time he would out brand any of them. They all laughed and said, "Well, Kid, you do have plenty of spunk."

They left right away and got to the pasture where the men had driven a whole lot of cattle the day before. They had stacked up a big pile of wood, a good piece from a bunch of trees. The chuck wagon headed for the trees, and Jake began to set up the chuck wagon. It wasn't long until he had a rowing fire going and began to make a pot of coffee. The men began to build a fire close to another pile of wood farther down in the pasture. They began to get out the branding irons and all kind of things that Tom had never seen before. He asked Bob what were all those things for. Bob told him that they were tools to brand the calf and castrate the bull calf so they would make larger bulls to sell for beef. After they castrated the bulls, they put the black tar-looking stuff on them to keep flies from getting in the wound. They had laid all their things out, and Bob told Tom they were waiting for the fire to burn down to hot coals so they could put the branding irons in them.

He told him the iron had to be hot enough to burn the brand into the hide of the calf. About that time Jake hollered, "Coffee ready, come and get it." They all went up to the chuck wagon and had a cup of coffee while the fire burned down. They were all kidding Tom again about what was his job going to be.

Tom told them, "Now, boys, you let me worry about that. I'll do one job at a time until I learn them all." And that really tickled the men. They all laughed and laughed. When they had drunk their coffee, and that included Tom (by then he could drink it as big as the next fellow), they went back to the fire. Some of the men got on their horses and went out to drive the cattle up closer to where the men would be working. Some of the other men went out among the cattle and began to rope the calves and drag them up to the fire. Tom asked Mr. Heart what he was supposed to do. He told him his job was to keep wood on the far side of the coals so they would have hot coals all the time. The men began to bring in the calves. They would jump off their horse and tie the legs together of the calf. Bob and two other men began to brand them while another man worked with each of them holding the calf down. When the branding iron hit the calf's hide, it began to smoke and the calf would bellow.

Mr. Heart was keeping count, and when the calf was branded, the man would holler out, "One heifer." Or if it was a bull, another man would castrate it and put the medicine on him and then holler, "One steer."

No one talked or kidded around. It was all business. They would turn the calves loose, and the ropers would have another calf waiting for them. Tom kept the fire burning so there were always hot coals for the men to put their branding irons in. Each man had two branding irons. He would take one out and put the other one in to heat. This went on all morning. About noon they stopped for dinner. They banked the fire up real good so they would have hot coals when they got back. Jake had plenty of hot water for the men to wash up with and plenty of soap. They all washed up, and Pete began to serve the meal with plenty of hot coffee. No one talked very much. They were all dog bone tired. Jim, one of the men that Tom had met on their way home the first time, did ask Tom if he still wanted to be a cowboy. Tom told him he did. After they ate, they all laid back and rested awhile. Tom saw that most of them went to sleep except Mr. Heart and Jake. Mr. Heart was busy figuring how many calves they had branded. He finally called to them that it was time to go. They all went back to their jobs, and it started all over again. Bob raked the coals up with a large stick, and they put their branding irons in them. He told Tom he could put some more wood on the other side of the coals. By the time Tom did it, the ropers had calves tied and ready to brand.

They had worked all afternoon, and just before they were going to quit, Mr. Heart told Bob he might as well show the kid how to brand a calf. Boy, was Tom excited. He walked over to where the calf was lying, as if he was just as big as any of them. Bob showed him how to hold the branding iron and then where to put the brand. He told Tom to put it down quick and flat so it would brand even. Then he branded the calf, and the man hollered "Heifer" and untied her. By the time it had run off, they had another one tied and ready for him. Bob handed him the branding iron and said, "It's all yours." Tom put the branding iron down just like Bob had showed him, and while Bob was branding, Tom had counted how long he had left it. So Tom counted the same amount of time and lifted the branding iron. The next one, Bob took Tom over to the fire and told him to always make sure the branding iron is hot and showed him how to put the branding iron into the fire so it wouldn't heat the handle. Tom took it and went back and Bob just stood and watched him. He did his best to put it in the same place as he did before and counted again. Bob said it was just right. He let him brand several then, each time watching him to make sure the brand was going to be in the right spot. Finally, Mr. Heart called, "That's all boys." Then they branded the last one on the ground.

All the men began to gather up everything, and they poured some buckets of water on the fire to make sure it was out. It wasn't long until they were ready to pull out. That morning they all had turned their horses loose in the pasture, and they were grazing up close to the chuck wagon. Tom helped the men take all the supplies up to the supply wagon. Then they all hollered for their horses. Tom hollered at Hart, and here she came. He saddled her and was ready when all the other men were.

They didn't talk a lot going back to the ranch. Everyone was too tired. Bob did say, "Kid, you did a real good job branding today. Give some time, and you'll make a top-notch brander." All the other boys said they agreed.

Mr. Heart asked Tom if he wanted to go back tomorrow, and Tom told him he did. Bob laughed and said, "Boy, is he ever a glutton for punishment." All the other boys laughed and agreed with him. Tom told them good naturally, just for them to wait until he has learned all the ropes and Mr. Heart made him foreman, that his first job would be to fire every one of them except Jake. They just roared. One of them said, "Listen at the cocky little rooster crow." They laughed so hard Tom thought they were going to fall out of their saddles.

The next day Mr. Heart told Tom, "Kid, I want you to go with the ropers and ride herd around the cattle to keep them from running off. Smitty and Slim will show you how." He had never met Slim, but he turned out to be a real swell guy. Smitty told him, "Kid, all you have to do is keep the herd from running off. If one of them starts to break through the line, just turn it back to the herd. Watch them and you will catch on."

Tom thought, *Boy, is this going to be a boring job*. But was he ever surprised. It seemed like he just turned one back to the herd until another one would decide it would try its luck at getting through. Hart did a beautiful job when she learned what she was supposed to do. She acted like it was another game they were playing, and she didn't miss a trick.

When one tried to break through the line, she was behind it and had got in front of it before they could get started. She would turn right in front of them, and they didn't have any place to go but back to the herd. You would have thought she had been trained already to be a cow pony. Tom talked to her each time and told her how proud he was of her and that she was the best horse in the whole world.

At noon, when Mr. Heart called them for dinner, they unsaddled their horses and rubbed them down. Then they turned them loose to graze. Tom didn't worry one bit about Hart not coming to him when time came for them to go back to work.

Mr. Heart asked, "Kid, how is it going?" And before he could say a word, Slim said "Boss, the Kid and that horse didn't miss a trick. That horse acts like she has been turning cattle all her life. When she found out what Kid wanted her to do, she didn't miss a one. I've never seen anything like it before."

After they ate and rested awhile, Mr. Heart asked him if he was too tired to ride herd that afternoon. Tom told him no, and besides he couldn't disappoint Hart. She was having too much fun, and Tom told him she acted like they were playing a game. Smitty told Mr. Heart he didn't think they could do without Kid. He is the best man they have ever had. Did Tom ever strut his stuff!

He told them, "You all had better start saving your paychecks for that rainy day when Kid learns all the jobs. He told you what he would do."

They all laughed and said they didn't know if they ought to finish training him or not. Tom acted like he was real serious and told them, "Now, boys, if ya'll will be good and finish training me. Then I'll promise to keep you all on when I make foreman."

They really got a kick out of that, and Pete said, "Well, there goes the little bantam rooster crowing again."

About that time Mr. Heart said, "Well, boys, let's go get 'um."

They all got up and called their horses and started saddling them. Hart was right there with all of them. Tom didn't lose any time saddling her and was ready when they all were. They worked all afternoon, and when the sun was getting pretty low, Mr. Heart hollered, "Time to quit, boys." So they rode around the herd and began to help gather up everything like they did the day before. Jake left right after the afternoon break.

They finished branding the following week. Mr. Heart told Tom, "We're taking the cows to another pasture to stay until shipping time." He told Tom he was going to leave Bob there with him, that Bob was the best roper he had and he wants him to teach him how to use the rope. Tom thought it was hard at first when he was trying to train Hart. Well, that was child's play compared to him learning to rope.

Bob told him, "We will start out by learning how to hold the rope and how to whirl it around your head." Then he told him, "See that post just sitting out there by itself. When you learn to whirl the rope without getting tangled up in it, then I will show you how to rope that post. Most all the cow hands at one time or another has learned to rope on that post."

Granny would let Tom go out right after breakfast every morning, and Bob would always be waiting there for him. Tom bet he whirled that rope a hundred times a morning. It always ended up around his head, on his feet, or on the ground. Bob didn't seem to get aggravated with him. Each time he would say, "That's okay, Kid. Just try to whirl it a little slower. Don't jerk, or here watch me again. See how easy it is."

They would stop at noon, and Tom would go in for his lessons. Granny told him, "You've been off long enough, and you need to get back on them." Each day she would ask him how he was doing. She acted like she was real concerned. Tom would tell her, and she would always say, "Tom, just have patience. Remember when you were trying to train Hart. Well, one of these days you will catch on and the rest will be easy." Tom told her, "I don't know what I would do without you encouraging me." Just knowing she thought he could gave him courage to keep trying. She would check his lessons that she had given him to do the day before. Then they would read, and then she would give him some more work to do. After that she would say the words Tom was waiting for, "You can go now and good luck." Tom would always tell her, "Thank you, Granny," and then he would tell her, "I will do my best." Tom always knew what her next words would be. She would always tell him, "I know you will, Tom." All the others called him Kid, but the whole time he was there with her, it was always Tom.

Tom tried and tried, but somehow, he just couldn't get that crazy rope to do what he wanted it to do. It always ended up around his neck or his feet. Mr. Heart came back, and he was still working on learning just the whirling. He asked Tom how it was going, and he told him not so good, that he was still working on the first part let alone the roping. Mr. Heart told him like Granny had, "Kid, it will take time. Don't give up." Tom told him he wasn't about to. If all those other cahoots could learn it, he could too. "I'll learn it or die trying," he told him. Mr. Heart laughed and said, "That's my boy. Go get 'em."

This went on for about a week. Every day he would try to whirl the rope over his head with Bob telling him what to do. Then one day Bob hollered, "Kid, that's it. That's just perfect. Now we are ready to start roping." They finished the day with him whirling the rope over and over around his head. Bob told him, "Kid, you're going to make a roper yet. Tomorrow we will start roping."

Tom couldn't wait to get to the house to tell Granny. As soon as he got within hollering distance of the house, he started hollering, "Granny, Granny." And bless her heart, here she came running toward him, hollering, "You did it. You did it." They met about halfway in the yard. She grabbed him and again they danced around the yard. Finally, they both had to stop because both were out of breath. When she could get her breath, she said, "See, Tom, I knew you could do it." When Mr. Heart came in, Granny met him at the door and told him, "Tom has got something to tell you." When Tom told him, he acted as proud as punch and really bragged on him. "Now the fun begins," he told him. "The rest will be easy." All during supper Tom couldn't talk about anything else. He knew he just about drove them crazy, but they never let on.

He told them he could hardly wait until morning to see if he could rope the post. Mr. Heart laughed and told him,

"Now hold on, big buddy, it will take time, just like the whirling did. Don't think that you will be able to do it tomorrow." Anyway, Tom could hardly wait until morning came so Bob and he could get started.

As soon as he ate his breakfast, he was in the yard waiting for Bob. He finally showed up and said, "Well, Kid, are you ready to get started?" Tom told him he was more than ready. They walked down toward the post together, or at least started together. Tom was so anxious to start that he was way ahead of Bob. Bob hollered, "Whoa, Kid, don't be in such a big hurry. We got all day." Mr. Heart was right. Tom wasn't going to rope it in one day. After he got started, he wondered if he would do it in a week. He would throw it, but it wasn't far enough or it would go on one side or the other. Bob kept telling him to aim. "Like this," he would say, and his rope would slip right over the post. Tom aimed and threw the rope until Bob told him, "Granny Heart is waving for you." Tom's arms and shoulders were killing him. Bob said, "I think we've practiced enough for today anyway, and I will see you tomorrow." Tom told him bye and went to the house. He didn't think he had ever felt so low. He was aching all over. If it hurt this bad, why would anyone want to learn to rope anyway.

Then he thought of Granny and how proud of him she was each time and he knew he had to keep trying until he learned how. By golly, if all those boys could do it, he could and he would. By the time he got to the house and Granny asked him how it went, he told her not so good but he would do better tomorrow. "That's my boy," she said and then told him as always. "You can do it. Just don't give up." After all that love and confidence, she had shown in him, he thought if she had told him to walk on water, he could have.

This went on for a whole week. Tom had thrown that rope until he thought his arms would fall off. Bob would tell him over and over, "Kid, don't give up. You can do it. It will just take time." Then one day, Tom whirled the rope around his head and took aim and threw it. To Tom's surprise it went around the post just like it was supposed to. He jumped up and down and hollered as loud as he could, "I did it. I did it."

Bob was laughing and clapping his hands, he said, "By George, I told you, you could." Bob went on to tell him, "Now, Kid, don't think you will do it every time. Even the best ropers miss sometime. How often he misses will show the real proof of how good he really is."

He left Tom to practice, and Tom practiced until Granny called him to come in. He hadn't roped it every time, but at least he had the knack of how to do it now. He put his rope up and ran to the house. When Granny saw him coming, she knew he had roped it and here she came to meet him and again they did their little special dance. She put her arm around his shoulder, and they walked on to the house with Tom talking a mile a minute. He told her that Bob said they would go to the pasture next week and rope a real steer. He would show him how to hold a tight line and they would train Hart at the same time. Again, they tried to study his lessons, but he was so excited he just couldn't keep his mind on them. Granny finally said it was all right, that she thought he needed a day off from school anyway, so they put up his lessons and just talked until time to fix supper.

Sometime Mr. Heart would be home for supper, and other times they would be too far from the house to come in, so they would just stay out on the range. They carried their bedrolls with them all the time, just in case. Pete always had plenty of food in the chuck wagon to last for a week. This was one of the times they stayed out all week, and Tom could hardly wait until Sunday to tell him.

Mr. Heart was just as excited as they were about it. He told Tom over and over how proud of him he was. Tom told him what Bob had said about going to the pasture and roping real calves. Again Mr. Heart told him, "Now, Tom, don't think you will be able to rope one on your first try. It will take time, just like it has to rope the post." Tom told him he knew it would, but at least he had the knack on how to do it now. Tom thought the weekend would never pass. He was so excited about going to the pasture and roping real steers.

They always had Sunday service whether all the men were home or not. Granny and Tom would dress for it and go down to the bunkhouse. That Sunday there wasn't too many of the men there, but the service was nice anyway. After lunch Tom asked Granny if he could go practice roping again, and she said yes. So he went down and practiced until almost dark. He wanted to be his very best when he tried to rope a live steer.

Monday morning they ate breakfast. Then Mr. Heart told Tom that he had decided to let him and Bob go to one of the pastures and check the cattle and fences while he was learning how to rope them. That way he would have plenty of calves to practice on and they could get the fence checked at the same time. He told him they would probably be gone a week or so.

Granny helped him get his clothes ready, and it wasn't long until Bob was there, ready to go. Mr. Heart told Bob for them to be careful and that he would see them in a week or so. Granny told Bob, "Now you take care of our boy and don't let him get hurt." Bob promised her he would. They walked down to the corral with Granny waving and hollering, "Now you all be careful and hurry back." Tom called Hart and saddled her while Bob saddled his horse. Then Bob showed Tom how to roll up his bedroll and tie it behind his saddle. Bob already had a pack horse ready to go. He told Tom, "Make sure your canteen is full of water. We'll need it before we get to where we're going." They rode until around four or five that afternoon.

They only stopped long enough to let the horses rest and eat a cold biscuit that Pete had fixed for them. When they got to the pasture where they would be staying, Bob told Tom that they would set up camp first thing. They camped under a tree that had branches hanging pretty low. Then they put their saddles next to the tree trunk and rubbed down their horses. Bob told Tom that they would hobble them so they wouldn't graze too far from where they were camping.

Then they started setting up their camp. He told Tom, "The branches hanging low will keep the wind from blowing on us and also will keep the dew from getting our bed wet while we sleep." A creek was just right down from them, so they had plenty of water. Someone else had camped there before because it had a place dug out already for a fire, so they just had to clean it out. There was enough dry wood to start a fire. Bob said he would start a fire and handed Tom a bucket and told him to go down and get some water. When Tom came back Bob had a real good fire going. Then they went looking for some more wood. There was trees everywhere, so they didn't have any trouble finding plenty of dead wood. Bob cut it small enough to go on their campfire, and Tom carried it back to their camp. When they had plenty of wood, Bob raked some hot coals to one side. He filled the coffeepot with water and put the coffee in it, then set it on the hot coals. It wasn't long until it was boiling. So all they had to do was sit down and wait for the coffee to make. Pete had fixed them some food, so they didn't have to worry about supper. When the coffee was ready, they ate and just sat and talked. Bob said it was too late to do anything today and they would get a good night's sleep and start tomorrow. Before dark they went out looking for some more wood. Bob said they would be real busy tomorrow and since they still had some daylight they might as well haul in some more wood. They worked until about dusty dark before they had hauled in their last load of wood. They sit down close to the fire as it had begun to get a little chilly, and the fire sure felt good. They talked about what they would do tomorrow. Bob said they would practice roping for a while, then they would check the fences for broken wires. He said he had brought along two hammers, some wire, and some staples. Tomorrow they would walk the fences and repair any breaks they found. He said it would take several days, and they would stay until they checked it all. Then he laughed and said, "Don't worry, Kid, we'll practice roping each day before we start mending the fences. By the time we get all the fences mended, I hope you will be able to rope anything."

Tom told him, "I hope I will too."

They talked awhile longer, then Bob told Tom that they had a long day ahead of them tomorrow so they better hit the sack. So Bob banked the fire, and Tom laid their blankets out and laid the other ones on top for them to cover with. They used their saddle for pillows. Bob pulled his boots off and placed them close to his head. Bob told Tom he didn't want any varmints carrying them off if they should come around. He took off his guns and laid them by his boots and put his hat on top of them. So Tom put his boots at his head and put his hat on top of his boots just like Bob had done. They both went to sleep as soon as their heads hit the saddle. Bob was right. The tree branches did keep the wind from blowing right on them, and they slept warm and comfortable all night.

Morning came sooner than they wanted it to. The first thing Tom knew, Bob was hollering, "Rise and shine." He told Tom to get a fresh bucket of water for coffee, and when he came back, Bob had the fire started. Tom added the water and coffee to the pot, and then they waited for the fire to burn down so they could rake out some hot coals to set the coffeepot in and also their skillet. Bob made some biscuits and put them in the Dutch oven. Bob placed the Dutch oven on some coals and covered it with some more coals. Tom raked some more coals out and placed the coffeepot on them while Bob sliced some dry salt bacon and put it in the skillet with some water to boil for a while to get some of the salt out of it. When it had boiled, he drained it good and put it back on the coals to fry. Tom broke the eggs in a pan, and it wasn't long until the bacon was done. They took the bacon up and poured the eggs in the same skillet. Tom stirred them while Bob uncovered the biscuits and poured the coffee. When the eggs were done, he put half in each plate and they were ready to eat. They sat down and propped their backs against the tree trunk. After they had finished eating, they washed their dishes and put them away. Bob had filled the Dutch oven full of water and put it on the coals, so they had plenty of hot water to wash their dishes.

Then they hollered for their horses. The horses were close by, and by the time they got their saddles, they were standing there ready to be saddled.

Bob said, "Well, Kid, today is the big day. Are you ready to learn to rope a calf?"

Tom told him he was as ready as he ever would be.

Bob grinned and said, "Well let's go get 'um."

It didn't take long for them to find where the cattle were grazing. Bob cut out a small calf and showed him how to rope it. He said, "Now, Kid, always throw a little in front of them because they will start to run as soon as they see the rope coming." He threw the rope, and sure enough the calf started to run, but Bob had thrown like he had told Tom, and the rope landed right over the calf's head. He got off his horse and let the calf go. He said, "Now, Kid, it's your turn." Tom did just like Bob told him, but his rope fell short. Bob told him, "Now, Kid, don't expect to rope one your first time, just keep practicing and before long you will get the hang of it. Now keep practicing just like I showed you. I'll be working on the fence and will see you about noon. If you get through before noon, come looking for me. Now just keep roping like you did on the post, and before long it will come just as easy. You won't rope one every time, but the more you rope, the better you will get. See you at noon." And he was gone.

Tom threw his rope and dragged it in what seemed like hours to him. He was beginning to think it was going to take a better man than he was to rope one of those calves. Then he remembered what Granny always told him. He could just hear her saying, "Now, Tom, you can do anything you set your head to if you just work at it hard enough." Tom started laughing and said, "Okay, Granny, if anyone else can do it, then I can too."

He kept on roping and dragging it in, until he thought his arms would come off and he had sweated until his shirt was wringing wet. He thought, *Don't let anyone tell you roping is not hard work.* About eleven he cut out another calf and threw his rope a little farther than he had been throwing it, and sure enough the rope landed around the calf's neck. Tom jumped off his horse and ran to it, hollering, "Yippee, yippee," with every step he took. After that he kept practicing the rest of the morning until he saw Bob coming.

He said, "Kid, how's it going?"

Tom threw his rope just to show him, and would you believe it, he missed.

Bob begin to laugh and said, "Well, Kid, guess that answered my question. Are you just trying to get out of helping mend fences?"

Tom told him, "No, fence mending would be easier than what I have gone through all morning. Just hide and watch." He cut out another calf. This time he took his time and sure enough, the rope went over the calf's head as slick as a button.

Bob laughed again and asked him, "What took you so long? I've been looking for you all morning."

They went to camp and rubbed their horses down, which they did each day to cool them off before they let them drink, then they brought them back close to camp and hobbled them. Tom grabbed their water bucket and ran down to get them a cold bucket of water Bob had put a pot of beans on before they left that morning. When Tom got back He had already started making some corn bread. Bob poured some of the water in it and put it in another Dutch oven, then he put the oven in the hot coals. While he did this, Tom made a pot of coffee. Then they sat down to rest while the corn bread cooked and the coffee boiled. They both was dog tired, Bob from walking and repairing fences and Tom from roping all morning, or at least trying to.

After they ate their dinner they rested awhile and drank another cup of coffee.

Bob said, "Guess we had better get started, Kid. Since you've become a famous roper, maybe now I can teach you to mend fences as well."

They both laughed, and Tom told him, "Yeah, maybe you could at that."

They worked until about four, then Bob said, "I think we've done enough for one day. It's about time for us to go rope some more calves."

Tom told him he was ready for that. They rode to where the cows were grazing, and they both roped calves until dusty dark. Bob said there wasn't any use for both of them getting down each time to release the calves, so they took turns. Once in a while Tom would miss, but it was a lot of fun. Bob missed some also, but Tom thought he did it on purpose to make him feel better. He told Tom that he was doing real good. By the time they brought the calves in for branding, he would be as good as any of them. That really made Tom feel good, and he knew Bob was telling the truth because he never lied about anything. When you did something good, he would tell you. But on the other hand, when you did something wrong, he would tell you also. He was a square shooter and always played fair with everyone. By dusty dark they were both tired and went in and took care of their horses, hobbled them again, and went down to take a bath. After that Tom as usual went after fresh water, and they ate their leftover beans and corn bread. Bob made them some coffee, and while it was making, they cleaned up their mess. Then Bob poured them some coffee, and they sat around the fire talking.

Tom asked Bob, "Do you remember when I first came to the ranch. After we came through the gate that had Heart's Ranch above it, I noticed a lot of the men pulling away from us. Do they not work for Mr. Heart?"

Bob told him, "Yes, they do. The ranch is divided into sub ranches, and each sub ranch has a foreman and cowboys that work for him. At roundup time they all bring their cattle that were to be shipped to join the main herd and also some of their cowboys go along to help with the drive. Then they all drive them to the railroad station to be shipped.

"Mr. Heart always went with the cattle and tends to the selling of them. Each foreman gives him a list of supplies to pick up and bring back. Then someone from each sub ranch stays with their wagons to pick them up when Mr. Heart gets back. Mr. Heart supplies a lot of men with jobs. Most of them are men that have been in trouble one way or the other, or runaway boys, or drunks, like I had been. They all think the world of Mr. Heart. He always shoots square with them all, and there is not one on the whole ranch that wouldn't give their life for him, if it came to it. He takes in men and boys that need a second chance, and he never asked questions. There's no telling where I would be if I hadn't met him, and not only me, but all the rest of the men."

Tom thought about that for a while and wondered just how much he should tell Bob. He finally decided to tell him as little as possible. So he told him, "Guess that includes me too, Bob. I don't know where I would be if Mr. Heart hadn't found me."

Bob didn't ask any questions, and Tom was glad. Because he just couldn't go back, and if his papa found out where he was, he would make him. Tom thought that part of his life was over and was best forgotten. Both of them sit there for a while saying nothing, both thinking about their own private thoughts and not willing to share them with anyone.

Finally, Bob said, "Well, Kid, guess we had better straighten up the camp and go to bed. We've a lot of fence to walk tomorrow. Do not ever leave leftover food around the camp because the wild animals would smell it and come into the camp to find it." They checked all around to make sure they had done a good job of cleaning up after they had eaten their supper. Bob put some green wood on the coals, and they rolled out their sleeping bags. It had gotten chilly, so they spread them close to the hot coals, and it didn't take them very long to crawl into bed.

Tom lay there thinking of what his life was before his mama died and blaming his papa for bringing Aunt Lou in to take her place. *We could have made it without her*, he thought. He finally dosed off to sleep feeling so bitter toward his papa and feeling so alone. The last thought he remembered was, *Mama, why did you have to die?*

They got up early and ate breakfast and were walking the fences by daylight. It took them three weeks to walk the whole fence around that pasture, but with Bob it was fun. They moved their camp every few days so they wouldn't have so far to go back to their camp each day. On those days they would stop early so they could fix supper before it got dark. Bob would always move them close to the river so they could have plenty of water for their camp and for bathing.

After walking the fence all day, they were always ready for a bath before sundown. Every day, except moving day, they would stop early enough to have a little time to practice roping. Boy, that was the highlight of the days, that and taking their bath. Tom didn't know how to swim, and each day Bob would work with him teaching him how. By the end of the first week, Tom was swimming like a pro.

Then one day Bob asked, "Kid, do you see where the fence turns back? That's where we had started. By this afternoon we will be at the corner, and tomorrow morning we will start home."

Tom was a little sad because he had really enjoyed the time out. They had really worked, grant you, but like he told Bob, working with him had been fun. He told him that he had learned a lot of things in three weeks. He told Bob he had taught him how to rope, how to swim, how to fix fences, and how to set up camp and that he really appreciate it. Bob acted like it was nothing, but to a boy of ten, it was everything.

During that day, while they finished walking the fence, Bob told him, "Kid, when you're out like this working, always try to camp under a shade tree so when you come in at noon, you will have a shade to rest under and at night to keep the dew from getting your bed wet. Stay close to the river so you'll always have plenty of water."

Bob had told him that before, but Tom guessed he wanted to make sure he didn't forget it. Tom pretended that he was hearing it for the first time and told him, "Yes, sir, I won't ever forget all the things you've taught me." Tom had no idea at that time how important all these lessons on setting up camp would mean to him all through the rest of his life.

They finished walking the fence about two o'clock. They had worked through dinnertime to finish it before they stopped. So they were tired, sweaty, and hungry. They went to their camp and rested awhile before they even ate their dinner. After that they laid down for a short nap. Tom went sound to sleep.

The first thing he heard was Bob saying, "Kid, are you going to sleep all day? I thought we'd go rope awhile, then go swimming one more time before we had to go home." Then he grinned and asked him, "That is, if you're game for that."

Tom jumped up and told Bob, "If you're waiting for me, you're wasting time."

They roped all the rest of the afternoon, just stopping in time to go for a long swim and get their supper before dark. They didn't stay up long, Bob told Tom he wanted to get an early start so they could get home before too late.

Morning comes early when you're camping out, so the next morning they were up and had fixed their breakfast. After they had eaten and while Bob cleaned up their mess, Tom ran down and filled up their canteens with fresh cold water. In no time they had everything packed, their fire put out, and were ready to go. Bob asked Tom, "Did you remember the first night we camped out and that there was plenty of wood to start a fire."

Tom thought back, and then he told Bob, "Come to think of it, there has been plenty of wood in every camp that we had camped in."

Then Bob told him, "That is another lesson for you to learn, Kid. All of our men have been told to always leave enough wood in each camp for the next ones that will be camping there. They may get in late at night, and it will be too late to get wood. Or someone might be caught out in an unexpected blizzard or snowstorm. The wood left here might just save their lives. So when you are out like this, don't ever leave a campsite without first getting in some wood to leave. Mr. Heart has taught all of us well about that, and if he finds one without wood, if you think he won't raise old Billy, heck, then just hide and listen."

So they got some more wood, then they were ready to go.

"Well, Kid," Bob told him, "it's been fun. You've made a good hand fixing fences and never complained one time. I'm real proud of you."

That made Tom real proud to hear Bob say that, but if Bob had asked him to walk through the fire Tom would have tried to. Bob had become his hero.

Bob went on to tell him, "When roundup time comes, you will be roping as good as the best of them."

Tom laughed and told him, "You wouldn't hurrah me, would you?" Tom knew he wouldn't because he had always told him what he thought, like it or not.

It took them all day to get home, and they didn't lollygag around either.

They stopped and rested the horses a few times and cooled them down before they let them drink. While the horses rested, they would rest also. They also hobbled them so they wouldn't wonder too far away grazing. They probably wouldn't, but Bob said it was best not to take any chances. After the horses had grazed, Tom and Bob would take them down to the creek, and while they drank, they would fill their canteen full of fresh cool water and drink some themselves.

Bob told Tom, "When you stopped to let the horses rest, always refill your canteen with fresh water, that way it will be cold when you needed it. You can't count on having a river running close by all the time."

Sure enough they left the river and headed across country about three, and you had better believe that cool water sure tasted good to them before they got home. They got there about sundown. They unsaddled their horses and cooled them down and then gave them some oats as they really had earned their feed. They acted like they were glad to be home and get a good meal. Tom knew he was, and he knew Granny would have one ready for him at suppertime. They turned the horses loose in the pasture. They both figured the horses would go for water when they got thirsty enough.

Bob told Tom, "I'll see you tomorrow. It's been fun, Kid," and headed to the bunkhouse.

Tom headed to the house. He could hardly wait to tell Granny what all he had learned. He was so excited, he was almost running by the time he got to the porch. Tom hollered, "Hello in the house."

And there was Granny. She was so proud to see him, and he was just as proud to see her. She hugged him and asked him, "What took you all so long?"

Tom started kidding her, "Well, you know how it is when fellows are roping calves and laying around the camp all day, they forget about the time."

She laughed and said, "Oh yes, I know Bob well enough that he wouldn't let you just lie around the camp all day, but did you really learn to rope real live calves?"

Tom told her, "Bob said come roundup time I'd be able to rope with the best of them." He strutted like a bantam rooster.

She told him, "I am so proud of you and what else did you learn?"

Then Tom told her, "Bob taught me how to mend fences, set up camp, and how to swim. It took us three whole weeks to walk those fences. That one pasture is as big as …" Tom started to say as his papa's farm, but he caught himself just in time and said, "A big town." He had never been in a big town, but that was all he could think of to say but the truth, and he sure didn't want to say "My papa's farm."

Mr. Heart wasn't home yet, but Granny said he would be in before dark. So Tom helped her finish getting supper, and by the time they had it ready, they heard him come up on the back porch. He acted as tickled to see Tom as Granny was, and Tom had to tell the story all over again with Granny adding to it. They washed up and ate supper, with Tom talking all the time about the camp out. Also, he told Granny how good the meal was, and it sure was after batching for three weeks. He helped Granny clean up the kitchen, and they all went in to the parlor and had coffee and talked some more.

Finally, Mr. Heart said, "Guess we'd better hit the hay. Morning will be here before we know it."

Boy, did that bed feel good after sleeping out on the ground for three weeks. Tom must have gone to sleep as soon as his head hit the pillow and he didn't even turn over all night. He woke up to the smell of bacon frying and got up and dressed real quick. He made his bed and went into the kitchen to help Granny finish breakfast.

She smiled when she saw him and said, "Good morning, Tom. I sure am glad to have you home, and I sure have missed you."

Mr. Heart came in, and they had breakfast. He told Tom he was giving him the day off and besides Granny Heart was complaining about him being behind with his schoolwork. Tom helped Granny clean up the kitchen, and then she handed him some pages of schoolwork. On one was a lot of words to learn to spell and on some more with arithmetic problems to do. She told him to work on these pages for an hour each and then she would be ready to help him with his reading. She also told him, "Tom, I know this is not your favorite thing to do. But if you don't learn how to read, write, and do your arithmetic, you won't be worth a flip when you get grown and start tending to shipping cattle yourself."

Tom thought that he wasn't going to be a bookkeeper, that he was going to be a cowboy like Mr. Heart and Bob. But he didn't tell her that, he only said, "Yes, ma'am." He took his schoolwork and went out to the back porch. He did his arithmetic first because he liked it best and he did better in it. After he worked all the problems she gave him, he started on his spelling. He went over and over the words she had given him for the rest of the whole hour, and when he thought he had them all memorized, sure enough here she came. He thought this will be a breeze, but I'll be doggone if she didn't start skipping around on them, and it wasn't a breeze after all. She told him they would practice on them again tomorrow. They did reading and then arithmetic. Tom did good on the arithmetic but not so good on the reading and spelling. After that she said he could go down and work with Hart awhile. Hart didn't need much working with, but anyway Tom sure was glad to stop doing that schoolwork.

He called Hart, and she acted like she was real proud to see him. He saddled her, and they just rode around for a while. Then Tom unsaddled her, and they just played around with him, calling to her, and she always came when he called. Then he told her to stay, and Tom would walk off a good piece and call her to come, and here she would come. She acted like she was really enjoying it. The time passed too quickly, and it didn't seem very long until Granny was calling him. He went to the house, and she was waiting with the spelling work. She told him she would start supper while he went over his spelling words that he had missed. Tom offered to help her, but she said no, that he had better study his words that he had missed.

Tom was still sitting on the porch, going over his spelling, when Mr. Heart came in. He grinned and said, "She's got you at it, huh?" Tom told him what she had said about him not being worth a flip when he got grown if he didn't learn his reading, writing, and arithmetic. Mr. Heart laughed and told Tom, "That's what she always told me too, and it just killed my soul to have to sit out there and work on all the work she gave me to do. I bet she was using the same lessons on you that she had me doing. But she is right, you do need to know how to read, write, and do arithmetic. Or how would you know if you were being cheated if you sold a herd of cattle and didn't know how to count your money. So just grin and bear it, Kid, and you'll thank her later."

Chapter 3

THE NEXT MORNING AT THE breakfast table, Mr. Heart asked, "Tom, would you like to go down in the west pasture and look for strays. Bob and the boys had taken the cattle from that pasture the day before and put them in another one. By rotating the cattle from pasture to pasture, it keeps the grass growing and the cows don't eat it down to nothing." He went on to tell Tom, "All you have to do is ride around and see if you could find any strays that they had missed." Tom told him he would be proud to. Both Granny and Mr. Heart told him, "Now, Kid, don't stay out until dark. Start home in time to make it before sundown." Mr. Heart told him, "Those pastures get awful dark after sundown, and it was easy to get lost. Tom, if you do get lost, don't try to come in after dark. There are a lot of gullies, and a horse could fall and break a leg. Take your sleeping bag and some grub and matches, and if you get lost, just find a good place to camp and stay there until daylight. The pasture is east of the house, so keep coming west toward the sun and you would find it. Don't panic, if you don't get home by breakfast time, some of them would come looking for you."

Right after breakfast Granny said, "I'll fix you some food to take with you." While she was fixing it, Tom went to the lot and called Hart and saddled her. They rode back to the house, and Granny had the food ready and packed in a flour sack. Tom rolled it in his sleeping bag and tied it behind his saddle like

Bob had showed him to do. Granny hugged him and told him to be careful. She said, "Now, Tom, don't you take any chances out there. You ride careful and watch out for danger. There's all kinds of animals and gullies, so watch out for them and be careful."

Tom told her he would and told her bye, then he rode off. He turned once and waved, and she was still standing there, watching him. She waved back and turned to go in the house. He was so excited that Mr. Heart had trusted him to go look for strays, also what a fun day it was going to be.

He rode to the east pasture, and he got down to open the gate. He told Hart to stay, and he went over and opened the gate. Then he called, "Come here, girl," and she didn't hesitate a minute. Tom petted her and told her she was the best horse in the whole world, but he told her that every time. He shut the gate, and they were ready to go. They rode all morning but didn't find any strays. Mr. Heart was right. The land was rugged with plenty of gullies and washes. Mesquite trees was growing everywhere, but the grass was good and thick. He was careful to look in and around the mesquite trees for fresh tracks of cattle, but he didn't find any.

About one o'clock they came to a creek. The water looked so cool, and there was a big shade tree right at the edge of it. Tom told Hart this is where they would stop for dinner and rest for a while. He took the saddle off her and rubbed her down. When he had finished, she hung around for a while, wanting to play, but he told her, "Not now, Hart, I'm hungry and tired. So go find some good grass and eat your own dinner while I eat mine." Tom got some fresh water and rolled his bedroll out. He put the saddle next to the tree and opened the sack that Granny had packed for him. She must have thought he would be starving at the amount she packed. Tom had enough for dinner and supper too. He ate about half of it and put the rest back in the flour sack. It would be good for a snack in the middle of the evening. He put his blanket on the saddle and laid back to rest for a while.

He must have gone sound to sleep because the next thing he knew he heard a squealing sound. He opened his eyes and saw a herd of wild hogs coming right toward him. They saw him about the same time that he saw them, and here they came. He just had time to climb the tree before they got to it. Tom guessed they smelled the food and came looking for it. They tore the flour sack apart looking for the food. Then they fought over it. You never heard so much snorting and squealing in all your life. They kept squealing and fighting until they tore the flour sack to shreds and ate his food, then they laid down right under the tree and went to sleep. Tom tried several times to ease out of the tree, but every time they would start snarling and squealing and snapping their jaws together, their tusks was about two or three inches long. They would look up at him, as if to say, "I dare you to come down." Now Tom thought, *I'm no coward, but those odds were too much in their favor.* He knew as soon as his feet touched the ground that he would be supper for them. Because they looked mighty hungry, and he saw what they had done to Granny's flour sack. Tom knew Mr. Heart would come for him, but his biggest worry was for Hart. He was afraid she would try to rescue him.

Sure enough, about an hour or so later, here came Hart. Tom was so scared for her, he hollered, "Run, Hart, run." He had hollered this to her when they were out riding to see how fast she could go, and believe me, she could go mighty fast. She saw the hogs just as they started toward her. She turned and ran. Tom knew they couldn't catch her, but he was afraid she would try to make a stand and fight them off. He hollered again, "Run, Hart, run," then "Go home, go home, Hart." Some of the hogs ran after her for a short distance, then came back to the other hogs that were under the tree, snapping their jaws together and snarling up at him. He thought he would be real still and they would forget about him and go somewhere else and look for food. But no such luck. Hart kept coming back, but each time Tom would holler at her to run, and each time they would run after her but not far enough to give him time to get down and escape. Finally, Hart stop coming and Tom was glad. He was so worried that she might get it in her head to attack them. He had kept telling her to go home, and finally, she left and headed that way. He kept hoping she understood him and was going for help.

Tom knew she couldn't get there before night set in, but he knew she was safe and Mr. Heart would come for him as soon as he discovered her the next morning. All night the hogs stayed there. Every time Tom moved just a little bit, they were up, snapping their jaws and snarling at him. They had ate his supper, and by nine or ten o'clock, he was hungry enough to eat a bear. He hadn't taken time to grab his water jug or his blanket when he saw them coming.

After the sun went down, it began to get cool but now it was downright cold. And Tom was so thirsty it felt like his mouth was so dry, he could spit cotton. It was pitch-dark. He could hardly see his hand before his face, and the only thing he could hear was those dad blasted hogs every time he made any kind of noise. The time just dragged, and he was beginning to get sleepy. Tom knew if he dosed off to sleep, he would more than likely lose his balance and fall out of the tree. He took off his belt and put it around the limb above his head, then he fastened the belt around his wrist so if he should doze it would keep him from falling. He knew what would happen if he did fall, so he began to sing and yodel at the top of his voice. Then he would fuss at the hogs, and he told them, "You ornery old cusses." If they were going to make him lose his sleep and keep him treed all night, then he would see to it that they didn't get any sleep either. They snorted and squealed all night, and every time Tom began to get sleepy, he sang. He believed that was the longest and coldest night he had ever spent.

Dawn finally came, and the sun began to come up. Tom could barely see it coming up in the east and did it ever look good. He was so worried about Hart. He was so scared she had started home and fell in a wash or gulley somewhere. Tom knew Mr. Heart and the boys would be out looking for him as soon as they could.

Sure enough about an hour or so after sunup, Tom heard them calling for him. Bless her, Hart had led them right to him. He started hollering at the top of his voice, warning them about the hogs. When they saw the hogs under the tree, they started shooting and you never saw hogs scatter so fast in all your life. They shot quite a few before they scattered. When Tom thought it was safe, he began to undo his hand. It was numb, and he decided he didn't want to take a chance of undoing it and falling out of the tree. Tom loosened the belt, then he rubbed his hands together and waited for the feeling to come back in it. Before the feeling was back in it good, the boys were there. They started kidding him as soon as they got there.

Bob said, "Boys, look at that big fat coon we got treed."

Mike had to join with, "Shall we shoot him or just let the dogs have him."

Mr. Heart came up about that time and hollered, "He's too tough to eat. Guess we had better just take him down. Kid, are you all right?"

Tom told him he was fine, but he sure hoped they brought a gallon of water along and plenty of breakfast.

Hart was right beside Mr. Heart. He told Tom, "Look what we found at the gate when we got up this morning." As dark as it was, she had found her way to the gate but couldn't get through the gate to get help. Mr. Heart said she was standing there waiting like she knew that we would come as soon as it got light. The minute they got there, she took off in a run, coming right straight to Tom.

Mr. Heart led her under the limb, and Tom tried to swing down on her back, but his legs were so numb the boys had to help him. As he started to swing down, they grabbed his legs and helped him slide on Hart's back and then to the ground. Slim handed them a blanket to wrap him in. He was cold and shivering so until he couldn't stand. They wrapped him up in the blanket, and Slim helped him sit down. Granny had sent breakfast and plenty of water. It wasn't long until they had a fire going and a coffeepot waiting to go on it as soon as it died down a little. Tom was so dry, he drank the water first, then started on the food, and boy was it good. He was so cold he could hardly hold the food still enough to eat. It wasn't long before the coffee was ready, and with the blanket and the hot coffee, Tom began to get warm. He told them he had never spent a colder and a hungrier night in all his life.

After he stopped shivering, Pete said, "Kid, now we would like to know how you got yourself in this kind of mess anyway."

Tom told them how he had hunted strays all morning and after he ate his dinner he lay down to rest. He had only planed on resting a little while, but he was so tired that he must have gone to sleep. The first thing he heard was the hogs, and they were almost up on him by the time he heard them. He told them he just barely had time to swing up in the tree.

Mr. Heart said, "Thank God you did, they would have torn you to shreds."

After they drank their coffee, Mr. Heart told them he guessed they had better be going. Granny Heart would be worrying herself to death.

They all called their horses. The hogs had torn everything up, but thank God they hadn't bothered Tom's saddle. He used the blanket Pete had loaned him to put on Hart's back. He saddled her, and they were all ready to go. Then Tom remembered to tell Mr. Heart that he hadn't found any strays. He told him he had looked in all the gullies and shady places that he had come to. He had found some old tracks but no fresh ones. Then for the heck of it, he told Mr. Heart, "Guess I won't get to fire these ornery cusses after all."

They all laughed and told him, "Next time, boy, we will just leave you up in that tree."

When they got to the ranch, Mr. Heart told Tom to go on to the house, that they would take care of his horse. Tom told him that he had always told him not to trust anybody to tend to his horse. Mr. Heart laughed and told him this was different, that Granny Heart had worried herself sick all night about him, so guess he had better go check in.

Tom told him, "I guess I'd better. I don't want Granny worrying about me." He petted Hart and told her, "Thank you, old girl." Then he headed toward the house. Granny met him at the door and hugged him, then asked him, "Where have you been, Tom," and in the same breath, "Are you all right?" She wanted to know what had happened to him. So he had to tell her the story all over again and assured her he was all right. Especially after he ate that good breakfast, he told her that he sure did thank her for sending it to him. They set and drank coffee and talked until Mr. Heart came to the house. He told Granny, "See, you just worried for nothing," and that he had told her Tom would be all right, that he was too tough and ornery for anything to happen to him. He told Granny, "If Tom had a gun he would have shot every one of those dad blasted hogs."

Granny told him, "Now you stop teasing him and go on about your business. Tom is going to stay here today and get some sleep. He looks dead tired."

Tom was but he wasn't going to let them know it. He told Mr. Heart no, he was all right and if he had something he needed him to do, he was ready. But Tom told him he was right about the hogs, if he had a gun with him, those ornery hogs would be lying out there for buzzard bate. Mr. Heart assured him that they could get along without him and left the house. Granny heated some water and told Tom she wanted him to take a hot bath and get to bed. It would keep him from getting so stiff, she told him. The water was nice and warm, and Tom began to realize how tired and sleepy he really was. He got out and dried, put his night clothes on, and helped Granny carry out the water. He got in bed, and he slept until noon. Granny had washed his dirty clothes and was bringing them in to him about the time he woke up. She handed him his clothes and told him to put them on and she would fix them some dinner. He told her he would help her. He put his clean clothes on real quickly and went to the kitchen. She asked him if he slept good, and Tom told her, "Like a rock." They ate, and Granny said she thought he had better get started on his schoolwork that he had missed so much lately. Then she gave him some sheets of homework to do before suppertime, and he worked all afternoon on his schooling.

Mr. Heart came in about dusty dark. They ate supper, then he told Tom as soon as he helped Granny clean up the kitchen that he wanted to talk to him. Tom said okay and then began to wonder what he had done wrong. As soon as he finished drying the dishes, he went out on the porch. Mr. Heart was waiting for him. He began by telling him, "Now, Kid you did real good hunting for strays and what happened to you could have happened to anyone. I want you to go and come as you please without all ways feeling uneasy. Smitty has some spare time, and I have asked him to take you back to the south pasture and start teaching you how to shoot." He told him that Granny and he had both agreed that he should learn to defend himself if he needed to. Mr. Heart went on to tell him a gun was not a play pretty. That it was a weapon to defend yourself with. That he wanted Tom to learn to shoot real good and fast so he wouldn't ever have to be afraid again. He told him if he had been able to shoot, then he could have killed those hogs. He laughed and started kidding him and he wouldn't have had to spend the night in that tree.

Tom laughed also and told him, "You bet your boots I wouldn't. I would have shot every one of them."

"I bet you would have," Mr. Heart told him. "But I want you to remember, Tom, what I said. A gun is not to be used as a plaything. It is a weapon and will kill anything that you point it at. Young man, I want you to always remember, don't point it at anything unless you want to kill it. Now, Kid, I know you are a little young for a gun. But this is wild country and you need to know how to defend yourself. I hope, Tom, you will take it serious and won't let me and Granny down." He laughed again. "Granny Hart would just about kill me if you got hurt."

Tom told him he would remember what he had told him and that he would always be careful. Then he told Mr. Heart that he wasn't a kid any more. He was twelve years old now. Mr. Heart laughed again and told him, "That's right, Kid, we all keep forgetting you are growing up." He told Tom the subject was closed and he would start learning to shoot tomorrow. "Now don't get discouraged. It will take time, just like everything else has."

Tom was so proud he went in the house to tell Granny, and he felt about ten foot tall. She also lectured him real good about the use of guns.

The next morning Smitty was there right after breakfast with their horse saddled to go. Granny had fixed them a lunch after telling him over and over, "Now, Tom, you be careful and remember what we told you." She handed him the lunch, telling him, "I don't want ya'll to get hungry and watch out for the wild pigs." They left with Granny waving and still telling him to be careful. She hollered, "Smitty, now you take care of our boy." Tom could hardly wait to get to the east pasture and start learning how to shoot a gun.

Smitty lectured him all the way to the gate about a gun was not a play pretty. Tom had heard the same story the night before and again that morning, but he listened and nodded his head in agreement because he knew they were right and was telling him this for his own good. But Tom did tell Smitty like he told Mr. Heart that he wasn't a kid anymore. Smitty laughed and said, "Kid, you've got a lot to learn."

They got to the gate, and Tom told Smitty he would open the gate and jumped down off his horse. Tom had it opened and called to Hart, "Come here, girl," and here she came. Smitty came through the gate chuckling, and he told Tom, "Boy, you had that horse trained so good. I think if you asked her to go to the creek and get you a drink of water, she would."

Tom laughed and told him, "Maybe I will teach her that next."

They rode about thirty minutes before they found a deep gully that Smitty thought they could get down without taking a chance of their horses stumbling and breaking a leg. Also, it was deep enough to keep the bullets from causing any harm if something or somebody just happened to come by.

Smitty put up some dry twigs along the bank. He told Tom he had to learn how to draw and fire quick. Sometimes he might not have time to aim. He told him, "Like this" as he turned, drew, and shot at the twigs that he had set up, knocking the tops off each one of them. Then he handed Tom a gun and told him, "Now it's your turn."

Tom raised the gun and pulled the trigger, and nothing happened but a click.

Smitty told him, "Kid, that's your first lesson. Be sure your gun is loaded. You won't always have time to check it if you need it right quick. Every morning when you put it on, check it to make sure it has a full chamber of shells." Then he handed him the holster and told him to strap it on. He told him today he would learn how to draw and shoot without shooting his leg off. Smitty told him, "You won't have any bullets until you learn to barely clear your holster and then fire." He told Tom for him to put his gun in the holster and let him see how he could draw and fire. "Just draw and fire as if your gun was loaded," he said.

Tom spent all morning drawing and firing while Smitty lay under a tree in the shade. Tom thought at first he had gone to asleep, but he soon found out different. Each time Tom would draw, Smitty would holler instructions at him like, "Slow down, Kid, you're drawing too fast," or "Kid, if a bullet had been in that gun, you would have shot your leg off," or worse still, "Now, Kid, you are not drawing for speed, you only want to clear the holster before you shoot. Now try it again and go a little slower."

Tom tried to do what Smitty told him. He practiced all morning. He was determined to learn how to do it right. Finally, Smitty hollowed, "Kid, why don't we stop and eat that dinner Granny Heart fixed for us." He told Tom he would build a fire and make some coffee while he rested a spell. Tom told him, "It sounds good to me." He wasn't about to tell him that he was about ready to collapse. Tom's arm was so tired he didn't think he could lift that gun another time, but he wasn't about to let Smitty know it. He went over and unrolled his bedroll and almost collapsed on it. He asked Smitty, was he sure he didn't need him to help him. He said no. He thought he could do it by himself, then Smitty told him, "One thing I can say about you, Kid, you sure do have the spunk. It will take time, but you will learn to shoot real good." He told Tom for him to go ahead and rest for a while. Tom laid back on his blanket with his saddle for a pillow, and he went sound to sleep as soon as his head hit the saddle. The next thing he knew he heard Smitty calling for him to come and get it. The dinner that Granny had fixed was real good. She had packed fried chicken and biscuits. For dessert she had made some cookies. Smitty talked all the time while they ate their dinner, telling Tom he did good but he had to do better before he let him have bullets in his gun. After they ate all their food, they had another cup of coffee and then Smitty said, "It's time to go back to work."

He took Tom's gun and loaded it. He said he wanted Tom to practice aiming at the twigs he had set up. He showed him how to aim and fire then told him it was his turn. Tom aimed and fired just like Smitty did, except he didn't hit the twigs like he had. Smitty told him it was all right, that he hadn't hit the target his first time either. He told Tom to keep aiming and firing, and he went back over to his shade tree. Tom kept aiming and firing all afternoon with him hollering instructions at him. "Well, are you going to shoot or stand there? Don't take all day, aim a little higher. You are shooting too far left. Bring it in a little, shoot to the right." Tom shot right, left, up, and down. He kept shooting, until he ran out of bullets.

Then Smitty said, "Guess that's all for the day, unless you want to practice drawing from the holster again."

Tom told him he would. So he spent the rest of the day practicing just drawing and firing with an empty gun. He wasn't going to give up.

Finally, Smitty said, "Kid, I think it time to call it quits. Let's call our horses and go home before dark catches us. I am not too thrilled about trying to go home in the dark from here."

So they called their horses, saddled them, and headed home.

Tom told Smitty, "Aiming and shooting is a lot harder than it looked."

Smitty told Tom he did good and they would try again tomorrow and it will get easier every day.

When they got home, Granny was waiting for them. She could tell by the look on his face that he didn't do so good because she said, "Never mind, Tom, you will do better tomorrow. You can't expect to learn it all in one day."

The next morning, right after breakfast, Smitty was there again ready to go. Granny had fixed them another dinner. They filled their water canteens at the well. And with Granny telling him, "Now, Tom, you be careful. And, Smitty, take care of him and don't let him get hurt," they were gone.

They got to the gully a little after sunup. Smitty said he wanted Tom to get an early start. He laughed and told Tom, "By tonight you might be shooting at everything in sight and hitting them too."

Tom said, "I hope so." He was expecting to have real bullets in his gun, but like yesterday Smitty handed him his gun empty and told him to practice drawing from his holster. Tom strapped it on, and he found some more twigs and placed them along the bank. He thought, what did he need twigs for with no bullets. But he did as he was told and didn't say anything to Smitty.

He just started drawing and shooting like he had a full chamber of shells. He did this for about two hours with Smitty hollering, "Kid, slow down. You're still drawing to fast. Raise it up a little when you fire," or "Kid, if there had been bullets in that gun, you would have shot your leg off for sure," and for him to "watch where you're aiming, that you have to learn how to aim and shoot at the same time," and "Kid, slow down, the fast draw will come later."

Tom heard all those instructions, so many times until he thought, *Boy, I bet I hear them all in my sleep tonight.* Finally, Smitty called, "Come on over and rest a while."

Tom went over and told him, "That's what I had been waiting to hear for the last hour."

Smitty laughed and told Tom again, "One thing about it, Kid. You've got plenty of spunk and are not a quitter. You're doing real good, a lot better than yesterday." Then he handed him his canteen. Tom drank and laid down on his blanket. He was tired again today, but he wasn't about to let Smitty know it.

Tom woke up about an hour later. Smitty was still sleeping. Tom got up and hollered, "Wake up, you old son of a gun." Tom told Smitty, he bet Smitty was just saying he didn't know how to shoot good so he could lay in the shade and rest all day. Smitty grinned and told Tom, "Now, Kid, would I do that?" Just for that he was going to give him some bullets and let him shoot at twigs. He handed him a box of shells and watched while he loaded his gun.

Tom started shooting at the twigs. Once in a while he would shoot one, but most of the time he wouldn't. When he did, Smitty would holler, "That's good, Kid. Keep on like that until you can hit them ever time." Finally, Tom got where he was hitting them almost every time, and he was proud as punch. But Smitty said, "That wasn't good enough. You're taking too long to aim. A cat or something could have you ate up while you still had your gun in your hand aiming at it." Smitty came over and drew his gun and started shooting at the twigs and hit all of them. He started to load his gun and told Tom to load his, and they would fire together. Smitty told him, "Kid, every time I fire, you fire too." That was fun, they both fired at the same time, and each time Smitty fired, he would hit the twigs. Sometimes Tom would, but most of the time he missed it. They kept loading and firing until dinnertime.

Tom got to where he was hitting them a lot more than he missed. They stopped and ate their dinner, and Tom was so excited he could hardly wait to start back again. But Smitty said they would rest awhile and wait until it got a little cooler before they started again. About three o'clock Smitty told Tom he was doing better but it still wasn't good enough. He told him he had the knack of it now but that he had to practice and practice until he could just draw and fire without even thinking of what he was doing. Smitty told him he had showed him how, now it's up to him to keep on practicing until he was as good as he wanted to be. "Tomorrow you are on your own," Smitty told him. He would come and watch to make sure he don't shoot himself, but he would practice by himself.

Sure enough, Smitty kept his word. He built a fire for coffee and sat down waiting for it to make, paying little attention to Tom. Tom loaded his gun and started setting twigs up to shoot at. He didn't put his gun in his holster but just aimed and fired. He wasn't quite brave enough to draw and fire from it yet. He did this all morning until Smitty hollered at him to come over and have a cup of coffee.

Tom told him that sounded real good, and by the time he got over there, Smitty had him a cup poured. They did this all week, just drawing and shooting, resting and napping in between. Smitty didn't have to tell Tom he was getting better. He knew he was. By the end of the week, there was no telling how many boxes of shells he had shot up. But now Tom was ready to start drawing from the holster and shooting, but Smitty told him, "Let's not get that brave yet." That he still needed to practice more, drawing from the holster with no shells. Smitty told him he was doing real good aiming and shooing but he wasn't ready to shoot from the holster.

He grinned and told Tom unless he wanted to take a chance of losing a few toes. Tom told him, "No, thank you," that he would wait until Smitty told him he was ready. Smitty said, "Okay, then next week we will practice just drawing from the holster until you are ready for bullets."

That night Tom told Granny what Smitty had said. She, as always, told him, "Tom, it will just take time, but I know you can do it."

Tom could hardly wait until Monday. He was sure he would be drawing and shooting with bullets before the week was out. Monday morning he was up and dressed waiting to hear Granny stirring around in the kitchen. As soon as he heard her, he went in to see if he could help her. She asked him why he was up so early. He told her he had got to thinking about his gun practicing and couldn't sleep. He told her that he hoped he would be drawing and shooting from his holster with real bullets before the week was up. He had been so excited thinking about it and wanting to get started, he just couldn't sleep. Granny laughed and said, "Now, whoa, boy, slow down. You have plenty of time to learn. The best way to learn is the right way no matter how long it takes."

As soon as breakfast was over and Granny had their dinner packed, Tom was ready and raring to go. He told Granny thanks for the dinner, hugged her bye, and headed toward the door. She hollered her instructions at him, for him "to be careful, young man, and good luck."

Smitty was waiting for him, so they didn't lose any time getting started. They got to the ravine just about sunup. Smitty told him to set his twigs up and get started. Then he went over and began to build a fire and make coffee again. He didn't pay Tom anymore mind than if he wasn't there. Tom set his twigs up, but he wondered what for. Without bullets, what did Smitty think he was going to hit. Nevertheless, he did what he was told. He remembered Smitty telling him once, "Now, Kid, you do what I say and we will get along just fine."

Tom drew from his holster and fired all morning without any bullets. Finally, Smitty hollered, "Kid," just like he hadn't been paying any attention to Tom at all, "you're drawing too stiff. You need to practice until you can draw and fire even with your eyes closed, and then you'll be ready for the bullets. Maybe then you'll be good enough to keep all five of your toes."

Tom hollered back at him, "Ha-ha, that's funny."

Well, Smitty sat down pulled his hat over his eyes and said, "Kid, go to it."

Tom was a little disappointed, but he knew better than to argue with Smitty. So he said, "Yes, sir," and started back drawing and firing.

Again Tom didn't think Smitty was paying any attention to him at all, but it didn't take him long to realize he was watching ever move he made. Without even raising his hat, he hollered at Tom, "You had better know what your aiming at before you pull your gun from the holster. Most of the time you wouldn't have time to aim after you drew it." He finally took the hat off his face, sit up, and told Tom, "You want to always know what you are going to shoot before you shoot at it. And never shoot at anything that you can't see. Because you don't know what might be hiding in the bushes. Each time find your target, then draw and fire." After that Smitty laid back down and covered his face with his hat as if he hadn't said a word.

Tom spent the rest of the morning trying to do what Smitty had told him to do—find his target, then draw and fire. It seemed kind of foolish to him because with no bullets in his gun, how could he tell whether he hit his target or not. But like he said, you don't argue with Smitty. About midmorning Tom stopped and rested awhile and got him a drink. His mouth was so dry he could hardly swallow. After a while he went back to practicing. At noon Smitty hollered for him to quit awhile, and every day they did the same old routine and ate their dinner that Granny always fixed for them. After dinner they laid back on their saddle and Tom always went to sleep.

Then one day, about three, he heard Smitty yelling at him, "Well, Kid, are you going to sleep all day or do you want to put some bullets in that gun and start shooting."

Man, it didn't take Tom long to come alive. Smitty helped him line up some twigs, and again he cautioned Tom about clearing the holster before he fired.

"Now, Kid," he said, "you make doggone sure you clear your holster before you shoot. Granny would never let me hear the last of it if I brought you back with a hole in your foot."

They both stood side by side and began to fire. Tom fired first, drawing real careful, and believe it or not, he hit his target. He and Smitty spent the whole afternoon drawing and firing. Smitty hit his target ever time. Tom hit his most of the time. When he missed, he got upset, but Smitty told him that he was doing real good and that it took a lot of practice to hit the target every time. He told him, "Right now it's more important for you to concentrate on clearing your holster than hitting the target every time. Make sure you keep your mind on clearing your holster, not on hitting the target each time. In a few weeks you will be hitting it ever time. But right now is the time to be cautious and concentrate on clearing the holster. Keep your mind on what would happen if you missed clearing it. Remember this, if you don't clear it, you could likely come up with no toes left or maybe a missing foot." Smitty told him this every day and always ended by telling him, speed and hitting the target would all come in time.

Smitty cautioned Tom all the time he was training him on how to use his gun safely. He told Tom over and over, "Now, Kid, don't ever draw your gun unless you intend to use it and don't use it unless it is absolutely necessary. Remember when you draw and shoot at something or someone, you are taking a life. Walk around a fight if you can. It's not worth having a man's life on your conscience."

They left a little later than usual that night, and it was dark before they reached the house. Tom was as proud as a peacock. He could hardly wait to tell Granny and Mr. Heart how good he had done. They both were real proud of him, and Mr. Heart told him, "Kid, all you need now is a whole lot of practice."

Smitty told them Tom was real good, that he didn't know when he had seen any one learn as fast and do so good as Tom had done. He told them, he had taught him all he needed to know. Now the rest was up to him. After that Tom practiced every chance he got. Mr. Heart put him up a target down close to the barn. He didn't know how many shells he used in the next few weeks, but Mr. Heart never complained.

Tom stayed at the house and helped Granny until dinner. After that she would always say, "Well, Tom, it's lesson time." Tom wasn't any different from any other boy. He hated those lesson times worse than anything. He could hardly wait until they were over, so he could go outside and start doing his own things. She would always tell him, make sure he worked with Hart first because she looks forward to seeing him each day. Tom guess she did because each day he would run down to the gate and holler for her, and here she came running. She acted like she wanted to say, "Well, where have you been? I have been waiting for you all morning." Tom would play with her an hour or so, then put her back in the pasture. Then he would go over to the target board and start practicing. Hart would stand at the gate and watch him until he finished. Later, he would go back to Hart and talk to her for a while. He knew to someone else it would sound crazy, but Tom would always ask her how did he do today. After a while he would tell her bye, then he would start toward the house. About halfway he would turn, and she would still be standing there. He would wave at her and holler, "Bye, Hart, see you tomorrow." Then she would turn and go toward the pasture.

Tom would try to get to the house in time to help Granny fix supper, but sometimes she would have it started before he got there. He always told her he was sorry he was late and ask her why didn't she call him. She always told him, "That was all right." A few times she told him she had come to the door and looked out, but he was having so much fun she decided to let him stay a little longer. She always said she would have called him if she had really needed him. Then she always asked him how he had done today. They would talk all the time they were getting supper.

Tom remembered helping Aunt Lou, and he hated it, but with Granny it was fun. It didn't matter if Mr. Heart was home or not, they always ate when they got it ready. They never knew if he would be home or not. If he was coming in, he would try to make it in time for supper. Nevertheless, Granny would always put him a plate in the warmer that was over the stove just in case he was late. After supper they would clean the kitchen and then go to the parlor.

If Mr. Heart wasn't there, they would play checkers or dominoes until bedtime. Tom got to where he was pretty good. Anyway it was fun, and they passed away a lot of nights that way. When Mr. Heart was home, they either just talked or if he had come back from shipping the cattle, he would always bring a bunch of newspapers and Granny would read to them. She would read the whole newspaper, from the front page to the back page. They would do that each night until she finished them all. They didn't get the newspapers only about once a year, and it was a big treat to them.

One night Mr. Heart asked Tom how he was doing with target practicing. Tom told him he was doing real good, that he thought he would start trying to do some fancy drawing and shooting. Mr. Heart told him right quick, "Now, Kid, I told you, when I got you that gun, it wasn't a play pretty. It is a weapon to defend yourself with only and that's what I want you to use it for." He went on to tell him, "Kill man or beast if you have to protect your own life, but don't ever try to aggravate any one to make him draw. If I ever catch or even hear of you doing that, I will skin you alive. I didn't have you taught by the best of them to make a killer out of you or a trick shooter. Kid, you are to use that gun only if you have to. With a man, try talking first and you won't have anything to regret. If you can't talk him out of it, then, Kid, you have been taught well enough until you can shoot the gun out of his hand. Only shoot to kill if you don't have any other choice at all. Believe me, it's not easy to live with yourself after you have had to kill someone to protect your own life, let alone someone that was aggravated into starting a fight or someone you could have talked out of it. Try everything you know first to avoid a fight, and you won't have any regrets out of it."

Tom was fifteen years old when Granny told him she had taught him, reading, writing, and arithmetic and that's all he needed to know to make a good foreman. Boy, was that good news to him. From then on he worked with the regular cowboys from morning until night. He still stayed up at the house. Granny said she would not hear of him moving down to the bunkhouse.

Chapter 4

That fall Mr. Heart asked Tom if he would like to go with them when they took the cattle to ship. Man, that was a dream come true. Tom had been hoping Mr. Heart would let him go with them ever since he had learned how to rope and shoot. Tom could hardly wait until roundup was over, and they had all the cattle separated. They would bring them from each pasture and put in a holding pen. It had a narrow lane with a fence on each side that they called a loading shout. They would drive the cattle through it. Mr. Heart would be standing at the end of it. As the cattle came through, he would holler, "Save" or "Ship" and some men would drive the ones to be ship into another holding pen. The ones to be saved would be turned back in the pasture. They did this for several days until they had all the cattle separated. Bob would stand by the gate where the ones to be shipped went and counted them. Mr. Heart only kept the best heifers for his breeding stock. He would have Tom stand there with him, and he would show him what to look for and how to judge the heifers for good breeding stock. He trained him well, and after a while, he was letting him help judge whether to keep or ship. As usual Tom didn't learn it overnight. It took quite a few years of watching and training to learn it.

After all the cattle had been run through the shoot to judge whether to keep or ship and had counted them, some of the men would drive the ones to be save back to another big pasture. Later they would all be taken to winter pastures where they would spend the winter. By the time they were out of the way, another bunch of men would drive another heard in from another pasture. Usually that bunch would be what they would separate the next day. Each year they worked from sunup to sundown, getting them all ready to ship.

That first year was no exception. With them staying so busy, the time passed faster than Tom thought it would. But not fast enough for him. He was so excited about getting to go on his first cattle drive, he could hardly wait. Then one day, Bob hollered, "That's the last pasture, boss." They finished it right before sundown. Mr. Heart told them they would take the next few days off to rest and leave on Monday morning at daylight. Believe me, they needed the rest. They were all dead tired, including Tom.

Granny helped Tom get his clothes ready. They never took much, just two pairs of pants, two shirts, their underpants, two towels, and some soap. For Tom's first trip, he didn't need a razor.

Monday morning Mr. Heart told Tom to make sure his gun was fully loaded and he had plenty of shells in his gun belt. You don't know when we might need them. He told Tom they would have plenty of shells in the chuck wagon if they needed them for later.

"Now, Kid, it is not always easy," he told him. "We have the weather and often wild animals to cope with. The men take turns guarding the cattle at night." And he said that he would take his turn along with the rest of them. Mr. Heart told Tom, "There's usually eight or ten men guarding them each night. We break it up in three shifts, that way ever one gets some sleep. The men guarding them are stationed around the herd and walk a circle around them all night. The first night I'll put you with someone to teach you what to look for." He laughed. "And to make sure you don't go to asleep and fall off your horse. After the first night, the rest of the time you will be on your own. There have been rustlers before, but not often." He laughed. "That's when you will use your gun that Smitty taught you to use. Also, be sure you fill your canteen with water. What you have in it will be all you will have until we come to a river or find a water hole. Now, Kid, the men won't share their water with you. If a man is so careless and doesn't fill up his canteen at each stop we make and he runs out, he just has to be without until they reach the next water hole. That may sound hard to you, but your water and your horse is what it takes real often to save your life. It's up to each man to take care of both of them. I guess that's all I need to tell you."

Tom took his canteen and filled it up real good. Then he went down and called Hart and put his saddle on her. He tied his bedroll along with all his personal belongings behind his saddle, then he checked it a second time to make sure it was tied good and tight. He thought of what Mr. Heart told him, and he thought, *I don't think they would share their bed with him either if I lost mine.* He also tied his canteen on real good and checked it the second time also. Granny came down to tell them all bye. She told Tom, for him to be careful and not to take any unnecessary chances. She hollered at Mr. Heart, "You take good care of our boy."

They left right after that, all the men spreading out until some were on both sides and the back of the cattle. Tom was at the back. He turned and looked back, Granny was still standing there waving at them. Tom thought, *Bless her heart, who could be more kind and loving.*

The back was called drag. They told Tom they all would take turns riding drag. It was the worse of the three because you got the most dust and dirt. Boy, were they right. Sometimes it was hard to breath, it was so dusty.

All along the way, as long as they were still on the heartland, they had herds of cattle and more men to join their herd. Tom knew it was some of the sub ranches of Mr. Heart's that Bob had told him about when they was out camping that first time.

About midmorning some boys from each side came back, and they swapped places with them. They still got some dust and dirt, but it wasn't as bad. About noon they came to a river that had plenty of water and a lot of nice big shade trees. Pete was already there with the chuck wagon. He had made plenty of hot coffee. Most of the men helped water the cattle. Some of the men stayed scattered out around the cattle to make sure they didn't wonder to far way. The rest unsaddled their horses and rubbed them down good. After they let them cool off a spell, they led them down to the water so they could drink. Then they hobbled them so they could eat, but not wander to far from camp, in case they needed them in a hurry. Mr. Heart told the men they could eat their dinner (it was the biscuits, bacon, and egg they all made each morning), then they could rest a spell while the cattle grazed. Then some of the men would go relieve the other men so they could eat also. He told the men there was plenty of grass there for the cattle to eat and they didn't want to push them too hard and run the weight off of them, that he wanted them as fat as they could keep them for shipping.

They ate their dinner in shifts so there would be men keeping the cattle bunched at all time. Their second day out, Tom's crew had finished eating and they had just gone to relieve the other men so they could come eat when all hell broke loose. No one saw these men come up. They must have been hiding in the thick brush and trees that was along the river. All a sudden here they came, hollering and shooting. Of course, that stampeded the cattle. It was a mess. All the men that were on horses started trying to keep the cattle from scattering. The rustlers that had stampeded the cattle were hollering and shooting in the air to make the cattle run faster and some shooting at them. They all were trying to keep the cattle from scattering and trying not to get shot at as well as shooting at the rustlers. They knew the other men would be there as soon as they could sit saddled. The outlaws' biggest mistake was they probably thought the few men there was all the men that were driving the herd.

Tom had never shot at any one and especially riding and trying to shoot his target. About that time, he heard a zinging sound. He ducked, but the bullet hit the top of Tom's hat, knocking it completely off his head. It was his new Stetson that Mr. Heart had bought him on his last trip. That made Tom so mad, he stopped, aimed real good, and shot the man plum off his horse. Tom didn't think the man was dead, but he was hurt enough that he would think twice before he shot at someone again or tried to steal someone's cattle.

By then all the men were there, and the rustlers decided they had bit off more than they could chew and pulled out fast. It took us quite a while to get the herd stopped. Some of the men that were on the outside started trying to turn them toward the river. When they got the herd turned that way, they could go only so far. There was so much brush and trees until they just stopped. Some tried to turn down the river, but there were so many cattle, they couldn't. All the men were dead tired, but no one was hurt. Tom was the only one that came close to getting shot. After Mr. Heart found out no one was hurt and they had the cattle settled down, Tom told him, "I'm going back and see if I can find my hat." Mr. Heart told one of the men standing close by that Tom didn't know, "Roy, you take two men and go with him just in case some of those rustlers are still hanging around."

The rustlers wasn't as lucky as they were. They found five of them dead along the way. Slim said, "It served them right.

They were just a bunch of no gooders trying to get something for nothing." Tom noticed Roy had tied a shovel to the back of his saddle when they left. As they came across the dead men, they would stop and bury them. Sure enough they found Tom's hat with a hole blown completely through it. Roy told the boys that they wouldn't go any further, just in case some of them would be coming back looking for their dead. He said they didn't want any more trouble if they could help it. When they got back to camp, some of the men were there drinking coffee.

Mr. Heart saw them coming and followed them in to the camp. He told Tom, "I see you found it."

Tom was so mad when he saw what a hole they had shot in his brand-new hat he threw it to Mr. Heart. "Yes, and look at it."

Mr. Heart took the hat and looked at it and threw it back to Tom. "Well, Kid," he said, "I would say you are one lucky fellow. That bullet missed your head by two or three inches, give or take one. If I was you, Kid, I would find me a quiet place and kneel down and thank the Lord that I was still breathing."

Tom hadn't gotten scared until then, but he did what Mr. Heart told him he should do. He went off to a quiet place and knelt down and thanked God he was still breathing.

It took them all the rest of that day and the next to gather up the stray cattle. Mr. Heart said they were about fifty short. Some were dead that had got trampled in the stampede. Others that were in the front had just kept running. He said they might pick up a few along the trail in the next few days.

The rest of the trip went just fine. They did pick up some more of the cattle along the way but not all fifty that they had lost. But Mr. Heart said they were lucky that they found as many as they did. With them losing two days of their time, they had to push a little harder than they would have liked to. They didn't have a choice. They had to be there when the train came in to load the cattle to be shipped. Mr. Heart had shipped cattle for so many years at this same time of year. He knew they would wait for him awhile, but he didn't think the conductor would wait for two or three days. Nevertheless, the cattle could only go for so long. So they would drive them as hard as they dared during the day and rest them at night. Mr. Heart knew all the places along the way where there was plenty of good grazing and plenty of good cold water for the cattle.

He told the men he didn't think the rustlers would be back after the beating they took, but he didn't want to take any chances. So they would use more men on each shift to make sure the cattle were well guarded. By doubling up like that, the men didn't get as much rest. Mr. Heart apologized to the men and told them he would make it up to them later. He told them he wanted to make sure the rustlers didn't decide to get more men and hit them again. He didn't know anything else to do. All the men agreed with him. As Bob told Tom once, all the men loved and respected Mr. Heart and would follow him to the hot place and back if it was necessary. They all proved it on this trip. Mr. Heart sent one man ahead to tell them they might be late. Mr. Heart told him to go as fast as he could, but make sure he make it on time.

They had the usual troubles—hot weather, sand blowing, and hard work—but the rustlers let them alone. The men worked hard keeping the cattle moving that at night they were all bone tired. They all were getting half the amount of sleep as they were getting before the rustlers. Some slept from dusty dark until twelve, then they would relieve the men on duty, and they would sleep until daylight. By the time they got to the railhead, they were all dead tired and filthy but not one complained. They had a job to do, and they did it. They got there about noon of the day that the cattle were supposed to be shipped that morning. Sure enough, the conductor had waited for them.

He told Mr. Heart he knew they would be there as soon as they could, that he had never been late before. And he hoped everything wasn't too bad. He asked Mr. Heart, "Did all the men come through without getting hurt?" Mr. Heart told him, "They were all just fine," that their only close call was one man got a hole shot through his hat.

While the men loaded the cattle, Mr. Heart went back to their camp to bathe in the creek and dress. By the time they had them loaded, he was back and ready to go. He called them all together and told them that he had been thinking that the rustlers would know they would have a lot of money with them when they started back and might try to rob them then. Rather than taking that chance, he would like for all the men to stay there at the camp until he got back. Most of the time the men that helped drive the cattle would go back to their sub ranches after they had helped load the cattle. Before Mr. Heart got back, some more men from each sub ranch would meet them in covered wagons to pick up their supplies. The wagons never came with them on the cattle drive, but Mr. Heart picked up all the sub ranches supplies. The covered wagons would come several days behind the drive so they wouldn't be in all the cattle's dust. They would always be there before Mr. Heart got back. The wagons were always waiting at the train station when Mr. Heart got back, to be loaded with their supplies, then they all went go back together.

This trip wasn't any different from any other one. After they had loaded the cattle, they all went back to the camp. The men took care of their horses, and by then Pete had coffee ready. So they all ate their biscuits and drank some coffee. Then they all grabbed their towels, soap, and clean clothes, then headed for a much-needed bath. Boy, did it feel good. They all soaped and scrubbed all the filth and sand off them. Then they just swam around and just enjoyed the leisure time of having nothing else to do. They had worked hard, day and night, with very little time for baths or rest, until it just felt good to have nothing to do. They washed their dirty clothes and hung them on bushes all up and down the creek. Then they all shaved, combed their wet hair, and went back to camp. Pete had them a large pot of coffee made, so they just sat around drinking coffee. They were still too tired for much kidding. They all laid down, and it wasn't long until they were asleep. The next five days they slept, ate, played cards, drank coffee, went swimming, and waited for Mr. Heart to get back. Tom, like all the rest, enjoyed the leisure time; but he was glad when Mr. Heart got back.

The day he was to be back, the men on horses and the men in all the covered wagons went to the train stations and were there waiting for him when he came in. Tom remembered the time he came in on that same train. It seemed like years ago, just a scared little boy, not knowing where he was going or what he would do when he got there. Then he looked around at all these men on horseback that had become his friends and his family. About that time the door of the train opened, and there stood Mr. Heart, a tall man with a heart twice as big as he was. Tom knew this was his home, his family, his life; and he wouldn't go back to his old life if he could. Mr. Heart hollered at them all, and they all hollered back. Then as always they asked about his trip and had he got a good price for the cattle. He told them the trip was the same as usual, and yes, he got a real good price for all the cattle. That he wanted to thank them for their faithfulness and hard work, that without them he would never have made it. Then, everyone, told him, "Boss, that's our job, and it wasn't any more than we should have done." But Mr. Heart told them he knew better than that and "Thanks anyway." Then he told those boys, "We are burning daylight, let's get this boxcar unloaded."

The wagons rolled up to the door, and as soon as the door opened, some of the men were inside and Bob was calling out what and how much went on each wagon. It didn't take them long to get all the wagons loaded. Tom stood there, remembering back at the little eight-year-old boy that was trying to hide his feelings and act like he was as big as the rest of them.

When the last wagon was loaded, Mr. Heart hollered, "Let's roll 'em," and like clockwork, they all began to pull out. They went down to where they were camped. As always Pete had a pot of hot coffee waiting for them. On a drive the cook was the most important man of the whole crew. If the men were lucky enough to have a good cook, they had it made and Pete was the best cook any one could have. Driving cattle was a tired, dusty, dirty job; and the men always looked forward to a cup of coffee when they got a chance to rest and a good hot meal at night. Pete saw they got it and that the men was well taken care of from headaches, cuts, and bruises to good coffee and food. They all sat around drinking coffee until supper was ready. They ate an early supper. Mr. Heart said he wanted to go to bed early so they could get an early start the next morning. When he said early, he meant eat breakfast and be ready to pull out at daylight

The next morning they did get up early, and by daylight they were ready to go. Mr. Heart hollered at Tom and said, "Oh, by the way, Kid, I had forgot to tell you. I had got you a new hat." He pitched him a new black Stetson hat. Tom caught it and told him, "Thank you." Mr. Heart looked real serious at Tom and said, "Now, Kid, try to be more careful with this one. Stetsons are too expensive to use for target practice. If you have got to practice on the job, then please see if you can find something cheaper to use rather than your hat." He never cracked a smile.

Tom took the old hat off and put the new one on. He wasn't going to let him have the last word, so he acted real serious and said, "Thank you and I will try my best to find something else to play with."

All the boys were dying laughing, and one of them said, "Wait until Granny Heart sees how you have been playing with it. Boy, will she ever hit the ceiling."

Mr. Heart said real quick, "Now, boys, this is our little secret," and he double dared any one of them to say one thing about the hat to Granny. He laughed and told them, "Do any of you want to get me killed? The hat story dies right here, and it will be buried before we get home. Get it?"

They all agreed with him. "That's right," they said. "The hat story will end right here, and this would be the end of it."

Bob, of course, had to add his two cents' worth. He raised his hand like he was being sworn to something and said, "We will all swear, Boss, that this will be the end of the hat story and of Kid playing gun practice with his hat while he was on guard."

They all started laughing and poking fun at Tom.

He wasn't going to let them get the best of him, so he told them, "Boys, you all don't have enough smarts to know I was just trying to protect you all. The next time I will just let the rustlers shoot all your hats off."

Mr. Heart said that with that smart thinking he guessed they had better get started.

The trip back was a lot easier than the trip going. They didn't lollygag along, but they did stop more often and let the horses that were pulling the wagons rest. They all were able to get more rest at night. Mr. Heart told them they would stand guard at night because he didn't want to be caught off guard, just in case the rustlers did try to rob them. He told them only three men would stand guard at a time, and they would change every three hours. That way all of them would get some rest. They stopped at night so they all could take a bath and wash their clothes. Also, the trip back was not as dusty as it was going, making it easier on both men and horses.

On the fourth day, Tom saw the house. It was still a good ways off, and he could just barely make it out. He remembered the first time he saw it and how tired and scared he was. That seemed like a hundred years ago. This time he was so excited. This was his home now, and he knew Granny would be waiting for them

They had started losing wagons as soon as they came through the gate with the big heart over it that read "Our Home." Now they had only three left. When they got to the house, one stopped at the house and the other two went on down to the bunkhouse. Bob and Slim helped them put everything on the back porch As soon as Granny heard them, here she came. She hugged Tom and said, "Welcome back, I sure have missed you all." She hugged Mr. Heart and asked him if they had a good trip. He never let on about the trouble that they had but told her just the same as usual, it was a long, old dusty trip. Not a word did he say about the rustlers or their shootout trying to protect the cattle, or their hard days of rounding them up, or of their hard trip trying to get there on time, and still was late, or anything about Tom's hat. He just smiled and told her, "Boy, are we looking forward to one of your good meals, a hot bath, and a bed."

She told him, she knew they would be all right, that she had prayed for them every day while they were gone. She told them as soon as they got the food in that she would put them away and get supper. The groceries consisted of things that they didn't raise and medicine they couldn't make. Most of their food they raised themselves. Each sub ranch raised their own hogs for butchering, had their own milk cows, and raised their own garden. It was up to them. If they raise a garden, they could eat good from it all year. Granny and Pete always raised a huge garden. Tom, and anyone else that had time off, would help them gather it and get it ready to can. Granny and Pete canned berries, fruit, and vegetables when it started coming in until it was gone. Thanks to Granny and Pete, they always had plenty of good food to eat.

Granny told them there was plenty of hot water in the reservoir for both of them and to get cleaned up before supper. After they got all the food in, Tom and Mr. Heart filled the tub with hot water. Then they put more water in the reservoir just in case. While Mr. Heart took a bath, Tom went down to tend to Hart. By the time he finished with her, Mr. Heart had finished his bath. He helped Tom empty the tub and filled it up again, and then it was Tom's turn. Boy, did it feel good to have a hot bath after all those weeks of cold water. He soaped all over and rinsed off real fast. He wanted to stay longer, but he knew Granny would have supper ready before he got dressed anyway. Sure enough, she called just as he finished dressing. She had laid out clean clothes for both Mr. Heart and him. It sure felt good to have fresh-washed clothes. They rinsed their clothes at night in the creeks and hung them up on brushes to dry. It wasn't like having them washed with hot water and soap. All they could do with cold water was get the sweaty smell partly out of them so they could stand to smell each other.

Tom went in the kitchen for supper, and man, what a supper. Granny had fried ham and fixed cream potatoes, red-eye gravy, and green beans. She had made hot biscuits and a peach cobbler also. Mr. Heart and Tom ate like they were starved to death, and they really were for a meal like that.

Mr. Heart told Tom, he thought they ought to take Granny along with them next trip, that they sure didn't have meals like that while they were gone. Tom agreed with him, but Granny laughed and said, "Oh no, you don't, I don't think they could afford to pay the wages that I would have to have. When Paw and I were just starting out, I use to go on every trip. We didn't have but few men and not many cattle to ship. If we could have gotten the men, we couldn't have paid them anyway. I worked beside Paw from morning until night branding, castrating, and anything else that had to be done. When it came time to drive the cattle to town to sell, I drove the chuck wagon and did the cooking. It was a hard, old life, but we made it. With the Lord's help and all our hard work, it paid off. Look at what we have accomplished."

They finished supper, and Tom helped Granny clean the kitchen. Then they all went in the parlor. Mr. Heart had brought some newspapers in as usual. Granny always said, "Just because we lived at the end of nowhere, that isn't any excuse for us being ignorant of what was going on in the rest of the world." Now you must realize back then a newspaper was a rare treat. Very few towns had a newspaper in those days. Even then they were just small papers and not a whole lot of news in them. But Granny would read them from front to back. That was one of the highlights of Mr. Heart's coming home, and Granny always looked forward to getting them. She would read to us each night until she read all of them. The amount of nights depended on how many papers he was able to get.

After that first trip, Mr. Heart let Tom go each time. They didn't have a lot of trouble. Just the usual rainstorms, heat, and dust to cope with. The trip was long hot and dusty. By then the rustlers knew that the Big Heart ranch had plenty of men to defend themselves, not only that but they knew that they would fight for that which was theirs and they let them alone.

Chapter 5

Tom will never forget one night right after supper when Mr. Heart said, "Kid, as soon as you and Granny get through cleaning the kitchen, come out on the porch." "I want to talk to you." Tom was so upset he couldn't keep his mind on helping Granny. Finally, she told him to go on out and she would finish up. Tom went out wondering what he had done wrong. He sat down facing Mr. Heart and asked him, "What's up?"

Tom guessed Mr. Heart saw he was real nervous. He said, "Now, Kid, you haven't done anything wrong. But there comes a time that we have to face facts."

Well, that really scared Tom. He thought Mr. Heart had found out who he was and was going to send him back.

Mr. Heart went on to say, "You know, Hart is getting old, and she is not going to be able to keep going on these round-ups. It's time that you started training another horse to take her place."

Tom had never thought about that. He had always just thought he and Hart would grow old together. Now here sat Mr. Heart telling him Hart was getting old. It just broke his heart. Tom tried not to show how upset he was, but tears started running down his face and he couldn't stop them. And as hard as he tried not to, he started crying.

Mr. Heart went on to tell Tom, "Animals age faster than humans. Hart loves you so much that she would kill herself trying to please you, but the fact is, she is getting to old to keep doing such hard work."

He just couldn't realize that Hart wouldn't be able to go as long as he did. Tom tried to tell Mr. Heart this, but he was so choked up he couldn't. Mr. Heart got up and came over and put his arm around Tom's shoulder and patted him. "I know how hard it is." He told him he remembered when his dad had told him he was going to have to put his first horse out to pasture and how he had cried his eyes out for over a week. He told Tom he still could remember his dad explaining to him, just like he was trying to explain to Tom. Mr. Heart went on to tell him his dad told him he had to love his horse enough to do what's best for her and he knew that Tom loved Hart that much also. He told Tom this didn't mean he had to put Hart out to pasture and forget her. He could still ride her around there some, but she was getting to old to go on long trips like they had to take.

Mr. Heart told him, he had picked him out a real good horse. He won't ever take Hart's place, but he will make his own place if Tom would let him. "Now in the morning, Kid, I want you to go to the barn with me and look at the horse, and if you don't like him, you could pick out another one. You know we have plenty to choose from."

Tom told him he knew they did have, but he had never looked at any of them close, that he had Hart and she was all he ever needed. Tom told Mr. Heart if he thought it was time to train another horse that he would look at them.

Granny knew what Mr. Heart was talking to Tom about and when he went in to the house she was there waiting for him. She came right over and put her arms around him. He had tried so hard not to cry. But when she came over, he threw his arms around her and started crying like a baby. She kept petting him and saying, "It's all right, Tom. It's all right. There comes a time in ever man's life when the tears have got to flow, you just cry all you want to." Tom finally stopped and told her how foolish he felt, crying like a baby, but again she told him it was all right.

The next morning, Mr. Heart took him down to the barn to see the new horse. He was a pretty thing. He was the same color as Hart, but he didn't have the four white stockings like she had and he was taller. He did have the heart in the middle of his forehead. Mr. Heart asked, "Kid, what do you think about the horse?" Tom told him he was okay. He tried to show some enthusiasm and tell him how pretty he was and that he was sure he could train him to be a real good horse. But the truth was Tom thought if he had to have a new horse, one was as good as another. Tom tried to hide the way he was feeling, but Mr. Heart knew how he felt because he had been there before. He told him, "Tom, he is really a good horse. In fact, one of our best. Give him time and he will be as dependable as Hart. He won't take her place, but he would come to love you as Hart loved you." He told Tom now if he wanted him, he was going to give him some time off just to train him like he did Hart. Tom told him that he was fine, and Mr. Heart said that's good then and that he could start training him tomorrow. Tom was glad he didn't say today because he didn't think he could have started with him right then. He had to have time to think and grieve. Also, he had to have time to explain all this to Hart. Mr. Heart told him, "Let's go back to the house, and you could tell Granny." Mr. Heart had showed him to her yesterday and she said she thought he would make a fine horse for Tom. She would be anxious to learn how he liked him. She was waiting at the back door when they got there. Tom tried as hard as he could to act proud of the horse. But Granny saw his face, and he just couldn't hide his feeling from her. She hugged him and said, "Give it time, Tom." Bless her heart she had made his favorite cookies for him. She didn't say they were for him, but he knew they were.

That was one way of showing her love and letting him know she understood. They sat around the table and had cookies and coffee and talked for a while. Mr. Heart told Granny that he had given Tom the day off tomorrow and he would start training his horse. She said that was fine because the sooner the better.

After Mr. Heart left, Tom asked Granny if she had anything she wanted him to help her with. She said no, that he could go down and take Hart out for a while. He hugged her and thanked her for the cookies. She told him "You're welcome" and there are plenty more when he wanted them.

Tom went down to get Hart. He didn't have to call to her. When she saw him coming, she came to the gate and was standing there waiting for him. He just opened the gate, and she came to him. He closed the gate, and she followed him like a little puppy. He petted her and told her what Mr. Heart had said about her getting to old to go on long trips anymore and that he had to train another horse to take care of him when he had to be gone. Tom knew all this sounded stupid and would to someone that had never had a horse and especially one that they had to depend on to save their life, like they all did. He spent all afternoon talking to her. He told her how much he loved her and that no other horse would ever take her place. Also, he told her that he had to start tomorrow there at the barn lot and that she could watch him if she wanted too. They rode around some, and Tom realized it was getting late. He put her back in the pasture and told her bye and that he would see her tomorrow.

Granny was already in the kitchen when he got there, so they finished getting supper together. Mr. Heart didn't get home by the time they got it ready, so they went ahead and ate.

Granny asked, "Tom, how did it go?"

He told her, "Well, I explained to Hart about the other horse."

Bless her heart she didn't laugh at him but said like it was the most important thing in the whole world, "Tom, I am glad you did, and I know she will understand."

They talked all during supper about it. Granny always knew just what to say to make everything all right, and by the time supper was over, Tom felt a lot better about it all. By morning he was ready to go down and start training the other horse.

Granny told him, "Now, Tom, he won't be Hart. But give him time and have patience with him like you did with Hart and he will do all right. You have to show him what you want him to do, and he will do it. In time to come, the horse will grow to love you and depend on you like Hart does."

After that talk Tom went down to the barn feeling good about it all. Mr. Heart had the boys put him in a stall in the barn. Tom was glad, that way he didn't have to go out and catch him. He put a rope around his neck and led him out to the same little pen where he had trained Hart. When Hart saw him, she came up to the gate and stood there watching him work with the horse and it just about broke Tom's heart. She just stood there and watched as if she knew what was going on and was letting him know it was all right and that she understood. He rubbed the horse down and talked to him and told him he was going to be his horse and they had to get acquainted. He seemed to like that. He was already broke to ride and was real gentle. The sub ranch that raised the horses would break them to ride, but the rest was up to the owner that got them. This time Tom had apples to start with. He gave him a piece of apple and told him to stay but sure enough just like Hart did, he followed him. Tom worked with him until about one o'clock. He saw Granny standing in the yard, waving and calling for him to come in. He took the horse over and turned him loose in the same pasture with Hart. She was still standing there by the gate waiting for him. Just as soon as he got the horse in the gate,

Hart went up to him. Tom thought that the horse would go on to the pasture but he didn't. He just stood there while he petted Hart. When Tom turned to leave, he went on off but Hart stayed there until Tom was almost at the house. Tom turned to wave like he always did, then and only then did Hart turn to go. Granny was there on the porch waiting for him, and as soon as he got there, she asked, "How did it go?"

Tom told her, "Just about like it did when I trained Hart. But the horse did stay at the gate until I turned to come to the house."

They went in and ate dinner and took a cold glass of water and went back to the porch. He didn't realize how tired he was until he stopped and sat down. They sat there talking until it was time to get supper.

"Tom," Granny asked him, "what have you named your horse?"

He told her that he hadn't thought of a name yet.

She asked him, "What had you been calling him?"

Tom told her he had just been calling him big boy until he could think of a name for him.

She said, "Well, one will come to you later, and it will be just right. But he had better name him soon or he will think big boy is his name."

They fixed supper and ate. Mr. Heart hadn't made it in by then. After that they played dominoes until time to go to bed. As hard as Tom thought, he just couldn't come up with a suitable name. The next morning he stayed at the house helping Granny. It was wash day, and they washed clothes all morning. They finely finished the last load and went in to eat dinner.

They were both tired and thirsty. Tom went after a bucked of cold water, and they had a glass of cold water with some ham and a cold biscuit that they had left over from breakfast. After that they rested for a while and then Tom went down to work with the horse. He was still in the pasture but when Hart saw him. She came to the gate, and he followed her. Tom petted Hart first and told her how much he had missed her. Then he put a rope on Big Boy and led him through the gate. Tom talked to him all the time he was rubbing him down. Tom did tell him that he had missed him too. They worked until suppertime. He acted like he was enjoying it. Tom petted him and turned him loose in the pasture again. Hart was standing there, and Tom made sure he didn't neglect her. She seemed like she didn't mind him working with Big Boy. Again, he just stood there while Tom petted Hart, and when Tom turned and went through the gate, he left again but Hart waited as always.

Mr. Heart came home right after Tom got to the house, so he told them both how the horse was doing. Both said, "Just give him time." Mr. Heart asked Tom what he had named him, and again Tom had to tell him the same thing he had told Granny. Mr. Heart told him, as Granny had, "Kid, if you keep calling him Big Boy, he will think that's his name. It's real important for you to name him as soon as possible. So while you are training him, he will learn his name and know when you call it and that name means him." Mr. Heart told Tom he didn't think Big Boy was a bad name for him. But to Tom, Big Boy just didn't suit the horse. He went to bed again that night still thinking of what he was going to name him. Tom knew he had to come up with something real soon.

The next morning, just after breakfast, Tom went down to work with him some more. Hart saw him coming, and here she came running as hard as she could. The horse saw what she was doing, and here he came. He was a good way farther out than Hart was, but he passed her like she was standing still. Tom watched him come and thought, *Boy, he runs like lightning.* And just out of the blue, it came to him. His new horse's name would be Lightning. When he got to the fence, Tom petted him and said, "Hello, Lightning, that will be your name." Hart came up about that time, and Tom took time to pet her and tell her the horse's name was Lightning. Then he asked her how did she like it. Tom led Lightning through the gate and began to work with him. Hart stood there watching them, like she wanted Tom to know she approved of the horse and also his name. He worked with him every day that week and the next. But he didn't get as anxious as he did with Hart because Tom knew eventually he would learn. Like Granny told him over and over with Hart, "Give her time and have patience with her and you can do it."

With Lightning, Tom had more apple slices in his pocket, and every now and then, Tom gave him a piece of one. Some of the times he would go over and give Hart a slice also. Then one day, by midmorning, Lightning seemed like he started catching on. By noon he was coming to him when he called, but Tom was still having trouble teaching him to stay. Tom just started leaving him and telling him to stay. By that afternoon he seemed to know what Tom wanted him to do, and he did it. Tom would call to him, "Come here, Lightning." Each time here he came, and then Tom would give him a slice of apple and tell him to stay, and he did. A few days later they worked on that, and by noon he was doing pretty good. After that the rest went easy. By roundup time Tom had him trained to drive cattle and the whole works, and boy was he good. He could turn on a dime, and no cow ever got by him. When they started rounding up the cattle and branding them, he was as good or better than any of them. Tom never had any trouble with him when he had to rope a calf. He seemed to know what he was supposed to do, and he did it every time. For the second time in Tom's life, he fell head over heels in love with his horse.

On one of the trips, Mr. Heart brought back three green horns, and they were green horns from the word *go*. Mr. Heart finally one morning called Tom in and told him, "Kid, will you work with them and see if you could make cowboys out of them."

It wasn't anything new for him to bring back men on his trips. Any one that was down and out and needed a helping hand always found one in Mr. Heart. It didn't matter if they were drunkards, thieves, outlaws, or whatever—if they wanted to straighten up and make a better life for themselves, they always found a friend in Mr. Heart. He always told them it's not what you were but it's what you want to make of your life now that counts. Very few ever let him down. Most of them did straighten up and made good hands. They seemed so grateful that someone was willing to give them a second chance.

It didn't take Tom too long to figure out these three guys were going to be the exception. They were buddies, and all they were looking for was a free place to stay and three squares. Tom tried to teach them how to ride a horse, but it was a big joke with them. Finally, Mr. Heart told Tom he wanted him to take them and go out to the north pasture looking for strays before winter set in.

He said, "And maybe they will at least know how to set a horse well enough to stay in the saddle by the time they get back."

Tom showed them how to tie their bedroll, a heavy coat, and what little else they would be carrying on the back of their horses. Jake fixed them a sack of grub, and Tom tied it on the back of the pack horse. He told them while they were tying their rolls on the horses, "Don't ever go out this time of year without a heavy coat. It's pretty now, but sometimes it can turn mighty cold in no time flat. Also make sure to take plenty of matches and a warm blanket."

They left right after that. They stopped at noon to rest and to eat their dinner. Jake had fixed them some biscuits and ham, so they didn't have to worry about dinner. Tom built a fire and made a pot of coffee. While the coffee was making, he told them to unsaddle their horses and rub them down good. They halfway did it and started back to where the camp was to lie down. Tom hollered at them and not real kind either, "Unless you all want to walk the rest of the trip, you had better hobble your horses." He showed them how to do it. Then told them that way the horses would be able to graze and rest while they ate. By then the coffee was made. Tom got the coffee cups and the ham and biscuits out. They leaned back against a tree and ate their biscuits. They all complained about the cold biscuits, that they didn't hire on to eat such crap. Tom tried to ignore them. He got up and leaned his saddle against the tree and laid down to rest. He thought, *If they don't have enough sense to follow suit, I'll be dog gone if I tell them, just let them rest any way they wanted to.*

They rested about an hour. Tom woke them and told them they had better get started if they were going to make it before dark. After, they all went out and got enough wood to replenish the wood they had used, with them complaining about it all the time. They saddled their horses, and Tom checked them to make sure the saddle was tight enough and they were on their way.

It took them until late that afternoon to get to the north pasture. They camped under a tree that had low branches. Tom told them what Bob had told him years ago, about always finding a tree with low branches so it will help keep the wind, rain, and dew off their blankets. Also, he told them to try to camp next to water if possible so they would have plenty of fresh water. Tom could tell it went in one ear and came out the other. Everything was just a big joke to them. Tom had done both. There was a big tree with low branches, also a beautiful creek just down below their camp. Tom had camped there many a time when they came each year looking for strays. They unsaddled their horses, and you would think that grown men wouldn't have to be told every time to rub them down and hobble them. Tom went over to his own horse out of habit and began to rub him down. They started to go lie down, but Tom told them, as he was told, "Always take care of your horse first. He is your guarantee of getting back home safe. To be caught out here without a horse it would mean your death." They halfway did it, and Tom was real ticked off with them. He told them that they were going to keep on taking halfway care of their horses and when they needed them, they were not going to take care of them at all. He also told them they had to treat them right, to let them build up their trust in them, then they will do anything that you all ask them to do.

They started joking and said, "Boys, did you hear that. If we take care of our horses, then they will do anything we want them to do. Well, maybe we can ask them to rob a bank for us, and we won't have to be out in this godforsaken land." They all got a big kick out of that and went off joking about learning how to speak horse language and playing nursemaid to a bunch of stupid horses. They halfway tended to them and went back to the camp and laid down.

Tom started supper. He had to tell them one by one, over and over, what to do. Every night he would tell, "Joe, go down and get some fresh water. Make sure you get it in a deep place so it will be clear and not muddy." Mike and Henry had to be told to find some wood and bring enough in so they would have plenty to last the night. He also told them, as he was told, when they left the next morning, they would leave enough wood to start a fire and last awhile for the next man that came along.

They all three wanted to know why should they cut wood for the next man. "Let him cut his own wood." Tom tried to explain to them as he was told, but they still always left grumbling. Tom would build a fire, then each night he would start supper. By the time Joe got back each night with the water, Tom would have a good fire going, biscuits made in the Dutch oven, and was slicing some ham in the skillet. The fire hadn't burned down enough to make coals, so he couldn't put the Dutch oven on it yet. He would make a fresh pot of coffee, and when the coals were ready, he would put it all on and sit back waiting for the meat to be turned. By the time Mike and Henry got back with the wood, Tom would have supper almost ready. They all three would go over and lay down under the tree and just wait until Tom got it ready, just as if Tom was the boy they had hired to cook and care for their needs. And every night they grumbled about roughing it. Not one of them ever offered to help Tom fix it. Each night, by the time Tom got the meal ready, he was getting pretty put out with them.

After supper he flat told them they would clean up their mess. They halfway did it, grumbling all the time. Every day Tom had to tell them over and over, "Now don't ever leave leftover food in camp for the wild animals to smell because they would come up to get it. Make sure there is nothing left to tempt them." After that they would made a second pot of coffee and talk for a while. Tom would always have to tell them, they had better hit the sack, that they would be up bright and early the next day. Tom told them they wanted to look for strays and get out of here as soon as they could, that sometimes winter came early up in these hills and he wasn't hankering to get caught up here when it did.

They were up early, and by daylight, they had their breakfast and were saddling their horses to go. Tom explained to them that they would check all the brushy areas and the ravines for cattle. They scattered out a good ways apart. Tom told them to holler if they found any stock. They hunted three hard days, and they found a few each day. Tom was surprised the boys worked hard. At the end of the third day, he told the boys they would drive the cattle to a gully that was close by and tomorrow they would head home. They got them in the gully and settled down. It made a perfect holding pen. It had high walls on all three sides, and the only side they would have to guard was the side they came in. Tom left Joe on guard at the gap to make sure the cattle didn't try to get out, and the rest of them went on in to set up camp. Tom had used this place before, so he knew where to go, where they usually camped. There was some firewood there, but they all three went to find more. They were back in no time flat, each with an armful. Tom fixed supper, and they ate. Tom told them that they only had the gap to watch, that they would break the night up in four parts and that way all of them could get some sleep. Henry went to relieve Joe so he could come in and eat supper. About midnight a blizzard started blowing in. Then it started snowing so hard they could hardly see their hands before their faces. Henry came in hollering that they better pack up fast and get out of here.

Tom tried to tell them that they wouldn't get halfway before they got lost. Their best bet was to stay there until it blows over. "Mr. Heart will send some help as soon as he can." They started arguing. Mike said the only thing Tom was thinking of was the cattle and they didn't mean doodle squat to them and they'd be dogged if they risk their lives for someone else's cattle. Tom told them they would risk their lives if they didn't stay. He tried to tell them again that as hard as it was snowing and as cold as it was, that chances were they wouldn't make it, cows or no cows.

Henry said, "Well now, it's no use arguing about it. Let's take a vote whether we go or stay."

Well, that made Tom mad, and he told them, "I don't care how many times ya'll voted. I'm staying here."

Joe told him, "I don't understand why anyone would send men out this time of the year knowing this might happen."

Tom kept telling them, "This is unusual. Winter usually don't come as bad this soon. Mr. Heart will send help as soon as he can." He tried again to tell them what their chances were, and finally, he told them that they wouldn't be able to go tonight anyway so why don't they wait and see what tomorrow would bring. They finally agreed. Tom told them, "Now let's get some sleep." He banked the fire up real good, then told them to put their saddles close together against the tree trunk and put all four blankets together and they all four would wrap up in them. That way all their body heat would help keep them warm. They all settled in, and sure enough they stayed fairly warm the rest of the night. Tom didn't think any of them got too much sleep. They were all worried about what the morning would bring. Sure enough, when they got up, it was still snowing, but not as hard as it was the night before and the visibility was a lot better. The night before, Tom had thrown his slicker over their woodpile to keep the wood dry. With the low limbs sheltering the fire, they still had some live coals. He put some wood on them, and before long they had a fire going. Tom fixed breakfast, not one time had they ask if they could help him. They just sat back and let Tom wait on them. They all ate with not much talking going on. They were all thinking pretty much about the weather and the fix they were in. Tom told them he thought the snow was letting up and they weren't so bad off as long as they had dry wood and a dry place to stay they could make it. They started grumbling about it. Joe said they didn't hire on to freeze to death under a tree out at the end of nowhere. Tom told them Mr. Heart didn't tell them it would be a picnic. He told them the same thing that he had told them over and over again, this is their only chance. If they started out in this, chances are mighty slim that they would make it. As long as they had this tree to knock the wind off them, dry wood to cook with, and dry blankets, they could make it until it lets up. As soon as it does they would start home. Tom tried to tell them he had lived here most of his life and he knew how tricky these hills can be when they are covered with snow and for them just to have patience and they would be all right. Tom had made enough ham and biscuits for dinner. Just out of habit he put his in his pocket, then told them he was going to check on Lightning and then he was going to ride a circle around the cattle if he could see that far. Not one of them offered to go check their horses or go with him. He told them he would be back before long for them to keep the fire burning.

Lightning had found a tree with branches hanging down low enough to keep the wind from whipping right on them, and the other horses were there also. He took Lightning back to the camp and saddled him. They told Tom, since they weren't going with him, they would leave their horses where they were, that they didn't care whether the cattle were alive or not. Before he left he told them, "If it gets light enough to see, you boys can find some wood and bring it in and lay it close to the fire to dry." They might need it later on. He told them to keep the fire going enough to keep the coals from dying out. Tom waved at them and told them he would see them later.

Lightning went right to the cattle just like he knew what Tom wanted him to do. They were hunkered down in a grove of trees close together, trying to stay warm. There were no tracks coming in to the gully, and chances were they would be all right. Tom wasn't too anxious to get back to camp to listen to their grumbling, so Lightning and he just rode around for a while, checking the area. It was about midmorning when they turned to go back to camp. He took Lightning to the camp to unsaddle him. Tom thought he would get a dry towel out of his pack to rub him off good and then lead him on to where Tom had found him under the tree. That way he wouldn't have to carry his saddle to camp.

When they got there the first thing he noticed the fire was out and everything was gone. They had taken all the groceries, all the blankets, and everything. Tom had put all the matches in the pack that morning to make sure they stayed dry. So he didn't have any matches to restart the fire. He tried to put wood on the fire, but it was too far gone. Undoubtedly, they had left as soon as he had pulled out that morning.

Tom knew his only chance was to stay with the cattle. By mingling among them, he would get some body heat from them. So he got back on Lightning and went back to the cattle. All that day Lightning and Tom stayed among the cattle. Once in a while he would get off and lead Lightning and just walk among the cattle. Tom guessed they got used to Lightning and him because after a while they didn't pay any attention to them.

By night he was so cold and hungry he didn't know what to do. He got off Lightning and ate some snow. Tom thought he would save his biscuits as long as he could. He didn't know how long this would last, and he thought he might need them later on, worse than now. Tom thought the night would never pass. Finally, morning came. He was so hungry he ate one of his biscuits and ate some more snow. By that afternoon, the snow had begun to let up. There were still some flurries, but by midnight, it had stopped and the stars was out. Tom was so cold and hungry and so sleepy he could hardly stay awake. He sang at the top of his voice, and then he would talk to Lightning, just anything to stay awake. He thought about Mike, Henry, and Joe, poor devils. He hoped they make it, but he had his doubts. The second morning, Tom ate his second biscuit and some more snow. By then, he was so tired and sleepy, and he was so cold he thought he would never be warm again. He knew better, but his reasoning was just about gone. All he wanted was just to be warm one more time. Some cows had lain down, and Tom thought he would go over and lay down in between them and get warm. By then they had gotten so used to Tom and Lightning that they didn't even move when he lay down between them. Tom didn't mean to go to sleep, but the last thing he remembered was Lightning nudging him trying to make him get up. Lightening kept pushing him, but he was past reasoning. Sometime during the morning, the cows got up and left him.

When Mr. Heart and the boys found him, he was just about frozen to death. His shirt was frozen to his back, and he was almost beyond saving. They took him back to where Tom and the boys had camped and build a fire. They had brought along the chuck wagon in case something had gone wrong. They had also brought plenty of emergency blankets and even dry wood.

Mr. Heart told them to warm the blankets as fast as they could, and he wrapped Tom up in them. Jake made some hot broth and coffee, and as soon as it was warm enough, Mr. Heart began to try to spoon it into his mouth. The boys kept warming blankets, and as they got warm, Mr. Heart would put them around him. When Tom came to, he was hurting all over. He told them he had never hurt so much in all his life, that it felt like someone was sticking pins all over him. He tried to get up, but Mr. Heart made him stay still. They kept wrapping warm blankets around him and spooning broth in his mouth. He was out two days, and some of them stayed right with him day and night, keeping warm blankets around him. Bless their hearts, they kept trying to spoon hot broth or coffee mixed with whiskey in his mouth. Mr. Heart was afraid Tom would take pneumonia. So they tried to get as much whiskey down him as they could. When he came to the next time, he asked about Lightning. They told him when they found him, Lightning was right there with him, that he had never left Tom's side. Tom was so proud of him, but he was so sick until he just went back to sleep. Sometime later he woke up again, and he was in his own bed with Granny watching over him. Sure enough, he had taken pneumonia. Mr. Heart had told the boys they had to get him home, that Granny Heart would know what to do. Sure enough, with mustard poultice on his chest and whiskey toddies with honey in it, she broke it up. She had some of the boys to stay day and night, keeping warm blankets on him and spooning medicine she had made up and warm broth or whiskey and honey in his mouth. The fever finally broke, and she said, "Tom is going to be all right." When he came to, he was so weak he couldn't get out of bed but she kept feeding him chicken broth and finally soft solid food until his strength came back.

At first, she would have the boys take him into the parlor and put him in a chair. He was so weak he couldn't stand by himself. Then finally he got up enough nerve to ask Mr. Heart if Henry, Joe, and Mike had made it back. Mr. Heart told him, "No, they didn't. The boys and me had found them along the way, frozen to death." Tom told him if they had stayed, as he tried to get them to do, that they all would have made it. Then he told him about them running off and taking everything. Mr. Heart told him he and the boys had figured as much when they found them along the way without him. He said he knew he had taught him, if something like that happened, to find a place to stay and dig in the best he could until it was over. Mr. Heart told Tom, "When we found Henry, Joe, and Mike and saw that you weren't with them, we knew you had so we kept looking until we found you. We found you just in the nick of time. If we had been an hour later, we couldn't have saved you."

Day by day he began to gain his strength and started walking on his own. Boy, was that a happy day. To celebrate, Granny fixed a big supper, and later, some of the boys brought their guitars and sang for them. Finally, Granny told them it was time for Tom to go to bed, that she didn't want him getting too tired. He thanked the boys for coming and told them how much he enjoyed the music. With some help, he went back to bed. He was real tired, but he enjoyed the boys coming up and singing for them.

Tom had to stay in all winter. Mr. Heart told him he had a real close call, and he still needed time to get over it. He told Tom in time he would gain his strength back, then he would be as good as new. "But it will take time, so don't rush it." By spring, he told him, he would be over this and doing fine.

When Tom got to where he could get out, he went down to see Hart. She was always at the gate waiting for him. Tom guessed she thought he was never going to come back because she wasn't at the gate like she always was. He had to holler for her. When she heard his voice, here she came. She acted like she was real proud to see him and acted like she wanted to say, "Well, where have you been all winter? I have been waiting for you." Whether she did or didn't, Tom explained to her that he'd been sick and hadn't been able to get down to see her. He petted her and talked to her some more. By then Tom was getting tired. He opened the gate, and she followed him over to the bunkhouse so he could sit down on the steps and rest. She stayed right with him. Tom knew she would. Come rain, hail, or sunshine, she would be right by his side. While he rested, she laid her head over on his shoulder and just stood there. He talked to her the whole time he was resting. To someone that never had a horse that they loved, it would sound silly, but Tom told her what a good horse she was and thanked her for taking care of him all these years. For some reason it seemed real important to him to let her know how he felt. After a while Tom put her back in the pasture and told her good-bye. He told her he would see her tomorrow if he was able and maybe by then they could go for a ride. Tom was weaker than he thought he was. By the time he got back to the house he was ready to lie down. Granny scolded him for walking so far. She gave him a glass of buttermilk and put him to bed. When Mr. Heart came in, he scolded Tom also and told him not to try it again, that he was still too weak to go that far. Tom didn't get up for supper. Granny Heart brought him some supper to the bed. He thanked her but told her he just wasn't hungry and couldn't eat it. That all he wanted to do was sleep.

The next day Tom was still tired. He did get up and offered to help Granny, but she told him no, for him to go back and rest some more. About noon Tom woke up smelling food cooking. He went to the kitchen, and Granny (God bless her) had made a pot of chicken soup for them. She told him to sit down, and she would have it ready before long. She poured them a cup of coffee, and they sat and talked until the soup was ready. Granny asked him how he felt by now. Tom told her he felt a lot better. Bless her, she always seemed to know just what to say to make him feel better. She told him it wouldn't be long until warm weather and he would feel a lot better then.

For the next two weeks Tom had to stay in the house and mostly in bed. The third week, there came another cold spell. It lasted almost all week. Then one morning Tom heard Mr. Heart and Granny talking in the kitchen. By the tone of their voices, he could tell something was wrong. He hurried into the kitchen and asked them what was wrong. Granny came over and told him to come and sit down. Then Mr. Heart told him that when the boys went down to the pasture to get their horses, they found Hart by the gate. She was lying down and was real sick. They got her inside the barn, but she was too far gone. She died right after they got her there. Tom was so stunned he just sat there. He couldn't say a word. He tried not to cry, but the tears just kept coming. Finally, Granny came over and put her arm around Tom's shoulders, and they cried together. Mr. Heart told them that the boys were digging a grave down in the pasture where some of their horses were buried. Tom wanted to go down, but Mr. Heart told him, "It's out of the question. Now, Kid, you can't do her any good, and it would just make you sick again. You know she wouldn't want you to take a chance like that if she could talk and tell you so. We will take care of burying her, and when spring comes, you can go down and say your good-byes." Tom told him he didn't know why, but he said his good-bye the day he went down to the pasture. He left, and Granny and Tom sat and tried to comfort each other. It was cold outside, so he stayed in all day, grieving. Tom told Granny, he guess people would think he was stupid grieving so over his horse. Granny seemed to always understand. Tom and she had been through a lot together. He told her all his problems when he was discouraged, blue, or just plain lonely. She seemed to always have time to listen to him. She tried to comfort him the best she could and told him Hart was getting old and tired. She knew it, and she knew she couldn't do the job she had been trained to do any more, and it grieved her.

Granny told him, "Give yourself time, Tom, and the hurt will get so you can bear it. You won't ever forget her, but you will remember all the good things and good times you all had together, and it will make it easier to bear. She did her job, and she did it well, and you should be thankful that God let you have her as long as you did."

Tom thought about it, and then he told Granny, "I've had a lot to be thankful for. You don't know how many times I have thanked God for letting Mr. Heart find me and giving me a home all these years and all the things you've both done for me. When Mr. Heart found me, I was so lost and so alone. I didn't know what I was going to do. I had just lost my mama, and you and Mr. Heart became my family. I don't know what would have become of me if Mr. Heart hadn't found me and took me in." Tom guessed that was the closest time he ever came in telling her about his life.

She just listened and said, "I'm here, Tom, anytime you need to talk to me."

Tom told her, "Thank you, and I don't know how I would ever have made it without you. In everything I tried to do, I always knew sooner or later I would learn to do it because you told me I could."

She turned away but not before Tom saw the tears in her eyes, but that was okay because he had tears in his also. He told her he had learned to love her as much as if she was his own grandma.

Granny told him, "Tom, you have been the son to John and the grandson to me that we were never able to have. That's why we would never let you stay down at the bunkhouse."

She warmed some soup she had made for their dinner, and they ate. She told him she wanted him to go in and rest for a while so he could continue to gain his strength. Tom didn't realize how tired he was until he laid down. He lay there thinking about Hart, but it wasn't long until he was asleep. The next thing he heard was Granny and Mr. Heart talking in the kitchen. Tom dressed and went in where they were. Granny was just finishing supper.

Tom told her he was sorry he had slept all afternoon. They both told him if he hadn't needed it, he wouldn't have slept that long. They sat down to eat, and Mr. Heart told him, "They had buried Hart, and Bob had carved a heart for a marker. All the boys said to tell you how sorry they were. As soon as the weather warmed up, I would like to take Granny and you down to see where Hart was buried."

The weather began to warm up, and it seemed Tom got stronger each day. Mr. Heart kept his promise, and one day he took Granny and Tom down to see Hart's grave. Granny and Tom stood there with their arms around each other just looking at it. Bob had done a beautiful job carving the heart. It was larger than Tom thought it would be, and in the center of it, Bob had carved her name.

Mr. Heart said, "Kid, I want to show you something." He walked over to another grave. The marker was a wood one, and it had "Roy" carved on it. Mr. Heart told Tom, "That was my first horse, and I had cried like a baby when she died, and Mama had put her arms around me, and we had cried together, just like she had with you. I don't know what I would have done without her. In fact, I don't know what I would have done without her all these years. She has been by my side encouraging me in everything I have done, just like she has done with you."

When spring came, Mr. Heart let Tom start doing light jobs around the barn so he spent his days helping Granny Heart in planting the garden along with Jake. They always had a big garden and canned all their vegetables for winter both for the bunkhouse and the house. Granny and Jake always took care of that.

If they didn't have anything for him to do, he would work at the barn. There was always plenty to do down there, things to mend like bridles, stirrups, saddles, and a million other things that the boys always wanted done yesterday.

Roundup time came, and Mr. Heart still wouldn't let him go. This would be the first drive he had missed since he was fifteen years old. He tried to tell Mr. Heart that he was all right, but he told Tom, "Now, Kid, you know how it is. We are out in all kinds of weather, rain or shine. We have to drive the cattle, and sleeping on the ground wouldn't do you any good. I don't want to take a chance of you taking pneumonia again. By next year you will be as good as new." He laughed and started kidding Tom. "Now you don't think we are going to coddle you from now on, do you?" Some of the boys were there, and they jumped right in and also started kidding Tom.

Smitty said, "Do you think this ornery little cuss took pneumonia just so we would have to wait on him?"

Most of the time Tom would get the last word in. He told them, "Well, it worked, didn't it?"

They all laughed.

Bob said, "Kid, you are all right. Guess we will keep you."

All the others chipped right in and said, "Yeah, even as ornery as he is, I don't know how we could get along without him."

They were all ready to go. So right after that, they all waved and hollered, "See you when we get back."

One of them hollered, "Keep your nose clean, Kid."

Another hollered, "Stay out of trouble," and they began to pull out.

Someone else hollered, "We'll miss you, Kid."

Tom stood there until they had all the cattle turned and were on their way. He hollered back, but he knew they couldn't hear him, "Yeah," and he would miss them too.

Granny was always standing outside waving each time when the herd of cattle pulled out. He hollered to her that he was going to take Lightning out for a while. All the time he was laid up Mr. Heart and the boys had cared for him. Lightning had come through the storm just fine. They went for a long ride. Then Tom put him back in the pasture and went to the house. He knew Granny would be worried about him. Tom knew she worried about the trail drive each year until they got back. So he didn't want to give her anything else to worry about.

Mr. Heart was right. When spring came, Tom had stopped coughing and his lungs began to heal.

By the following year, when roundup time came, he was as fit as a fiddle and roaring to go. They got the cattle in from the summer pastures without any trouble and the separating them went just fine. They were through early, and of course, the boys had to hurrah him about it. They said, "The Kid is back. That's why we got through so much faster."

Tom told them, "I'm older now, and I know the difference." But boy, it sure use to make him fill big when he was a kid.

The drive went well, and they were soon back, and another year finished.

Chapter 6

THE NEXT ROUNDUP CAME AGAIN, and Tom didn't know it then, but this was to be the cattle drive that would change his life again. They didn't have any trouble getting the cattle to the train station to ship. They hadn't been bothered with rustlers in years now. Guess they finally learned they could and would take care of themselves. They loaded the cattle as usual and waited for Mr. Heart to come back. The trip back went well, and when they got home, Granny was waiting on the porch as always. They ate supper and went into the parlor. Mr. Heart had brought the newspapers as always. They sat down, and Granny began to read to them. As Tom had said before, this was a big thing for them to find out what was going on in the rest of the world.

Granny was about halfway through with the first paper. She turned the page and said, "Well, what do you know, listen to this. Some man has an ad in the paper wanting to know the whereabouts of his son. He is offering a twenty-five-dollar reward to anyone that could tell him anything about a Tom Brisco. He ran away from home when he was eight years old and hadn't been heard of since. He would be almost twenty-two years old by now. It went on to say he didn't want him to come home if he didn't want to, but he would like to know if he was alive or dead."

Tom was so shocked, it was like someone had knocked all the wind out of him. Granny finished reading, but he didn't hear another word she said. Right after she finished reading the paper, Mr. Heart said, "Tomorrow will be a long day, guess we had better turn in."

They said good night and went to bed, but Tom didn't sleep much all night. He kept remembering that ad. The next morning, at the breakfast table, Tom told them that he was Tom Brisco. That was his papa that had placed the ad. Of course, he had to tell them the whole story of why he had run away from home. Tom told them he had hardly slept a wink all night and finally decided early this morning that he had to go home.

By the time he finished, Granny had tears running down her face. She told him, "I know you have to go, Tom, but what in the world will we all do without you. We all have learned to love you, and you have been my very own grandson ever since you were eight years old. We was planning on turning the whole spread over to you when the time came."

Mr. Heart said, "Now, Mama, don't make it any harder on Tom than it has to be. We knew someday this might happen."

She said, "I know, but I had prayed night and day it wouldn't happen."

Mr. Heart told Tom, "Now, Kid, you know what time we ship the cattle each year. If you will wait until this next shipment, I will drop you off the same place I picked you up." Tom wanted to go right then, but he knew with winter coming on he would be better off waiting until winter was over. Looking back later, Tom could see they thought if he waited until then he might change his mind. Tom told them he guessed that would be best because he didn't want to be caught in another snowstorm and before he got there, he very likely could be.

So it was settled. He would stay until they shipped the cattle in the fall and ride the train back with Mr. Heart to where he had picked him up. The winter came early that year. Outside of repairing their riding equipment and checking the cattle, when the days were pretty enough that they could, there was mighty little to do. When it snowed and the cattle couldn't find food, they did pitch hay out for them. Also, some of them would check the water holes and make sure they had plenty of water and that the water tanks weren't frozen so hard that the cattle couldn't break through the ice to get it. They always carried an ax along, in case it was frozen, then they would chop holes in the ice big enough for the cattle to drink.

It was a hard winter, but finally, spring came, and they took the cattle up to the spring pastures so they could find plenty of fresh green grass. Tom was so restless after he had made up his mind to go. He wanted to go right then. But he knew it was best to wait and go with the drive, that it would be safer that way. A man traveling alone was always in danger in this part of the country.

Spring and summer came and went. They had taken the cattle out to the summer pastures. Mr. Heart said the new calf crop was looking real good, that their herd was really growing because of the amount of new heifers they had kept each year. Some of them would be bringing calves this year. Mr. Heart said that when their calves got big enough to ship in two years or so, they might have to start shipping twice a year. This time of the year they didn't have a lot to do except walk the fences looking for broken wires, then check the cattle.

Fall finally came. Tom was so anxious to get everything done so they could be on their way. All went well, and early in August they were ready to go.

The night before they were to go, Mr. Heart, Granny, and Tom went into the parlor. They told him they had something to talk to him about. They all sat down, and Mr. Heart told him, "Now, Kid, you know that the whole time you have been here, we have never paid you a real salary. Mama and I had talked it over a long time ago, and we have been putting your wages up every year. So if this time ever came, you would have a tidy little nest egg to help you get started."

Tom couldn't believe what he was hearing and told them so. He told them, "Ya'll don't owe me anything. Ya'll bought my clothes and gave me room and board for all these years and have treated me like I was your own son and grandson. What else could anyone ask for?"

Nevertheless, they said they wanted him to have enough to get started, somewhere else if he felt like he had to go. Mr. Heart told Tom, "You know you will always be welcome back here. As far as treating you like you was my son, you have been ever since the first day I saw you. When I first saw you, Tom, standing there, it just broke my heart to see you was barefooted, with no shirt on and your overhauls was filthy. I could tell that you had been crying for a long time." He had been watching him a long time and thought, *There is a boy that needs a friend.* When the policeman came up and started talking to him, he thought that was his chance to help him.

Tom told him he would never forget and that he sure did need a friend, that he didn't know what he would have done without him. He told Mr. Heart he was standing there thinking, *What was I going to do? What's to become of me?* The only thing he knew was he couldn't go back. He was so tired, hungry, and cold. He didn't know what to do. He had run and cried all night, and he was about ready to start crying again. They both would never know what they all had meant to him and that they had given him so much. There is no way that he could take money from them now.

Granny said, "Tom, you know you will always have a home here. Why don't you go see you papa and stay awhile and come back?"

Tom told her he couldn't promise because he didn't know what he would find when he got there, but that he would think on it. Granny ripped the lining of his jacket out under the arm and sewed the money bag that she had made right in the front of the lining. She resewed the lining and handed him his jacket. She told him, "Now, Tom, don't you let anyone know you have this amount of money. People have been killed for a lot less. Don't you take it out until you get there."

Tom didn't know how much it was, but he promised her he wouldn't bother it until he needed it. They left early the next morning. The hardest thing Tom had ever done was to tell Granny good-bye. She hugged and kissed him bye. She was crying and didn't make any effort to hide it. She whispered in his ear, "Tom, come back. Don't stay gone too long."

Tom had tears running down his checks too when he turned to go. This had been his home for over fourteen years. She had loved him more than any one had. She had taught him, laughed with him, cried with him, and been so proud of him in all the things that he had learned to do. He could still hear her gentle voice saying, "Now, Tom, you can do it, just have patience." And he always knew he could because she told him he could.

The trip went smoothly, and they were on time at the train station, ready to load the cattle as they had done so many times before, only one thing different this time Tom would be going to. Another hard thing he had to do was tell Lightning bye also. Tom talked to him like he had talked to Hart and told him how much he appreciated him taking care of him all these years and if he could he would be back. He told all the boys bye, with one thing different this time, there was no kidding. They all had something to say like "Kid, don't stay gone too long," or "Hurry back, we will miss you," or "Kid, what will we do without you?"

The whistle blew, and Mr. Heart and Tom got on the train as they had a long time ago. The only difference was, the first time, a scared, lonely, bitter kid had said good-bye to his world that had fallen apart. This time a grown man was saying good-bye to the life and family that he had known and loved for so long. Mr. Heart and Tom slept and woke and talked the whole trip. Mr. Heart told him, as he had long expected that the reason he never would let Tom go with him was, he was afraid someone would recognize him, and he told him now, "Kid, I know this was selfish, but Mama and me were so scared of losing you. You had brought so much joy and happiness into our life that we couldn't bear losing you. We knew some day this would happen, but we always prayed that it wouldn't. God forgive us for being so selfish, but our life was so empty before you came into our life that we just couldn't bear losing you. Tom, you know you will always have a home with us. Kid, I hope you will do like Mama said, go home and visit awhile and come back to us. I will look for you each trip we make, and we will be praying that you would make it soon."

When they arrived, Tom helped unload the cattle. Then Mr. Heart said, "Well, guess we had better find you a horse to ride home." But Tom told him, "I think I'll just walk the rest of the way." Tom didn't know why, but it seemed it was the only way to go. He said his good-byes to the man who had been his idol, his friend, and just like a daddy to him for so long. Mr. Heart hugged him bye, with great big tears running down his face. He told him, "Kid, hurry back. Our life will be so lonesome without you." Tom told him, "Thank you for all that you and Granny have done for me, and I will always love ya'll." Then he turned and walked away. He didn't look back. He was afraid if he did, he wouldn't go. Again, like the ragtag little boy, the tears began to fall. Tom wanted to turn around and run back as fast as he could, but he knew he had to go on. He walked and cried for a long time, and then night came. But there were no buggers this time, just sad memories.

Chapter 7

Tom didn't know what he would find when he got there, but he knew what he was leaving and it broke his heart. Tom said out loud, "Why, why, did Granny have to read that article. I was so happy where I was." A time or so, he stopped and turned around to go back, but each time, he told himself, "Tom, you have to go on. You owe that much to your papa." Like Granny said he could stay awhile and then go back. Tom argued with himself all the way there. He felt like he owed more to Mr. Heart and Granny than he did to his papa anyway. They had taken him in and raised him and been his family all these years. By the time Tom got there, he had made up his mind. He would stay a week or two and go back. Tom knew Mr. Heart would wait for him at least two weeks and that would give him plenty of time to visit with his papa and let him know that he was all right and that he had a good job with people who had raised him and had cared for him all these years.

Tom got there about one o'clock that morning. The house was more rundown than he remembered it, but that had been fourteen years ago. Of course, it had aged just like he had. It was still neat with a white picket fence around the yard and flowers growing everywhere.

Tom hollered, "Hello in the house," and he didn't have to holler but about three times when he saw a light come on. Tom heard Papa say, "Lou, you come back here. You don't know who that is," and she hollering back, "Oh, yes, I do, Jim. That's Tom's voice." And here she came in her nightgown. She threw her arms around his neck and started crying; and between sobs she said, "Oh, Tom, you've come back. You've come home. I have prayed all these years that you were alive and that you would come home someday."

By then Papa was there; and he grabbed him also and kept saying, "Tom, you're alive. You have been alive all these years. Oh, Tom, you don't know how I had prayed and prayed you was." He told Tom he had just about given up hope. But Lou, bless her heart, never lost faith. She kept telling him, every time he told her that he thought Tom was dead. If not, surely they would have heard something by now. She would always tell him, "Now, Jim, keep praying. We just can't give up. Someday, somehow God will answer our prayers. And I just know he can't be dead." Then his papa asked, "What are we standing out here for? Let's go in the house." Aunt Lou built a fire in the kitchen stove and put on a pot of coffee.

Tom had to tell them all about his life and how he had found such wonderful people to raise him. They talked and drank coffee until about daylight. Aunt Lou said it's no use going to bed, that they were so excited they wouldn't sleep any way. About daylight his papa said, "Well, Tom, I don't know how to tell you this." He had tried to several times, but he just didn't know how to start, but he guessed the only way is to come right out with it. "Lou and I are losing the farm. We've had a crop failure and borrowed money to plant last year's crop. Then I took sick and wasn't able to work it. They have given us to the end of this month to come up with the money or they are going to take the farm. We don't know what we're going to do. Sally and Lou tried to work it as much as they could, but they only made enough money to see us through this coming winter with nothing to pay on the mortgage."

Tom handed Lou his coat and told her, "Rip out the lining under the sleeve." She did and then he told her to "rip out the bag and hand it to me." Tom handed it to his papa and told him, "No one is going to take your farm away from you. I think there is enough there to pay off the mortgage."

Tears came into his eyes, and he told Tom, "We can't take your money."

Tom told him, "What choice do you have?" I will stay here and work the land until you get all right and when you are able to work the land again and have the money you can pay me back."

Lou fixed breakfast, and as soon as they ate, they went to the bank and paid off the mortgage. The banker told Tom he could just pay what was owed and they would carry the rest over, but Tom told him no. They would just pay it all and clear the farm. They went back to the farm where two happy people kept trying to tell him how much they thanked him. Papa said they didn't know what they were going to do or where they were going to live. He told Tom they had sent Sally to Mary Ann's in Weatherford. She was married and lives there. They talked all afternoon.

Before dark Tom helped Aunt Lou with the night chores. He told her he would milk the cow while she gathered up the eggs. After she had finished getting the eggs, she came into the barn and told him how glad she was to have him back home, that his papa really needed him. And she said he had been ailing ever since early fall. Tom told her he would stay and put the crop in and help him until he got better.

The next morning he told them he was going down and look at the fields and see what had to be done. Aunt Lou told him, "They are a mess," and she was right. Tom knew he would have to work with them all winter if he got them ready for planting in the spring. He could never remember seeing his papa's farmland so grown up and in such bad shape. Brush and weeds had almost taken it over. He went back to the house and told his papa he would start clearing the land and plowing it the next day. His plans of staying a week or so had to change.

Now he knew he couldn't leave his papa in such a mess. Tom worked like a demon from morning until night; and before real bad weather set in, he had it cleaned and plowed, ready to plant when spring came.

Spring finally came, and he got the crops in by working from morning until dark. Tom hated every minute of it. He was no farmer, and he didn't want to be one. His mind and his heart were back with Granny and Mr. Heart and the boys. Every day as he worked he thought of what they would be doing on the ranch and hoping Papa would soon get well so he could go back. He wrote Granny and told her what he had found when he got home and that in a year or so he hoped his papa would be well enough so he could take over and he could come home.

She wrote him back and said, "Tom, you wouldn't be the boy I raised if you did less. Stay as long as you are needed and then come home. You know we miss you so much, but we know some times we have to do things that are not what we want to do, but what we have to. Just remember that we love you so much and come back home when you can."

The weather was good for crops that year, and they got good rains when they needed them. So they made a good crop. They made enough money to last all winter, buy their seed for next year, and some to save. Papa tried to make Tom take the savings in on what he owed him, but Tom told him they would put it in the bank for a rainy day and worry about what they owed him later. Tom's greatest worry was his papa. He didn't seem to get any better. He planted the crops that year, and the next, with little hope of getting to go back home anytime soon.

Then the letter came, and going back didn't matter anymore. This time it was from Mr. Heart telling him, "Granny had passed away. She just went to sleep and didn't wake up. I went in to check on her that morning, because she had never slept pass breakfast time, and she was gone. She went the way she wanted to and now she is with my papa. Kid, she loved you so much and was waiting for you to come home. She always said you had a job to do, and when it was over, you would be back. Don't grieve for her. She is with Papa now, and they are happy." He went on to say, "I want to thank you for all the love and happiness you had given us while you were with us. Remember, Kid, you still have a home here when your job is finished there, if you still wanted it."

Tom had taken the letter to the field with him to keep Papa and Lou from knowing how homesick he was, and he was glad he did because he sat there reading it and crying. Again, he blamed himself for not being there and letting Granny down when she needed him, like he had done when mama died. Tom had the same horrible empty feeling as he had back then. He hollered, "Why, God? Why did you have to take the two women that I loved more than my own life away from me? God, why couldn't you let her live until I could get back to see her?" He knew then that he would never get to go home again. Tom worked and cried all the rest of the day. He could only think that he had let her down, just like he had done his mama, and the more he thought about it, the more he cried

The years passed, and Papa didn't get any better. Tom stayed on and ran the farm for him. Every year he thought his papa would get better and would be able to start running the farm himself, then he could go back home. But each year he and Aunt Lou both seemed to get worse instead of better. Sallie came back to help Tom with them, but it did make it easier on him.

Then the second letter came when he came home for dinner one day after they had sat down at the dinner table. Sally said, "Oh, I almost forgot Tom, you got a letter this morning." She got up and went to get it and handed it to him. This time it was from Bob. As soon as Tom saw Bob's return address on it, he knew it was bad news. He didn't want to upset any of them, so he stuck it in his pocket and told them he would read it later. Tom knew they were curious about it, but none of them said a word. He guessed they thought it was his business, and if he wanted them to know anything about it, he would tell them

Again, he waited until he got back to the field where he had been plowing. His hands were shaking so he could hardly open it. He just knew it was bad news and sure enough it was. Bob told him, "Kid, I had rather be kicked by a horse than have to tell you this, but we all thought you ought to know. So the boys elected me to do it. Mr. Heart died this morning. He just grieved himself to death after Granny Heart died. He just couldn't get along without her. She was the one that held everything together, and after she died, it seen like he didn't have anything to live for. Now, Kid, try not to grieve too much. They understood you being gone and knew it was the only thing you could do. They both said over and over, 'Tom wouldn't have been the boy we raised, if he had done otherwise.' That you had a job to do. And when it was over you would come home. We all send our condolence and our love. Come home when you can." He signed it, "From all of us."

Tom cried until he felt like there wasn't a tear left in him. He cried over and over, "Why, God? Why, God, did You have to take them now? Why? Why couldn't You wait and let me see them just one more time. You didn't even let me tell them goodbye, God." Then he kneeled down and thanked God that He had given him such wonderful people to raise him and asked God to forgive him for complaining.

Tom got up and went to work. He still had a job he had to do. Now it didn't matter anymore. He knew he would never go back home because without Granny and Mr. Heart there wasn't a home to go back to anyway.

Another year came and went; and just like he lost Mama, Granny, and Mr. Heart, he lost Papa. They buried him next to mama, Papa on one side of her and little Becky on the other side. John and Mary Ann came home for the funeral. Some of Lou's kids came home for the funeral, but they didn't say one word about taking her home with them.

Tom knew he couldn't leave her, so again, he and Sally stayed on to care for her and run the farm. After everyone left, Aunt Lou told Tom she wanted to go to town while she was dressed and asked if he would take her. Tom told her he would, and he went to the barn and hitched the horse to the buggy. By the time he got it ready, Aunt Lou and Sally were waiting in the yard to go. He didn't ask her why she wanted to go to town, but when she got there, she went straight to the bank. Tom didn't know what she was up to, but he didn't think it was any of his or Sally's business, so they waited in the buggy.

When she came out, she handed Tom a slip of paper and told him she had put all the savings that they had accumulated over into his account. She said, "Now, Tom, I don't want you to argue about it. Every bit of that money is what you had worked for, and if it hadn't been for you paying off the farm to begin with, your papa and I wouldn't have had any place to go. You had made it possible for your papa to spend the last days of his life in his own house and that, Tom, you don't know what that meant to both of us. Your papa told me to do this as soon as I could, that it was the last thing he told me the night he passed away, so now I have fulfilled his last request. We both knew that my kids would come in and try to take it all, if it was left in their name. So now it's done, and it's only the right thing to do, and Lord knows that don't began to pay you for all you've had to do. Also, it sure don't pay back the money that you used to pay off the loan."

So they went home to an empty house. His clothes were there. The house was as neat as they had left it, but the man that had made it a home was no longer there, and so it was just an empty house. Tom finished working the crop, and again, they made a good harvest. And again, Aunt Lou insisted that the money from it went into Tom's account. She told him all she needed. She knew he would take care of and that way the money is safe from the vultures. None of them had been back to see her since the funeral, and it had just about broke her heart.

Sally and Tom did all they could do for Aunt Lou, but in six months she was gone. Her children buried her next to their papa in the same cemetery where Tom's mama and papa was buried. After the funeral they all went back to the house. They wanted to settle the estate as soon as possible so they could all go home. The next day they all went to the only lawyer that was in town. He already had Papa's and Lou's will. He told them that Aunt Lou and Papa had made it out right after Tom came home. In the will Tom was to get back the amount he was out when he paid off the mortgage. The only thing with that is, they didn't have enough in the bank to pay it back. Lou's kids argued they had worked just as hard while he was gone, as he had when he got back. That he owed his papa something as well as they did. If it hadn't been for them, there wouldn't be a farm left to sell. They told the lawyer they would fight it until there wouldn't be anything left. Tom told the lawyer, rather than cause hard feelings and an uproar, they would just divide it equally. That satisfied them, but they found out Papa and Aunt Lou had willed their half of everything to Lou's children and Papa's half to John, Mary Ann, Sallie, and Tom. They both had stated that since there was more of Lou's children than there was of Papa's, they thought it was the fair way to do it. Aunt Lou's kids didn't like that and told the lawyer so. He told them plainly that there was nothing they could do about it. The lawyer told them, "Ya'll are lucky. Tom could insist on getting his money back for paying off the farm, and also, he and Sallie could ask for wages for working it and for taking care of your mama all these years. The will stated, and your mama signed it, that Tom was to get his money back if he insisted on it. And ya'll could sue until you were black in the face, and Tom and Sallie would still get their money. By that time, there wouldn't be anything left to divide. So you had better be satisfied with what you were getting."

They finally agreed on the terms and told the lawyer that they had been checking around ever since Papa died, and they were sure they had a man who was ready to buy the farm. It turned out to be Henry Butler, the neighbor next to Papa's place. He had tried to buy it after Papa passed away. He was wanting to enlarge his farm. What they didn't take with them, they sold to Henry. He bought all the farm equipment, Lou's buggy, and the livestock, which made it easier because all the money was paid to the lawyer. By the next day it was sold, the money divided, and the house stripped clean. It was all right because after Papa's funeral, Lou had given to Mary Ann and Sally their mama's things that she had saved for them. And Mary Ann had taken them home with her at that time. Sally, Mary Ann, and Tom didn't have a bed left to sleep in when they got through. They spent the night in a hotel, and after breakfast the next morning, Tom put Mary Ann and Sally on the train for Weatherford. He told Sally he would come for her as soon as he had a place to stay.

Tom stood and watched the train until it was out of sight, then he went to the bank to put his money from Papa's estate in the bank. Tom sure didn't want to do it while Lou's kids were there. Mr. Harper, the banker, and Tom had a lot of occasions to get acquainted during the last few years. He had put the rest of the money that Granny and Mr. Heart had given him in the bank after he had paid off the farm. Mr. Harper asked Tom what he was going to do now. Tom told him he didn't know, that he might look around for some land to start a ranch, that he didn't have any particular thing to do right now. Tom didn't tell him, but he didn't have any place to go either. He knew he would never go back to the ranch. Granny and Mr. Heart were no longer there, and it would never be home any more.

They talked for a while; and he told Tom, "I don't know how many acres you're talking about, but I know a man that has six hundred acres he is wanting to sell. His wife died, and right now he has some share croppers living there and just working the farmland. If you're interested in it, you might get it pretty reasonable. With what you've got in the bank, you could get a loan and have some left to buy some cattle to get started on." Mr. Harper went on to say the bank would be glad to loan him the money to buy it. Tom told him he would like to see it. He drew Tom a map and told him it was just pass the third town he came to, going west. If he wanted to see it, he could go see the land first, then if he was interested in it he could come back to the second town. Anyone there could tell him where J. B. Rogers lived. He told Tom, "Now he will feel you out first, don't act too excited about it and don't give him the first price he asks for it. Try to Jew him down as much as you can before you buy it."

Tom thanked him for telling him about it and told him he would do his best if he liked it. Tom told him, "I'll need a good horse" and asked him where he might find one.

Mr. Harper sent him down to the stables and told him to "ask for Pete Potter and tell him I sent you." Mr. Harper told Tom, "Pete's a good honest man and will treat you right."

Tom told him, "As soon as I've found out about a horse and get a grub stake, I will be back. I don't want to draw out any more money than I have to right now."

They parted with Tom saying thanks a lot and that he would be back in a little while. Tom went to the stable first, and the man he asked for was Mr. Potter. Tom told him what Mr. Harper had said. He said he did have two good riding horses, and in fact one of them had been trained to work with cattle. Tom looked at both of them but ended up buying the one he said had been trained to work cattle. He was a far cry from Hart or Lightning, but Tom knew he would need one if he got some cattle. He was a pretty roan. Mr. Potter told him the horse's name was Roy. Tom called to him, and he came to him. He asked Mr. Potter if he had a saddle that he could use. He went in the barn and came out with a pretty good-looking used saddle and blanket. He said, "In fact this is the saddle and blanket that was with him. If you like him, I could make you a pretty good deal on the whole lot."

Tom saddled him and rode out a piece. He seemed to be real gentle and handled good. He asked Mr. Potter what he would take for the whole works. He quoted him a price. Tom saw immediately he was just feeling him out to see what he would pay. He told him he thought that was a little high and asked him what was the rock-bottom price cash on the barrel head he would take. He quoted him another price, and this time it was a fair one, so Tom told him he would take him. He told him he had to go to the store and pick up some things, then to the bank, and as soon as he got through he would be back with the money.

When he got to the store, it wasn't busy. Mrs. Wood asked if she could help him. Tom handed her the list that he had made out of groceries and asked her if she would help him get them while he got the other things he needed. He told her he wouldn't ask her, but he was in a hurry. She said she would be glad to. Tom bought a skillet, a small Dutch oven, a coffeepot, two cups, two plates, two knives, forks, and spoons, a canteen, a blanket, towel, and a washcloth. Then he asked her for some shells for his gun. He had brought it with him when he left the ranch. Mr. Heart had told him he would feel better if Tom took his gun along with him as it might come in handy before he got to his papa's house. Tom had wrapped it in one of his shirts when he got settled in, and he hadn't taken it out until he began to get his clothes together after Aunt Lou's funeral.

Tom knew it would take him several days before he got to the ranch, and he thought the gun might come in handy again. When they both finished getting what Tom needed, he told her if she would figure it up he would go to the bank to draw out his money to pay for them. When she finished figuring it, he told her he would be right back with the money. Mr. Harper was waiting for him and asked him if everything went all right. Tom told him everything went fine and told him how much he wanted to draw out to pay for the things he had bought. Mr. Harper gave him the money, and Tom told him he would see him as soon as he got back.

Mr. Harper asked him, "When are you leaving?"

Tom told him, "As soon as I've paid for my things and saddled the horse. I don't have any place to stay, so I thought I might as well be on my way."

Mr. Harper wished him good luck and said be careful.

Tom told him he would try and left.

Tom went by to pick up his supplies. She had everything ready for him, and she had wrapped them in a nice bundle, all except the shells. She said she thought he would like the shells handy so he could load his gun. Tom had taken the shells out of the gun when he had wrapped it and had not realized it was empty, so he thanked her and paid her for his supplies. Then he hurried out. He was anxious to get started now that he had made up his mind. Mr. Potter saw him coming and brought Roy out. He still had the saddle on him. Tom paid for him and thanked him for having Roy ready. He tied his gear on the back of his saddle and left. Tom wanted to cover some miles before dark.

Chapter 8

THEY TRAVELED UNTIL ALMOST DARK. The more he rode Roy, the better he liked him. Tom stopped in a wooded area far away from the road so they wouldn't attract attention. In fact, someone would almost have to be looking for them to find them. He built a small fire, and while it burned down, he took the saddle off Roy and rubbed him down good. A creek was close by, so Tom led him down to it, and while he drank, he got some fresh water for coffee. He led Roy back and hobbled him so he wouldn't wander off. Tom soon saw he had nothing to worry about. Roy stayed real close to camp, as if he was trained to do so. By the time Tom finished hobbling him, the fire had burned down and he had plenty of coals to make biscuits in the Dutch oven and put it and his coffeepot on the coals. While they cooked, he sliced some bacon, and by the time it was done, the coffee and biscuits were ready. Tom made some red-eye gravy. He had been so busy all day until he hadn't thought about eating, and he was plenty hungry. The whole time he was eating, Roy was grazing right at the camp.

As soon as supper was over, Tom washed his dishes, got his blanket, and put his saddle right at the trunk of the tree, and started to lie down. Roy was still eating right at the tree. Tom got up and petted him and told him to go on and eat, that he would call him when morning came and when he was ready to go. He still just ate around the tree. Tom had a busy day, and he was dog tired. It didn't take him long to go to sleep.

Morning came early. He fixed breakfast, and they left right after breakfast. Tom was in a hurry to get to the ranch. They traveled all that day. At noon he stopped by a creek to water Roy and let him graze for a while. While Roy grazed, Tom was so eager to get there until he just ate a cold biscuit with a slice of bacon and drank some cold water. He rested awhile, and then they were on their way. He got there on the fourth day out, about ten o'clock that night. Tom decided it was too late to check with the people at the house.

He made a dry camp in the pasture not too far from the house. He didn't want to alarm anyone in the house. That night he didn't hobble Roy. By then he knew he would be close by when morning came. Tom laid down and just waited for morning to come. In spite of his excitement, he did get a good night's sleep.

The next morning he did make a pot of coffee and ate some more cold biscuits and bacon. He waited until about seven o'clock and then went to the house to talk to the people and let them know what he was there for. When he hollered, "Hello in the house," a woman came to the door. Tom introduced himself and told her what he was there for. She called her husband, and he came to the door, and again Tom told him who he was and why he was there. He invited Tom in and told him, "I'm John Rucker. This is my wife Dora, and yes, we're the share croppers." He offered Tom a cup of coffee. They sat down at the dining room table, and while they drank their coffee, Tom told him he wouldn't be interested in the farmland right now, but if he decided to buy it, they could stay on if they wanted to. He told them in fact right now he wouldn't have any tools to work it with. The only thing he would want right now was the pasture.

Tom asked them if any one there could show him around the boundaries of the place. The man said his son would as soon as he got the morning work done. They had another cup of coffee, and it wasn't long before a young man about eighteen or nineteen came in. The woman asked Tom if he would like to see the rest of the house while the boy was getting ready. He told her he might as well, so she showed him through the house. It was a nice six-room house. It had three large bedrooms, a nice-size kitchen with a huge table where they had sat and drank their coffee, a large dining room, and a good-size sitting room that was as clean as a pen. By that time the boy was ready. He had saddled an old horse, and when Tom came out his papa said, "Tom, this here is Jim." Jim told him hi, then said he hoped he had plenty of time as it would take all day to cover the boundary lines. Tom told him that he had as long as it took. They rode all morning looking at the pastures, and Tom had never seen such good pastures in all his life. The grass was about knee high. Jim told him there were three pastures and they were broken up into one hundred acres each. There were good fences around all of them. A creek ran through them. Jim said it was spring fed and never ran dry. There were enough trees in every one of them to have good shades for the cows to lie under. Another hundred acres was in a meadow, and it already need cutting.

They stopped at noon to let the horses rest. Jim told Tom his maw had made a lunch for them. Tom asked him if he drank coffee, and he said he did. So Tom made a fire, and while he was doing that, Jim got some cold water from the creek. They watered the horses, rubbed them down, and turned them lose to graze. By then the fire was ready, so they put the coffee on and set back against a tree and talked until the coffee was ready.

Jim asked Tom what he thought of the place. Tom told him, "So far I like what I have seen." Again, Tom told him, "I wouldn't be able to work the land by myself and would welcome ya'll to stay on and work it on the thirds and fourths." In fact, he would really need the money from it to help him get started. Jim said he was pretty sure his papa would be glad to do that because there were nine kids to help work the land and it was pretty hard to find a place with enough land to support eleven people. He said they planted mostly cotton and corn as that was good crop money. Tom told him the planting of the crops would be up to them if he got it. By then their coffee was ready. They poured them a cup, and my, what a lunch Mrs. Rucker had packed for them. They ate until they couldn't eat anymore and still had some left. After that they laid back on their saddle and rested while the horses grazed.

Finally, Jim took him to see the farmland. It was as impressive as the rest of the land was. They got back to the house about suppertime. Mrs. Rucker had supper ready for them, and boy, what a supper. After supper they talked some more, and Mr. Rucker said he would be glad to stay on.

They wanted Tom to stay all night, but he told them he would just camp out. He wanted to get an early start in the morning, that he wanted to find Mr. Rogers and find out what he could do. The next morning Tom left way before daylight. He was so excited about the place.

Tom got there the next day, late that afternoon. Sure enough the first person he asked told him where he lived. He didn't have any trouble finding it, and by seven o'clock Tom had introduced himself and told him what he was there for. Sure enough, he tried to feel him out before he told him what he wanted for the place. He asked Tom how he liked it. Tom was ready for him. He told him it was just fine, then went on to say it could use some fixing up, especially on the house and barns. Mr. Rogers quoted him an outrageous price.

Tom told him, "Now, Mr. Rogers, you know that place is not worth that much. If you don't sell it soon, you are going to have to have someone do something to those pastures or the grass will be so tall and tough, cows or nothing else will be able to eat it." Tom didn't know that for sure because Mr. Heart didn't let his get that tall, but he just took a wild guess, that he didn't know that for sure either.

He quoted another price, and it was way out of line too.

Tom told him, "Now, Mr. Rogers, you know blame well that you aren't going to get that much money for the place. No one but a millionaire would have that much money, and I'm no millionaire. In fact, I will be doing good to buy the place at a decent price. Now if you want to quote me a decent price for it, here is a letter stating that Mr. Harper at the bank in Springtown will give me a loan to buy the place at a reasonable price. Now if you want to get down to business and quote me a reasonable price, then I will listen. If not just tell me and there will be no hard feelings and I will be on my way."

Mr. Rogers chuckled and said, "Did I hear you say you would have to lease the land out to the Ruckers. If you do buy it, then where are you going to live?"

Tom thought it was none of his business and started to tell him so, but he thought about what Granny had always told him, that the least thing he could always do was be polite and listen.

So Tom told him his papa and step mama had passed away, that he had been staying there and taking care of them. He had always wanted a ranch, and now that they were gone, he wanted to try his luck, if not here then somewhere else. Tom went on to tell him that he had worked on a ranch and saved his money, and now since he didn't have any place to go, he thought it was now or never. Tom told him, "To answer your question where I would live. I noticed a place in the first pasture where it looked like at one time a home might have been there. It looked like someone had built a cellar there. If I get the place, I thought

I would restore it and live there until I could do better." Tom told him he didn't have anyone but himself to worry about and it would do just fine for right now. The main thing is that he wanted to get some cows growing on the land right away.

Tom noticed his eyes had blurred as if he was about to cry, so he told him, "Now, Mr. Rogers, I don't blame you if you don't want to sell. It's your land, and if you didn't want to sell it, then that's your business and I wouldn't hold any hard feelings against you. I'm going to find me some land, and if you don't want to sell yours, then let's stop dillydallying around so I could be on my way because I have a far piece to ride before I get back to Springtown."

Mr. Rogers said, "Son, it's not that I don't want to sell. It's just when you mentioned the dugout, there was no house there. It's where mama and I lived when we first came out here. We didn't have enough money to buy the land, build a house, and buy cattle to stock it at first. So we build the dugout and lived there until we could do better. Mama and I worked mighty hard, and it took us a long time before we were able to build the house where it is now."

Tom told him he was so sorry to hear he had lost his wife and he could sympathize with him, that he had lost his mama, the woman, and man that raised him and his papa and stepmama in the last few years, that he knows how he feels. Tom got up and told him it was nice meeting him and that he had to go. He wanted to cover a few more miles before night.

Mr. Rogers got up too and said, "Now, whoa, son, I thought you wanted to buy the place."

Tom told him, "I did, but it don't look like we can come to an agreement on it."

Mr. Rogers said, "Now let's don't jump to conclusions this fast. Maybe I was a little high on it and just maybe we could come to some kind of terms. If you would let me help restore the old dugout. You know, boy, this task you have decided to do is not going to be easy. It will be a lot of hard work and sweat, with hard times and bad times as well as good times."

Before Tom thought about what he was saying, he said, "Nothing I have ever done was easy. Besides Granny Heart always said, if it was too easy it wasn't worth doing."

Mr. Rogers looked kind of funny and said, "Was you talking about Bill Heart and Granny down in the hill country? You said the couple that raised you." And before Tom could answer, he said, "You are not Kid Allen that they raised, are you?"

Tom told him he was and that it was a long story. Mr. Rogers saw that he didn't want to talk about it, so he just dropped the subject. Tom didn't want to hurt his feelings so he went on to say, "Maybe someday I will tell you."

Mr. Rogers laughed and said, "Son, I bet I could tell you a lot of things, if we had the time. Bill and I shipped our cattle from the same place. Bill talked about you all the time. He was mighty proud of you."

Tom laughed and told him, "At his age, I bet you could and a lot of the things sure would help me get started too."

Mr. Rogers said, "About the place," and he quoted him a decent price and said he wouldn't take a penny less. Tom told him he wouldn't ask him to, that he thought that was a fair price. Now if Mr. Harper would keep his end of the bargain, he would take it.

Mr. Rogers said, "Now the bargain is, that you will let me help restore the old dugout or no deal."

Tom laughed and said, "You know, I don't know a thing about building a dugout. Believe you me, all of your help will be appreciated. When do you want to meet with me at the bank?"

He said, "One step at a time, boy. Why don't you stay the night, and we could go tomorrow. I would enjoy camping out anyhow and haven't done that in a long time."

Tom agreed, and Mr. Rogers said, "Its pass suppertime. Let's eat, then we can talk some more."

They ate, and he told Tom all about him and his new wife coming out West and how they had chosen the ranch. He said he was a green horn and had to learn everything the hard way. That he hoped Tom would let him help and maybe then both wouldn't make as many mistakes as he did. Tom told him he would welcome all the help and advice he could give him and that he was as green as grass. That he had worked on a ranch ever since he was eight years old, but he had never managed one. Then again, he told him, Mr. Heart had always done the managing and selling. He didn't ask any more questions, and Tom was glad. But it was so easy to talk to him. He finally said, "Well, guess we better hit the hay if we are going to get an early start tomorrow." Tom was so excited he couldn't sleep. He was like the little boy that Mr. Heart told of. Tomorrow he could go with Bob on his first camp out.

They got up about daylight and were ready to go in no time. Mr. Rogers had packed a lot of food, his blanket, a few clothes, and a canteen and was ready as soon as Tom was. They rested several times, more than he would have if he had been by himself. On the way to the next town, he told Tom that Mr. Engles lived a few miles down the road and he had heard he had some cattle he wanted to sell. It wouldn't be much out of their way to swing by and check them out. Tom told him that would be fine and if it worked out, he could get a loan on them at the same time.

When they got there, he introduced Tom to Mr. Engles and told him what they were there for. He said that he did have about a hundred head and he wanted to sell all of them and his bulls at the same time. Mr. Rogers asked if they were good cattle and in good shape. He told them they were and the only reason he was selling them was his health had gotten bad and he was going to sell them and go live close to his kids. They went down to look at them, and he was right. They were in prime shape, and they were all young cattle.

Mr. Rogers asked him what he would take for all of them, and before he could say anything, he said, "Now, Jack, you know with that many cattle you are not going to find a buyer, and you will have to ship them. Tom could take them off your hands, and you wouldn't have to pay shipping cost. That way you could sell them cheaper, and you both would get a good deal."

Tom saw Mr. Rogers was going to get him the best deal he could, so he just backed off and listened. Mr. Engles finally agreed to knock off all the shipping charges. Then Mr. Rogers told him that Tom was a young boy just trying to get started and asked him if he could come down some.

Mr. Engles told him, "J. B., you drive a hard bargain, but I will come down." And he quoted him the price and said, "That's my rock-bottom price, take it or leave it."

Before Tom could say a word, Mr. Rogers said, "We will take it."

Then Tom told him about having to get the loan and showed him Mr. Harper's note. He said if old Josh had said it was okay that way, it was all right with him. He went on to say his hands would have to drive them to the station to ship, so they might as well take them over and put them in the pasture.

Tom told him, "Now hold on. I haven't got the loan yet."

Mr. Engles told Tom, "If old Josh had written that note then, we don't have anything to worry about. His word was good as gold."

Tom thanked him and said, "We'll see you as soon as we get the loan settled and can get back with the money."

They shook hands on it, and he turned toward Mr. Rogers and laughed. He told Tom he wasn't worried about his money.

If he didn't come back, he would have old J. B.'s hide. He knew the land because he asked Tom what pasture did he want them in. Before Tom could say anything Mr. Rogers said, "You know where the old dugout used to be, just put them in the pasture next to it and tell John to keep a watch out for them until we get back. Tom is buying my place, and he is going to fix the old dugout up and live there until he gets on his feet."

Mr. Engles said, "I figured as much."

Tom thanked him, and they shook hands.

He said, "Good luck, kid."

Then Mr. Rogers shook his hand and told him thank you too.

Mr. Engles told him, "You all be careful, you old reprobate." And to Tom he said, "Take care of this old thief. He a good one."

They left there with Tom buying six hundred acres and a hundred head of cattle plus the bulls without a nickel in his pocket. They camped out all along the way, and Mr. Rogers acted like he really was enjoying himself. It took three days because Tom didn't push it. Tom used the excuse that they didn't want to wear the horses out. Mr. Rogers didn't say anything, but Tom didn't think he bought his story, about them needing to let the horses rest. But he went along with it anyway. They spent the last night in his papa's pasture, and the next morning they went on to town and to the bank.

When Mr. Harper saw them, he came around the counter to meet them. He shook Tom's hand again and said, "I guess you bought the ranch, or you wouldn't have this old scaly-wag with you." Then he shook Mr. Roger's hand. "Hello J. B., how are you?" They talked like long-lost buddies for a while. Then Mr. Harper said, "Well, Tom, are you ready to get down to business?"

Tom told him he was ready whenever they were.

Again Mr. Rogers took right over and told him about the cattle that they had bought from Jack and he thought Tom had got them at a good price. When Mr. Rogers told him how much they paid for them, Mr. Harper said, "For that price, how many did ya'll steal while his back was turned?"

Mr. Rogers laughed and said, "Now, Josh, you know I wouldn't do that."

Mr. Harper turned to Tom and said, "Tom, watch this old scaly-wag in a trade. He will steal you blind."

Mr. Rogers told him, "If you thought I was bad, you ought to see Tom in a trade. He was wheeling and dealing that I thought for a while Tom was going to ask for my shirt for boot."

They both laughed, then Mr. Harper asked about Jack and said to tell him hello for him.

Mr. Harpers drew up the papers, and Mr. Rogers and Tom both looked them over, and both told him they looked fine to them. Under his breath Tom thanked Granny for teaching him how to take care of his own business. Mr. Harper told Tom how much money he needed to pay down on his loan. And said he had made it on the ranch and cattle, also that way Tom would have only one note and only one payment to make each year. He handed the papers to him. Tom looked them over good and told him they looked all right to him, and he signed them. Then Mr. Harper wrote a check for what Tom owed Mr. Rogers. Mr. Rogers told him to put it in the bank because he didn't have any use for it right now. So Mr. Harper made out a receipt for him, then asked Tom how he would like the rest of the money. Tom told him he would need cash money to pay for the cattle. After that Mr. Harper gave him the rest of the money that was left in his account. It wasn't very much, but Tom knew he would need it to get started on. They both thanked him, and Tom told him he would see him when his payment was due. Shortly after that they left with Mr. Harper wishing Tom good luck. Tom thanked him and told him he would need all the luck he could get.

They camped in the same grove of trees that he had camped in the first day he left going to see the ranch. They took care of their horses as soon as they got there. After that Tom made a fire in the same pit he had used the first time. It wasn't long until supper was ready. They ate, and after that they just sat back and talked about the ranch. Mr. Rogers was real eager to get started on the dugout. He told Tom there was a lot of cleaning out before they could get started. Tom told him give him a few days and he would have that done before he got there. Finally, they decided they had better get to bed and go to sleep or they weren't going to get up the next morning, and both had decided they wanted to get an early start.

The next morning, they were on their way about daylight. They both were so excited. They wanted to hurry and get home so they could go to work on the dugout. They stopped at Mr. Engles and paid him for the cattle. While they were there, with Mr. Rogers help, Mr. Engles sold Tom a milk cow named Susie, a hog named Miss Molly that was about ready to have pigs, a dozen hens, plus a rooster. Also Mr. Engles said he had some furniture if Tom was interested in it. Tom told him he would need some because he didn't even have a bed but he couldn't afford to pay too much for them. They looked at it, and with Mr. Rogers dealing, they got a bed and mattress, a table with four chairs, a cook stove, and two rockers for almost nothing. Then Mr. Rogers made him throw some lumber he had lying by the barn and also some nails. He told him, "Now, Jack, you know blame well you wouldn't be using them and we sure would need them to build a place to put Tom's food and dishes." He also asked him if they could leave them until they got ready for them and if he could bring them over to the house in a few days.

When they got ready to go, Mr. Engles asked him, "Is there anything else you want to steal from me before you leave?"

Mr. Rogers didn't bat an eye and said, "As a matter of fact there is, an old chester drawers on the back porch that we could use. Now, Jack, you know most of these things you couldn't sell at all. You would probably have to pay someone to haul them off, and Tom sure could use them."

So Mr. Engles threw it in too. While they were getting ready to go, he said, "Tom, do you have any sheets or anything like that?"

Tom told him, "As a matter of fact I don't. I hadn't thought that far ahead. The only thing I have was my blanket and camping gear."

Mr. Engles told him, "I have some old sheets and pillowcases, also some dishrags, cup towels, and some towels. They were old, but they would do you until you could get some. I won't need them. In fact, I had them in a pile to throw away."

Tom thanked him and told him, "You don't know how much all this means to me."

Mr. Engles told him, "Oh shucks, Tom, it's just junk that I was going to throw away."

Tom told him, "When you don't have anything at all, your junk sure looks good to me. It sure would help me get started." Then Tom paid him for what he said he owed him.

Right after that they left, with him promising to bring the things in his wagon in a few days. Tom was leading a cow named Susie and the hog named Miss Molly, and boy, did they have trouble getting that hog to Mr. Roger's. They thought if they led the cow that the hog would learn from the cow what she was supposed to do and do it. Boy, were they wrong. Finally, Mr. Rogers got on one side of her and Tom on the other. They took the rope off her and just drove her and that wasn't easy. She kept trying to run off. The cow led just fine, so the only thing they had to worry with was that dad blasted hog. When they got to Mr. Rogers place, they decided Tom would never get her home by himself so they decided to leave her there and Mr. Rogers would bring her in the wagon when he came.

Tom thanked him for all he had done to help him.

He said, "Shucks, Tom, I didn't do anything."

Tom told him, "Oh yeah, if it hadn't been for you, I would still be back there trying to buy the cattle, let alone all the other things." Tom laughed. "But I wish we had left that dad blasted hog there."

Mr. Rogers said, "Oh yeah, when you get her home and she has you a bunch of pigs, you will be glad we didn't." He asked Tom to spend the night, but Tom told him he wanted to get as far as he could tonight so he could make it home as soon as possible to check on the cattle.

Mr. Rogers said he was going to have a mighty unhappy cow before he got home if he didn't milk her before he left. Mr. Rogers got a milk pail, and Tom milked her. They parted with Mr. Rogers telling him he would see him in a few weeks. Tom waved and left, leading Susie. He didn't get home that night. Tom found out right fast he wouldn't make as good of time leading a cow as he had when he came. It took him a day longer going back as it did when he came the first time. The next morning he had to milk Susie just out on the ground. Each morning and night he had to do the same. The last day he got up real early and was there before Susie got to unhappy. Then he realized he didn't have a bucket there either to milk her. He saddled Roy and went up to the Rucker's to see if he could borrow a bucket.

When he got there, he hollered, "Hello in the house." Mrs. Rucker came to the door. Tom told her he had bought the place and asked her if she had a bucket that he could borrow that he had bought a jersey cow and he had forgot to buy a bucket.

She told him she had plenty of lard buckets and that was what they milked in. Tom told her they would do nicely. She gave him two. Tom asked her if they could use some milk, that he knew the cow would give more than he could use. She said they would be real happy to get it, also she would send one of the kids with him to bring it back. She called one of her children and said, "Mike, you go with Mr. Tom and bring back some milk he is going to give us and be careful coming back and don't spill it."

Tom asked her if Mr. Rucker was there, and she said he and the rest of the kids were in the field. Tom told her he wanted to see if he could borrow an ax and shovel from him for a while, if he has them and didn't mind him using them. If he would just set them out somewhere, he would pick them up in the morning. She said they would come in for dinner about twelve and she would have him set them out. He could get them any time that afternoon. Tom thanked her and said also he would have more milk for her that night if she could use it. She laughed and said with nine children they could use all the milk they could get and they sure would appreciate it. Then Tom called Roy to come. He stepped up in the saddle and asked Mike if he wanted to ride. You would have thought Tom had asked him if he wanted to go to the moon. His eyes got big and he asked, "Could I really?" Tom told him to give him his hand, and Tom swung him up on the saddle behind him. His mama handed him four buckets and said, "One for now and one for tonight and two for Mr. Tom."

As soon as they got there, Tom just rode on into the pasture to find Susie. She wasn't too far from the place where the old dugout had been. He helped Mike off, buckets and all, and got off. Tom turned Roy loose. He went just a little ways from the camp and started eating. They drove Susie to where Tom had camped. He milked her and got right at two gallons. He told Mike that he would keep a half gallon and they would take the rest of it to his mama. Tom didn't have anything to strain the milk through, so he used the wash rag he had bought at the store, with Mike holding it while he poured. After they put the lids on all the buckets, they took his and put it in a little shallow creek that ran close to the dugout. There was a small stream of water running out of a spring there, and it was ice cold. Mike told him the little spring never went dry. Mike and Tom dug out a shallow place where the cold water would run into it. They had to dig it with their hands and a stick. It wasn't easy, but they finally got it fixed so it could act as Tom's icebox. Then they fixed a place to set the milk bucket so the cold water would run around it.

Tom took the full bucket and told Mike he could carry the small one and they would just walk back to keep from spilling the milk. When they got there, his mama met them and Tom told her he would bring the milk up that night so he could pick up the ax and shovel if Mr. Rucker had one. He left, with her thanking him and she was sure John would have what he needed. After that Tom checked on the cattle, and they were just fine. There was a fence about an acre or better around the dugout, so he started checking it to see how much repair it was going to take. He walked around it, and it looked like it was in pretty good shape, but he would need some staples to staple some of the loose places back to the post. He thought as much grass as there was around the dugout, he could let the chickens stay in the yard and eventually they would get it eaten down. He would need a small chicken house to put them in at night so the varmints wouldn't get them. After that Tom started looking around to see where he could put it. When he got the ax, he would start cutting down some small trees to make it out of. Tom knew he would need a pen close to water to keep the hog in. So he looked outside of the fence down below the spring, and luck was with him. He found another place he could dig out pretty easy so the water could run in and out, giving the hogs a perfect wallowing place so they could stay cool.

There were some trees growing close by, so the hog would have a good shade most of the day. Tom knew he would need it as soon as the hog got there, so he decided he would go up after dinner and see if he could get the ax and shovel so he could get it started that afternoon. He waited until about one o' clock and walked up there. He thought that would give them time to eat and be back at work. They were still there.

Mr. Rucker said, "We rest an hour or so after dinner while it is hot, then we work late when it gets cooler." They were planting their crops. He showed Tom the shed where the tools where and told him to take what he needed. Tom told him thanks for loaning them to him. They talked a few minutes. Then he asked Tom if he was going to have a garden.

He told him, "I hadn't thought that far ahead, but I guess it sure would help me with my food supply for the winter."

Mr. Rucker told him, "When you get ready, I could send one of the boys down to plow it for you."

Tom told him, "I sure would appreciate it, and any time that they had time would be fine with me, that way I could get started cleaning it up."

Mr. Rucker told him, "That's what neighbors are for."

Tom asked him, "Do you know anyone who I could get to cut the hay in the meadow on the half's. It sure needed cutting, and I don't have a way to cut it."

Mr. Rucker told him, "Mr. Buck would probably cut it," and told Tom how to get to his house.

Tom thanked him, and Mr. Rucker waved and said, "Help yourself to the tools you need."

Tom went to the toolshed. He had never seen so many tools. He took a shovel, an ax, a post hole digger, and a sickle.

When he got back to the dugout, he decided to go see Mr. Buck about cutting the hay. It needed cutting right now. His place wasn't hard to find, and as luck was with him, Mr. Buck was there. Tom told him what he wanted and asked him if he would cut it in halves. He said he would be glad to. Tom told him that he didn't have a barn that he would have to put his in a haystack. Mr. Buck said that wasn't a problem, that he could do that. He told Tom he needed all the hay he could get. Tom made arrangements for him to cut one pasture and the hay meadow in halves. He told him that would be all the hay he needed and if he wanted to cut the rest of it and the second cutting, he would sell it to him for the going price.

Mr. Buck said, "I will be glad to get it."

Tom told him, "It is ready to cut right now."

So Mr. Buck said he would cut it that week.

Tom put the cattle in the next pasture as soon as he got home. With as much grass as they had, Tom didn't think they would bother the haystack but he didn't want to take any chances. Sure enough, Mr. Buck came over that week and he had it cut, and Tom's part stacked in a nice large haystack by the end of the second week. Tom had told him to make the haystack in the pasture next to the dugout so he could save that pasture for his winter pasture. With that problem solved, Tom knew he would need something to put the hog in as soon as they got there. By night he had something put together that would hold her, but Tom didn't think it could be called a hogpen. He had dug a channel from the creek through the pen so she would have fresh water all the time. Then he had dug a pretty good-size place for a hog wallow. Anyway, it would do until he could do better.

By the time he finished, Mike was there so they milked the cow. He must have told his mama how they had to strain the milk because Mike handed him a white cloth and said, "Mama sent this to use to strain the milk."

Tom told him, "Tell your mama thank you for it."

Then they strained the milk and put it in the spring. Tom still had some cold milk there, so he asked Mike, "Would you like to have a cup of milk?"

He said, "That would be good."

So they took it up to the camp and got the cups out and poured some, and they sat down under the trees where Tom was camped and drank their milk. Then Tom helped him carry the two buckets up to their house. When they got there, Mrs. Rucker was waiting for them at the door. She had some butter for him and some buttermilk. Tom thanked her and told her how proud he was to get some good old butter and buttermilk.

She told Tom, "It's kind of foolish for you to milk the cow and send most of it up here. Why don't you bring the cow up here, and we could feed and milk her and bring you what you needed each day. We have plenty of sweet feed here for her. Also I would have some butter and buttermilk for you every few days."

Tom thanked her again. He told her if that was all right with her, it would be fine with him because he didn't have any feed to give her and that she was only getting grass. She told him Mike had told her so and she said with some sweet feed it will make the milk better too. So Mike went back with Tom, and they put the buttermilk and butter in the spring, and they got Susie and took her back up to their house. Mike insisted he could lead her up there by himself, but Tom told him he would go along, that he didn't know how gentle she was with children. By the time they got there, he knew Mike could have lead her anywhere. She was as gentle as could be. He put her in the lot, and again Mrs. Rucker was out on the porch. She said she had some jelly for him and had forgotten to give it to him when he was up there before.

Tom thanked her for it and told Mike he would see him tomorrow.

When he got back to the camp, he made a fire. While it was burning down, he made a pan of corn bread, all except the milk. Then he went down to the spring and poured some milk into it and stirred it up. When he got back to the camp, he put some grease in the Dutch oven and poured the corn bread in it. He sure wished he had an egg to go into it, but he didn't, so he just made do with what he had. By then the fire had burned down, so he put the Dutch oven in the coals and covered it good. Then he sat back and thought about what he had gotten one that day. Tomorrow he would clean a larger place out in the spring. With the shovel, he could do a better job fixing it. But first he would try to find a place to put the garden so he would know where it was to go before they came down to plow it.

The next morning he got up early. He was so eager to get started on everything. Tom made a pan of biscuits and a pot of coffee. He got the butter and jelly out of the spring, and as soon as it was ready, he sat down and began to eat, and did that butter and jelly taste good. He raked the coals in a pile and made sure they were all right, then he put the butter and jelly back in the spring again. A little way behind the trees that were around the dugout, Tom found another place where there was some wire. He walked around it and again found out it could be mended. It was all grown up, so he got the sickle and started cutting the grass away from the fence so he could see how big it was. Tom worked all morning, just cutting around the fence. It would be a pretty good-size garden, maybe close to a half acre. He stopped and ate some cold corn bread and buttermilk and rested for a while. He knew if he was going to get it ready for planting, he had his work cut out for him. Tom knew he would have to worry about the chicken house later. They would have to stay in the chicken coop that Mr. Rogers brought them in at night until he could get the garden cleaned and planted. Tom worked all afternoon cutting the grass down so it wouldn't be so hard to plow. The next day he got up early, and as soon as he ate breakfast, he started working on the garden again. He got it finished about sundown, and just in time, Tom had just got a cold cup of water and sat down to rest when he looked up to see Jim coming with the horse and plow. Tom had found an opening where a gate had been. By the time he got there, Tom had it open and was ready for him. Jim plowed the garden just deep enough to get the grass roots and told Tom as soon as he got them pulled out he would be back and plow it deeper.

They sat down to rest, and Tom asked him if he would like a cold glass of milk, and he said, "Right after I have a cold drink of water and rest for a while." So they took their cups and went down and got a cup of ice-cold water. Then they poured them a cup of milk and went back and propped their backs against a tree that Tom had cleaned around at his camp. After they drank their milk, Jim said guess he had better go. He got up and handed Tom the cup and said, "Thank you for the milk."

Tom told him, "Thank you for plowing the garden."

Jim said, "That was fine and to let us know when you are ready to have it plowed again."

Tom told him let me know when they needed the tools that he had borrowed, and he would bring them home. He told Tom it wasn't likely that they would need them. They had several, but he would if they did and for him to keep them as long as he needed them.

The next morning Tom started on the garden, trying to pull the roots out. By the time Mike came down with the milk Tom knew he was going to need a potato fork to get the grass roots out. The land was sandy, and it wouldn't be hard if he had the right tools to work with. They put the milk away, and he walked back with him and borrowed a potato fork and went back. That made it a lot better, but he still worked all morning. By noon he didn't have it half cleared, but what Tom had cleared looked good. He would put the roots in a pile, and when he got a good pile, he would stop and throw them over the fence so what he had cleared was in good shape. Tom stopped at noon, and boy was he tired. He ate dinner and laid back and went sound to sleep.

He got up about three thirty and went down to the spring and drank a cup of cold milk, then started working on the roots again. He worked all that day and the next before he got all the roots out.

The next day, when Mike brought the milk down, he told Tom, "Mama said Susie was giving more milk now since she was getting some sweet feed, and if you needed more milk or butter, just let her know."

Tom told him to tell his mama, "Thanks, but I am doing just fine on what I am getting." And Tom told him to tell Jim, "I have the garden cleared and is ready to have it plowed again."

The next day Tom used the cycle and cut under the fences around the garden, then he took the sharpshooter and took the roots from under the fence. Again, it took him all day. When he got through, he checked everything. It all looked real good now. All he had to do was wait until Jim came back and plowed it. The fence wasn't the best of shape, but he would finish it when he got some staples from town. That afternoon Jim came down and plowed it the second time, and now it was ready to plant.

Chapter 9

Tom made up his mind that he would go into town and get some staples before he planted the garden. So the next morning he saddled Roy and went by to tell the Ruckers he was going to town after the staples. When Tom hollered, one of the boys came to the door and invited him in.

Mr. Rucker was still drinking a cup of coffee, and he asked him to have a cup with him. Tom sat down, and while he drank his coffee, he told him his plans for the day. He said the staples were all right but he needed to check with Dora because she saved her seed and would probably have enough to share with him. She came in and helped Tom make out a list of what seed he would need. He asked her if he could pick up some things for her, and she made Tom out another list of seeds and groceries she would need. Mr. Rucker suggested Tom take their wagon and get her things that she needed and that would save them a trip to town. Tom told him he would be glad to. He put Roy back in the pasture, and while he did that, she finished making out her list. By then the boys had the horses hitched to the wagon and ready for him. The older boys were trying to get the fields ready to plant. The girls and Mike didn't have anything to do in the field, so Mike asked if he could go with him. Before Tom could say anything, Mr. Rucker said, "Now, Tom, wouldn't want to fool with you."

Tom told him, "I would be happy for him to come with me as he could keep me company and show me where the stores are."

He told him, "There is only one store and a hardware store, but between us both, we can carry everything."

Right after they left Mike took Tom at his word and talked all the way to town. He showed him where the hardware store was and told him the other one was just next door. They went to the grocery store first and left their lists. Tom told them he would pay for his things. The woman there said she would be glad to fill them for them while they were next door.

Tom bought the garden seed that Mrs. Rucker said he would need, staples, some nails, and a hammer. Tom knew he couldn't really afford to buy it, but he knew if he got the fences fixed, he had to have one. They looked around for a while, and by the time they went next door, she had their orders almost filled. Tom's was ready, and he paid for it and had her add a penny worth of candy on it. By the time they got it loaded, Mrs. Rucker's order was ready also. They loaded it, and by then Tom realized they didn't have anything to eat for dinner, so he asked Mike if he liked cheese and crackers. He said he did, but they didn't get them very often. So Tom went back in and bought a dime's worth of each for their dinner. As they were driving home, they ate their cheese and crackers. Tom's canteen was almost full of water so they had plenty of water to drink with their dinner and enough to make it home.

When they got there about dark, all the kids came out and helped unload. Tom gave Mrs. Rucker her bill.

She told him, "We have supper ready, and it is time for John to come in. By the time you both get washed up, he should be here."

Sure enough, just as they were finishing, here he came. He washed up, and they went in the house together. The supper was delicious. Mrs. Rucker had fried chicken and had cream potatoes, gravy, green beans; and for dessert, she had made a peach cobbler. Tom told Mrs. Rucker he didn't need his milk that night. He thanked her for the supper and Mr. Rucker for the use of his wagon. He told them now that he had the staples he wanted to get an early start tomorrow so he best be going. Mike hollered thanks for letting him go with him and "See you in the morning." Tom called Roy, and Mike handed him the supplies. As soon as he got to the camp, he turned Roy loose and went to bed. He was tired, and he would have a busy day ahead of him tomorrow.

Tom was up by daylight. He had made the coffee and went down and got the butter and jelly out of the spring. He just warmed some cold biscuits in the skillet he had left over from the day before. He ate real quick and was in the garden before the sun was up. He walked the garden fence and stapled all the places that were loose. He repaired the gate where it would close, and now it was ready to start planting.

Tom had just finished the gate when Mike came down with the milk. Mrs. Rucker had already strained it, so all he had to do was take it to the spring. Tom had some left from the day before, so he and Mike drank it, and then they washed the bucket so Mike could take it back. He had also brought the seed that Mrs. Rucker said she could divide with him. Tom never saw so many seeds. She had sent green beans, pinto beans, butter beans, black-eyed peas, sweet corn, okra, and squash.

Mike told Tom, "Ma said to tell you, it was time to plant all of these now. She also said she would have tomato plants, sweet potato plants, and pepper plants as soon as they were ready." She said to cut the potatoes' eyes off the potatoes that you bought yesterday, that you needed to get them ready and put in a shady place to dry some before you start planting the other seed.

Mike grinned and said, "She said I could stay and help you if I wouldn't be in your way."

Tom told him, "You sure wouldn't be in my way, and I will be glad to have you to show me what all to do."

That really pleased Mike, and he told Tom, "I plant the seed for Mama while she covers them. And I know just how to plant them too. You take a short step and drop two seeds until you get them all planted."

Tom told him, "With you knowing how and with me covering them, we will get through pretty quick." They finished their milk, and Tom told him, "Well, guess we had better get started planting."

Mike told him, "Not before we get the seed potatoes cut up and put out to dry, we don't." Mike showed him how to just cut a chunk off the potato. "Now it is not necessary to use all the potato, just cut a chunk out that has the eyes on it, and when you get through, you will have some of the potato left, and you can cook it. That's the way Mama does it."

Tom did it like Mike showed him, and sure enough they had quite a lot left on each one to cook later. Mike told him, "They will turn dark, but Mama says it don't hurt the potato. You can peel the dark off and still have plenty of potato to cook when you need it." When they finished cutting them, they spread them on a piece of tin they found. Mike said it wouldn't hurt to get them dirty. They took what was left over of each potato, and Tom wrapped them in his clean towel to cook later and laid them on his saddle to dry. Mike told him, "Now we could get started planting the seed and by the time we need the potato eyes they will be dry enough to plant." Boy, was Tom proud of the seed. If they made good, he wouldn't have to buy much all winter, except staples, and that would sure help. His share of the crop money and the cutting of hay and the baby pigs that he planned to sell will tide him over just fine.

Mike was a lot of help. He told him what seed his mama planted next to each other, so Tom planted them that way. He said, "She always saves the first row for onions, the second row for tomatoes and radishes, the third row for carrots and peppers. Mama said they gather them more often, and if it rained, they wouldn't have to go out in the mud to get them. Of course, your rows won't be as long as ours because you won't need as much."

So they planted the bunches of onions they had got in town on the first row and skipped a place long enough for the tomatoes and at the end planted a short piece of the row in radishes. On the third row they planted the carrots and left plenty of room for the pepper plants. They didn't get through by noon, but they stopped and Tom fixed some dinner. Mike acted like he sure enjoyed them cooking over a campfire.

After dinner Tom told Mike he was tired and that he bet he was too and why don't they lie back and rest for a while. Tom removed the potato pieces they had put there to dry and let Mike lie back on his saddle. Tom told him that was the way cowboys had to do when they were out taking care of the cattle. Mike asked him if he was really a cowboy. Tom told him he was raised on a ranch from the time he was eight years old until now. Mike asked him one question after another like, Did he have his own horse? What was his name? Did he have to go to school? And in one breath said that he didn't like school very much. Tom told him he was homeschooled, but Granny Heart was real good and real strict. Then Tom told him what she had told him about—if he didn't get his schooling, he wouldn't be worth a flip when he got grown, that he wouldn't know if someone was cheating him or not if he couldn't read or know his numbers. Tom told him, "She was right because if I hadn't known all that, how would I have bought this place."

Mike told Tom, "I hadn't thought about that. When I get grown, I want a place just like this one."

Tom told him. "Then you had better make sure you go to school and learn all the things you need to."

Mike said, "Sure enough."

And Tom told him, "You bet your boots."

Mike hadn't let up talking the whole time they were resting. Tom finally said, "Guess we had better get up if we are going to get the rest of the garden planted."

He informed Tom that "we probably won't get it done today anyway, but I could come back tomorrow if you want me too."

Tom told him that would be nice.

Mike was right. With him telling what to plant beside what and how many rows to plant, it took them longer than Tom thought it would. But Mike said, "We sure did make a big dent in it, didn't we?"

Tom told him, "We sure did, and tomorrow we will finish it."

They stopped a little before sundown. Tom told him, "You need to get home before your papa and the others came home from the field. If you come tomorrow and if we get through in time, maybe you could stay for supper and after supper we could go rabbit hunting. I had noticed there are a lot around here, and they sure will play whaley with our gardens when they come up. Make sure you tell your mama that you are going hunting with me and tell her I will bring you home before dark."

Mike said, "We need to kill all we can because, like you said, rabbits will play whaley with our gardens, and I know it will be all right."

Tom told him just the same, for him to make sure he asked her. They left right after that, with Mike, just as happy as a boy could be after someone had said he could go hunting. It was almost too late to hunt for rabbits, but Tom was hungry for meat, and like Mike said, they sure would play whaley with their gardens. Before supper, Tom went back to look at the garden. He was so proud of it. This was going to sure help him through the winter. He would have plenty of food, and it wasn't going to cost him a whole lot. Then Tom called Roy and went to see about the cattle. He had been busy and hadn't checked on them in a few days, and he wanted to make sure they were all right. Then he ate supper and went to bed early again. He wanted to finish planting the garden tomorrow.

Mike came early. Tom had waited on him because he didn't want to hurt his feelings by starting without him. Tom was down at the hogpen when he came up. Tom was trying to wire some of it together with some old wire he had found.

Mike asked him, "What is it for?"

Tom told him it was a hogpen and that he had bought a mama hog that a man was going to bring to him in a few days.

Mike walked around it twice before he said anything. Then he said, "Well, it sure don't look like a hogpen."

Tom could hardly keep from laughing, but he said, "I just made this real quick to have a place to put her until I can do better."

Again, he could hardly keep a straight face, he said, "I don't think it will ever hold her," and in the same breath he asked him, "Did you say a mama hog? Does she have baby pigs?"

Tom told him, "No, but she is going to."

Mike walked around the pen again and said, "It sure will be crowded with a mama hog and her babies."

"Maybe I will make it larger before the babies get here." And with that, they left to go plant the garden. Tom told him, "We better get started so we can get through before dusty dark, so we can go hunting."

They went by and put the milk in the spring, both of them in their conversation about the hogpen had forgotten the milk. They worked until noon. Tom had put some pinto beans on earlier, so they would be done for their dinner. By dinner he knew they would have plenty of time to finish planting the garden that afternoon and after that they rested for a while. They had worked hard, and Mike was beginning to look tired. Tom knew better than to ask him if he wanted to go set in the shade and let him finish. To a farm boy that would be an insult because they are taught you don't stop until the job is done.

When they finally stopped, Tom told Mike, "Sit down and rest, and I will finish getting dinner ready." But Mike would have no part of that. He wanted to help him fix it. Tom emptied the beans out of the Dutch oven into the skillet, then washed and dried it. He told Mike he could go down and get the buttermilk. Tom made corn bread, and by the time he was ready for the buttermilk, Mike was back. Tom had put some wood on the fire, and it had burned down. He put the buttermilk in the corn bread and stirred it good, then poured it into the Dutch oven. Then he raked the coals back and put it on some hot coals. He put the lid on it and covered the lid with some more coals. All the time Mike was watching him and asking why he did everything that he was doing. Tom explained it all to him as he went along. After he got the corn bread on, he raked another spot out in the coals and set the skillet with the pinto beans in it. Mike wanted to know why he didn't cover it too, and Tom told him they only wanted to keep it hot because it was already cooked. Tom asked him if he liked green onions with his beans, and he said he did. Tom told him he saw some wild onions close to where the pigpen was and that they would go down and get some while the bread cooked. They pulled what they wanted, then took them by the spring and washed them. He put the buttermilk back and got some butter and milk. After that Tom pealed and washed the onions. He told Mike he could carry them and he would carry the sweet milk and butter, but he told Tom he could carry them. By the time they got back to the camp, the corn bread was done. They filled their plates with the beans, green onions, hot corn bread, and plenty of butter, then poured them a cup of cold milk. Tom told him he could lean back on the saddle and he would lean back on the tree trunk.

Mike sat down and starting eating. He looked up and said, "Ain't this the life?"

Tom told him, "Come to think about it, yes, I suppose it really is."

After they ate they took the dishes down below the spring and washed them. Mike dried them while Tom washed them. They went back to camp and laid down, and again, Mike began to ask questions. He asked Tom where he had learned to cook like that and told him it sure was good. Tom told him that they had to cook their food like that when they were camped out fixing fences or looking for stray cattle. Tom told him the corn bread would have been better if he had an egg to go in it. Then he told him he had a dozen hens coming. Mike wanted to know when, and Tom told him the man that was going to bring the hog was going to bring the hens also.

Mike said, "Well, guess we had better get the garden finished so we can build a henhouse. You do know you will need one, don't you?"

Tom told him he did, but until the man came, he didn't have any material to build it with.

Mike then asked, "Where are you going to keep them until you get one built?"

Tom told him, "I figure I could let them run out during the day and put them back in the crate at night until I get one build."

"Guess that will be all right, but you better not forget to put them up or the varmints will have them eaten in one night." With that, Mike said, "Guess this ain't getting the garden finished. Maybe by then the man will be here and then we can get started building the henhouse." He got up. "Well, let's get started." He wanted to make sure they got it finished in time to go hunting.

They finished the garden late that afternoon. Mike was real eager to go hunting, but Tom told him it was better to go at dusty dark. They went to the spring for a cold cup of water. It was ice cold. Then they rested for a while.

Mike told him, "Oh, I forgot to tell you. I will be late tomorrow because all of us are going to plant our sweet potatoes. It won't take us long with all of us planting."

Tom asked him, "What time will you all start planting?"

Mike said, "About sunup."

Tom told him he would see him then.

Mike tried to tell him, he didn't have to come up.

"Now, if you are going to help me, it's only right that I help you in return." To make him feel better about it, Tom said, "And besides, I have never planted sweet potatoes and I need to learn how."

So it was settled. He would be up at daylight. Mike told him right after they got theirs planted, it won't be long until they will be big enough to get his. Mike told Tom he thought they were ready for them anytime, didn't he? Tom told him he thought so too. Mike told him, "I will let you know, and we will go up and get them together so we could plant them the same day, so they wouldn't wilt." They had saved two rows for the sweet potatoes and one left for tomatoes and bell peppers.

Mike was so eager to go hunting about six, he said, "It's going to be sundown before long, don't you think we had better get started so we will have time to skin them before dark." It wasn't, but he was wanting to get started so bad, and can you blame him? He was just a boy going on his first rabbit hunt. Right then that was the most important thing in his whole life. Mike had brought a lantern with him that morning. He said,

"Papa said we might need this to see, to skin all those rabbits with. He has already filled it up with coal oil."

It still wasn't time, but Tom told him he expected it was. So Mike got the lantern while Tom got his gun. When Mike saw it, he got real excited and said, "Wow, a real gun. I bet you could kill anything with that."

Tom told him, like Mr. Heart had told him, "It's a weapon, not a play pretty. Don't ever point it at anything that you didn't want to kill, and don't kill anything but for food or defending yourself." Tom could still remember a little boy hearing those same words, as he went on to say, as Mr. Heart said to him, "Now, Tom, always remember that because it's real important." Tom's mind went back to that little boy as he heard the same words, "I will, I promise I will." And once again, he became so homesick. Right after that, they left. Tom didn't think they would find any rabbits that early, but what did that matter, they still would be on the hunt and looking for them. They walked down in to the pasture close to the big creek. It was a good ways from where his camp was, but Mike didn't complain once. When they got there, they sat down behind some bushes, close to where the cattle came down for water.

Tom told Mike to be real quiet and maybe some rabbits would come out for water before long. Sure enough, they hadn't sat there long until Mike punched him and pointed at the creek. Tom let them get a little closer before he shot. When he did shoot, he aimed at their heads. He got three before they had time to scatter. Mike went down and got them and again they waited, but they didn't see one rabbit. Tom told Mike, "Guess they had better find another watering place," so we moved up the creek, to another place where more of the cattle had been coming down to drink. Again, they hid in some bushes, and before long, here some came, and he shot and got some more. They walked and hid until about dusty dark, and by then they had gotten seven, and they all were nice and fat. Tom told Mike guess they had better go get them cleaned before it got too dark to see how to clean them. They took them below the spring. Mike held them while Tom dressed them. They had gotten two buckets when they came by the camp, but the two wouldn't hold them. Mike took the lantern and ran to the camp and got two more buckets. They washed them real good in the cold water at the spring. Tom took one rabbit, and he told Mike that would be enough for both of them.

They came by the camp, and Tom filled his bucket with cold water and put it in the spring. It would stay plenty cold until morning, then he would cook it in the Dutch oven. They washed up and took the rest of them up to Mike's house. It was dark by then, but they weren't worried because Mr. Rucker had said if it was after dark it would be all right. Tom carried two buckets, and Mike carried one and the lantern and walked ahead of Tom so they both could see.

Mrs. Rucker was real proud of the rabbits and said she didn't think they would get that many. Mike told her how many they got, and he was just as proud as punch. He told them they got seven, and every time Tom hit them right through the heads. He told them, Tom said, that way they didn't waste any meat. Tom told her if they were going to have gardens, he guess he had better keep killing them, but when the weather gets hot they won't be "fit-ten" to eat, and he didn't think they could eat them as fast as he killed them. Mrs. Rucker told him not to worry about that. They would can them as long as they are good. Some of the boys can skin and dress them while he shot them. Besides, they have been griping because they didn't get to go too. So it was settled. Each night, as long as the meat was good, they would hunt. Before it got hot, they had killed quite a few rabbits and it helped in two ways—the rabbits wouldn't eat their garden and they made good meat for the winter. With all of them hunting, they sure made a big dent in them.

The next morning, Tom was up early and had a fire made. He got the rabbit from the spring and in the Dutch oven by the time it burned down. He had re-peeled the potatoes that they had bought and cut the eyes off, added the carrots he had also bought, and some wild onions. By the time he had added all that, he had a real good meal in the Dutch oven. He cleaned out a place in the coals and set it in them. He put some more coals on top of it, and by dinner, it would be ready. Tom got to the Ruckers just as they were coming out to start pulling the potato slips. Mrs. Rucker showed him how to pull them, then she said she and Tom would pull them while the girls dropped them in the rows and the boys planted them. Mike would go back to the potato bed and get the plants every time they got a bunch pulled so that way he kept the girls in plenty of plants. Tom didn't know how many rows they planted, but about eleven they ran out of plants. Mrs. Rucker said as soon as they put on new plants, that they would finish planting theirs and then would still have plenty for him. They all watered the potato slips, but it didn't take long with three watering and four carrying water from a spring that was close to their house.

After that, Mrs. Rucker thanked him, and he started to leave. Mike asked if he could go help Tom.

His mama said, "Now, Mike, Mr. Tom don't want you around all the time."

Mike told her, "But, Mama, he has a whole lot to do and no one to help him."

Tom told her, "I don't mind him coming down to the camp, but I don't want to take him away when you need him."

Mike said, "Please, Mama, let me go. That's all we have to do for the day, ain't it?"

She said, "Oh, all right, but don't you get in Mr. Tom's way, and you help him."

Tom told her it was just plain Tom, and she said okay as long as it's Dora and John. So Mr. and Mrs. Rucker became Dora and John.

As soon as they got to the camp, Tom told Mike, "You run down and put the milk in the spring, then rest while I go to look at the garden again." Tom was so proud of it. He just wanted to look at it again. For a man that didn't know how he would have food for the winter, he had come a long way.

Mike came up and said, "It sure does look good, don't it?"

Tom told him, "You bet it does."

Mike asked him, "What are we going to do today?"

Tom told him, "I guess we had better get busy on the dugout because if it rained, I wouldn't have a place to stay."

They got the shovel and ax and went to see what they could do. Tom dug the dirt off the top so he could see what had to be done to it. All the top was bad, so they began to take the old timber off it. They just barely got started good before it was dinnertime. They went to camp, and sure enough their rabbit and vegetables were ready, with some good gravy to boot. Mike went after the milk and butter. Tom thought that he would give a dollar for a hot cup of coffee, but he didn't want to take time to make it. He warmed some corn bread that he had made the night before. By the time it was warm, Mike was back with the milk and butter. They sat down and ate, with Mile telling him all the things that they had to get done before winter.

When they finished eating, Tom told him he was tired and he thought they would rest for a while. Mike looked tired, and Tom knew he wouldn't rest if he didn't, so they laid back for a while, and Tom went to sleep. About an hour later Mike woke him and told him, guess they had better get busy if they were going to get it finished before winter so he would have a place to stay in when it got cold. They finished getting all the dirt dug off and all the old logs tore off and stacked close to their campfire. Tom told Mike they would use it all for fire wood later. When they finished that job, they measured the length of the logs they would need. There was a grove of trees about a block from the dugout that needed cutting anyway. So they started cutting them down and dragged each one to the dugout. They put them in place on top of the dugout. This, Tom did for two reasons—one, because he wanted to make sure they fit and, two, about how many they would need to cover it. Right now he didn't want to cut any more than he had to. It took them the rest of the day to cut all the logs they would need. They dragged them up to the camp, and by then it was time to stop for the day. He told Mike, "We will layer them on top tomorrow, to make sure we have enough. Then we'll take them off so we can clean the inside. This was the hard way, but I don't know any other way to do it." After that, the boys were down to go hunt rabbits again. They came down every night about dusty dark.

The next day Tom was up early and was waiting for Mike to get there. They placed all the logs on the top, and sure enough they had cut the right mount. After that they took them all off and stacked them in a neat pile far enough away so the logs wouldn't be in their way. The inside was filthy. Some varmints had used it for their den, but from the top they could see that there wasn't anything in it now. They looked for snakes, and they didn't find any. So they went down with a rake, an old broom, and a shovel. Tom had also borrowed a half bushel basket from the Ruckers. They first swept all the walls down, and they were in pretty good shape, only a few would have to be replaced. Then they started raking the floor and shoveling all the crude into the basket. When they got it full, Tom took it out while Mike raked some more up. It took them several hours to get the floor raked out, and then they swept it good. After they had repaired the walls, Tom told Mike, "Now we have to go look for some clay." They went to the large creek, and sure enough, they didn't have to look far until they found a bank with plenty of wet clay. With a shovel Tom dug enough to fill an old bucket he had borrowed and carried it back to the dugout. Mike carried the shovel asking questions all the way, about what they were going to do with all that mud and why. Tom told him, "Just wait and I will show you." When they got to the dugout, they went after some water from below the spring and poured enough into the clay to make a thick paste. They took some old rags that Mrs. Rucker had sent down and tore them into strips. They wet them with the clay, then stuffed them between the cracks. After that they took more clay and filled the cracks up real good. They had to get quite a few buckets of clay and water, so they didn't get a lot done until it was time to stop for the night.

Chapter 10

FOR WEEKS AND WEEKS THEY had hunted rabbits every night, first to can, then after, they weren't good to eat, just to get rid of them so they wouldn't eat their gardens up. Tom was so glad when they stopped finding them; now he could get some rest. After he checked the garden, Mike went home and Tom went straight to bed. Tom was tired, and he slept real good all night and was up at daylight. He ate breakfast and was down working on the walls before Mike got there. He had brought the sweet potato plants, the tomato slips, and the pepper plants. So Tom had to stop on the dugout, and they planted them. By the time they got them all planted and watered, the morning was gone. They stopped and ate dinner and rested for a while. Mike was shaking him about one thirty, telling him if they were going to get through, they had better get to it.

Tom told Mike, "Don't let anyone tell you, raising a garden is not hard work."

"Yeah," Mike told him, "but it's worth it. Look at all the good food you are going to have."

Tom thought about what Mike said and told him, "You sure are right about that."

It took all that afternoon and all the next day to get all the walls filled. After they finished the walls, they brought water from the spring and wet the floor real good and dried them the best they could. They had clay already on them pretty heavy, and it was in good shape. Now the only thing they had to do was wait until it all dried and for Mr. Rogers to come. Tom didn't know how to put the roof on.

The next week Mr. Rogers and another wagon came. Tom saw them from a good distance before they got there. He couldn't tell who was driving the other wagon, but he knew one would be Mr. Rogers. When they got close enough, he could see Mr. Engles was driving the other one. The wagons were loaded to the brim. Tom thought they must have spent the whole month gathering up things to bring. He waved and ran down to meet them. He told them, "I had wondered what had happened to ya'll, but now I know you had been going around all month gathering up stuff to bring."

They laughed and said, "Its things people wouldn't ever need anymore and things you will need. So we thought we would just as well bring them and dump them off on you in place of the dump grounds."

It was a gold mine to Tom, and he told them so. He told them how proud he was to see them and told Mr. Engles, "Seeing you was a surprise. I wasn't expecting to see you."

Mr. Engles laughed and told him, "You didn't think I was going to miss all the fun, did you?" His wagon had the hog and chickens on top of ever thing else he had in it. "Guess we all had better get the hog and chickens out of the crates so they could get some water before we start unloading the wagons."

Tom told them, "I don't have much of a place for the hogs and nothing for the chickens." He told them that he had thought the chickens could stay in the crate until he could get something built in the next few days.

They took the hog down to the pen, and they agreed with Mike that the pen wouldn't hold her overnight if she wanted out. They said the water idea was great, and they could build a better pen around it. They let her out, and she went over to the wallow hole that Tom had dug out, drank some water, and laid down. Then they took the chickens up to the dugout, and he found a pan that they could put some water in to water them They put the two crates that the chickens were in, together, with the doors open, to give them more room, then sat it close to the place where they would be sleeping so they would be safe for tonight. The wagon was loaded down with all kinds of lumber, nails, staples sheets of tin, and a gold mine of all kind of tools. Plus, the chickens and the hog were in crates on top. Tom told them it was like someone handing him the whole world on a silver platter. He hadn't seen anything that they were unloading that he couldn't use. On the other wagon, it was loaded with the bed, mattress, and all the other things Tom had bought for the house. They had brought dishes, pots, pans, two sets of sheets, two pillows, two sets of pillowcases, some quilts, cup towels, dishrags, washrags, a kettle to heat water in on the stove, a big washpot, a tub, a can sealer, and cans for canning, and at that time, the Lord only knew what else. They pulled the wagons close to the camp and unhitched the horses and turned them loose in the yard around the dugout.

Mr. Rogers said, "There's plenty of grass for them that need to be eaten down."

Then the three of them took some of the lumber and nails and went down to build Molly a pigpen. With the three of them, it didn't take them long. Tom cut the poles that they needed and they laid out the size of the pen. Then with the post hole digger, Tom dug the holes to put the post in. They showed him how deep to dig them so they couldn't be rooted up. He dug and put the post in as he went, and each time they were right behind him, nailing boards to the post. It didn't take them long until they had it finished, and Molly had a good home with plenty of room. They also had brought some sacks of feed for Molly and also the chickens.

Mr. Engles said, "In a few days we will let the chickens out to eat the grass seed, and with us feeding them, in the two crates, they will come back at night for their food and we can lock them up until we can get a chicken house made."

After that it was getting close to suppertime. Tom was real worried because he didn't have but two each of dishes and things. Again, Mike had come to his rescue. When Tom got back to the camp, there he stood with two plates two cups, two knifes, two forks, and two spoons. Tom hugged him and told him how much he appreciate him.

Mike said, "Aw shucks, it wasn't nothing. I told Mama you had two visitors and didn't have but two plates. So she told me to bring them down and for you to keep them as long as you needed to."

Tom told him, "It sure was something too," and told him to thank his mama for him. Mike told Tom he would and hollered, "Bye, see you soon," and left. They had brought their own bedrolls and some groceries. They all three cooked supper, then ate and sat around, making plans for what they needed to do first. They all agreed that a chicken house should come first. They spread out their bedrolls and laid down.

The next morning, they looked around. Mr. Rogers said the perfect place was between the dugout and garden, so they choose a place there to build it. And he also told Tom how good the garden looked. After that Tom cut the logs for it. This time he had the horses and wagon that they had brought the lumber and tools in. They had unloaded one wagon earlier and boy was it easier. Tom loaded the logs on the wagon and brought a whole load up at one time. They notched and placed the logs, and as he brought a load of posts up, they would be about out before he could cut another load and get back.

Mike had come down and bought a whole gallon of sweet milk and some butter. He had put it in the spring already.

Tom told the men, "I see you have met Mike. He is the boy I told ya'll about that helped me with all I had got done."

"All except the pigpen," Mike told them, grinning. "That he did by himself."

Mr. Rogers told him, "You should go see it now. It is a humdinger."

Mike told them, "Guess I had and besides I want to see the hog." And in the same breath, he asked, "Has she had babies yet?"

Tom told him, "Not yet, but any day now."

While he ran down to see the hog and the pen, Tom unloaded the logs. Mike came back and told Mr. Rogers, "You are right, it is a humdinger."

Tom was just getting ready to leave, and he asked Mike if he wanted to go with him. He told Tom, "That's what I'm here for. What are we going to do now?" He talked all the way to where Tom was cutting the logs. Mike helped him load them as he cut them, and it didn't take long until they had another load. It took them two days to build the henhouse. Everything was logs except the door. They made the door out of some boards that they had brought with them using a piece of leather that they had cut into strips for the hinges, and it worked just fine. Tom nailed a small oblong board on the door frame so when the door was shut, it would turn cross ways and keep the door shut. The crate that the chickens and hog came in, and they nailed inside the henhouse on the wall for nest boxes. Mr. Rogers had put dividers in the boxes, and they made real good nest. Mike and Tom pulled some grass and put in them. With every one helping, they got through about six that evening.

Mr. Engles said, "We had better get the chickens in the henhouse before night," and that took them a good while as they had stayed pretty close together. Mr. Engles had put chicken feed out, but the chickens were getting plenty of food.

They didn't seem to be interested in the chicken feed. It was a race for your money. They had to catch each one of them and carry them to the chicken house. By the time they got them all in and counted them, they were about ready to have chicken and dumplings the next day.

The guys had a long day, so Tom told them he would fix supper. Mike told them bye and told the guys he was glad to meet them. Then he told Tom, "I won't be back for a few days. I have to help my mama hoe the garden. Also, now you had better keep the sweet potatoes, tomatoes and peppers watered real good each night until they start growing good or they will die. Also, the garden will need hoeing soon." Tom thanked him and told him he would and for him to come back to see him when he could. Dora had given Tom some of the cans of the rabbits she had put up. He put two cans in the Dutch oven with the rest of the potatoes and carrots and covered the Dutch oven with hot coals. When it was ready, he put it all into the skillet and placed it on the hot coals to stay warm. Then he washed the Dutch oven and made biscuits in it. Again, he placed the Dutch oven back in the hot coals and covered it to cook. He also made a pot of coffee. While they cooked, he went down to the spring and got the butter and a jar of jelly that Dora had given him. By then the bread was done. Tom raked the coals off the Dutch oven and told them to come and get it. They filled their plates and sat down next to the tree for a back rest. Tom poured them a cup of coffee and took it to them. Then he got the butter and jelly and took it to them, but they said they would save the butter and jelly for dessert after they finished their rabbit stew.

Tom filled his plate, then and poured them all a cup of coffee, then sat down too. They both told Tom how much they were enjoying the rabbit stew.

Mr. Engles said, "I hadn't had rabbit stew in I don't know when."

Mr. Rogers told him, "Now see, Jack, what I had told you. Now, isn't this better than sitting around feeling sorry for yourself. And besides, Tom needed us and it sure feels good to be needed again."

Mr. Engles said, "It sure does."

They finished eating their stew and had another cup of coffee with a buttered biscuit and jelly. They talked for a while, making plans for what they would do tomorrow. After that, they said they thought they would turn in as they would have a long day tomorrow and wanted to get an early start in the morning. They spread out their bedrolls and laid down. Again, Tom thanked them, got his pistol from force of habit, and put it under his blanket just where he could reach it and went to sleep, but not before both of them did. Tom heard them both snoring as he drifted off.

Tom woke up just as it was barely light enough to see. He slipped out of bed and took his clothes and boots and went away from the camp so he wouldn't wake them up. He put them on and got some buckets and went down and got water and started to water the garden. He was just finishing, when they woke up. They ate breakfast, and while they ate, Mr. Rogers said, "Jack and I had been talking about what we needed to do first. We decided, if we made the kitchen cabinet first, we would have more light to see to build it."

So right after breakfast they started on the cabinets. Tom left the chickens in the chicken house until noon, hoping by then they would lay before he let them out. J. B. told him to give the chickens a little feed right by the henhouse and maybe they would come up that night for their feed. When he went to let them out, some were on the nest already, so maybe they would have some eggs that night. Tom just propped the door open and sprinkled the feed right in front of it. Some of them came right out and began to peck at the feed, but the others didn't seem like they were in too much of a hurry to come out. So he just left them with the door open so they could come out when they got ready and went down to feed Molly. She had her pigs during the night. She had ten little pigs, and all of them looked strong and healthy, and Molly didn't look any worst for having them. Tom put the feed out and hurried back to tell the guys. Mike had got there with the milk, and he had already put it in the spring. He told Tom he had brought milk, butter, and some buttermilk and that there was plenty, if after a while they wanted some to drink. When Tom told them about Molly, all work stopped and every one had to go see Molly's family.

Mike said, "Mama said for me to come right back so we could get started hoeing the garden, but she wouldn't mind me taking time to see the pigs."

So they all went down to where they were. Molly didn't mind them looking at her piglets, but they didn't get into the pen to check them for males or females. They did try to check and thought it was pretty close to half and half, but really, they couldn't tell for sure. Tom was so proud of them. This was another way of him having money to help him make it through the winter. He could keep some and sell the rest.

Mr. Engles said, "If it was me, I would keep two of the little females for breeding. That would give you some cash money each year when they had their babies."

So it was agreed that Tom would keep two. Mr. Rogers told Tom, "You will need a male and maybe Jack and I can find someone that has one before you need him and can swap one for one with him. And be sure and hold one back for that purpose."

Tom told them, "I will keep one to butcher, but that still leaves five to feed out and sell."

Mike said, "Guess I had better get to the house and get to hoeing out the garden, and by the way yours probably needs it too."

Tom told him that he had been pulling weeds each night, ever since they planted it, and he thought it was in pretty good shape and told him thanks for reminding him. The garden was coming right along. They had a good stand of everything.

They left Miss Molly to her pigs and went back to the house and started building the cabinets. Tom brought the lumber to them, and they worked on the cabinets. They did as much outside as they could. J. B. and Jack, as they had insisted Tom call them, had built a table effect that came out far enough for a cabinet top. Then they had made the shelves to set at the back of it. Now all they had to do was to let them down in the dugout. They had made them, so they could let the bottom half down and put it in place. It was a little harder to do than the top part. Jack and Tom let it down while J. B. guided it until it touched the floor. They nailed it in place, then let the shelves down the same way. It took all three of them to lift it and put it on top of the bottom part. Jack nailed the side of the shelves to the wall so it would sit down on the counter, then they nailed it down real good to secure it to the countertop. The shelves came all the way to the ceiling, or at least to where it would go when they got the ceiling in. Jack finished nailing it to the wall. He made sure he found a log to nail it to and not in-between. They were crude, but Tom sure was proud of them. By the time they finished, it was dinnertime and they were all tired and ready for a break. They ate, and while they rested, Tom checked the garden. Then he pulled weeds until he saw them stirring around. He went to the dugout, and they started on the roof. They told Tom to hitch the horses to the wagon and go cut more logs. He had cleaned the grove where he had been cutting, so he had to find a new place to cut. It didn't take long to find a new place.

He cut a wagon full as long as the trees were. When Tom got there, they were waiting for him. J. B. said they had just finished and had just sat down, so they rested for a while, then they went back to work. Tom pulled the wagon close to where they were working and unloaded as many logs as they said they would need. They told Tom to unload the rest by the henhouse. So he pulled the wagon over there and unloaded the rest of them and went back to help place the logs where they needed to be. It didn't take long until they had the rest of them in place.

They had left a square hole in the roof for the chimney. When they had finished putting all the logs in place, they went back to the square hole and started working on it. Jack told Tom to bring them the chimney pipe. They put it down in the hole to form the chimney. While they were doing all this, they told Tom to take the wagon and go get a load of clay from the creek. "Make sure it's good and wet," J. B. told him.

When he got back, they had the chimney finished and were waiting for the clay. Tom handed them a bucket of clay, and they told him to add more water to it to make a paste. So he added a little more water, and they started putting it around the pipe that came up through the hole to form the chimney. After they got it finished, they sent Tom back after more clay. Again, Tom made a thick paste, and they began to put it all over the logs that were on the roof. They did this all day until by night they had a thick coat of clay all over the roof.

After they finished, J. B. said, "Now all we have to do is let it get hard, then we will be ready for the dirt to be put back on it."

It was getting late so they stopped for the night. They still had the chickens to get in and supper to fix. They put some feed by the henhouse door again and called for the chickens, but they didn't come up as Tom hoped they would. So again they had to go down and catch them and bring them up. They put them down where they had sprinkled the feed, so they could learn to come up for it each night. By doing this they hoped the chickens would finally learn if they came in at night they would get some feed. They ate it all, then turned around and just walked into the chicken house, just like they knew that was what they were supposed to do.

Jack said, "Maybe if we left them in the house each day until noon, that way they would lay there and we wouldn't have to look for the eggs and they might learn they were supposed to come there each night to sleep."

Tom said, "Anything was worth a chance."

So it was decided that was what they would do.

Tom fixed supper again while the boys rested. They had a long hard day, and Tom knew with them not being used to working that hard, they needed some rest. After supper, he made another pot of coffee and put it on the coals while it made he cleaned up the dishes. Then they just sat around talking and drinking coffee until bedtime. They were so eager to get all the things done.

J. B. finally said, "Well, tomorrow is another day. Guess we had better get to bed, so we will be bright eyed and bushy tailed come morning."

The next morning, Tom made some biscuits and put them on to cook. Then he sliced some bacon and put it on in the skillet to boil some of the salt out of it. The day before the hens had begun to lay again, and today they would have eggs with their bacon and biscuits. While the bacon was cooking, he went after the milk, butter, and a jar of jelly. By the time he got back, the meat was boiling. He drained all the water off and put it on to fry. Tom made a pot of coffee, and while it finished perking, he scrambled some eggs. Tom couldn't remember when he had scrambled eggs, and they were so delicious. J. B. said it was the camping out and cooking it over the campfire. Jack said he didn't know when he had such a good time.

Tom cleaned up the dishes and went down to feed Molly and check on her brood. They were fine, and Molly had introduced them to the water hole Tom had dug out for her. He made a memory note that he would have to make it larger when he had time. It was pretty crowded for ten pigs and Miss Molly. The larger the pigs got, the more crowded it would be.

He came back by the henhouse, and two hens were trying to nest. So Tom decided to save some eggs that night for them to hatch. When he got back to camp, the guys had poured them some coffee and Tom had never seen such excited men. They were talking about all they had got done and said they didn't know when they enjoyed themselves more. They told Tom that they felt useful and needed again. Something they hadn't felt for years. Tom told them that he had sure enjoyed having them to help him, that he didn't know how he could have gotten along without them. They seemed so happy, sitting there drinking their coffee and planning all the things they wanted to get done before they left.

Tom put some beans in the Dutch oven and J. B. said, "Tom, why don't you go down and get some clay, and I will show you how to bake a ham in the coals." They had brought two small hams with them when they came. J. B. told him, "Now make sure you get it off the bank, so it will be good and clean." Tom got the clay, and J. B. added more water to it to make a thick paste and rubbed it on the ham real good. Then he dug out a deep place next to the hot coals. When it was as deep as he wanted it, he raked the hot coals into the hole and placed the ham on the coals. He covered it deep with more hot coals. After that he put a few more logs over it to make more coals. He told Tom by dinner it will be done. Tom put the Dutch oven a good piece out from where he had put the ham because it wouldn't take the beans as long to cook. Tom only wanted to simmer them. Then close to the Dutch oven he put some sweet potatoes that Mrs. Rucker had sent down. That completed their dinner, and it would be ready when they wanted it.

Mike came down and told Tom, "Our two cows had their calves, and Mama said we were getting plenty of milk now. Also, you would need all the milk you could get to feed the baby pigs. So if you wanted to bring Susie back home, you could bring her down."

Tom told him, "That would be fine, but I will come and get her tonight because I want to make sure your mama doesn't still need the milk."

Mike told him, "That will be fine because we are still hoeing all day, every day."

After that the guys told Tom to take the wagon and go down along the creek and pull a load of grass sprigs where it was a little damp. It being sandy land, it was easy to get. He used a pointed shovel and was able to get big hunks at one time. After he had got a good wagon load, he took it back to the dugout. Tom put the wagon in the shade while the guys cut the sprigs off a little above the roots. Tom put all the dirt back on the top of the dugout and started planting the sprigs. Tom planted it pretty thick so it wouldn't take long for it to cover the top. As Jack said, "The sooner the better." Tom carried water from the creek and watered it good. By night they had it finished; and the boys told him, "Well, Tom, you are ready to move in."

The next morning the guys helped Tom move in. They brought the stove in first, and while they were finishing connecting it to the chimney, Tom began to unload the wagon. He sat all the things out until he found the bedstead and took it in and set it up on the north side of the dugout. By then the guys were through with the stove; and they helped him bring in the springs, mattress, and chester drawers. They put the chester drawers at the end of the bed on the east wall. The stove was at the back on the west side, between the cabinet and the bed.

J. B. said, "That way the stove, in the winter, would keep the bed warm at night."

They put the table on the east side next to the cabinet. That way the table, the cabinet, and the stove would be close together.

Then they said that Tom could bring the dishes and things in because he would know where he wanted them. Tom put away the things all day. The dishes, he put on the third shelf from the top. He could reach them, and it was completely full. He never saw so many things in all his life. He had plenty of everything to cook on the stove with. The churn and milk buckets, he put under the cabinet on the floor along with the tin can sealer and the cans. They would come in handy when the garden came in. Tom put the sheets, cup towels, dishrags, pillowcases, and his clothes in the chester drawers. He made the bed and put a pretty quilt on it for a bedspread. There was even a tablecloth to go on the table. Then he went out and brought in the chairs and put them around the table. Jack and J. B had also bought two rockers. Tom put them in the spot between the table and the bed. That finished up everything that went inside. It was a nice-size dugout, and he didn't have any trouble getting everything inside. Just guessing, Tom would say it was around fourteen or fifteen feet wide and a little longer than it was wide. Now that's just guessing as he didn't have a way to really measure it. Anyway, it was big enough to hold all he had and a bed to sleep in. Grant you, it was crowded.

Anyone else would look at it and think how crude and awful it was, but to Tom, it was like a dream come true. He had his ranch, his cattle, a roof over his head, a bed to sleep in, and soon he would have plenty of food to do him all winter. Who could ask for more? Tom felt like he was the luckiest person in the whole world. By the time Tom finished, the men had finished building the outhouse and were working on a smokehouse. They stopped on it and said, "Reckon it's time to get the door built in front." The door was the only thing that really showed. All the rest was mounted up like a dirt cellar. It had steps leading down to the dirt floor. It faced on the south side, and when they got through with it, it looked like a door propped up on the end of a large grassy mound. It was crude as it could be, but it was a home for Tom, and he was proud of it. They worked on it the rest of the day. J. B. and Jack had brought the door and frame that they had gotten somewhere.

Tom helped them until it was time to do up the night work. And here came Mike with the cow. Tom fed Molly and her family and milked the cow, and would you know, when he got to the henhouse there stood the chickens ready to go in. Tom could hardly believe what he was seeing. He sprinkled the grain in front of the door, then waited until they had eaten all of it, then he put them inside the chicken house. After that he went back to help on the doors. By then they had it finished. Tom told them, it looked real good. Somewhere they had picked up a doorknob to go on the door to keep it shut. They were just finishing putting it on, and Tom helped them finish it. By then it was almost suppertime.

About dusty dark, Mr. Buck came over to check on the hay meadow. Tom told him he had plenty to do him all winter.

Mr. Buck said, "If you want to sell the rest, I will buy it and cut it."

Tom told him, "That sounds fine with me."

Then he told Tom, "Your other two pastures are knee high. Are you going to need them?"

Tom told him, "My cows haven't come close to eating down the second pasture, and I have the first one, still with plenty of grass to do them until it turns cold."

Mr. Buck told Tom, "I could use them and would like to lease them."

Tom told him, "I don't want them overgrazed, and if you want to put a limited amount of cattle on them, then I would lease it to you."

They agreed on the amount of cattle he would put on them and for how long. He told him he would pay him, or if Tom would like to take it out in cattle, he would be glad to swap him some young heifers. Tom told him to let him see how the crops turned out and they would go from there, that he would really like to have some more cattle and he thought he would be able to trade but he would let him know before shipping time. So they agreed, and he finished cutting the hay. Then he said he would bring some cattle over in a few days, and before shipping time Tom could let him know what he wanted to do.

After he left they just sat around, drinking coffee and talking. J. B. said, "I guess when we get the smokehouse done, that we had better go home."

Tom told them, "I sure hate to see you go. I sure have enjoyed ya'll being here, and I don't know what I would have done without you both. I would probably still be trying to figure out how to get the roof on. You both will never know how much all the things ya'll brought meant to me. If it hadn't been for you two, I still wouldn't have a bed to sleep in or a stove to cook on, or as far as that goes not anything else. What did you think about the deal that Mr. Buck had offered?"

They both said, "We thought it would be great if you could swing it."

Tom told them, "I wouldn't have to buy any things but staples. Thanks to you two and I have all the money from one cutting of the hay and would have the crop money. Also, Jimmy and I have planned on hunting all winter. There is a lot of rabbits around here." He figured that would offset the money from the crop money and what he needed to make his bank payment.

They talked a while longer about Tom's plans. Then again Tom told them he sure hated to see them go, that he had really enjoyed them. Also, Tom told them again, he didn't know what he could have done without both of them. That there was no way he could have done all they had done by himself, even if he had known how, which he didn't. He told them, "Do you all realize because of both of you, I have a roof over my head with furniture in it, dishes, pots and pans, a way to cook, a way to can my vegetables, a mama hog with her pigs, chickens, this ranch and my cattle, the chicken house, the smokehouse, the toolshed, the outhouse, and the Lord only knows what all else. What in the world would I have done without you? To me it was just a miracle from God."

They just got the dugout done in the nick of time. It rained that night, and they had to move into it. Tom told the guys they could take the bed and he would sleep on the floor. At first they were not going to have any part of that, but Tom told them he had slept on the ground so long that he probably couldn't sleep in it anyway and besides there were two of them and only one of him and he would take up less room on the floor. They finally agreed. So they all got settled in and went right to sleep. It was real comfortable in the dugout. It was nice and cool, and they couldn't even hear the rain beating down. It was raining pretty hard when they came in. Tom was afraid the roof hadn't had time to seal good, but it didn't leak one bit all night.

The next morning it was still raining. Tom built a fire in the stove and cooked breakfast. Even with the fire in the stove, it was still comfortable. They opened the door enough to let some fresh air come in. They had just gotten breakfast over with and the kitchen cleaned, when they heard someone hollering, "Hello in the house."

It was John. He said, "Since it was raining and we couldn't do anything in the field, I thought I would come down and sit a spell. I am sorry I hadn't got down to see J. B. and Jack sooner." He hoped they understood that this time of year they had to stay busy as long as they could to get all the hoeing done.

Jack and J. B. acted like they were real proud to see him. They sat around the table while Tom finished with the few things he had to do, then he went out and milked the cow and strained the milk and took it to the spring. When he came back, they asked him if he knew how to play dominoes.

Tom told them he shore did, so he got the dominoes out that J. B. and Jack had brought and they spent the rest of the morning playing dominoes. At noon, Tom fixed them some eggs and bacon. He had brought the butter and jelly back from the spring along with some cold milk. He put the coffeepot on and made biscuits. By the time they were done, the eggs, bacon and coffee were ready. Jack set the table, and they ate and went back to their dominoes. Tom sure was proud of the dishes they had brought. They were old, mind you, some had chips and they didn't all match. But he had enough to set a table, and that was what counted. They played until time to do the night chores. John said guess he had better go and help the kids. It was still raining but not as hard as it had been.

J. B. told John, if it was too wet or still raining tomorrow, come back and Tom and he would beat him and Jack again. He said he might do that, but he didn't think they could beat them twice in a row and that they all just had a streak of luck. Tomorrow it would be different. He waved and hollered, "See you tomorrow if it's raining."

Jack and J. B. said they would get supper while Tom did the outside chores. He milked Susie and went in and strained the milk. Then he took it to the spring and brought back some cold milk and butter. He had enough milk to churn again. He didn't know why, but he hated churning worse than anything. Tom dropped the milk off and went down and fed Molly. The pigs sure were growing. He had plenty of buttermilk to feed them, and by winter, they would be big enough to kill. John wanted two males to butcher for meat and a female to keep for breeding. J. B. was going to trade one for another male, so Tom could raise him for breeding purpose. Tom wanted to give one to Mike for helping him, and he had planned to keep two himself to raise from. The only ones left were a male and one female to sell. After he fed the pigs, he went by the henhouse. It had almost stopped raining. He sprinkled a little feed just inside and just opened the door. They had started coming up each night. Now all they had to do was shut the door at night and lock it. Tom gathered up the eggs. Two more hens were still setting on the nest. Tom had noticed them that morning, but it didn't occur to him that they were trying to hatch the eggs. Tom put some eggs in two other nest that wasn't being used, then moved the hens on those nest. He had plenty of eggs in the house to do them. That made four hens sitting. Tom was so proud of them. That would give him more laying hens and some males to have to eat. By the time he got through, Jack and J. B. had supper ready. They ate, and Tom cleaned up the kitchen.

The next morning Tom had just barely gotten through with the outside work when John got there. Two more hens were wanting to nest, so Tom put them in two more nests that wasn't being used with one egg under each of them. He didn't have enough eggs left for both of them, but he would have tomorrow. It had stopped raining. The sun was shining, but John said it was still too wet to hoe. He said tomorrow they would be able to get back in the fields. They played dominoes the rest of the day. This time John and Jack beat and boy did they crow! They told Tom and J. B. that they only let them win yesterday, so they wouldn't hurt their feelings.

The next day it was dry enough for Jack and J. B. to work on the smokehouse, and Tom worked in the garden. It was beginning to bear, and he gathered them a mess of green beans and some fresh tomatoes. Tom took them in and snapped them and put them on for dinner. He went back and pulled weeds until it was time for dinner. Tom found enough squash and gathered it also. He went down and got the milk and butter before he went in the house.

He made corn bread, and while it cooked, he fried the squash and sliced the tomatoes. He set the table and hollered for the guys to come and get it. They ate, and they just went on and on about how good it was. J. B. told Tom that guess they would get the smokehouse finished today and they would go home tomorrow. They had decided that Jack would move in with him in place of his daughter. So they wanted to get home and get him moved in.

Tom told them again how much he enjoyed them and how much he appreciated all the work they had done. "You guys don't know how much I will miss you." Also, he asked them, "What am I going to do without you two?"

Jack laughed and said, "Probably better," but he didn't know how much they had enjoyed it. They told Tom, "You have given us something we needed so bad, and that money couldn't buy it." Tom had given them hope and made them feel like they were useful again. They both were just sitting around with no hope, just waiting to die, but now they felt like they still had something to live for. J. B. said they would be back before winter sets in and bring him the male pig. Without these two wonderful men, Tom could never have done all this by himself, not counting all the furniture, tools dishes, cattle, pigs, chickens, and everything else they had helped him with. Then his third blessing was, now as he had a wonderful family that had taken him in and helped him in every way they could. Tom thought about all of this. Then he just bowed his head and said, "Thank you, God." Right now, he could say, all in all, he was one lucky fellow.

Chapter 11

THEY LEFT EARLY THE NEXT morning. Tom was so lonesome, he worked in the garden all day. It was still damp, and that made the weeds easier to pull. He went in at noon and just ate some leftovers. It sure was lonesome without the guys, but while he was eating, he just stopped and counted his blessings. His first blessing was to have two wonderful men like them to care for him. His second blessing was that a few months ago he didn't even have a roof over his head, a bed to sleep in, and no place to go, or anyone to care for him. Thanks to them, he had all that, plus a chicken house and twelve chickens, a toolshed to store his tools in, an outhouse, and a pigpen to boot.

The next morning, Tom checked his clothes and got them ready for Sunday. The Ruckers had told him they went to church just down the road. Tom hadn't gone so far because he didn't want to embarrass them. Up until J. B. and Jack came, he didn't have a way to press his clothes. They had bought him an iron and ironing board with all the rest of the other stuff, so now he could heat it on the stove and press his clothes. Tom had missed church, and each Sunday he could just hear Granny say, "Now we don't want the Lord to think we are just heathens, do we?" Oh, how Tom missed her and all the boys each Sunday when they went down for their Sunday service. The church people were real friendly, and it wasn't long until he was just a part of them, and he went every Sunday.

Tom still had a lot of things to get done. He had six hens that were hatching baby chickens, and he didn't have a place to put them. All that week he made some chicken coops out of some wire the guys brought to him. He wanted to put them outside as each hen hatched, but he knew he would need something to put them in to keep the varmints from getting them. So Tom made six square pens with a top on them but no bottom so he could drag them around the place. That way they could scratch for seed and insects, and at night he could put them in the toolshed or smokehouse either one since he wasn't using them right now. The pens weren't too big, so they would only hold one hen and her babies. That way Tom could drag the pens to a new place each day before he put the chickens in them.

The rest of the summer he worked in the garden. Tom had something to gather and canned every day. He had helped Granny, and he knew how to get them ready, but he didn't know how long to boil them in the washpot. He had to ask Dora how long to boil them. Every day when he got them on, he went down and cut a load of wood for the next day. It took a lot of wood to keep the pot boiling for as long as they needed to boil.

J. B. and Jack had left one wagon and the two horses. Boy, did they come in handy. With them, Tom could load the wagon with the dead wood from under the trees and bring a whole load to the house. That way he could watch the pot and cut it up at the same time. Each time he canned a different vegetable, he had to go ask Dora how long to boil them. Tom ran out of cans and salt before he got the vegetables all canned. So he had to go to town and get some. Tom asked Dora if they needed anything from town. She sent Mike along with a big list of things to pick up. Tom had almost a week of eggs, so he took them along to see if he could trade them in on his grocery list. It took them all day driving the wagon in, but they couldn't have brought all the things back without it. Tom got the things he needed. He made sure he got plenty of cans and salt to do him. He didn't want to run out again. The lady took the eggs and said she could use them each time he came in. They got home in time to do up the night work before it got dark.

In August, Dora sent Mike down to tell Tom it was time to plant his mustard greens and turnips. She sent him enough seed to plant two rows of each.

Mike said, "Mama said to plant them where you had dug your potatoes and any other rows you had empty."

By September, Tom had canned all the vegetables. John came down, and he and Tom decided where to dig a row to store his sweet potatoes for winter. John told Tom they needed a place that had a real good drain. He told Tom he wanted a place where the water wouldn't stand on it because if it did, it would seep into the potatoes and rot them. They finally chose a place on the far side of the last row in the garden. John said he thought it would be a perfect place for it and also it would be out of the way. He showed Tom how to dig a row deep enough to store his potatoes. He told him he would probably get it dug by tomorrow afternoon and he would come back when he came from the field and show him how to fill it with hay and how to store them.

The next morning, after he had milked the cow and strained the milk, he took it to the spring. It was time to churn the clabbered milk he had already put it out, so it was ready. When he finished churning it, he went to the spring and got a bucket of ice-cold water to rinse the butter in. Then he molded it in the butter mold that the boys had also brought and took it and the buttermilk down to the spring. While he was there, he got the old buttermilk to take to Miss Molly and her brood. They all were growing like weeds, and he would have some to butcher before spring. They wouldn't be as big as he would have liked them to be, but he sure was looking forward to having some good old pork to eat.

After that Tom got started digging on the ditch, as deep and as long as John had showed him to do. He dug with a sharpshooter by hand and as long as the garden rows. It was hard work and took Tom most of the day. He stopped at noon and let the chickens out. By now the baby chickens were big enough that he didn't have to keep them in the cages, and it didn't take him as long to tend to them all. In fact, they were small pullets, and he had just started killing and eating on the roosters. He grabbed him some leftover food from the night before and went right back to work.

He wanted to get the row dug before John came back to show him how to store the potatoes. He got it finished, then hitched the horses to the wagon and went after a big load of hay, and he pulled it right up to the side where he had dug the ditch and unhitched the horses and put them back in the pasture. He had used the hay fork to load it with and left it on top of the hay. He wanted to be ready when John came. It was late in the afternoon when Tom got it all done. He hurried and did the night work so he would be through when John came.

He had just got through with all the night work and was sitting down with a cold glass of water to rest a while when John hollered, "Hello in the house." Tom went out real quick, and they started on the ditch. John showed him how to put hay in the ditch and how to lay the sweet potatoes and also to make sure they didn't touch each other. Then he showed him how to put more hay on top, then how to put the dirt back on and how deep to cover it. He showed Tom how to mound it up so it would shed the water so it wouldn't go into the ground deep enough to get the potatoes wet. He told Tom, if they did get wet, they would rot. John just showed Tom on a small piece of the row how to do it. He told him it was real important to put them right, and he showed Tom the second time how to place them. Also, he showed him how to put a post, where Tom started the row and where it stopped. That way it would make it easier to know where they were when he went to dig them. John also laughed and told Tom, "Now tomorrow you are on your own." That he would come back and check it out after they came in if he wanted him to. Tom told him he hated to put him out, but he would feel better if he would check and make sure he had done it right.

Again, that morning Tom got up early and did the outside work so he could get started on finishing with storing his sweet potatoes. First thing he did was go down into the pasture and cut two small saplings big enough to make his post. He took them back to the garden and dug a hole big enough and deep enough to put his post in, making sure it was standing as straight as he could get it. Then he put the dirt back around the post and packed it real good. He brought some water from the spring and poured around the post, making sure it was packed real good, then finish filling it with more dirt. After that he put the rest of the hay down, then put the potatoes in just like John had showed him. He made sure they weren't touching, so if one started rotting it wouldn't cause the other one next to it to rot also. Each step he took he made sure he had done it right before he took another step. He put the straw on top, checking John's sample, to make sure he was putting enough hay on them. After that, the dirt was easy to fill in and make sure the mound was as high as John's was. Tom left a small place at the end. Then he dug another hole and put the other post in.

That night, John came back to check the rows. He told Tom he couldn't have done better himself, that it was just fine. Tom was so proud of it. He told John how proud he was, that it meant more food for him in the winter. John told him, he knew just how he felt. Tom told him he couldn't have done it without him, that he didn't know it could be done. John told him he was glad to help and call on them when he needed them.

Tom had let some of the beans and peas from the last gathering to dry for seed so he could gather them for next year's seed. So the next day he gathered them. He had helped granny wind blow beans and peas, so he knew how to do it. After he gathered them he got a worn-out sheet that the boys had brought for rags, telling him he could always use rags sooner or later. He laid it on the grass and poured the beans on it, then he folded it in half. He got a flat board and started pounding it lightly to get the beans out of the dead shells. Granny had always told him they would come out good this way if they were good and dry. After that he took out as many of the large hulls as he could and put the beans in a basket and shook the sheet to get the rest of the hulls off. He laid it back on the ground and began to pour them back and forth to let the wind blow what hulls were left in them out. When Tom had finished blowing them, he put them in a lard bucket and stored them under the cabinet. Then he gathered the peas and did them the same way. Early in the year Mike had showed Tom how to pull his onions and tie then three or four in a bunch. They had used some of the rags that J. B. and Jack had brought and tore them in strings. Mike told Tom make them long enough to tie the onions with enough left over to tie on the nails. They had old nails hanging up in the shed. When he had gotten them all gathered and hung, he had a whole row hung across one side. It would be enough onions to do him all winter.

By the last of September, he had everything gathered and stored away except the greens and turnips. They would be ready probably sometime in late September or October. Also, the last of September J. B. and Jack came back with some more stuff that they said Tom could use and also the male hog to trade for Tom's. J. B. said if he hadn't sold the little female, they had a man that wanted her also. The male was larger and older than Tom's pigs and was a real good hog for breeding stock. They unloaded the stuff and put it in the shed, and sure enough Tom could use every one of them. Along with everything else, they had brought some more lard buckets and Tom sure did need them. He had used the last he had to put the dried beans and peas in. The rest of the stuff was all tools that any one on a farm could use. They didn't stay but a couple of days. They said they wanted to get back before it got cold. On the third morning, they loaded the two pigs in the large crate that they had brought Tom's in. After they had tied the crate down good in the back of the wagon, they told Tom bye and crawled upon the wagon seat and waved, and they left. Tom stood and watched them until they were out of sight. He sure enjoyed them and had told them so. It did his heart good to see how happy they were, living in the same house and having someone to talk to and to share meals with. After they left Tom called Roy and went down and checked on the cattle. From the looks of them, he would have a good calf crop this early spring.

The corn had made real good, and John ground enough for Tom for the chickens and for the hogs to do him all winter. Also, he ground enough for Tom to have cornmeal to last until the coming year. Tom put it in gallon buckets and stored it under the bed. In the shed Tom built two bens, one to store the hog and chicken feed and one for the maize. Tom still got a little money for what was left over for his part of it. John said the cotton crop was looking real good. So Tom told Mr. Buck that he would take the hay out in trade for some heifers.

Tom had money to buy coal oil for his lamps. There was plenty of wood to cut for his stove, and he had plenty of water. He would have money to buy what staples he would need to last him. When the cotton crop came in, he would have enough money to buy what seed he would need for the following year and make his payment to the bank. Tom stopped right there and just thanked God for all He had given him. He had blessed him in so many ways, it was hard to believe it was possible.

The next week after J. B. and Jack had left, Tom started canning on the mustard greens. It was slow work getting them gathered, checking for bugs and worms, and taking the large stem out of the center. After he got all that done, the rest was easy. It was no trouble to wash them real good, wilt them and put them in the cans. When he got all that done, he put them in the pot and filled it up with water, then he would build his fire around the pot. Then he had to find out from Dora how long to boil it. When he got back, it was almost boiling. Tom put some more wood around it and started timing it. J. B. and Jack had brought him a big clock that stood on the floor and chimed on the hour and on the half hour. Now all he had left to do was watch the time and make sure to keep enough wood around the pot to keep it boiling.

Each day Tom put a canning of greens on, waited for it to start boiling, put some more wood around it, and checked the time. While it boiled Tom took the wagon and went after a load of wood. He would always pull the wagon close to the pot so he could make sure it always had a good fire around it. Then he would unhitch the horses and turn them loose in the pasture. While he watched the pot, he would cut up the wood. The greens had to cook longer than the other vegetables so he had to have more wood than with the others. After he finished with the greens, he started pulling the turnips. Tom knew they wouldn't be as hard to do as the greens were, but pulling the turnips and canning both the greens and turnips took that whole week. It took longer to do the greens, then it had any of the vegetables, but it would be worth it this winter. Nevertheless, Tom sure was proud when he got them finished. Each time he finished canning, he thanked the Lord for them and what he had gotten done that day.

After he got the greens canned, Tom started cutting more wood for his stove. He wanted to get enough cut before winter set in. He cut that day and the next, then he stacked it at the side of the dugout. He probably had more than he needed, but Tom thought, he had rather have too much than not enough.

John came down and got his pigs. He said, "I am sorry we had to leave them so long, but we had to build a pen for them."

Tom told him, "It wasn't any trouble for me to feed them along with mine."

They had been furnishing the corn for all of them, and Tom had furnished the milk to soak it in. He put the corn to soak each morning, and each night and by feeding time, it was good and sour. They sure went after it, and they were growing by leaps and bounds. John wanted to pay him for the hogs, but Tom told him, "No way, everything you and your family have done for me and you think I would charge you for the pigs." Mike was with him, and Tom told John, "There is only one thing before you get your pigs. Mike gets to pick his out first." They both looked real shocked, but Tom told them he wanted to give Mike one for helping him.

Mike got in the pen. He looked them over real good, then picked each one up and examined every one. He did this over and over again and finally decided which one he wanted. He acted so proud of it, but he kept telling Tom that he didn't help for wages and he didn't expect nothing.

Tom winked at John and said, "Oh well, guess you don't want one after all. Guess you had better pick out yours."

John grinned and said, "That one he is holding looks real good to me, so I think I will take it."

Mike stepped back real quick and said, "Oh no, you don't, you're not getting this one."

They both laughed, and John said, "Well, guess I will have to get second choice." He didn't take as much time as Mike took. He said any two of the four would be all right with him as they all looked like they would make good breeding hogs. So they both got in the pen and caught two for him. Tom told him that J. B. and Jack had brought him a male hog to trade for one of his males when time came. He was welcome to use him for both his two and Mike's also.

He looked him over and said, "He looks like a real good male hog to me. You can count on J. B. and Jack. They know how to pick good stock."

John and Mike had come in the wagon so they could take them back. So Tom helped them put them in tow sacks and put them in the wagon. Mike crawled back with them to keep them from getting out. He didn't want to put his in a sack, but his daddy told him he had better, rather than taking a chance of it getting loose and trying to jump out and getting hurt. So in the end, he didn't want to but he finally did. His daddy told him he could hold the sack and that way he would know which one was his. They left with Mike hollering, "Thanks, Tom. Thanks for my pig. See you soon."

Jimmy and Tom hunted coons all winter, and they found plenty. They skinned them and stretched them on the outside walls of John's barn to dry. Jimmy's dog had pups, and he gave Tom one and kept one for himself for them to train for coon dogs. They were just plain, old ordinary dogs, but before the winter was over, they planned to have them trained for real good hunting dogs. They both were trying to think up names for them. Tom came up with Skitter, and Jim said he liked Scottie. So that was settled. Their dogs would be Skitter and Scottie. They were still young, but in time they would be as good as any hunting dog. Jim came down each night, and they built them each a doghouse.

When the dogs were old enough, every day before dark, Jimmie and Tom would take turns pulling an old coon hide around the dugout or the barn to leave the scent. The other one would hold the dogs so they couldn't see what was going on. They would let the dogs smell the hide, then one of them would drag the coon hide around, and then he would hide it somewhere. Each of them would take their dog and try to teach them to pick up the scent and find the hide. Like Hart and Lightning, they didn't train them overnight. Tom told Jimmie how he had used apple slices to train Hart and Lightning. So they started saving all their meat scraps and biscuits to give them if they did good. They sure were a lot harder to train than Hart was. It took them all winter working with them and pulling that coon hide until Jimmy and Tom both dreamed of pulling it at night while they slept. Tom told Jimmy what Granny Heart and Mr. Heart told him about not getting aggravated with her. Talk to her and always speak kind to her, then one of these days she would understand what he wanted her to do. He told Jimmy guess that would work with dogs also. Tom told Jimmy, Mr. Heart once told him to train any animal, you first had to be smarter than the animal. Then he laughed and told him, he didn't think either one of them were as smart as these dad blasted dogs. But one night they finally understood what Tom and Jimmy were wanting them to do. After that they couldn't stop them. They were like Hart. They thought it was a game. They were playing for the food they were getting, so they acted like they were real happy to go along with it if that's what it took to please the boys so they could get the food.

After that Tom told Jimmy, "I think it is time to take them out, to see what they have learned." They let them smell the coon hide, then turned them loose and hollered, "Go get 'um." And boy, did they ever go. Tom and Jimmy let them run with their mama, thinking she would help them learn what they were supposed to do, but they ran completely off and left her behind. She couldn't keep up with them at all. Jimmy and Tom were trying too, but they left them behind also. They would stop and sniff the ground, then here they would go again. Finally, Tom heard them baying. He told Jimmy, "Listen, they have one treed." Sure enough, when they got to where the dogs were, there was a big fat coon in the tree. The boys gave them a piece of meat and petted them and told them how proud they were of them. From that day on, they were either with Tom or Jimmy all the time, unless they had locked them up in their doghouses.

Chapter 12

THE LAST OF JANUARY IT turned real cold. John came down and asked Tom if he was ready to kill hogs. They were hoping to wait longer, but John told Tom they needed time for the meat to cure out before it started getting warm. So they decided to kill them the next morning. John told Tom he had everything they would need up at his house, so they decided to kill them up there.

The next day, by the time Tom got up there, the boys had a big barrel filed with water and a fire going under it. Tom told John he had never killed hogs before, so they would have to tell him what to do. The boys had a platform at the side of the barrel. When the water started boiling, they brought the first hog over and John knocked him in the head. They had rigged up four long posts with a pulley on them, and John and Tom tied a rope around the hogs back feet and let him down in the hot water to scald so they could scrape the hair off him. After the boys lowered it up and down a few times, two of the boys guided it and the other three swung him over to the platform. After they got it dressed out, John cut him up enough that they could carry him over to another table. He finished cutting him up, and Dora and the girls took over while they did another hog. They put the sugared cure on the hams and, with John helping, got it ready to hang up. It took all day, but they got them finished before night. Dora said that tomorrow they would render the lard and then make the soap but it would take a couple of days. The girls had taken some of the backstrap and went in and cooked supper. They had fried the backstrap, made gravy, creamed potatoes, and hot biscuits. Dora said, "You are staying for supper. The girls has it all ready." So he did, and boy was it ever good. They hadn't stopped for lunch because they were trying to get through before dark. The womenfolk had brought them some hot coffee, and they had drank it in between dressing each hog. They all were plenty tired, cold, and hungry. Tom left right after that. He asked what time would they start in the morning, and Dora said as soon as they got the morning work done and could get out there. Tom knew on a farm that meant as soon as you could see.

Tom went home and built a fire in the stove and put some water in the reservoir to heat, then he went out and did the night work. By the time he finished, the water was hot. He brought the tub in and took a real good hot bath. He was plenty cold and tired. As soon as he finished his bath, he went right straight to bed. He was up early the next morning. He built a fire in the stove and fixed breakfast. He ate and was outside by the time it was barely light enough to see good. He milked the cow and brought it in and strained it. He left it in the house. As cold as it was, it would be all right. It still wasn't light enough to go up to the Ruckers, so Tom locked Skitter in his doghouse and went in and drank another cup of coffee. It was still plenty cold outside. He got there just as they were building a fire around the washpots.

Dora greased the inside of the pot and left some of the grease in the bottom so when they put the fat in it, it wouldn't stick. The girls and the younger boys had taken the fat off the meat yesterday so all they had to do was put it in the pot and start stirring it to keep it from sticking while it cooked. Tom told Dora he had another big pot if they wanted to start another pot. She said that would help to get through faster. So all the boys and Tom went down, hitched the horses to the wagon, then went to Tom's and loaded the pot. They all decided that they would need more wood and went to the first pasture close to the dugout and got a large load of dead limbs that had fallen off the trees.

When they got back to the Ruckers, Dora and the girls had a place fixed for the second pot and was ready for them to sit the pot on it. They build a fire around it. Dora put some water in it to get hot and washed it out good, then she greased it and put some more grease in it to get it started so it wouldn't burn until some of the fat began to cook. The girls began to put some more fat in it that was to be rendered out for the lard. The fat that didn't melt that had lean meat on it would be strained out of the grease and saved for cracklings. The boys and Tom unloaded the wood from the wagon. Tom asked Dora if they needed some more wood, and she said it wouldn't hurt because they would be needing it for making the soap tomorrow. So while Tom cut the wood up, Jimmy and two of the other boys went close to their house and got another load of wood. The rest of the kids started taking the fat off the intestines for the soap grease. Tom would get through cutting up the wood before they got back each time so he would go over and help them take the fat off. Mike showed him how and told him, "Now be real careful and go slow, so you won't break any of the intestines," and he didn't have to tell Tom that twice. He had barely got started until he broke one and the odor was horrible. They tied it off on each side of the break, and with a small bowl under it, they tried to pour some water over it. By doing this they thought they could wash off some of the manure that had leaked out of it. By the time they got through, they had gotten most of it and had smelled it so long until they couldn't smell it anymore. Anyway, that taught Tom a lesson—you take your time when you are fooling with the intestines.

Every time he left to go cut up the wood, when he came back, as soon as he got there, they would all holler, "Now take your time. Make sure you don't break another intestine again."

Mike hollered, "If you break another one, we are going to fire you."

The others laughed but agreed with him and said, "Yeah, we are, and we won't ever hire you back again."

They all laughed, and Tom told them, "I learn real fast, and ya'll won't never have to tell me not to break one again."

They got through with rendering the lard and dipped the cracklings out of it. They let it cool enough so they could pour it into the lard buckets. Tom had brought his from home that Jack and J. B. had brought him. Dora gave him half of the lard. Tom told her that was too much, but she insisted he take it. She said after all he gave them the hogs to begin with. Tom tried to tell her the hogs didn't half pay them for all they had done for him. But Dora told him, this way they all would have meat and lard. But Tom only took a third. He told them that was only fair. By the time they got everything cleaned up, it was still too hot to take home so he had to leave it until later.

The next morning he took his lye and went up right after he finished the outside work. Tom had five dozen eggs. He knew he wouldn't be going to town any way soon and he didn't want them to go bad, so he took them and asked Dora if she could use them. Dora said that she sure could use them and was real proud to get them. She said she thought they had better get their sausage made and put away today instead of making soap. They had already made real narrow bags about two or two and a half feet long. Tom told her he had a food grinder also if they needed it, and she said it would sure help. So he went back to the dugout and got it. While he was there, he decided to take an extra-large dishpan that he had hung behind the stove. Tom had wondered at the time what he would ever do with anything that big when he hung it up. He put the grinder in it and took it along just in case they did need it. Dora said she was real glad he had brought it as that way she could mix more at a time. Jimmy and Tom ground the meat, and Joan and Jan, the two oldest girls, fed it into the grinder for them, keeping up with them all the time.

Tom was beginning to learn all their names. The boys were John Junior, Jimmy, Billy, Mark, and Mike. The girls were Joan and Jan, who were twins, then Martha and Mary. Mary and Mike were twins. When they got enough meat, Dora would take it. Then she put it in the big pan and began to put the spices into it. When she got it made, she would fry one to make sure it was just right. Then the rest of the kids began to stuff the sacks. Each time they got enough ground, she would mix it and cook one, and if it was all right, she would take it over for the younger kids to fill the bags. This went on until almost lunchtime. Dora stopped and fried a big plate of the sausage, made biscuits, gravy, and scrambled some of the eggs that Tom had bought up, and boy, were those sausages good.

While they ate the kids laughed and joked all during the time they were eating. But while they were working, there was very little playing going on. It was all work until they finished. Back then all the kids were taught to work. The more kids you had, the better off you were, and the more land you could work. The whole family worked the crops and did all the work at the house, whether it be gardening, canning, or fieldwork. They got through about four or five o'clock. After they finished stuffing all the bags, the boys put some lard in the pot and build a fire under it. When the lard got hot, they dipped each bag in the hot lard to seal it good, making sure it was covered real good with the grease, then hung them in the smokehouse. It was still cold outside, so it didn't take them long to cool.

Dora said that as soon as all the meat hangs a while, that Tom could bring the wagon and they would help him load it all so he could take all his home to put in his own smokehouse. Tom helped to hang all of it in their smokehouse, and he measured about how far apart they had hung everything. So when he took his home he would know how to nail the nails to hang his meat. When they finished hanging the sausage, Tom went home and did the outside work and went in and fixed a bite and went to bed. They had a long hard day and would have another one tomorrow.

The next morning Tom got up early and did all the work outside. On a farm, the outside work has to be done, come rain, hail, or high water. The animals don't know the difference between one day and the next, and so the cow has to be milked every day, twice a day, and the chickens and hogs have to be watered and fed. Also, the eggs have got to be brought in to keep the hens from getting back on the nest the next day and breaking them. Tom thought, on a farm, like the old saying goes, you work from sunup until sundown and don't let anyone tell you living on a farm is an easy life. But it is a good life.

When Tom got up to the Ruckers, they had just got a fire made under the first pot and were fixing to build one under the second one. Tom had cone up in the wagon so if they needed to haul in more wood, they would have it and sure enough they did. They had already started taking the fat off the rest of the intestines. Tom helped them finish, with them still kidding him, "Be sure and take your time, we don't want a repeat, of the day before yesterday."

Tom acted real serious and told them, "Now I learn fast, and ya'll won't ever have to teach me how to do this job again."

They got a big kick out of that, and they all said, "We sure hope we don't."

While they finished up, Dora, Joan, and Jan loaded the fat into the pots and Dora put the lye in it to make the soap. She and the girls cooked it until all the skin, chunks of fat, and everything was dissolved by the lye. Nothing else was left in it but liquid. The girls stirred it off and on as long as it cooked.

After a while Dora told the girls it was ready. The boys had brought up a big long container that John had made to put it in until it got hard. It was long and wide, but it wasn't over four or so inches deep. They raked the fire away from the pot and started dipping the soap out of the pot into the long container to harden. Tom noticed they only dipped about two inches of the soap into the tub. When they had finished, they put the rest of the fat into the pot and started again. When Dora and the girls got it mixed, the boys rekindled the fire and again the girls stirred it as before. After a while Dora told them it was ready. The boys had brought up another long and wide container to pour it in. By the time they got it all poured up, it was about two or two-and-a-half-inches thick in each pan. Dora told Tom they would leave it until it hardened and dried out some and then they would cut it into bars. She told him she and the girls would finish cutting it when it was ready. They all finished cleaning up their mess. Tom told Dora if he could help them tomorrow, just let him know. Dora told him that was all they had to do and he had been a lot of help. After that Tom went home.

The next morning, he got up early, and after he got through outside, he cooked breakfast and he just sat down and just took his time eating. He had a second cup of coffee and just rested for a while. Tom hadn't cleaned the house or churned since they started killing the hogs, and he had plenty of milk to churn. He had been just skimming the cream off it and giving the hogs the sweet milk. He had put the ground corn in it each night to let it sour and had been giving them that. Tom went to the spring and chopped the ice from around the buckets and brought all the cream and milk that was ready to be churn. He set it next to the stove. He would churn it that night or when it was ready. He cleaned the house, and then he build a shelf in the smokehouse on the north side of the wall, big enough to put the butter, eggs, and anything else he needed to put on it.

After he finished it, he went after the butter, milk, and jelly and put them on the shelf. It was cold enough to keep it in the smokehouse now. Tom was getting tired of having to take the milk twice a day and go back and get it whenever he needed it. He had been toying with an idea of making a ditch from the spring through the smokehouse and out again to keep the milk and everything cold. It was still cold, but in the smokehouse, it was out of the wind. So he thought he would begin his project. He dug a channel from the west wall to the east wall, then he made a frame about a foot or more longer and wider than the channel would be deep, and he nailed a piece of net wire over the frame. After that he dug the channel out a little wider and deeper just outside of the smokehouse, where the channel would come through the wall. He cut a hole out and took a sledgehammer and gently drove the frame into the opening. When he got it in place, he nailed it to the wall real good. Later on, when it got warmer, he would haul in some rock and pack it in the deeper part so the rock would come to just where the water ran through the opening that he had cut in the wall.

After he placed the big rocks in place, he would pour some small pea gravel and clay mixed with water to make a thin paste all in the rocks, then let it dry real good before he opened the channel all the way from the spring. That way nothing could dig under it and the water wouldn't wash it out. Tom got both ends finished before he stopped for the night. He would finish digging out the rest of the inside channel tomorrow, if nothing came up that he had to do first. If it was cold tomorrow as it was today, Tom didn't think he would be able to do too much in this kind of weather. He didn't realize how cold it was until he stopped for the night. When he got to the house he was shaking all over. He put some more wood in the stove and put a pot of coffee on. As soon as it was made Tom drank a cup, sitting as close to the stove as possible. The coffee and the warmth from the stove helped warm him up. After a while he stopped shaking. He put some more wood in the stove and poured him another cup of coffee. By the time he drank it, he was warm enough to go out and do the night work. Susie had already come up from the pasture for her feed and to be milked. Tom milked her first and took the milk in. By the time he strained it, then took it to the smokehouse, she had eaten all her feed. Tom turned her back into the pasture so she could go to a group of trees close by to help her stay warm, and he went to tend to the chickens. They hadn't strayed far from the henhouse all day. They were smart enough to stay in where it was warm. So he fed them in the henhouse and gathered up the eggs.

After that, Tom went down to feed the hogs. They were hunkered up together in the little shelter he had made for them. He poured the ground corn and buttermilk into their trough, and they did get up and come over to eat it. Then Tom went in the house to get warm. It had gotten a lot colder since they had killed the hogs earlier in the week. Tom sure was glad they got everything done before it got as cold as it was now. He put some more wood in the stove, and it was just as warm as could be inside.

He warmed the leftovers from dinner, and while they were warming, he drank another cup of coffee to help him get warm again. As soon as he finished eating, he cleaned up the kitchen and put some more wood in the stove and turned the damper down and crawled in bed. It was nice and warm under the covers, and it wasn't long until he was fast asleep. Tom woke up during the night and put some more wood in the stove and went right back to bed.

It was too cold to do much work the next day. He did the outside work that had to be done and stayed in the rest of the day. By the third day it had warmed up some. The wind was blowing real hard, but as long as you weren't in the wind, it wasn't too bad. So he went out and dug on the trench through the smokehouse. By early in the afternoon, he had done as much as he could in the smokehouse and it was still too cold to work outside. Tom went in and made a pot of soup and just sat around waiting for it to get done. He decided to do the outside work early before it got colder, and when he came back, the soup was ready. It was good and hot, and it sure tasted good in this kind of weather. He went to bed as soon as he got the kitchen cleaned. The dugout was nice and warm, and it didn't take him long until he was fast asleep. Tom slept in the next morning. There wasn't anything he had to do, so he just stayed in bed and rested, something he hadn't done since he didn't know when. There is not much rest to be had living on a farm.

He finally got up and went out to do the outside work and after that ate breakfast. By then it had started getting a little warmer. Tom decided to work on the channel outside. The wind wasn't blowing so hard, and as long as you had a wind break, it wasn't too bad. Mike came down about noon and asked if Tom would like to have some company. Tom told him he sure would and that he was about ready to go in and get warm. Mike commented on how warm the dugout was.

Tom told him, "I have a pot of soup on the stove warming, if you would like to stay for dinner." So Tom got the bowls out. He had a pot of coffee on the stove too, and Tom asked him, "Do you want a cup?"

Mike said, "I think I had rather have milk, and I will go and get it."

Tom told him it was in the smokehouse.

When Mike came back he asked, "What in the world were you doing in the smokehouse?"

And while they ate Tom explained to him what he had in mind. Tom had a brown piece of paper that he had made a sketch on of what he wanted to do. So as Tom explained it to Mike, he showed him on the sketch. Mike looked it over real good and said it just might work and he wanted to know if he could help him build it. Tom told him if his mama didn't care, he would be glad to have him. Then Mike told Tom, "Oh by the way, my mama sent me down to tell you, the meat was ready to bring home any time now and also the lard. We all will help you load it." Then he grinned. "Oh, I almost forgot, the soap also."

So, after they finished eating, they hitched up the horses to the wagon and went up to get it. All the boys and Dora came out and helped him load it. With all of them working it didn't take long until they had it all loaded and were ready to go. All the boys wanted to go and help Tom unload it. Their mama said it was okay with her if it was all right with Tom. He told her it was just fine, so they all piled into the wagon. Tom was going to keep his project quiet until he found out if it worked or not, but when they all saw the ditch running through the smokehouse, they all wanted to know what was going on. So, of course, Mike had to explain it to them. He told them Tom had a drawing of it in the dugout and maybe when they got through unloading the meat and things, he would let them go in and see the drawing and explain it to them. So they finished unloading the meat, lard, and soap; and all went in to see Tom's drawing. They hadn't seen inside the dugout and were quite impressed with it. They were all real impressed with the drawing also. All of them seemed to think it would work. They all said that since they didn't have anything to do for a while, they would be glad to help him. So it was settled. Tomorrow, they would come down and bring their shovels to help him dig the channel to the smokehouse and away from it. They put the lye soap in the toolshed and unhitched the horses so they could go back to the pasture and try to find a place to stay warm. It was too cold to do anything outside, so Tom suggested they go in and play dominoes. The rest of the afternoon they stayed in and just played. They seemed to really enjoy themselves. They stopped in time for them to go home so they would have time to do their night work before dark, promising they would see him tomorrow.

    After they left, Tom went out to the smokehouse and just stood there looking at all the meat. Again, he thanked God for all the blessings He had given him. No one knows what it's like to have nothing and not knowing where you are going to sleep or eat, then have some wonderful people to help you get started. The dugout wasn't a mansion, grant you, but it was a roof over his head and God had blessed him with all this food.

    The next morning, Tom made a great big pot of soup. It was still cold out, but not as cold as it had been, but he thought the soup would warm them up when they came in at noon, and also it would be ready for them, and they wouldn't have to stop their work and take time to cook dinner. They all got there just as Tom was finishing the outside work. Tom saw them coming, all bringing their shovels, ready to go to work. They told John what Tom was going to do, so here he came with them. He wanted to see how Tom was going to make it also, so Tom showed him the plans, and he agreed it ought to work. He went on back in a little while, and they all lined up, some on the side going out and some on the side coming in.

By noon, they had the channel almost finished on both sides. Tom told them he wanted to haul the rock and gravel and fill the holes up even to where it came into the smokehouse first and then let it dry before they dug through to the spring. That way it would have enough rock in the hole so it wouldn't wash it out and it would be deep enough so anything couldn't dig in and get the meat. They went in to eat and rest for a while. Tom put some wood in the stove. Mike and Billy went out and got an egg, some butter, and the milk. While he was getting the corn bread ready, Jimmy made the coffee. Mark set the table while John poured the milk for those that wanted it. Tom put the corn bread in a long oblong pan, so it didn't take it too long to cook. When it got done, John poured the coffee. Tom didn't have but four chairs, so two of them pulled up the rockers to sit in. After they ate, they rested a while, then went out and hitched the horses to the wagon and went down and loaded some rocks. When they got them placed like Tom wanted them, they went back and got some clay and some pea gravel. They mixed it with water until it was a very thin paste and poured it in the cracks where the rocks were. Everyone agreed it looked real good. They couldn't do anything else until it dried real good, so they went in and played dominoes until they had to go home. Tom told them it would probably take about three days at least for it to get good and hard. They said they would come back in three days and help him finish it.

    Sure enough, on the third day, bright and early, here they came. They opened the channel right where the spring came out of the ground and let the water circulate through the smokehouse and back in to the creek right below the spring. They opened the one going in first, and it did just fine. It didn't take long until it was almost at the entrance, and by the time they got the other end opened, here the water came.

Mike shouted, "Here she comes!" They all were so excited about their achievement. They just stood there watching the water running in and out of the smokehouse. Then Mark said, "Let's go in and see how cold it's getting inside." Of course, it hadn't run long enough to change the temperature much, but it was working, and before long it would be cold. They went back out and just stood there watching the water running. You would have thought they had struck oil. They were so proud of it. Eventually the water would be clear, and Tom could get his drinking water right there also. It didn't have far to go and the ground was level. Tom thanked them all for helping him and told them he would have been weeks getting it done without them. Soon after that they went home, and before long John came down to look at it. He was quite impressed with it. He said, "You know, Tom, I think it will keep it cool all summer."

Tom told him, "That is what I was counting on."

The next day, early, John and another man that Tom didn't know came down. John told him he had brought some bad news to them. The man said, "J. B. sent me to tell you that Jack had died and the funeral would be day after tomorrow at two." Tom thanked him and told him to tell J. B. he would be there. John said to tell him he would be there too. They left, and Tom went in the dugout, and as hard as he tried, he couldn't hold back the tears. He thought about all the good times they had working, getting everything finished, that they had done on the place so Tom could have a place to live. Then all the things he and J. B. had given him and of the love that had grown between them. The bond had grown between the three of them until no brother could be any closer than they had been. Tom thought of all the times he had wanted to go see them and had just kept putting it off with the excuse of being too busy. He kept telling himself as soon as he did this job or that job he would go. Now it was too late, and then the tears really came. Tom cried and cried because again, he had failed someone that had helped him so much and someone Tom had learned to love.

The next day Dora, John, and Tom got up before daylight and left so they would be there in time for the funeral. It would take them that long to get there. All of Jack's children were there, and the neighbors had been so kind to J. B. and fixed dinner for all of them. After the funeral they visited with J. B. and Jack's children for a while. Tom tried to get J. B. to go home with them, but he said not now, that he would come later.

The next morning, they left real early so they could get home before too late. The ladies had insisted on packing a lunch for them. It was enough to do them for dinner and supper each day until they got home. When they got there, the boys had already done the night work. So Tom didn't have anything to do that night. Tom thanked the boys for doing everything and also John and Dora for going with him. Then he went home and went to bed. He was dog bone tired from getting up so early each day so they could hurry and get back home. He lay there thinking of all the things Jack and J. B. had done for him and thanked God for letting him know two wonderful men like them. Tom promised J. B. he would be back to see him soon. This time he would keep his promise.

Chapter 13

THE NEXT MORNING, TOM CALLED Roy, and when he heard Tom's voice, here he came. Tom saddled him and went to see about the cattle. They didn't have to go far before they found them. They were in the second grove of trees, and they didn't seem none the worse because of the cold spell. Tom counted them, and they were all there. In the early spring, they would be dropping their calves and he was expecting to have a real good calf crop.

When the weather broke enough for them to get out at night, Jimmy and Tom started back coon hunting. They were afraid that the dogs had forgotten all they had taught them. As soon as they turned them loose and hollered, here they went and it wasn't long until they heard their baying and they knew they had one treed. They kept going toward their baying until Tom saw them, and sure enough they had one treed. After they killed and skinned it, they turned them loose again. Tom and Jimmy were trying to keep up the best they could, but before long they were way behind. They came by the haystack, and there was a big buck deer. He had jumped the fence and was eating on the haystack. Tom asked Jimmy if they liked deer meat. He whispered, "Love it," so they waited until he had settled down. When the deer heard the dogs, he raised his head and was ready to run, but when the dogs just went on by without looking his way, he went back to his eating.

They crept up until Tom could get a good shot at him. They didn't have a rope big enough to hang it up to field dress it. Jimmy said that he would go get Dad, and the boys to come and help them while Tom watched after the deer, that they sure didn't want anything carrying it off while they both went. Tom told Jimmy to go by and hitch up the wagon and go that way as it would be a lot faster. Tom called off the dogs. They didn't understand it. They were ready and raring to go, but nevertheless they minded Tom and came to him. When they saw the deer, they ran over to it but Tom told them to lie down and stay and they did as he told them. He hated to call them off like that, but the deer meat was more important right now.

Jimmy must have run all the way because it wasn't long until here they all came. They loaded it on the wagon and took it a good ways from the hay meadow so the varmints wouldn't smell the blood and come too close to the hay meadow where the cows would be. Tom didn't want any of them coming up too close to where the cows were when they started having their calves. They threw the rope they had brought over a big limb, and all of them carried the deer over and tied the rope to its hind legs and pulled it up high enough to field dress it. After that they took it to the house and skinned it with all of them working on it, they had it done in no time.

John said, "As cold as it was in the smoke shed, we could let it hang and it would cure out some, then we could cut it up later."

The channel was working just fine. It was cold as it could be in there all the time. Jimmy and Tom were so proud of the deer, and everyone bragged on how big and pretty it was. John said it would dress out a whole lot of meat and that sounded real good to Tom.

The day after they killed it, Tom went to the potato mound and got enough potatoes to cream for dinner so if they came down today they could have some deer steaks. Tom hadn't had any deer since he left the ranch, and he sure was hungry for some. He got down four pints of green beans, so they would be handy. By the time he ate breakfast and did the outside work, they were there waiting on him so they could start cutting up the deer. Tom hung up one of the front and back legs. As cold as it was in the smokehouse, it was almost frozen and it would stay plenty cold to have deer steaks along. With the rest of his half, he was going to make some deer chili and can it. John wasn't going to take half of it, but Tom insisted he did. He told him, both he and Jimmy had killed it together and they all helped with it so half was theirs. They all were real proud of it.

John said, "I don't know what Dora will do with it. She will probably make chili out of some of it too." He told Tom, as many of them as it was, it would probably take most of the front leg for one day. They hung their part in the smokehouse also, and he told Tom, "As cold as it is in there, it would stay better than it would up at our house until Dora decides what she wants to do with it."

They helped Tom get his chili meat cut up. After that they took it out to the spring and washed it real good. Tom kept telling them, he could do it, but they said they didn't have anything else to do. So if he didn't care, they would just stay and help him. Tom, of course, told them he didn't mind at all. In fact, he was glad to have them. After they had washed it, they all took turns grinding it for the chili. When they had finished, Tom put the ground meat in the big dish pan and they took it out to the smokehouse. He would let it stay there, and later on, he would make it into the chili.

By then it was noon. Tom asked them to stay and have deer steaks. John again told Tom they didn't want to eat up all his meat. Tom told him that was what it was for. They cut some deer steaks and went into the dugout to fry them. While

John fried the steaks, two of the boys peeled the potatoes and put them on to cook. Tom made biscuits, and Jimmy put the green beans on to cook. One thing about them, they all pitched in and helped regardless to what was being done. Tom had two large skillets. John filled both of them with steaks, and it didn't take long until he had a large platter fried. And by that time the biscuits were ready, the boys had the potatoes creamed. While they were doing that, Mike and Mark went to the smokehouse and got some butter and milk and some preserves. By then the rest of them had set the table. John made gravy, and they all sat down to eat. Boy, was it good. Tom told them it was twice as good because he had someone to eat it with.

After they finished eating, they all helped clean up their mess and took some of their share of the meat for supper that night and went home. Tom went out and got the ground meat and brought it in so he could get started making chili. He had helped Granny Heart make chili, so he knew how to do that. While it cooked, he went out and carried enough water from the spring to put in the pot. He placed the wood around it, but he didn't start the fire. He would wait until he got the chili ready and in the pot, then he would start the fire. Tom went in to check on the chili. It was boiling, and it was ready to start canning. He put it in the cans and sealed it. Then he took it out and put it in the washpot and started the fire. Now all Tom had to do was keep the fire going around it, until it was ready to take out. When it was ready, Tom took it out while it was still partly hot and dried the cans. The heat would finish drying them, so the cans wouldn't rust. Tom took it in and put it on the shelf. Now he had plenty of good chili for when it was cold and when he wanted it.

The rest of the season, there wasn't much left to do. So Tom and Jimmy went coon hunting every night and got several each night. When the season was over, they had quite a few to show for their winter hunt. They let them all dry good, then took them to town and sold them. They brought a good price, and Jimmy and Tom split the money that they got for them. They were both proud of what they had made from them. Also, Tom had gotten his share of the cotton crop, and he was able to send all of it to the bank on his loan. He bought an envelope and stamp and mailed it to Mr. Harper and asked him for a receipt and his balance. Tom told him to mail it to the post office there, and he would pick it up when he was in town.

Jimmy's mama had sent a list of things for them to pick up, so they both filled their orders. Tom got some more coffee, flour, baking powder, sugar, and some syrup. He was out of bacon, so he bought a small slab to do him until his was ready. He had brought some eggs in. She took the eggs in trade, then he paid her the difference. Tom asked her if she had any honey. She said she didn't, but told him Mr. Jackson had bees and would have some. She told them where he lived, and it wasn't too far out of the way as they were going home. Jimmy's order was a lot larger than Tom's and also he paid their bill where they had been getting things all winter. As soon as they got them all loaded, they headed to Mr. Jackson's place to see about some honey. It wasn't hard to find, and sure enough he did have some honey. Tom bought a quart, and Jimmy asked if it came in gallons. Mr. Jackson told him it didn't, but he would knock off on four quarts, enough to make up for the difference. So he bought four quarts. He asked Tom where they lived, and Tom told him he had bought J. B. Rogers place, if he knew where that was.

Mr. Jackson told him, "Quite well, and what has become of the Ruckers?"

Tom told him, "They are still there, and I am living in the old dugout. This is Jimmy, John's son."

"Sure enough!" Then he told Jimmy, "Tell your dad hello for me."

They kept talking, and before Tom left there, he had bought three beehives. They waited until almost dark, so the bees that were out would be back inside the hive. All the time they were waiting, Mr. Jackson was telling Tom about how to raise bees and how to tend to them. Tom didn't tell him, but he was hoping John would know how to tend to them. They stuffed rags in the mouth of each hive like Mr. Jackson told them to do and then loaded them before it got too late and were on their way. Tom laughed when they got out of hearing distance and asked Jimmy if John knew how to take care of bees. He said he didn't know that they had never had any that he could remember. He went on to say, he bet his dad did, that his dad knew how to take care of just about anything.

They drove the horses at a steady pace and didn't stop except to let them rest. They got home way after dark. When they got to the house, John wanted to know what had kept them so long. They had begun to get worried, and he was about ready to come looking for them. All the kids helped unload the supplies and asked about what he had in the boxes. Tom laughed and asked John if he knew how to care for bees. John told Tom he did know a little about caring for them and asked him where he was going to put them. Tom told him he hadn't thought that far ahead and asked him where he thought would be a good place. John told him if they were his, he would put them close to the farmland. He told him, "That way the bees would pollinate the crops and the blooms would give them plenty of nectar to make the honey from."

So it was settled. The next morning, they would come down and help Tom unload them close to the farmland. Tom told John if he would help him learn how to take care of them, that they would go in halves with them. He said that wasn't necessary, that they would be glad, just to be able to get some honey each year. Tom told him no, that he thought if he helped him with them, it was only right for it to be on the halves. So it was settled. Tom and John would take care of them on the halves. Tom told them he would see them tomorrow and went home and got the night work done before it got any later.

The next morning, John and all the boys came down and they took the bees to the farmland. They were still on the wagon, so all they had to do was call the horses and hitch them to the wagon. It didn't take long, and they were on their way. When they got there, John and Tom got out and found a suitable place that was level and partly shaded. They all unloaded them, and after a while, John and Tom, real easy, took the rags out of the openings and got back as fast as they could. It wasn't long until some of the bees started coming out. John said the hives were real heavy and that meant that there was plenty of honey in the hive to do them all winter. He went on to tell Tom, "When you buy beehives, make sure they are heavy, that means there is plenty of honey in them. If the hive is real light, it means the hive is almost empty, and this time of year there is nothing left for the bees to make honey out of and your bees will starve to death. If the hives are light in the spring and there is plenty flowers and fruit trees blooming, then it's okay. If the bees get sick or have a disease, a lot of people will panic and try to sell them right fast to keep from losing money on them. You have to watch for all this when you are buying hives."

They watched them for a while, and John said, "With these as heavy as they are, I don't think we have to worry about anything." They went to the dugout, and Tom made coffee, and they sat at the table, drinking coffee and making plans for their bees. John asked Tom, "Do you know we will have to have three more empty hives before swarming time. We will want to be ready to catch our new bees when they get ready to leave the hive. Also, we are going to need two bee nets and some gloves, before we rob them. I wouldn't even attempt to rob them without nets and gloves." He went on to tell him, "We could make our own smokers with some rags wrapped around some sticks real good and just a little coal oil sprinkled on them to help them get started. Mr. Jackson might have some empty hives, he would sell to us. If not, we would have to get some wood and make them before we start planting because after then we wouldn't have time. We need to see about them and the sooner the better."

So the next day they hitched the wagon up and headed back to Mr. Johnson's place with all five boys going with them. John told Tom, "Dora reminded me that when it came time to rob the hives, we would need jars to put the honey in. We won't need them any way soon. We could get them later, but if we are going to be partners in this, I will pay for half of everything we are out."

Tom told him, "No, I hadn't thought about all of these things we would need to start raising bees." Tom laughed. "I thought I would just buy them and come time to get the honey, we would rob them."

John laughed too and told him, "You know, Tom, on a farm nothing comes that easy and that cheap."

When they got to Mr. Jackson's house, he was making some hives. Tom and John shook his hand. Then he laughed and told John he knew they would be back to see if he had any spare hives and that he had already made some.

He told John, "I knew you could tell him all he needed to know about raising bees."

John told him, "Now, Frank, why didn't you tell Tom what he would need, that way you would have saved us a trip."

Frank laughed and told John, "You old scoundrel, I was hoping you would come with him to get the hives. You don't come very often, and I thought that would be a good way to get you to come in and see me."

They talked for a while, and finally John said, "Well, do you have any hives to sell or not?"

Frank laughed and told them, "What do you think these are for?" He had started making them the next day after the boys left. "When Tom told me who they were and one was your son, I was hoping you would come back with them. I have been working on some ever since Tom and Jimmy left. I have three just waiting for ya'll, and the hardware store will have everything else you will need."

John told him, "Now, Frank, that was a dirty trick you pulled."

Frank laughed and told John, "I know it, but it worked, didn't it? Now let's go to the porch and chat for a while."

They didn't stay very long as John told him they had to get the other things from the hardware store. John told him, "If you were so sure we would come, why didn't you have them here ready for us, and we could have stayed longer?"

Frank laughed and told John, "I thought about it, but I didn't know how many jars ya'll would need."

John told him, "You old hypocrite, I bet you could tell us to the last jar how many we would need."

They laughed and hugged each other, and Frank told him, "John, come again. I get so lonesome since Milley died." He turned to Tom and said, "Boy, this old scoundrel can teach you all you need to know about bees."

Tom told him, "Come out and see us when you get lonesome and need someone to talk too. We'd be glad to see you."

Frank told them, "Don't make promises ya'll don't want to keep. I might just show up one of these days."

Tom told him, "That would be fine. We will be looking for you." Tom paid for the beehives while the boys loaded them. They all waved to him and left. They went to the hardware store, and Tom told John, "Do you think we need to pick up the jars now? I could pay for them."

John said, "I think that might be a good idea because when canning season comes, jars get mighty scarce."

So they got the amount Frank told them to get plus an extra dozen just in case. Also, they got two bee nets and two pair of gloves. John said the three hives would do for this year but next year they would need six, if they were lucky and got each hive when it swarmed, and that they were sure going to try too. He said they wouldn't need all the jars but they would have them whenever they needed them.

When they got home, the boys put them and the hives in their toolshed. John said, "Well, Tom, now all we have to do is wait for the bees to do their job." Tom went back home and put the horses in the pasture and called Roy. He saddled him, and they went to check on the cattle. Tom thought it was about time to turn them in on the haystack. It was time to stop milking Susie. Her calf would be due in the early spring. If it was a heifer, Tom wanted to keep it, to raise another milk cow so he could have milk all year. It was going to be tough on him and the hogs, trying to get along without milk until her calf came. The hogs were really growing. Molly was already expecting another litter of pigs in the early spring. That way they would have more growing time before hog-killing time. Tom drove Susie into the pasture with all the rest of the cows. There she would stay until she had her calf.

Chapter 14

THE YEARS CAME AND WENT, and Tom thought how good God had been to him. Each year had been real good. By his fourth winter, he had 250 head of cows and their beehives had doubled every year. Mr. Buck was still cutting the hay, and with his half, he had a haystack large enough to feed the cattle all winter. By rotating them from pasture to pasture, Tom had plenty of grass. He had five breeding sows, two milk cows, three dozen hens, and plenty of feed to feed them each year. He was able to pay all the money he got from his calf crop and half the cotton money on his note each year and still have plenty to live on.

Jimmy and Tom still went coon hunting every winter, and that made them good money also. God had blessed him in everything he had tried to do. The fourth winter, about the first of October, Tom had everything gathered and stored or canned. So he decided to go see Sally and Mary Ann. He had written to them, but he hadn't seen them since right after Aunt Lou's funeral. He asked Jimmy and Mark if they would see to the milk cows, the hogs, and the cattle while he was gone and that he would settle up with them when he got back. Also, they could have all the eggs for tending to the chickens and the milk and that they could saddle Roy and ride him to check on the cattle about twice a week.

Tom left early Monday morning. John Junior and Jimmy took him in the wagon to the train station.

Dora said, "I need some things from town, and the boys had just as well take you in the wagon and bring it back. There is no use paying to leave the horses and wagon for two weeks when the boys can take you and come and get you."

Tom stopped at the store when they got there and bought two pair of pants and two shirts and a suitcase to carry them in. Tom put his other belongings in it and headed to the train station. John and Jimmy walked with him. They didn't have long to wait before they heard the train whistle. Tom bought his ticket to Weatherford, and he was ready to go when it got there. He told John and Jimmy bye and told them not to wait that he didn't know how long it would be before the train pulled out. He told them he would see them in two weeks. They waved bye and hollered, "We'll be here. See you then." By the time they got the train loaded, it was late in the evening before it was pulling out.

It took them until about six the next afternoon to get there. The train stopped at every station to take on cargo and people and unload some. When they got there, Tom asked someone at the train station where High Burger Hill was. They asked, "Who are you looking for?" Tom told them, and they told him exactly how to get there. It didn't take him long, and by seven he was there. He hollered, "Hello in the house." Sallie came out first, and God had another blessing in store for Tom. Standing just outside the door with Sallie was the most beautiful girl Tom had ever seen. She had coal-black hair, down to her waist, and the darkest brown eyes he had ever seen.

Sallie hugged him and said, "Oh, Tom, what took you so long?"

He told her, "Building a home so one day you could come and live with me."

Then she turned to this beautiful girl and said to Tom. She wanted him to meet Ettie, her very best friend. "Ettie, this is Tom that I have been telling you about."

She came over and shook Tom's hand and told him how glad she was to meet him at last. That she had heard so much about him. Right then Tom wanted to take her in his arms and hug her, but instead he took her little delicate hand and said he hoped it wasn't all bad. She said. "On the contrary, it was all good."

Mary Ann came outside about that time, and Tom went over and hugged her and told both of them how proud he was to see them. They all went in, and Tom had to tell them all about the ranch and what all he had done since he last saw them. Tom also told them about the dugout where he lived and the story about it, being the same dugout that J. B. and his wife's first home and how he and Jack helped him restore it. The night passed real fast, and before long, Sally said she and Ettie had to get to bed as both of them had to be up bright and early in the morning. They had to be on their jobs in time to cook breakfast. Tom told them good night and asked Ettie if he would see her tomorrow. She said she usually came over and visited with Sally after they got off from work. Tom went to bed wishing the night and day would hurry and pass so he could see her again. He felt like he had been waiting for her all his life. Most of the time, Sallie had to work later than Ettie. He so hoped she would today. He wanted to talk to Ettie alone. He wanted to feel her out to see if she cared for him like he did for her.

Tom told her again about the dugout. He told her it was okay for him, but he couldn't expect a woman to want to share anything like that with him. Tom told her it would be a while before he could have anything better to offer any woman, that he was trying to get the ranch built up enough so he could make his payments real good and right now, even if he could take the ranch house, he couldn't afford to and that right now, he wouldn't have money to even buy furniture to go in it.

She looked at him with those big brown eyes and said, "Tom, if a girl loved you enough, she would be glad to live with you in a dugout or any other place he could afford. I know I would." When she realized what she had said, she blushed and dropped her eyes.

Tom couldn't help but kid her, and he said, "Would you really?"

She didn't look up but said they were talking about his life and not hers. Again, Tom told her he thought they were talking about both of their lives. She turned red again and didn't look up or say a word.

Tom told her, "You would love it there. It has big trees around the dugout and a little creek with a spring that runs all the time. I had made a swimming hole just past the house deep enough to go down at night and take a cool bath when I come in from a day's work or just go down and go swimming."

At that she looked up and said, "But, Tom, I can't swim."

He told her, "At one time I couldn't either, but a very good friend of mine, who loved me very much, taught me to swim. I bet I could teach you how real fast."

Tom saw a sparkle come in her eyes, and she said, "I would like that."

Sally came up about that time, and they didn't have time to say anything else, but Tom was about ready to shout, she did care for him like he did her.

That was the fastest two weeks Tom had ever spent. The days were long, but the nights were gone before they got to say hardly anything. Most of the time Sally or Mary Ann was there with them, so Tom didn't have a chance to feel her out much more. He did believe she cared for him as much as he did her.

The last night he was there, Sally said, "Tom, don't stay gone so long this next time."

He looked right at Ettie and said, "I sure won't. You have my word on that. I will be back before you know it." He told them the spring and summer was real busy for him. With all the animals having their babies in the early spring, the hay season, garden time, and everything else that had to be done on a farm and ranch, it was really hard to get away during that time. Most of the time it would have to be in the winter months, and even then it was hard to get away.

They said their good-byes that night because they all had to get up early and go to work. Also, his train left early for Jacksboro too, and Tom had booked it as early as he could so he could get home as early as possible. Tom knew John and Jimmy would be there waiting for him. He walked with Sallie and Ettie to where he had to turn off to go on to the train station. He told them bye again. This time he hugged and kissed Sallie on the cheek, then he hugged and kissed Ettie on the check also and told her he would be back as soon as he could. Tom didn't have too much time to wait before the early train pulled in, and it wasn't long before they were on their way.

Sure enough, the boys were there when he got there. Tom stopped and bought some shells and paid the boys, just in case they wanted to buy something before they left town. They said they didn't, so right after he paid for the shells, they started home. They asked Tom how his trip was and how he was told them the trip was just fine and it was nice to see his sisters, that he hadn't seen them since just before he bought the place and moved here. Tom asked how everything was going, and they said just fine, no problems at all.

They had picked up some things for Dora while they were waiting for him, so when they got home, Tom helped them unload them. They asked him if he wanted them to help him do any of the night chores, but he told them he would do it and thanked them for asking anyway. Tom drove the wagon on down and unhitched the horses and turned them into the pasture. Before, the place always looked good to him and he was always so glad to get back to it, but this time it looked so lonesome. He didn't know he was so lonely until he met Ettie. Tom went in and put his clothes up, and the dugout was so cold and dreary. He built a fire in the stove so it would be nice and warm when he came back in. Then he went down to see about the hogs. The boys had some ground corn, soaking in some buttermilk. So he fed them. They looked like they had grown a whole lot while he was gone. Molly was getting pretty heavy, and the other sows were beginning to show that they were pregnant also. They would have them early in the spring but not as early as Molly. Tom had bred the cows at different times so he would have milk all the time. Sara, Susie's calf, was expecting a calf; but he was still milking Susie, so he was still getting plenty of milk and butter. She was standing at the gate when he got back from feeding the hogs, waiting to be milked, so Tom fed and milked her, then turned her back in the pasture. When he took the milk into the smokehouse, Dora, bless her heart, had sent buttermilk and butter down for him to have when he came home.

    Jimmy and John had also left a half gallon of the morning milk so he could have some to drink tonight. Tom took some of the buttermilk and part of the sweet milk from tonight's milking and took it to the shed and put ground corn in it. By doing it tonight, it would sour for the hog's morning feeding. He went by and fed the chickens. They had already come into the chicken house and were waiting for their supper also. He gathered the eggs and took them to the smokehouse so they would stay nice and cool.

    While he was there, Tom realized he hadn't eaten all day, so he decided he would have some sausage and eggs for supper. So Tom took some in with him along with some milk for gravy and biscuits. The fire had burned down, but it didn't take long until the stove was hot again, and as soon as he got the biscuits ready, he put them in the oven. He sliced some sausage and made a big pot of coffee. By the time the coffee and sausage were done, the biscuits were ready and Tom took them up and made gravy and scrambled the eggs. He set the table and poured him some coffee and sat down to eat. Tom was always proud of the food, and each night he would thank God for it, but tonight he was so lonesome. He thanked Him for it, but he also asked him to work things out so he could have someone to be with. Tom told Him he never knew how lonesome he was until he met Ettie.

Tom ate his supper, and even as hungry as he was, nothing tasted as good as it used to. He finished and sat there drinking a second cup of coffee, even it wasn't as good as it always was. Now the dugout seemed so big and empty. He cleaned up the kitchen and went to bed, but Tom just laid there. It wouldn't be right for him to ask her to share his life here in the dugout even if she would. Tom had paid all he had made on the cattle and his part of the share crops in on the mortgage. He had done that each year, and Tom didn't dream he would need it for anything else. Even if he could get the house, he knew he couldn't afford to buy furniture and all they would need to live there. There was no way he could work the farmland. He didn't have the equipment to work it with, and he would still need the crop money to pay on the note this fall. Tom finally went to sleep about midnight. He had come to the conclusion that there was no way he could ask her to marry him with nothing but a roof over her head and three meals a day, and that's all he had to offer her. By morning Tom was more depressed than he was when he went to bed. He fixed his breakfast, but for the first time he didn't eat much of it. Tom went out and did up the morning work. Then he saddled Roy and went down to check on the cattle. The weather was beginning to get colder, and it wouldn't be long until their winter would set in. He tried to tell himself how lucky he was. He had plenty of food, and he didn't need anything for the winter. Then he thought, on second thought, maybe some more wood and that he would start cutting it as soon as he checked the cattle.

Tom thought of his first winter and how he had worried all summer about whether or not he could make it. Then God had opened doors for him, and by His great miracles, He had given him everything Tom needed to make the winter and more than he needed. Tom just stopped Roy and bowed his head and thanked Him for all the wonderful blessing He had given him. The cattle were just fine, and the calf crops should be real good this year with 250 calves. And if the prices stay up, he should be able to give Ettie a home this coming winter. Anyway, Tom planned on going back and asking her to marry him before long.

As soon as he checked all the cattle, he went back and unsaddled Roy and put him back in the pasture. He called the two horses and hitched them up to the wagon. He had to do something. He just couldn't stay in the dugout all day and sit there thinking about Ettie. Besides there was no way right now that he could take a wife. Maybe this coming fall, but right now there was no way. All the money had been paid on the mortgage note. God had blessed him so much. Tom was tickled to death because he could pay all he had made this year on the note. Even if he hadn't, he still couldn't take the house. He still needed the Ruckers to work the land. Tom scolded himself. He kept telling himself, "Now, Tom, just have patience. Everything will work out in time if it's meant to be, and by next year I will be able to marry her if it's God's will."

Tom cut wood all day. He had to have something to do to keep his mind off Ettie. When handling an ax, you better keep your mind on it or you could come up missing a leg and that was all Tom needed right now. The day passed faster than Tom thought it would. By late that afternoon he had cut a whole load, and by the time he got it to the dugout and unloaded, it was time to do up the night work. He now knew for sure. He would have plenty of wood to do all winter. Tom stacked all the wood just outside the dugout's door in a neat stack. Tom realized he hadn't stopped all day, not even for dinner, and he was hungry. He went in, made a fire in the stove, and cooked a large meal just to have something to do. When he had finished supper, he cleaned the kitchen and went to bed. Tom went to sleep promising himself that he would go and ask her in the next week or two, then he would know if she would marry him this fall or not. That way it would give him something to look forward to and to work harder for.

On the second Sunday after he came home, Tom went to church with the Ruckers. By then he had almost talked himself into going back this next week. He told the Ruckers that he had some business to take care of and he thought he would tend to it before it got any colder. When it got real cold, he thought he needed to be there to see to the livestock. He asked John and Jimmy, "Could ya'll watch after everything for the next week or so."

They said, "We would be glad to."

Tom told them, "I have turned the cattle in the front pasture, where the haystack is, so ya'll won't have far to go to check on them. I will take the wagon and team and drive in and just board the team out while I am gone, that way ya'll won't have to take me because I don't know just when I will be back."

So Monday, Tom headed back to town to catch the train going to Weatherford. He took the team and wagon to the livery stable and told them his plans. They said that would be fine, that he could get them any time when he got back and pay when he came to town next trip. Tom thanked them and headed down to get his ticket. The ticket salesman said, "The train should be here soon." It wasn't long until they heard the train coming. Tom boarded the train, and it wasn't long until he was on his way. Then he began to get scared. Tom thought, *Now, Tom, why are you doing such a fool-headed stunt like this? You ought to have waited until fall. Right now you can only offer her a bunch of promises, and they are just maybes and hope so. What kind of girl will accept a proposal like that. Dummy, you will do more harm than good by going through with such a hair brain thing like you have in mind.*

By the time Tom got there, he was about ready to get back on the train and hightailed it back home as fast as he could. He had walked up the road toward Sallie's and Mary Ann's, and just where the road turns up to go on to their house, Tom stopped. He was standing there thinking about turning around to go back to the train when he looked up and there she was waving at him as she was coming up the road. She was just coming home from work. Tom hurried to meet her as fast as he could and hugged her. She asked him what he was doing back so soon. Tom knew he had to tell her, here and now, or he would lose his nerve. He put his arms around her, and before he could think any further, just blurted it out. He told her he came back to ask her if she would marry him this fall. Tom told her, "I don't have anything to offer you right now, but if I have a good calf crop this fall and the cotton makes good, then I will be able to take the house back and buy some furniture. Even then I won't have too much to offer you except a roof over your head and plenty to eat until I get the ranch paid for. I know even then it won't be easy, but I love you and want you for my wife."

She looked up with tears in her eyes and said, "Tom, that's a whole lot more than I have now, and if a girl loved you enough, she would be glad to share the dugout with you as long as it took for you to do better."

Tom told her, "Ettie, I dared to even hope, but do you love me that much, that you would live in a little more than a cellar until we could get started."

She looked up with tears still in her eyes and told him, "I loved you ever since the first day I saw you."

They talked some more, and Tom promised he would be back in the fall to get her. She and Tom walked on up the hill hand in hand. Tom was so happy he didn't think his feet hit the ground. If you would have asked him, he would have sworn he was walking on air. They decided to keep it quiet and not tell anyone until he could ask her mama. Sallie came home shortly after they got home. Ettie, Tom, and Mary Ann were sitting on the front porch waiting for her. Sallie knew something was up, but she didn't say anything in front of Mary Ann.

Sallie, Mary Ann, and Ettie fixed supper; and after that they sat around and talked. Mary Ann asked Tom how long he was going to stay, and he told her probably just a day or so, that he had to get back before it turned cold to see to the livestock. Mary Ann's husband, Ross, came home, so they went in to fix his supper. They said good night, and Mary Ann told Tom she would see him tomorrow. Finally, Sallie said she hated to break up their party, but if they didn't get to bed, those youngsters wouldn't have any breakfast in the morning. Tom walked Ettie home and asked her if he could kiss her good night.

She told him, "Tom, if you didn't, I will have my feelings hurt."

Tom laughed and told her, "I guess I had better then," because he sure didn't want to hurt her feelings. Tom told her he would see her right after she got home and he would ask her mother.

"You aren't scared are you," she teased.

Tom laughed and said, "You better believe I am. What if she says no?"

She kissed him on the cheek, saying, "Then I will go anyway. But, Tom, I don't see why we can't get married now. If the dugout is good enough for you, it will be good enough for me also. It would be more than I have ever had. And you promised me three meals and a roof over my head. We didn't always have that."

Tom thought the time would never pass, just sitting there on the front porch waiting for Ettie to come home. About noon he went in and warmed him some coffee and took it back to the porch. It wasn't long until Ettie's mother came by. She spoke and hurried on by. She cleaned houses for some elderly folks, but she didn't have to stay all day. Ettie told him "I have two little sisters and a brother, and Mama goes early to work so she wouldn't have to leave them too long after they woke up. Mama leaves their breakfast on the table, and they were dare some to come outside until Mama gets home about two or three o'clock, and I usually get off about three."

Tom saw Ettie coming up the road. When she got closer, he saw she was crying. She ran by, and Tom didn't think she even saw him. Her dress was torn, and she was almost in shock. She ran into the house, and Tom didn't wait to be invited in. He opened the door and just walked in. When she saw him. She ran over still crying and said, "Oh, Tom, oh, Tom," and just grabbed him and started crying again.

Tom petted her and kept telling her, "Now, now, it's going to be all right." With her in his arms, he looked across her head at Mrs. Coker. She got Tom's message of what's wrong and told him quietly, "The old man that she worked for tried to rape her."

Finally, Ettie said, "He didn't succeed. I fought him and fought him. That's how he tore my dress. I finally shoved him down and ran out of the house real fast and ran all the way home. I was so scared he was going to come after me."

Tom petted her some more and kept telling her it was okay until he got her calmed down. Her clothes were sopping wet where she had cried and run all the way home. When she had calmed down where she could talk some, she started crying. Her mama went over and started petting her.

Ettie told her, "Mama, I just can't go back there anymore. I just can't."

Mrs. Coker came over and took her in her arms and said, "You won't have to, baby, not ever again."

Tom told her, "You are right." They were going to ask her mama if he and Ettie could get married this fall, but this changed things. He told her, "I want to marry her now and take her home with me. Right now." Tom took her in his arms again and said, "Baby, you won't have to go through anything like this ever again."

Mrs. Coker looked real funny and said, "Tom, do you know how old my baby is."

Ettie spoke up real quick and said, "I am almost nineteen."

Mrs. Coker told Tom, "My girls had to grow up fast. Their daddy fell dead over my bed right after I had given birth to a baby boy. I had four little girls, just stair steps. The little boy died a week after I buried my husband. I had tried to make them a living by cooking in a restaurant. Then later I got on at a hotel cooking and cleaning the rooms. We got our room and board and a very small salary, but we had to work like dogs for it. The girls helped make beds and clean rooms from the time I had gotten the job. We didn't have hardly any money for nothing. We stayed there until the two oldest girls were just barely in their teens. The hotel owner was nothing but a devil. He tried to pull the same stunt on my first girl, as this one tried on Ettie. She came crying to me, and that same day we got a house and moved. I was hoping that this would never happen to any more of my girls. I didn't know what we were going to do without a job or any money, but God blessed us by me finding a job that very week, and the girls were able to find jobs, staying with elderly couples when the wife was sick. None of the jobs paid much, but with all of us working, we were barely able to pay rent and buy a few groceries. I had started cleaning houses and cooking for people that were sick and needed help or any other kind of work I could find to do. We didn't make much, and we had a tough time of it, but I kept my girls safe until now. When their wives died, the two older girls married the old men because they needed someone to take care of their children. That's what this old devil wanted, but Ettie wouldn't go along with it. Then I married and had two more little girls. Later on, the oldest girl died in child birth, leaving a baby boy behind, and I took him to raise. I was able to stay home and take care of them. Then another heartache came into my life, my second husband died leaving me with three girls and a little boy to raise. Again, we moved into a cheaper house, and Ettie and I went back to work, keeping house and taking care of elderly people. Thank God, the two little girls were able to take care of Willie while Ettie and I were at work. Tom, I am telling you this so you will know what Ettie has already been through and why she has had to grow up so fast. She has been through enough, so don't marry her because you feel sorry for her. Search your heart and make sure you love her and don't just feel sorry for her. She doesn't need that."

Tom assured her that he loved her and that he wanted her for his wife to love and cherish and not for a slave. Tom told her, "I don't have anything to offer her right now but a roof over her head and three good meals. As soon as the ranch starts paying off we will have a home and all the things we need."

She said, "Tom, that's more than she has right now, but the thing she needs more than anything is someone to love her. Are you sure you could do that and was not just feeling sorry for her."

Tom answered her as truthful as he knew how, he said, "Mrs. Coker, with all my heart and with all my life, and as for as feeling sorry for her, yes, I was sorry this had to happen to her, that it shouldn't happen to any girl. But I had already asked Ettie to marry me before this happened. In fact, that was what I had come back for. We were going to wait until this coming fall, but now, we can't wait because I don't want her to take a chance of this happening again."

With tears streaming down her face, she said, "Then take her with all my blessings. And, Tom, be good to her." Then she told Tom we will need some time before the wedding to get everything ready.

The next day, Maw, as Tom later called her, Ettie, and him went to town and bought some material to make Ettie a dress. Tom told Maw, "She would be better off doing something to get her mind off what happened." Ettie found two pieces she liked and couldn't make up her mind which one she liked the best, so Tom told her to take both of them. He thought she would need them both for Sunday dresses anyway. They found a pretty pair of shoes for her also.

Maw said, "We had better get home so we can get the dresses made. We will need at least two days to get everything ready, so we had better go so we can get started."

When they got back to the house, Tom told them, "From now until you get the dresses finished, I would only be in the way, so I will make myself scarce and see ya'll them later. Anyway, I want to pick up Ettie's train ticket."

Maw said, "Tom, don't you think, you and Ettie need to go down and see the preacher first and see when he can marry you before you pick up the ticket."

Tom laughed and told her, "Yes, I guess that does come first, doesn't it?"

She told them, "Why don't ya'll go down and talk to him, while I start getting things ready. After that you could drop her off and then go do whatever you need to do."

So they left, hand in hand, promising they would be right back as soon they could.

The preacher was busy, and they had to wait for a while. When he came out, he said, "Hello, Ettie, I didn't expect to see you until Sunday. What's brings you here today, and who is this nice-looking boy you have with you?"

All in one breath, Ettie told him, "This is Tom, and we came to see you about getting married."

He congratulated them and then said, "Let's see, I am leaving early tomorrow and I won't be back until Saturday afternoon. What day did you all have in mind?"

Ettie told him, "Tom needs to get back as soon as he can. He has livestock that he has to take care of and he told the boys that's watching them for him he would be back as soon as he could."

Chapter 15

"IN THAT CASE," THE PREACHER said, "why don't we have it Saturday at about seven in the afternoon? The last train leaves at eleven and there is no train on Sunday."

They told him, "That would be just fine."

He asked her, "Now where are you planning on having it?"

Ettie said, "At Mama's, I guess."

So it was settled. Saturday at seven at Ettie's house. Tom walked her home and left her and her mama with their sewing while he went down to get her ticket. When he came back by the road leading up to where they lived, he saw Sallie just coming home from work. They talked for a while, and he asked her where did Mr. Thompson live, the man that Ettie worked for. She didn't know about the trouble as they had decided not to tell anyone. She told Tom, "It's just outside the city limits on the right side of the road, you can't miss it. It has a "For Sale" sign in front of it."

Boy, that was his clue. Tom didn't know how he was going to get in to see him and do what he came to do, but that was his way. The next day when he got there, Tom knocked at the door and he came to the door.

Tom told him, "I saw your sign, and that I might be interest in it, if the farmland was any good."

He said, "It was real good."

Tom told him he would deliver if it was what he came to find. The man called the horses and hooked the wagon up. He talked all the way to the farmland, and then to the back pasture he stopped the wagon. Tom got off and told him, he thought this would be far enough for what he had in mind. He got off, still talking, when Tom told him what he came for. He turned as white as a sheet and said he wouldn't fight him and started to get back on the wagon.

Tom told him, "No, you are too big of a coward, but you would fight an innocent girl, wouldn't you?" Tom grabbed his foot and pulled him off the wagon. He sure was kicking and fighting, trying to get loose from Tom, for someone who said he wasn't going to fight. Tom told him that wasn't what he had in mind, that he had planned on using his belt but there was a stick about the size of a good-sized switch. Tom picked it up and told him he intended to whip him as if he was a teenage boy that had pulled this kind of stunt. Tom jerked his feet out from under him and turned him over before he knew what he was doing, and Tom gave him the whipping he needed. Tom guessed he had never had a whipping because he hollered and cried worse than a teenage boy would. He kept crying for mercy, but Tom didn't show him any. The more he hollered and cried, the more Tom whipped him. He told him he hadn't showed Ettie any mercy. When he finished, Tom was wringing wet with perspiration and so was he. Tom helped him on the wagon and drove him to the house. After he got him on the wagon and before they left, Tom told him, "You have three little girls and maybe this will save them from this happening to them or to some other person's daughter." If he ever heard of him pulling this kind of stunt again, he would come back and this was just a sample of what he would get next time. Tom told him he would pay for Ettie's dress he almost tore off her and a year's salary. The man began to say, "Oh, I don't have that kind of money." Tom told him, "Then get it. That beats a trip to the pen, don't it?" He began to beg Tom not to do that and said he would get it. Tom told him he knew he would and he would be back tomorrow after it in cash. Tom told him he didn't need it or Ettie but her mama would, and Tom intended that he would remember this from now on, and like Tom told him, maybe this would save another little innocent girl from this happening to her. When they got to his house, Tom took him in and put him in bed, then Tom doctored his backside. He told him he would be back after lunch tomorrow for Ettie's wages and the money for her dress. If he was smart he would have it. If not, he could play stupid and call the law, but he had Tom's guarantee, he would spend the next few years in jail, not counting the disgrace it would cause him and his family.

Tom went back to see how the dresses were coming along. They said they were doing fine on them and what took him so long. He started kidding Ettie and told her, "You didn't think I had left without you, did you?"

She laughed and said, "You had better not."

After that he went over to Mary Ann's, and he and Sallie sat on the porch and talked for a while. She said she thought Ettie would be home before now. Tom told her she was home and how about us going over there for a while. Tom knew Ettie would be dying to tell her, and he had held it back as long as he could. As soon as they knocked, Ettie came to the door and asked Tom, "Did you tell her?"

Sallie looked dumfounded, then said, "Tell me what?"

Ettie was so excited she blurted out, "Tom and I are getting married Saturday."

Sallie was real tickled about it and told Ettie, "Now you will be my sister, as well as my best friend."

The next day, Ettie and Maw were still sewing. Tom told them he would stay out of their way. Tom asked Maw if she had anything for bruises. She gave him some salve and told him to rub it on the bruised place real good, that the salve would keep it from getting infected. About twelve thirty, he started over to collect the money. Tom knew it would be after one by the time he got there anyway. Tom thought he had just as well go, so he could get it over with. When he got there, Tom noticed, Mr. Thompson was barely creeping around.

He came to the door to let Tom in. "Boy," he told Tom, "I don't know who you are or where you came from, but you sure worked me over."

Tom told him, "You deserved ever lick you got."

He said, "I wasn't complaining and I know I did. Here is the money. I am real sorry about this. I wish it had never happened."

Tom told him, "I do too. Maybe you have learned your lesson, and it won't happen again."

He said, "There is no maybe to it. After that lesson from you, I don't ever want a second one."

Tom told him, "Keep your nose clean, and I won't be back. Mrs. Coker sent some ointment over. If you would like me too, I will put some on your backside. She said keep it greased good and it would keep it from getting infected and help it heal faster."

He said, "I would appreciate it if you would." So he rubbed it real good. "Tom, do you know you are a heck of a fellow. That you beat me until I almost pass out, put me in the wagon, brought me home, put me in bed, then come and doctor me. In my book you are quite a guy." Then he said something that kind of shocked Tom. He thanked Tom for everything, including his lesson.

Tom told him, "I didn't have anything against you. In fact, I think you are a pretty good person that just had to learn a lesson the hard way."

Then he sure enough did surprise him. He asked him, "Would you tell Mrs. Coker to come to see me as soon as she could. Tell her I would come up there." Then he grinned and said, "But right now I don't think I am quite up to it."

Tom promised him he would, but he couldn't guarantee she would come. Tom told him he would check on him tomorrow. Shortly after that Tom left. Tom didn't stop at Sallie's to see if she was home; he just hurried right over to Ettie's. Now the hard part was to come. Tom knew Mrs. Coker had not approved of what he had done and would approve less when he told her about the money. When Tom hollered, Mrs. Coker came to the back door. Ettie had her lap full of the dress she was hemming. That gave him time enough to tell her he had to talk to her alone. They went in, and Tom went over and told Ettie hello. She asked him where he had been all afternoon, and Tom told her, "I was out trying to find a beautiful girl to take home with me."

She laughed, then said, "Did you find one?"

He kissed her and said, "I sure did, right here."

About that time her mama asked, "Tom, would you like me to get you a cold drink from the well, or better still would you rather have a cup of coffee."

Tom told her, "I thought you would never ask, and a cup of coffee sounded fine. In fact, I will even help you make it."

So they went into the kitchen on the pretense of making coffee. Tom handed her the money. She asked where he got it and told him flat she wouldn't take any money from him, that they were doing all right. Tom told her where it came from. Tom thought she was going to explode. He expected her to get mad but not that much. She told him in no certain terms that she did not need his filthy money. Tom asked her to let him explain before she murdered him. He told her, he wanted him to remember real good, so if he was ever temped to do anything like this again, and he didn't think he would after this, that it was going to cost him, in skin as well as in money to get out of it. Tom told her by her helping him teach him this lesson, she just may save it from happening to some other poor girl. He will think twice before he does this again if he knows it will cost him plenty. Tom said that he had promised him more of the same, if he ever heard of him doing anything like this again, but he needs this little boost also. He told her she needed the money to help her get on her feet. This will help her, and besides, a dollar and a half a week for a year is not going to break him. He doesn't need it to just hog it up. The bruises will heal, but he will remember the cost longer.

She finely agreed but said, "Tom as long as you live, you are never, and I mean never, pull this kind of stunt on me again."

Tom told her, "I will try not to, but the situation called for drastic measures."

She told him, "Tom, it's not your place to dish out the punishment for another person. You are not God or His judge or jury."

Tom told her, "Maw, I knew all that, but someone had to help God, the judge, and the jury a little bit."

She really got mad at him then and told him, "That was no excuse for your stunt. Neither God or the judge or jury needed your help."

Tom told her, "Would you forgive me? I will try to do better next time."

She told him, and her voice was kind and soft again, "Tom, I know you were only trying to help, and I appreciated it, but next time please don't try to help that much. Next time try to turn the other cheek."

Tom always being full of mischief said, "Now, Maw, I thought about that, but I remembered you telling me about another man like him, that was just a devil. Well, I thought hard about that and I was afraid if I had turned the other cheek, I would have hit it too so I just did what I thought was best."

He could see she wanted to laugh, but instead she said, "Well, next time don't think so hard and maybe you will do the right thing."

Then Tom said, "Oh, I almost forgot, here is the fifty dollars for Ettie's dress."

She did explode then. She told him, "You beat anything I have ever seen in all my life. If you ever do anything like this again, I will forbid you to come to this town again, let alone my house. If this gets out, I won't be able to hold my head up in this town again."

Tom told her, "It won't get out, that I promise you. He will never breathe a word of it. He is too ashamed to let anyone know what he did. Because it would disgrace him badly. He would be the one leaving town, not you. Also, he knows it will disgrace not only him, but his whole family and he don't want that."

She told Tom, "I will take the dress money because he did tear her dress completely up, and she deserves another dress, but not that much."

Tom told her, "I didn't know how much a dress cost, and I didn't have anything to do on setting the price. Mr. Thompson did that himself."

About that time Ettie hollered, "Is it going to take all day to make that coffee?"

Mrs. Coker told her, "It is just about ready. Why don't we all stop and have a cup."

Ettie said, "That is fine, and I have just finished hemming the last of the dresses."

Then Mrs. Coker told her about the money Mr. Thompson had sent for the dress, also to tell her how sorry he was, that he didn't know what made him pull a stunt like that. Ettie said she bet he is, and Tom told her he knew he was.

Her mama said, "Yes, Ettie, I think he has more than learned his lesson, and he will never pull a stunt like that again."

Tom didn't think Ettie noticed the sarcasm in her voice, but he sure did. Then Tom and Mrs. Coker drank their coffee. Ettie told Tom she didn't drink coffee.

After that Mrs. Coker asked Ettie if she would like to go to town and buy some things with the money. She first said she didn't want his filthy money, but Mrs. Coker said, "Now, Ettie, it was your dress he tore up, and it's not wrong to make him pay for it." So they decided they would go and get some things with it. Tom walked part ways with them. Then he told them he would make himself scarce and he would see them later. Tom walked around town just killing time. He saw a small little shop that had wedding bands in the window. Tom stood there looking at them wishing he could buy one for Ettie. He thought it won't cost anything to look. He went in, and the woman asked if she could help him. Tom told her what he was looking for and told her he couldn't afford anything expensive. She said she thought she would have something he could afford and showed him several for fifteen dollars and under. Tom found four that he liked and asked her if she would hold them until tomorrow, then he would bring back his girl to see which one she liked.

Tom asked her, "What if they don't fit?"

She said, "I have them in almost any size. How small is her hands?"

Tom told her, "Real small."

She got the four out in two small sizes. She said, "This is the smallest size I have, and these are next."

Tom told her, "I think one of them might be the right size. If you would hold them, we will be back tomorrow." He had paid for her ticket and had thirty dollars in his pocket. He thought that would do them until they got home and then they would be all right. He would have money from the eggs, butter, and honey if they needed anything. He had already laid by all his winter supplies. Tom didn't think they would need anything until they sold their coon hides in about February or March.

After that he went back to see Mr. Thompson to doctor his backside. He was better and was able to get around good, but he couldn't get to his backside to doctor it.

Tom asked him, "Do you want me to doctor it for you again?"

He said, "If you don't mind. It is a lot better, and in a few more days it will be in pretty good shape." After that they talked awhile. He asked Tom, "Would you like a cup of coffee?"

Tom told him, "I never turn down a cup of coffee in my life, unless I think someone put poison in it."

He laughed and said, "As tough as you are, you would drink it and never know anything was the matter with it. You would go home and brag about how good it was."

They went in and made the coffee and sat around and talked some more. Tom told him he would be leaving Saturday night so he wouldn't be by any more to see him. Now for him to take care and maybe he would see him again someday. They shook hands, and he said he hope so, but under different circumstances. Tom told him if they ever did meet, he knew it would be a lot better.

Tom left, and by the time he got back, Ettie and her mama was back. She was tickled to death. she told him, "I had bought some undergarments, two gowns, a pair of everyday shoes, another dress, a pretty purse, and a bag to put my things in. And, Tom, I still have money left."

Tom told her, "You can put it in your purse and spend it later."

"Tom, the dress was so pretty," she told him. "I just had to buy it. It is going to be my wedding dress, so you can't see it until tomorrow night." She hugged him, and he left right after that so he could spend some time with Sallie and Mary Ann. Ross had already come home from work, and they were just sitting down to supper.

At the supper table, Tom asked him, "Would you be my best man?"

He smiled as he said, "Tom, I will be glad to. Ettie deserves a good man, and I believe she is getting one."

Tom went around to shake his hand and thank him and then told him, "I hope I will never let you down."

They sat around for a while with Tom doing most of the talking about the ranch. He told then about the cows and that he was expecting a full crop of calves this early spring. If the prices are as good as they have been, the ranch would begin to support itself, plus the five sows. The bees had doubled each year ever since they got them, and they had a good market for their honey each year. Then Tom remembered about the honey that he had brought them. He went after it and told them he had forgotten to give it to them. Tom held it up to show them how pretty and clear it was. Ross said it was real pretty, that he could see why they had a ready market to sell it. He also said he guessed they had better get to bed, that tomorrow was Saturday and they had a big day before them.

Tom went to bed, but he rolled and tumbled all night. He was as nervous as a pussycat. Tom thought he would never go to sleep. But he finally did because he woke up to bacon and eggs frying. He got up and put on some jeans, then said, "Thank You, Lord," that he had put in his suit, thinking they might go to church. They ate breakfast, then he went over to ask if he could borrow Ettie for just an hour or so. Tom left Mary Ann and Sallie making cakes, and Ettie and her mama was cleaning house and, as they said, cooking for the night meal, that everyone was coming there for supper. Everyone meant Mary Ann, Ross, Sallie, Tom, and them, he thought.

Ettie asked him where they were going that was so important. Tom told her it was a secret, that they would hurry and be right back. When they got there, she said, "Now, Tom, what are you up to?"

About then the lady brought out the four rings, and Tom told her, "This is the secret I wanted to surprise you, but I didn't know what size to get."

She picked out one, and it just fit. The lady congratulated them, then they were out the door and back on their way home.

Tom told her, "See, I told you, it wouldn't take very long."

She kept telling him, "Oh, Tom, it's so pretty. It's so pretty. Could I show it to mama as soon as I get home?"

Tom told her she could, then he would take it and she couldn't have it back until she said "I do" tonight.

She said, "I can't hardly wait."

As soon as they got to the back door, she rushed in the house and hollered, "Mama, come see the surprise."

Her mama told her how pretty it was and how proud she was for her. Tom told them, "I will go now and let ya'll get started so you can be through by seven." Then he started teasing her, "Don't you all be late." He hugged her, and she said, "That will be the day, and you just make sure you are there on time."

That was the longest day Tom ever spent. Ross and he sat on the front porch and talked while Sallie and Mary Ann worked with the cakes all day.

Tom thought it would be Sallie, Mary Ann, Ross Mrs. Coker, Ettie, the preacher, and him; but a little after six, people began to come up, bringing dishes of food and tables. The men began to set tables up, and the woman put tablecloths on them as fast as they got them set up. By seven they had the yard full of tables and chairs. At the back they had tables full of food, and people just kept bringing food in. At the front they put an archway, then some ladies covered it with English ivy, then put some bows on it. When they were through, it looked real pretty. They got through with it right at seven.

All the people began to sit down around the tables facing the archway. The preacher came over and told Tom it was time. Ross and he had dressed earlier, and he thanked the Lord again that he had brought his Sunday suit. The preacher led the way over to the archway, then showed them where to stand. Tom didn't know it was going to be like this or he would have been scared to death. As it was he didn't have time to get very scared. Some guys with guitars and banjoes started playing "Here Comes the Bride," and here came Sallie, then Ettie right behind her. She had the white dress on she had bought. It wasn't a regular wedding dress, but they had put lace and a veil with it, but with the flowers she carried, it looked like one. She looked so beautiful coming down the path they had made from the house to the archway. When she got there, Tom whispered to her, "I didn't know I was marring an angel." The preacher and Ross smiled along with her and that made her more beautiful. Tom couldn't tell anyone what the preacher said except telling them to join hands and Ross punching him to say "I do." Then he asked if they had a ring, and Ross gave it to him and the preacher told Tom to place it on her finger and repeat after him. Tom was so glad that the preacher went slow because he was so scared. At that moment he didn't think he could have told them his name. Anyway, they got through with their vows, and the preacher said, "I now pronounce you man and wife. You may kiss your bride." Then he had them turn and face the congregation. "May I present to you Mr. and Mrs. Tom Brisco. Everyone is invited to stay for dinner."

After dinner they had them go over to another table with gifts on it. Ettie and Tom opened all the gifts, and there was a car load. They thanked them all for the gifts and for all of them coming to help them celebrate their wedding. After that they all came by and congratulated Tom and Ettie, then they began to tell everyone bye and that they would see them next time they got to come back.

It wasn't long until they were all gone; and Tom and Ettie were left with Mrs. Coker, Sallie, Mary Ann, and Ross. They all started cleaning everything up. Sally said, "With all of us working, it won't take us long." The biggest job was packing all the wedding gifts. Mrs. Coker had planned ahead and gotten boxes before the wedding to put all the things all in. Tom never saw so many wedding gifts. The preacher and his wife had given them a whole set of dishes. He said, "They were from the whole church." They were already packed, so they didn't have to do anything with them but load then on the wagon.

Ross had borrowed a team and wagon to haul all their things to the train station. By the time they got it packed, they had twelve big boxes. They had towels, cup towels, dishcloths, sheets, pillowcases, all kind of scarves and crochet things, a complete set of matching tea glasses, water glasses and fruit bowls. And thank goodness, they were already packed in the box also two quilts. Sallie and Mary Ann made one, and Mrs. Coker made the other one. Mrs. Coker said, "You had better keep one of the quilts out to cover with. It would be cold at night on the train."

Tom thought they had everything they needed to start keeping house including pots and pans. Tom didn't tell them, but he didn't know what they would do with them when they got to the dugout, but Ettie would find a place for them he bet. After they got it all loaded on the wagon, it was almost ten o'clock. They all got on the wagon and went down to the train station. By the time they got, there it was ten thirty but the ticket agent said the train would be at least an hour late. Tom told Ross, "It's no telling when it will get here, so why don't we unload everything so ya'll can go home and get to bed. It has been a long day for the women, and church time would come mighty early in the morning." So they got it unloaded. Tom and Ettie told them all good-bye and thanked them for all they had done.

Mrs. Coker told Tom she needed to speak with him, so they walked off while all the rest was saying their good-byes. She told Tom, "Mr. Thompson had offered me a job when I went to see him. He said he would give me the amount I was making now plus room and board for me and my children. If it had not been for the trouble, I would take it in no time flat."

Tom told her, "Take it, and you won't ever have any trouble with him. He guarantees that, and it will help you and him both."

She said, "I had been wanting to tell you, but I had been so busy. This was the first time I have had time to ask you what you thought about it."

Tom told her, "If you could forget what happened, then I think it would be good for both of you. That way you can be with your children all the time and help him raise his, and they sure are needing someone. Also, that way, you won't have to worry about how you are going to make ends meet. He has learned his lesson. You and the girls will be safer there than anywhere."

Right after that they left, and Ettie and Tom sat down on a bench right next to their things to wait for the train. It was almost twelve when it finally got there. Tom and Ettie were the only ones boarding, so they helped them load their things and it wasn't long until they were ready to pull out.

Ettie was so excited. She said, "I can't hardly wait to get to our home."

Tom kept telling her, "Now don't expect too much. It's just a little more than a big cellar."

She told him, "Tom, anywhere with you would be heaven, after what I had lived in."

Tom told her, "I hope I don't ever disappoint you."

It took them all night. The train made several stops taking on freight. It was around noon or after before they got to Jacksboro. They unloaded the boxes and luggage. Tom asked the ticket agent to keep an eye on Ettie while he went down and got the wagon. He said he would be glad to. Tom told her not be afraid, that the ticket agent was going to watch after her while he went after the wagon. Tom sure was glad that he had insisted on bringing the wagon. Tom rushed down to get it. It being Sunday and that late, he knew the caretaker wouldn't be there. Tom got the horses and hitched them to the wagon and hurried back to Ettie. The ticket agent helped him load everything, then they stopped at the restaurant and ate. Tom introduced them all to Ettie. It didn't take them long to eat, so in a little while they were on their way home. Ettie wanted to know how long it would be before they would be home. Tom told her if they hurried and with luck, maybe they would get there around seven or eight o'clock or so if they pushed it. She told Tom, "Then let's push it," that she was so anxious to get home and see everything.

Chapter 16

THEY GOT THERE A LITTLE after seven. If she was disappointed, she didn't act it. She told him, "Tom, its fine. It's a permanent place, and it's ours." That's more than she had ever had. Both of them and the horses were dog tired. He had pushed them as fast as he dared so they could get there before too late, also the excitement of Saturday, then being awake most of the night and the long drive home.

As soon as they unloaded the wagon and put them all on the other side of the bed, Tom told her he would help her put it away tomorrow, that he was almost asleep standing on his feet. She told him she was tired but she was so excited she didn't think she could go to sleep. Tom built a fire in the stove and told her he would go tend to the horses, then he would get them some supper. She told him getting supper was her job, so he went out to the smokehouse and got some sausage, eggs, and milk. He showed her where everything was, then while he went out and tended to the horses real good. She fixed them something to eat. He drove the wagon close to the smokehouse, where he kept it, unhitched the horses, and brushed them down good, then put them in the pasture.

He knew when he wasn't there by time to do the night work that the boys would have come down and done it, so he didn't have to worry with that. By the time he finished and went back to the dugout, Ettie had supper ready. Tom got some jelly down that Dora had given him, then they were ready to eat. Ettie told him "Tom, this is our very first meal together in our very own home." He asked the blessings, then they began to eat, and everything was real good. Tom was to learn that she was an excellent cook. When they got through, they cleaned up the kitchen, then she wanted to go out and see everything in the yard. But by then it was getting dark. Tom told her he had checked and made sure everything was all right, that tomorrow he would take her out to see it all. He showed her the empty drawers in the chester drawers and where he had a wire stretched across the corner at the foot of the bed to hang their Sunday clothes. He helped her hang up some of her Sunday clothes, then to bed.

The next morning, she was so excited she could hardly eat her breakfast. She was so eager to go see everything. They went out to milk Maud. She wanted to try to milk, but she was afraid she would squeeze too hard and hurt her. Each day she would try, but she never did learn how to milk. (Tom always had to do the milking. She would try so hard, but she could never get any milk to come out.) He showed her how to strain it, and then they took it to the smokehouse. She wanted to know what they were going to do with so much milk. Tom told her they would drink all they wanted, the rest they would churn and make butter and buttermilk. What milk they didn't use they would put ground corn in it, let it sour, and feed it to the pigs.

After that they went down to feed the pigs. Tom told her all five of them were pregnant and getting big, but Molly would be first. She wanted to know when Molly would have her babies and how many would she have. Tom told her it will be the last of February or the first of March, usually she had nine or ten and that he hoped and prayed the weather would turn warmer by then.

THELMA INMAN

They came back by the swimming hole, Tom told her he used that for his bathtub in the summer, that it was nice and warm all the summer months. She asked what about the neighbors seeing him. Tom told her he took his bath at night, that way no one could see him, but if he just went swimming he left his underclothes on. She told him again she couldn't swim Tom told her not to worry about that. He would teach her. That it wouldn't be long until she would be swimming like a duck.

Coming back they went by the spring, and Tom showed her where he got his drinking water before they had channeled it to the smokehouse. Tom told her it stayed cold all year around that they always had ice-cold water to drink. She wanted to feel how cold it was, then asked what kept it so cold. Tom had to explain to her it was fed by a spring coming out of the ground, no telling how far down. When they got to the smokehouse, Tom showed her how he had channeled the water through it to keep the milk and everything cold. He told her he got tired of having to go back and forth to the spring every time he needed something. So he came up with this idea. She was real impressed with it. Tom told her all the Rucker boys helped him dig it, or he probably would be digging on it yet. But with five of them digging, it didn't take long.

He told her she could get water from there for the household water also, but the coldest was just when it came out of the ground there at the spring. They went arm in arm to the henhouse. Tom told her, "This is the chicken house," and how many chickens they had. He told her they would open the door and let them out later on so they would have time to lay their eggs, then she could see them.

John and Jim came down right after that. They told Tom how much they had missed him, and everything had gone just fine while he was gone. Tom introduced them to Ettie, and they both said they all wondered why he had went back so soon.

John said, now they knew. He told Tom, what he wondered now is, what took him so long. If he had a wife that pretty, he would have gone back faster than Tom did. They all laughed, and right after that they left. Ettie told Tom, "They thought you came back after me and that we were already married." They both laughed at that, and he told her, "We will correct it when we see them Sunday, if not before."

Tom asked her, "Would you like me to saddle Roy, and we could ride down into the pasture to check on the cattle. That way we wouldn't have to wait for them to come up tonight."

She was real excited. She told Tom, "But, Tom, I have never rode a horse."

So he called Roy. It didn't matter whether it was days or weeks between the time Tom called him, he always came and he always acted proud to see him. Today was no exception. As soon as he heard him call him, here he came, tickled to see him.

Tom told Ettie, "He is real gentle, and you could pet him if you want to." Again, she was real excited. She acted like a little girl seeing her first animals. She patted him and talked to him, like he was a human, and Roy liked that. He laid his head over on her shoulder, and she said, "Tom, look, he likes me already."

Tom told her, "Of course, he does. Everyone and everything will like you. You don't have to worry about that." He saddled Roy and stepped up in the saddle and told her to give him her hand and swung her up behind him. They had to ride a good way to find the cattle, but she was enjoying every bit of it.

When she saw them, Tom had never seen anyone so excited before. She kept saying, "Oh Tom, are they all ours?" Then she asked, "Tom, are you kidding me? How soon will they have babies? Can I pet them?" all in one breath.

He told her, "Yes, they are all ours. No, you can't pet them, but when Maude has her baby, each time, you can pet it and Maude, either one. The cows will have baby calves in the early spring." Then he laughed. "Now, did that answer all your questions?"

She laughed and told Tom, "There is so many things to see that you just take for granted. I bet you think I am crazy going on so, but I had never seen so many cows in all my life."

Tom told her, "Just wait until the calves are born, that's when you will get excited."

She hugged him and said, "I can hardly wait." She wanted to know if he would let her help him take care of them.

He told her, "That's the mother's job, and they do a pretty good job of it. All we have to do is make sure wolves and other varmints don't get in and kill them."

When they got back, he told her, "It is close to noon, so we will let the chickens out so they can go scratch around for bugs and any seed that might be left."

She wanted to know if it was time to get the eggs. It was still early, but she was so eager, Tom gave her a pan and he just stood back and watched her. You would have thought she was a little girl on her first egg hunt at Easter. She was going from nest to nest. Each time she found some, she would say, "Look, Tom, here are some more." She got quite a few, and Tom was so glad that the hens had done good that day because she was so excited over each one of them. They put the eggs in the smokehouse, and again she was so excited over having plenty of eggs, milk, and butter. She wanted to know, "Do we always have this much?"

He told her, "This much or more."

Then she wanted to know, could she use all she wanted to.

"As many as you want. Then we will take what you have left to town and sell them to the cafe or trade them to the grocery store for things that we need."

That night when Tom was doing up the night work, she was right there with him, still asking questions. It just amazed her that they were going to get that much milk twice a day and so many eggs every day. She told Tom, "We have never had that much in a whole month, let alone each day."

By then the chickens had come up, and he let her feed them. Tom guessed if a person had never raised chickens, it was a pretty sight to see all those chickens in one bunch. Then he thought back to the first week after he got them and remembered how excited he was over them and how glad he was when he got his first egg. She wanted to know when they would have babies.

Tom laughed again, then told her, "They don't have babies. When the time comes, we will have to put eggs under them, then the eggs hatched and you have baby chickens."

Again, she was so excited. She said, "Tom, can we have some babies right away."

Tom told her, "No, the hens will let you know when they are ready to hatch some babies, then you give her the eggs."

She wanted to know, "How does the hen let us know?" Before Tom could tell her, she told him, "Oh, Tom, don't laugh at me. I have to know so I can give them eggs when they want them."

He told her, "When they want eggs, they start staying on the nest all the time. They are not hard to spot."

Ettie wanted to know, "Where do I get eggs to put under them?"

Tom told her, "You take the eggs you gather from all the nest and pick good-shaped ones, then put them under her."

Again, she asked, "The hen want mind if they are not all her eggs?"

Tom told her, "No, she will hatch anything that is put under her, even turkey, duck, or guinea eggs."

She asked, "Can we get some of each and let them hatch them?"

He told her, "I don't know what you will do with ducks and guineas, but I guess we could if you want to. First thing, we will have to find someone who has some eggs that we could get."

She was so excited, Tom told her, "Ettie, I haven't handed you the moon on a silver platter."

With tears in her eyes she hugged him and said, "Tom, you don't know it, but yes, you have. You have given me a roof over my head, plenty of food to eat, and someone to love me and take care of me. What more could a girl ask for? Ever since Daddy died, we hadn't had any of that. Mama tried so hard, but there was no way she could pay rent and buy groceries on a dollar and half a week. If we were lucky she might get two dollars but that was very seldom."

Tom put his arms around her and promised her, "You won't be hungry again, and I will take care of you from now on."

Everything amazed her, and she was so eager to learn it all. Tom showed her where he had stored the potatoes and hung the onions and asked her if she would like to have some fried potatoes for supper. Then he showed her the sweet potato row and how to dig into the ditch and get them. She wanted to know, "Is that all potatoes?" She was so excited over so much food. She wanted to know if they could have baked sweet potatoes for dinner tomorrow. Tom told her they could have them any time they wanted them. After that they went by the smokehouse, and Tom sliced some venison steak off a deer he had just killed and dressed out right before he came for her. They took the meat, some onions, and the potatoes into the dugout. Tom asked her did she know how to cook the meat. She told him they never had meat at home, but yes, she did know how to cook it. She was amazed at all the food they had. She was a real good cook, and it wasn't long until she had a supper fit for a king. She fried the potatoes and steak, opened some green beans and corn, made gravy and hot biscuits. Tom kidded her about where was the company, but it sure was all good. She made a pot of coffee for him, and she tried to drink some with him, but he could see she didn't like it. He thought back to a little eight-year-old boy that had done the same thing years ago. Tom told her, you don't have to drink it just because I do." But she, like Tom had, said, "Oh I know, but I like it." So after that first night, he would drink milk with his meal and his coffee later, and each time she would pour her a cup also and try to drink it with him. They would clean up the kitchen, then sit down in their rockers, have their coffee, and she would tell him all she had done that day, unless she had been with him all day. Then they talked about what they had gotten done that day. She asked Tom to say grace always at every meal and thank God for all the things He had given them. Tom said, "I always say grace at every meal." Then she would say, "Now, Tom, always thank Him also for what we have accomplished today, regardless of what it was."

She was so eager to do her part, she told him, "Now feeding the chickens, the hogs, and gathering the eggs is my job."

Tom told her, "You can feed the chickens and gather the eggs, but the hog feeding I will do. The buckets would be too heavy for you to carry."

She wanted to know, "Can I go with you then, just in case you did need me."

Tom hugged her and told her, "Always."

Jim and Tom went coon hunting at night as long as it wasn't too cold. He hated to leave her, but he told her they would need the money the hides brought to help them until they got the crop money and sold the calves and hogs this fall.

As soon as they went to town, Tom bought an extra gun for her and started teaching her how to shoot it. She learned fast, and it wasn't long until she could shoot and hit her target real good. Tom didn't teach her how to draw from a holster because he didn't think she would need to know that.

Tom told her, "This gun is to be used to defend yourself in case I'm not here and someone or something threatens your life. Don't be afraid to shoot it, if necessary. I want you to feel free to come and go at all times around here without being afraid, so when I won't be here, I want you to have the gun with you or close by at all times."

She said, "Tom, I don't think I could shoot at something or someone."

He told her, just like Mr. Heart told him, "Now, Ettie, if something is threatening your life, make up your mind. It's either you or them, and this is your home, and they don't belong here. Talk first, if it's a man, but don't let anyone get close enough to take your gun. God gave you the right to defend yourself and to protect your life. Your life is just as important to you as his is to him, and you belong here and he doesn't."

They went to church their first Sunday home. Ettie worked all Saturday making a cake and fixing food to take. She was so excited about fixing it and kept wanting Tom to taste to see if it was all right. She wore the white dress she wore when they got married. She still looked like an angel in it. Again Tom told her he didn't know God had given him an angel. She hugged him and said. "Oh, Tom, I hope you will always be proud of me." They stopped by and picked up the Ruckers. Tom introduced Ettie to them. They all said they had been dying to meet her ever since John and Jim had told them about her and, yes, she was just as pretty as they said she was. Dora had quilts to put in the wagon for all the children to sit on. They all got in, and Dora got up on the seat beside Ettie and Tom.

After church, the preacher had Ettie and Tom come to the front. He said, "I know all of you have been wondering who this beautiful young lady was, that's with Tom today. Let me introduce to you Mr. and Mrs. Tom Brisco. Now I want all of you to make Ettie feel welcome and make her feel like she is just one of us."

They all came by and congratulated them, and all the ladies hugged Ettie. After the service they all went to the kitchen and put their food on the tables. The preacher blessed the food, and everyone bragged on Ettie's dishes. They were all real good. Her cake was outstanding. Several ladies asked for her recipe. She just beamed. She was so tickled over it. She told them she would bring it next Sunday.

This area was a country community. Everyone came in wagons or buggies, some coming several miles. They all had night chores to do. So on Sunday, they had Sunday school, then the worship service. After that they had dinner, then the woman cleaned up everything while the men played dominoes or just talked about their crops or cattle. The small children played and were cautioned not to get their clothes dirty. The teenagers had their own way of laughing, teasing, and playing games. After the women got through, they sat around talking, exchanging recipes, and the usual women's talk. About three o'clock they went back and had another brief service and went home to get the chores done before it got dark.

Ettie was so excited about the service and getting to meet the ladies. She and Dora talked all the way home. When they got to the ranch, they went by and dropped off the Ruckers. They left with Dora promising she would come down and visit with Ettie as soon as she could. As soon as they got to the dugout, Ettie ran in and changed her clothes while Tom unhitched the team. Before he was finished, she was back out going to feed the chickens and to gather up the eggs. She was through by the time Tom got his clothes changed and had got the hog feed ready to go feed them. She always went with him to make sure he didn't need her to help him, and wherever Ettie went, you could count on Skitter being right there beside her.

When they finished feeding the hogs, she took the buckets to the shed and put the hog's corn in them while Tom got Susie from the pasture to milk. While he milked Susie, if they didn't have plenty of buttermilk or needed more milk, she would skim the cream off yesterday's milk so they would have the milk to pour over the hog's corn. When he finished milking, Tom took it into the dugout to strain. Ettie would always ask, "Did you fill Skitter's bowl?" She always made sure Skitter had his bowl of warm milk every morning and every night. She would strain the fresh milk, and Tom took the old milk and poured it over the corn so by morning it would be soured for the hog's breakfast. They tried to use the buttermilk, but on days that they didn't have enough, they used the leftover sweet milk. She churned every other day, so most of the time they had plenty of buttermilk.

The next Sunday after church, the ladies gave them another wedding shower. They got several quilts, and Tom never saw the likes of pretty knickknacks for their house. Ettie was so proud of everything. With tears in her eyes, she thanked them for everything and told them she could use every one of them.

After they got home, Tom helped her unload all the gifts. They did the night work and had supper. Tom told her, "While you look at all the gifts, I will go down and check on the cattle, and when I get back, I will help you put them away." Tom saddled Roy; and Roy, Skitter, and he went down to see about the cattle. When they got about even with the haystack, there was a great big buck eating there. Tom always took his gun, just in case he needed it. He shot it, and left Skitter there to protect it while Roy and Tom went back to the dugout. Tom had trained Skitter to guard his kill each time, and you better believe nothing got near it until he got back. When Tom got to the dugout, he hollered for Ettie and told her, "I have killed a deer, and I am going up to tell the Ruckers so they can help me hang it."

She told him, "Do what you have to do, and I will go tell them."

Tom helped her into the saddle. While he hitched up the horses to the wagon, she went to get them. They were back by the time he had everything ready. They field dressed it and loaded it on the wagon and brought it to the dugout and finished dressing it out on the wagon. The boys brought water from the spring and washed it good. They helped Tom hang his half in the smokehouse with a bucket under it to bleed out until tomorrow. They left their half on the wagon, and John drove it to his house and said, "As soon as we unloaded it, I will send the wagon back." With the deer meat and all their pork, they had more than enough to finish the winter with. Tom was tired after they got the meat hung, so he told Ettie they would just go to bed and they would put the gifts away tomorrow.

The next morning, they hurried and got the chores done, and right after breakfast, they started cutting up the deer. Ettie said, "I wouldn't mind having some dear roast," so they left the part that was steaks and roast hanging without cutting it up. The rest they saved for chili meat. It was so cold in the smokehouse. They took it in the dugout and ground it and made the chili. Ettie didn't know how to make chili or can it either, so Tom showed her how and they did it together. After they got it ready, they put the cans in the washpot and covered the cans with water. Tom built a fire around the pot, and he told her how long they had to cook it. As soon as the water started boiling, they started timing it and went in to get warm and to clean up their mess. They put away their wedding gifts while the chili cooked.

Tom asked her, "Would you like a roast for supper. Since we have to keep a fire going outside, we could cook one in the Dutch oven."

She was so excited about cooking outside like that, but she told him, "But, Tom, I have never cooked outside and I don't know how."

"Then we will do it together," Tom told her.

So they went by the smokehouse and got a roast he had already. The fresh deer meat would hang and bleed out. It was so cold in the smokehouse, they had nothing to worry about. It would keep hanging until they needed it. They went by the shed and got some onions and potatoes and the Dutch oven. They took it all into the dugout, and Tom showed her how to season the meat and put it in the bottom of the Dutch oven. Then they put the potatoes and onions on top of the roast and sprinkled some pepper and salt on top of them, then added some butter on top to season their vegetables. Later on, they would add some canned carrots. Ettie wanted to go out and see how Tom cooked it outside, so he showed her how to dig out a place in the hot coals and put the pot, then cover it with some more hot coals. Tom told her, "We don't have to worry about it until suppertime." He put some more wood around the pot, then told her, "While you go in and get warm, I will go down and see about the cattle since I didn't make it yesterday." Tom laughed. "I promise you, I won't kill another deer."

She told him, "I don't mind if you do."

But he told her, "We don't need it right now, and we only kill one when we need it for food." Tom told her what Mr. Heart told him about never killing anything unless it's for food or to save your own life.

She said, "He must have been quite a fellow from what you have told me about him."

He told her, "He was," and turned and went out with the longing in his heart just to see them both just one more time and knowing he would never see them again in this world. Again, Tom prayed, "Oh, God, why couldn't You have let them live until I could get back to see them just one more time." Then he thought, oh how they would have loved Ettie and how Granny would have spoiled her rotten. He smiled, then said out loud, "That's all right, Granny, I will spoil her enough for both of us."

Tom wiped the tears out of his eyes and went on down to saddle Roy so he could go see about the cattle. They were doing fine in spite of the cold weather. They were at the haystack eating, all counted for and all in good shape. He went by and checked the water to make sure they had a place to drink. He had taken the ax with him just in case he had to break a hole in the ice. But it still had a hole and was beginning to thaw some. When he got back to the house, he unsaddled Roy and turned him loose so he could go eat with the cattle and find a good place out of the cold wind. He went by and put some more wood under the pot. The chili was boiling real good. Tom raked some more hot coals over the Dutch oven and went in to get warm. Ettie had made some coffee for him. She poured him a cup, then she asked about the cattle. He told her all was fine, and again she wanted to know about the mama cows. Tom told her they were fine, that they were used to the cold weather. She said, "Oh, Tom, I will be so glad when March and April get here so we can have some baby calves."

They brought the chili in. When it finished cooking and after it cooled, they stored it on the shelf behind the old cans of chili. Tom told Ettie to stay in, that it was too cold for her to go out. But nothing would do her, she had to go out and help also. She told him, "Now, Tom, it will be just as cold on you, so I will help, and that way we both can get it done faster and get back out of the cold faster." So she fed the chickens, gathered up the eggs, and made sure they were locked in the henhouse. By the time she had put the eggs away, Tom had finished milking. She took it in and strained it and put it in the smokehouse after he fed the hogs. He came back, and she had put the corn in some buckets and poured the milk over it for the hog's breakfast. Tom took the dirty buckets he had and went in and washed them. Then they got the roast from out of the coals and went in for supper. Ettie added the carrots and just simmered it until the carrots were hot and the flavor went through them. She took all the vegetables up and made gravy and a pot of coffee. She had begun to drink coffee with their meal when the weather was cold. She bragged and bragged on the roast and how tender it was. She told him, "You will have to show me again, how to cook it so we can have it more often."

March finally came, and it was still cold but not as cold, as it had been. Also, Miss Molly had her babies. She had ten little pigs, all in good shape, and Ettie was so excited she got in the pen and told Miss Molly how proud of her she was. All the animals would come to her when she called to them. She seemed to have a way with animals, and all of them seemed to love her. Tom had not named the other two pigs, so she had named them Dolly and Polly. She wanted to know when they would have their babies. Tom told her, "It won't be long now." Miss Molly was feeding her brood, so Ettie got down and looked at each one to see how many males and females they had. Tom had to show her how to tell the males from the females.

About the middle of April, the cows started dropping their calves and Tom stayed busy checking on them. He wanted to make sure that none of them had any trouble calving. Dolly had her pigs, and a few days later Polly had hers. Dolly had nine, and Polly had only six. This worried Ettie because Polly had such a small litter, but Tom told her it was her first litter and probably she would do better next time.

Chapter 17

BY MAY, MOST OF THE cows had calves, and did they look pretty. Ettie and Tom would just go down and stand and watch them when they had some time. They were staying pretty busy planting the garden. They had to go in and get the seed and onion plants they needed. Tom had learned what seed to save and had most of them they needed. They had made their sweet potato bed earlier, and by the last of May they had little slips coming up. Not too long after Easter, they had the garden planted. Ettie was so proud of it. She was like a little girl. She wanted to have everything. They had cucumbers, beets, and several different kinds of squash that people had given her a start of at church. Also, she had planted radishes, cantaloupes, beans, and a few hills of watermelons. You name it, and if she could get the seed, she had planted it. Tom had to dig an extra row on each side of the garden because someone told her not to plant her watermelons and cantaloupes next to each other.

She had managed to find someone that had some turkeys, guineas, and ducks and had offered to trade some hen eggs for some. Of course, they gave her a start of each of them. Tom learned that is how country people were. If they have something that a neighbor didn't have and wanted a start, they were always glad to share it with them. So one week a woman brought her twelve guinea eggs. She put some guinea eggs and hen eggs under two hens to make a good sitting for them both. She wanted to give every hen that started nesting some eggs, but Tom told her they didn't need all that many baby chickens. By the time her guinea eggs hatched, her turkey eggs, duck eggs, and hen eggs had hatched. They had babies everywhere. Tom had to get more wire and make her extra pens for them.

He told her, "When they hatch, you can give some extra baby chickens to some of the hens, that way they won't have so many pens to drag around."

"I don't want to," she said. "It isn't fair taking the babies away from their mamas."

But after several days of dragging them around each day, she decided to give about fifteen to five different mothers.

Tom told her, "The other mothers would forget in a few days, and after a while they would start laying again."

She didn't like it at first and neither did the mother hens, but sure enough in a few days they went on off to their own business of hunting bugs, worms, and looking for seeds. That satisfied Ettie, and she was happy with not having to drag all those extra pens around each day.

Tom told her, "I don't know what we will do with that many chickens."

But she assured him that they could keep some more for laying and the roosters they could eat or sell. She told him, "Mrs. Butler at the grocery store said she could use all we had."

Tom laughed and told her, "Mrs. Butler wasn't counting on fifty some odd per day."

She told him, "Now, Tom, don't you worry, I will find places to sell all of them."

He told her, "You can have all the egg money for your very own."

By the time the chickens were pullets and started to lay, another cafe had opened in town and Ettie had made arrangements with both of them to sell them eggs. So sure enough, she sold all she had to the grocery store and the two cafes. She was quite a businesswoman. She would cull the eggs, and they used the small ones, and she sold all the large ones. The rest of the small ones she sold at a discount. They had to take them in twice a week. She got to where she drove the wagon as good as any man. Sometime she would go by herself, and sometime Dora would go, if she needed to get some things or if she didn't have anything to do. It didn't matter with Ettie. She went twice a week and took her eggs to her customers. Rain or shine, she would go. She said, "They were expecting them and needed them, so I won't let them down." She hatched more each year. Tom finally had to build her a larger henhouse. Also, she made arrangements with the cafes to take her roosters to kill for fried chicken each year, as long as she had some. With her egg money, the money from the hides and all the honey they sold, they made it just fine. She had built up quite an egg route. She continued hatching more eggs each year to replace her old hens and to make sure she got enough eggs to take care of her route and to have plenty of eggs for them.

Sometime in June, John and Tom would rob their beehives. Dora and Ettie put it in jars, and John and he would deliver it to their customers. The hives had doubled each year, and now they had quite a few hives, but they were able to sell all the honey each year and have plenty left over for both families. The garden produced real good each year, and Ettie and Tom canned all they needed each year. Some of the things she had planted Tom didn't know how to do, like cucumber pickles and beets, so she would go up and ask Dora. Also, when the fruit trees began to produce, she went up to help Dora with them. Ettie, Dora, and the girls gathered the fruit and canned it. They made all kinds of jelly, jams, and preserves. They ran out of jars and sent Tom to town for more sugar and jars to finish up with and to deliver eggs. They gathered blackberries and made blackberry jam and canned some for cobblers. Ettie said the cobblers would be real good in the winter. When canning season was over, each year they had enough canned for two winters.

Ettie always told Tom, "We don't know if the garden will produce this good next year, so let's can it while we have it." She was so proud of it. She said, "Oh, Tom, look we won't have to have anything but flour, sugar, salt, and baking powder to do us all winter. And the egg money will buy that, Tom. We are so lucky. God has given us a warm shelter to live in and plenty to eat."

Tom went over and put his arms around her and said, "And someone to love."

Right then and there they just stopped, held hands, bowed their heads, and thanked God for all the blessings He had given them.

After the first year Ettie told Tom she knew he had been worried about them living here, but it was everything they needed right now. They still needed the money from the crops and cattle to pay on the note, just like he had been doing.

"Why don't we tell the Ruckers that we want them to continue working the land and let's stay here and save the money to buy furniture when we need it. Also, we could continue paying big payments on the note. By the time we are able to take it over, we would have cash money to buy the furniture with. You won't be able to work all the land that they are working and that we do need the money from all of it."

So that night they went up and asked them if they would stay on and work the land as usual. They said they had been looking for a place to farm and hadn't found any so they would be glad to stay on. Tom told them they would still need the money for a few years to pay on the note and for them not to worry about looking for anything else for a few years. He told them, "And besides, there is no way Ettie and I could work that much land by ourselves." So it was settled. They would stay on, and Ettie and Tom would stay in the dugout. The Ruckers asked Ettie if she was sure that this was all right with her. She told them, "God has given us a roof over our heads that is warm and dry, a bed to sleep in, and plenty of food to do us all winter, what more could anyone ask for? And that one of these years, when God gives us children, we will need a larger place. But right now, we are happy and contented with what we have. That it was big aplenty for the two of us." They told them they would see them Sunday and left holding hands, as happy as they could be, and so were the Ruckers. They both had a home

They had everything pretty well caught up, so Tom asked Ettie if she would like to go with him to see J. B. They asked John and Dora to go with them, but they said they were still picking cotton but maybe next time they could. They said the boys would do the night work for them so they wouldn't have to hurry back. Tom thanked them and told them they sure would appreciate it. That way they could stay a little longer. Tom got up real early and did the outside work while Ettie got breakfast and packed their lunch. They took a coffeepot and a skillet along with some coffee, a stick of sausage, and some potatoes for their supper. They would stop and let the horses rest and cook supper and spend the night, that way they would get there early the next day. It would give them more time to visit with J. B. Ettie had made two cakes the day before, one for them to eat on the way and back, then one to take to J. B. She had put in some butter, honey, eggs, and another stick of sausage to take to him.

By the time Tom finished outside. She had breakfast ready. The food all packed and was ready to go. They ate real fast, and while Tom was getting ready, she cleaned up the kitchen. They loaded their food in the wagon and were pulling out before daylight. They camped before dark, and Ettie told him she would get supper while he tended to the horses. Tom made a fire for her, then he went to tend to the horses. That was Ettie's first time to cook over a campfire, and she really seemed to enjoy it. They slept in the back of the wagon, and it was also Ettie's first time to sleep out like that. It wasn't too comfortable, but bless her heart, Ettie never complained. She snuggled as close to Tom as she could get and said, "Oh, Tom, look at all those stars. I never knew before, there was so many."

As soon as they pulled up, J. B. came out; and as soon as he hugged Tom and told him how glad he was to see him, he asked, "Who is this beautiful lady you have with you?"

Tom was proud as punch when he told J. B., "This is my wife, Ettie. Ettie, this is that old scaly-wag J. B. that I have been telling you so much about."

He shook her hand and said, "I hope it wasn't too bad."

Ettie told him, "On the contrary, it was all good."

He asked, "Have you eaten yet?"

Ettie told him, "No, but we have brought some sausage and potatoes, and I will fix dinner if it's all right."

He told her, "Now I should do the fixing, but as Tom knows, I am not much of a cook and for a good home-cooked meal, I am not going to argue with you. Come on in, and I will show you where the kitchen is." He built a fire in the stove for her and showed her where everything was that she would need.

She told him, "Now if you would show me where the flour is, I will make you some hot biscuits."

That tickled him. He told her, "For a good homemade biscuit, I would walk a mile."

She laughed and told him, "Now don't get your hopes up to high. I don't know how good they will be."

Tom was just standing there, listening to them. J. B. seemed so pleased to see them. He, like everyone else, had already taken to Ettie. Tom told him, "She is leading you on, just wait and see, they will melt in your mouth." Tom had brought the cake in, and he handed it to J. B. and said, "Just like this chocolate cake she made."

He was so proud of it. He set it down at the table and went over to Ettie and said, "Young lady, it's been a long time since anyone had made me a chocolate cake. For that you deserve a big hug and kiss." He hugged her and kissed her on her forehead. When he turned, tears were running down his cheeks.

That was too much for Ettie. She put her arms around him, kissed him on his cheek, and said, "It won't be the last time. Now you guys go in the other room and talk while I get our dinner. Tom almost killed those poor horses driving them so hard to get here so you would have more time to talk."

It wasn't long until she called them. Her meal was fit for a king. She had fried the sausage and made gravy. She had creamed the potatoes instead of frying them and had hot biscuits.

J. B. said, "Tom, you were right. They do melt in your mouth." He told Ettie, "Young lady, I haven't eaten any biscuits like these since mama passed away. It takes a special woman to follow a man to the end of the earth and live in a dugout like we did, and Mama was one of them." He turned to Tom. "I think you have found one also."

Tom told him, "I know I have. I don't know how I ever lived without her."

She made a pot of coffee, and J. B. cut the cake. He just went on about how good it was and ate a second piece.

After dinner Ettie shooed them out of the kitchen and cleaned up everything. They talked and talked. He wanted to hear about everything and how it was doing. Ettie joined them, and they talked all afternoon. The day passed so fast, and it wasn't long until it was suppertime and then time to go to bed. The next morning Ettie fixed breakfast, and before they left, she switched the cakes and left him the whole one.

She told J. B., "The leftover cake will be enough for us, and that will be more for you."

He thanked her and again told her how good it was and that chocolate was his favorite cake. He told her, "I have some things to give you for a wedding gift." He told her they were Mama's and he hadn't found any one he wanted to have them until now. He gave her a beautiful butter bowl, honey bowl, some beautiful glass bowls. He told her that all of them were given to them in their wedding shower. She hugged him and told him how much she would treasure them. He told her, "I know you will, and that is why I want you to have them." He also gave her some beautiful quilts, and told her, "Mama spent many a day setting in that house and working on these. She would be happy knowing that when she and Tom get to move into it, that the quilts will be going back home."

Tom thanked him and told him, "Ettie will take good care of them."

J. B. told Tom, "I know she would."

Shortly after that they left, with him waving and thanking them for coming and to come back soon.

All the way home, Ettie talked about what a nice man he was. They did keep their promise and went back several times. Always Ettie would take him a chocolate cake. She got where she fixed a whole meal to take with them. She would fix some kind of good desert, such as pies, cobblers, or cakes, but she would always make a chocolate cake to leave with him. He was always thrilled to death to see them and learned to love Ettie just like she was his own daughter, and she did him. She told him he was the daddy she had never had. After a few visits, it wasn't J. B. anymore, but it was Papa.

Tom had a real good calf crop that year, and when he shipped them, the prices were good. He shipped them to the same place that he had first met Mr. Heart, and each year, he could hardly stand to go back. It always brought back the memories of the little rag-tailed boy standing there all alone and a kind man picking him up, taking him in, and giving him a home all those years. Each year he went there, it just broke his heart. Just knowing he could never go back to let them know how much he loved them and how much he appreciated everything they had done for him. One lesson he had learned that he would never forget was tell those you love how much you love them and how much you appreciate what they do for you every day because you can't go back to yesterday and relive it. Tom stood there talking to them, but they never heard it. One thing he did do, he promised Granny Heart he would tell Ettie how much he loved her and how much he appreciated everything she did for him every day. Tom thought if anyone was around to hear him, they would have thought he had lost his mind because out loud, he said, "And maybe that will make up for the many times I didn't tell her and Mr. Heart how much I loved them both."

That year they had a better calf crop than they had ever had, and they brought more than Tom had ever dreamed they would. When he got home and told Ettie, she was thrilled to death. She told him that with this they would be able to make a larger payment on the land. Tom told her the biggest payment they have ever made and they would still have some money to put back to save for their furniture and everything when the time came.

Tom had also bought her a buggy and a horse. When he got back from taking the cattle, he had stopped to pick up Roy at the stable. He saw Mr. Anderson, the stable owner, had a buggy sitting in front of his building. Tom asked Mr. Anderson if it was for sale, that he would like to buy one and a gentle horse for his wife. Mr. Anderson told him he had just bought it and a horse that went with it. He told him the horse was as gentle as a little dog. Tom looked at it and asked him, "What is the least you will take for it, cash dollars?" He finally came down to what Tom thought was a fair price, so he told him he would take it.

Tom tied Roy behind the buggy and took it home for a surprise for Ettie. She had been driving the wagon back and forth to deliver her eggs. Tom wanted her to have something better. She was inside when he got there, so he tied it on the henhouse door. After they had talked for a while, he asked her if she thought it was time to gather up the eggs.

She told him, "No silly, I never gather the eggs this early, you know that."

Tom told her, "Well, let's go out and get them early today."

She didn't want to, but finally she went with him. When she saw it she began to holler, "Oh, Tom, oh Tom, is it really for me?"

Tom told her, "Every bit of it, horse and all." She was so proud of it, and he told her, "It is a 'I love you' gift, to show you how much I love you and how much I appreciated all the things you do for me. From now on, you can drive it in place of that old wagon you have been driving."

She wiped the tears from her eyes and said, "Tom, I didn't mind driving the wagon."

Tom told her, "I know you didn't, and you have never complained, but I wanted my wife to have something better."

Ettie had a special knack with animals. They all seemed to love her, and she loved them too. If any of the animals got hurt, she would doctor and pet them until they got well. They always seem to know that she was there to help them and they always let her doctor them without too much trouble. The horse took to her just like all the other animals did, and it wasn't long until she was driving the buggy everywhere.

That winter went by real fast. It was cold most of the time, so they stayed in and only got out to tend to the animals and bring in wood. Tom delivered Ettie's eggs for her, but when it wasn't real cold, she would go with him. They wrapped up real good, and in the buggy it wasn't too bad. The buggy kept the wind from blowing on them, but they took them in once a week instead of twice.

Chapter 18

SPRING FINALLY CAME, AND WITH it the usual work of planting the garden and caring for all the babies that were born that year. One morning Tom went down to check on the cattle and see how many babies that had been born that night. Skitter was always with him. He kept running over to some bushes and barking, then coming back to Tom, as if he wanted him to follow him. Tom went over to where he was, and there was a dead mama coon. She had babies, and he guess something had killed her while she was fighting to save her babies. They had all starved to death except one, and it was about starved. Tom put it inside his coat and took it in to Ettie. She would know how to care for it. She was so proud of it. She wrapped it in one of her towels and put it next to the stove, talking to it all the time, telling it not to worry she would get it warm and give it some warm milk and then it would be all right. She warmed the milk and spooned it into its mouth. She didn't give it much at a time, so it could digest it slow enough, to kept it from making it sick. It drank like it was starving to death, and each time wanted more. She rocked it and held it next to her body to keep it warm all afternoon. That night she put it in a small box and wrapped it with a towel, leaving part of the top open, and when they got ready to go to bed, she put the box on the far side of the bed, next to her.

Tom teased her about her baby, and she told him, "Now, Tom, I have to keep it warm." She got up every few hours all night and warmed some milk and fed it. That went on for several weeks. By then its eyes were open, and it was going everywhere. She had Tom grind some meat to give it. She made the meat in little balls and put it on the floor and put a bowl of water next to it. She would wet the meat in the water and give it to him. She kept doing this hoping he would realize what she was doing and do it for himself. Finally, she just made the balls and would hand them one at a time to him and take him over to the bowl of water and dip his paw with the meat in it into the water. In about a week, he was doing it on his own and was running all over the house. In the daytime, he would get in his box that Ettie kept sitting close to the stove when he wanted to take a nap, but at night he would go over to the bed to sleep next to Ettie. She would put his box next to her, and he would crawl into it and go sound to sleep. At night, if his box wasn't on the bed when he got ready for it, he would climb upon the bed and lie there waiting for her. He tolerated Tom, but to him, Ettie was his mama and he didn't like Tom getting too close to her. When they sit down in their rockers after supper, he would always climb up in her lap and lie there, with her rocking and singing to him until bedtime.

The years came and went, and before long Ettie and Tom was celebrating their third anniversary. He had kept his promise to Granny. Every night before he went to bed he would tell Ettie how much he loved her and how much he appreciated all she did for him. Each time he had to leave her to take the cattle or hogs off, he would bring her some little something back to let her know how much he cared for her. He would always tell her how happy she had made him all these years.

That fall, John and Dora came down to talk to them. They told them that they were going to have to give up the place.

That John and Joan, both, were getting married; and Jim and Mark had been offered real good jobs on a ranch. That there was no way that the rest of them could work that many acres. That John's health wasn't as good as it used to be. John told them they had found a ranch to manage that paid a salary and furnished a house. He said that would be easier on all of them. Tom told him that he understood and wished them the best of luck. John told them they weren't moving too far away, that they would be able to come to church on Sunday and that they would see them each week at church. Ettie told them, "I don't know how we can ever manage without ya'll. Ya'll both had taught us so much." She laughed. "I will probably have a list each Sunday of things that I need Dora to tell me how to do. We will miss you, but God always knows what's best for all of us."

Tom asked John, "When will ya'll be leaving?"

He said, "As soon as we can finish getting the crops in. The people want us as soon as possible." He told him about a family that wanted to rent some farmland to work. They didn't want the house but only wanted to rent the land on the thirds and fourths like he was doing. Tom told him he would talk to them, but he wanted someone that was honest and dependable. John told him, as far as he knew, that Mr. Yodel was. He has a small place but not enough land to make his large family a living.

That night, Ettie told Tom, "You know, Tom, God takes care of problems a lot of time before we even know we have them. Oh, Tom, isn't God wonderful."

He knew that there would be a time when the Ruckers would have to quit farming and would have to move and by then they could afford to move into the large house. Tom asked her, "Are you getting tired of the dugout?"

She said, "No, Tom, but I thought it would be awful crowded with a baby crib in it, don't you?"

Tom was so shocked he didn't know what to say. He finally said, "Ettie, are you sure? It's been so long."

She told him, "Yes, Tom, I am sure, the Lord has finally answered our prayer."

Again, Tom asked her, "Are you sure?" He didn't want her to get her hopes up and be disappointed.

She told him, "It is true, and I am about two months. I didn't want to tell you until I was absolutely sure and now I am. Are you as thrilled as I am?"

Tom put his arms around her and told her, "I am so shocked I can't think of anything to say. I had just about given up hope that we would ever have one of our own."

She told him, "I had too, and it just broke my heart to think that God hadn't let me have children. I had prayed and prayed that God would give us a baby."

They started making all kinds of plans that night. Tom told her their little town wouldn't have any furniture and they would have to go somewhere else to get the furniture they needed. So they started making a list of what all they would need.

Ettie told Tom, "We will only need two-bedroom suites, a living room suite, and a dining room suite. Our stove is perfectly good, and so is the table and chairs for the kitchen." She wanted to know if they had enough money in their household money to buy all this.

Tom told her, "I think with what we have been saving each year we will have plenty."

Ettie told him, "I have all my egg money. That way I could buy what the baby will need with it."

They went to sleep planning on what they were going to do to the house and about all the plans they had for their little one. The last thing Tom remembered her saying was, "I can hardly wait until Sunday to tell Dora. I didn't tell her tonight because I wanted to tell you first. Tom, isn't it wonderful?"

That Sunday, they told them about the baby. They were tickled to death for them and said, "We had wondered what Ettie meant when she said, 'God would work it out for all of us.'"

Dora said, "John and I had talked about it, and John had said, 'Wonder if she is expecting at last.' He hoped so. John said Tom deserves a son of his own, he is so good with children and has so much to teach a son."

The next morning, they decided to go get their furniture while the Ruckers were still there to see to the place and the animals for them. They wouldn't be able to go after they left because someone would have to be there to take care of the livestock while they were gone and gather up the eggs and deliver them. Tom went up to the Ruckers to find out if the boys could take care of the livestock while they were gone. They said they would be glad to. It was almost two days' drive to a town that was big enough to have a place to buy furniture, so they would be gone at least five days. They packed their clothes, some quilts, some food, a Dutch oven, and a coffeepot. They would be camping out one or two nights, going and coming. While Tom packed everything, Ettie made a cake for them to take along. They filled the water containers up, and it wasn't any time until they were stopping at the Ruckers to tell them that they were gone. Tom didn't push the team real fast that day, and they stopped to let Ettie and the horses rest along. They stopped at noon for lunch.

Ettie had fried some sausage and put them in between some biscuits that morning, so Tom made a pot of coffee. They leaned back against a tree trunk and ate their sausage and biscuits and drank some hot coffee. Tom got a pillow and some quilts out of the wagon and told Ettie he wanted her to lie down while he cleaned up everything. There was a creek close by, so he went after some water and put it on to heat. It wasn't long until Ettie was sound to sleep. Tom finished cleaning up and put everything back in the wagon. He checked the horses to make sure they were hobbled good. He wanted to make sure they couldn't wonder off to far while they slept. Then he got a pillow and laid down beside Ettie and went to sleep also.

They slept for about an hour before Ettie was calling to him to wake up. She told Tom, "Don't you think we had better get started, so we can get halfway there by tonight." Tom knew they wouldn't, but he didn't tell her because he didn't want to push too fast. Tom wanted to make sure she didn't get too tired. They had the little one to think of. Later on, he stopped for another break. He made the excuses that they had to let the horses rest for a while. So he hobbled them so they could graze while they rested. They had been lucky. They had the creek beside them all morning. Like Bob always said, "You can't always count on it being there," so he went down and filled their canteens with some cold water so if they left the river they would still have plenty of cold water. They rested for about thirty minutes, by then Ettie was raring to go. She told Tom, "If you keep stopping every hour or so we are never going to get there." She assured him she was all right and she wasn't going to do anything to hurt the baby, that when she began to get tired she would tell him, then they could stop.

They had to camp out three nights. Ettie, as usual, never complained once. When they stopped at night, Tom would make sure it was a nice shady place with trees big enough to camp under to sort of protect them, as Bob told him. With the low-hanging branches, it would help keep the dew or rain from getting their bedding wet. They would make their beds in the wagon and the sideboards kept the wind from blowing right on them. He would build the fire, and while he tended to the horses, Ettie would fix supper. She always had a good meal for them, and they would eat and talk about their plans for the little one. Then they would clean up their mess, bank their fire, and go to bed. It wasn't the most comfortable bed in the whole world, but it wasn't that hard either. They were so happy about the baby, getting furniture, and at last being able to move into their own house it didn't bother them at all.

They came to the city limits on the morning of the third day. It had taken them a lot longer than if Tom had come by himself, but he wanted her to pick out the things she wanted for the house. They had barely got inside the city limits when they saw this man putting up a sign in front of this real nice house. Ettie said, "Look, Tom, it says 'Furniture for Sale.' Let's stop and look."

The man told them, "I want to sell out fast so I can get back to my own home." It reminded Tom of when Aunt Lou died and how her kids had done. The man took them in to look. He had three nice bedroom suites, a nice dining set with a beautiful china closet, a couch, two chairs, and some nice tables in the sitting room.

Ettie told Tom, "They are nicer than what we could afford to buy right now."

The man told them, "I have to sell real fast and get back to my job. If you would take it all, I would let you have it real cheap."

Ettie told Tom, "I would be perfectly happy with it."

Tom asked the man what he would take for all of it, and he quoted him a price that was dirt cheap. Tom told Ettie, "I really wanted to buy you some new furniture. Are you sure you would be happy with this?"

Before she could answer him, the man told them he needed to get back home as soon as he could and he had to get rid of it before he left, that he had the place sold but they didn't want the furniture. He told them if they would take it today and clean out the whole house, they could have everything in it—

lamps, dishes, what's in the china closet, and everything. All he asked, is they leave it clean for the people that's buying it. He quoted another price lower than he had already said.

Before Tom could say anything, Ettie said, "We will take it."

Tom laughed and said, "Whoa now, how long would we have to get it out and the house cleaned if we decided to take it." Tom told him their situation and how far they had to take it.

The man said, "The people won't be coming down for a month or two. I am to mail the key to them when I have everything out and it was ready. So I could leave the key with you, and as soon as you have everything out, you could mail it to them. But they did insist it be left perfectly clean as they would be shipping their furniture with them when they come and wanted to move right in. They said that meant dusted, swept, moped, and everything. And if I didn't want to agree to those terms then, they wouldn't buy it. They won't be closing the deal until they get here." So he wanted Tom's word that if they bought the furniture, they would leave it spotless.

Tom told him, "We will clean it from top to bottom, but it will be according to how long it will be, before they get here, whether it stays that way or not. You know, if they don't get here before two months, it will be dusty again. There is no way we could come back, as far away as we live, to dust it every week. If they want it perfectly clean and dusted right before they move in, you would probably have to hire someone to dust it that week before they get here. You know as well as I do that it won't stay clean for two months."

Mr. Scott thought about it and finally told Tom, "I guess you are right. I hadn't thought of that. I guess I had better find someone here to dust it the day before they are to get here."

Tom told him, "We will take it at the deal you quoted us, and we will leave it as clean as it can be left. That means house, barn, and yard. But the last-minute dusting you would have to see to that."

He agreed and told him, "I will have to let you know where to leave the key under those circumstances."

Tom paid him and got a receipt and asked him, "Where could we find a furniture store? We will be needing a baby bed also."

He congratulated them and told them how to get to the closest one. He told them, "I can help you load the wagon if you plan on taking a load with you."

Tom told him, "I would appreciate it, and we will be back as soon as we check on a baby bed. If you are going to find someone to dust it and a place for him to leave the key, you could ride down with us."

So they all got on the wagon and went down. It didn't take them long to find the furniture store, and they did have a baby bed. Ettie suggested they buy it and let them hold it until the last load. That way they could carry a bigger load of things they needed to move right now. They agreed, so Tom paid them and got a receipt. Tom told Ettie they would stop at the grocery store and pick up a few groceries they would need for the trip back. Mr. Scott was at the grocery store. He had made arrangement with the lady there to dust the house and for Tom to leave the key when he was through with it. They got their groceries, then went back down to load the wagon. The kitchen drawers were full of cup towels and dishrags.

Ettie asked him, "What are we supposed to do with them?"

He told her, "You will need them to wrap the dishes out of the cabinet and the china closet in."

There were several tubs outside, so he got them for her, and she started packing the dishes. They decided to take all the mattresses, bed lamps, dishes, and pictures first. That way they could pack the beds in between the mattresses so they would not get scarred. On top of the mattresses, they could put the dining table upside down and inside the table they could put the dishes. Then they could fill in with whatever else would go. That way they would have all the breakable things packed and moved while Ettie was there to wrap them. They left plenty of quilts and sheets to wrap the chester drawers, dressers, couch, and other tables in so they wouldn't get anything scratched. By late that afternoon they had the wagon loaded to the brim and were ready to go. Tom had made sideboards for the wagon before he left home, and he sure was glad he had.

Tom found enough rope in the barn and tied everything down good so nothing would fall off and get broken. Mr. Scott told Tom again, "I want the house, barn, and everything completely cleaned. I do mean spick and span when ya'll finished up. I don't want anything left outside or inside."

Tom told him, "It will be."

Mr. Scott told him, "When you finish, just leave the key with the woman at the grocery store and I will let her know when to dust and finish it up."

They put a few odds and ends in the barn so no one would take them. Then he locked the door, shook his hand, thanked him, and was ready to go.

Tom promised him, "Now you don't have to worry. It will be spick and span inside and out when I finish and give her the key."

He and Ettie, both, thanked him again, waved to him, and were on their way.

Tom told Ettie, "I would like to make a few miles before dark, but we won't travel to fast and when you need to stop, let me know."

She promised Tom she would.

They had picked up some cheese and crackers and an onion for their dinner, but being so busy they hadn't stopped to eat. They had filled their canteens up right before they left the Scott's place. They drove along, eating their dinner just as happy as two kids could be after getting their first furniture and for getting to move into their first home, for the baby, and everything that God had given them. Right then they stopped the wagon and just bowed their heads and thanked Him for it all.

Tom had tied the quilts they had brought from home over the whole load so he could get to them to make a pallet for them to lay on when Ettie got tired. About three, Tom found a real shady place with plenty of good grass for the horses to eat and a creek close by. He told Ettie this is where they would stop and rest for a while. She began to protest, that she wasn't tired, but Tom told her, "No, but the horses are." So he took the quilts off the wagon and made her a pallet and told her. "Lie down while I unhitch the horses and water them." He hobbled them so they could rest and eat, and then he laid down beside Ettie. It wasn't long until she was fast asleep. At about four she was calling him, she said, "I think the horses have rested enough." So Tom got up and hitched them up again and tied the quilts back over the wagon, and it wasn't long until they were ready to go again. They stopped in plenty of time to get supper before it got dark. Tom tended to the horses, then made a small fire. He told Ettie he would lay the quilts out and she could lie down while he got supper. But she would have no part of that. She said, "Now, I will get supper while you rest for a while." They finally compromised, and they both got it. Tom fixed the coffee while she made biscuits, then they peeled some potatoes and fried them along with some sausage. By the time the biscuits were done, the potatoes and sausage were ready also and the coffee was done. They leaned back against a tree trunk like two kids on a picnic. They still had some of the cake left, some butter and jelly, bacon and eggs. So they ate some of the cake with a second cup of coffee. The eggs, butter, bacon, and jelly, they would save for breakfast each morning.

On the way up, they had slept in the bed of the wagon. But now they had a full load, and Tom made them a pallet on the ground. Ettie was afraid a snake would get on the bed, so Tom kept a small fire burning next to her side of the pallet so she could see. He didn't think she slept very much all night because every time he woke up to put some wood on the fire, she would beat him to it. So he just made sure there was plenty of wood for her each time. She was up before daylight, putting more wood on the fire and starting breakfast. Before it was light enough to see, they had eaten breakfast and had everything packed, back into the wagon, and ready to go. Tom went after the horses and stopped by the creek to make sure they had a good drink before they started out. He took them up to the camp and hitched them to the wagon, and they left before daylight.

In the middle of the morning, Tom had to insist that they stop and rest for a while. She told him she wasn't tired, but he told her, "Yes, but the horses are. They are pulling a heavy load." He put the quilts down and told her to lie down and he would make them a pot of coffee, but before it was ready, she was fast asleep. Tom drank a cup and laid down beside her. They both sleep for about an hour before they finally woke up.

He hitched the horses up, and they were ready to go again. She was so afraid of something getting on their bed at night until after that first night. They traveled a lot at night and slept more during the day. It still took them a little more than three and a half days to get back. On the fourth morning, Tom started worrying where they were going to put all this stuff. Ettie said, "Don't worry, we can put it on the long porch at the Ruckers until they move, and we can cover it good like we have it now." The Ruckers had already been taking some things that they didn't need over at night, so the porch was empty. They helped Tom unload the wagon and cover it up good. Tom tied some of the rope he had brought from the Scott's around it like he had done on the wagon. Tom told the Ruckers what he and Ettie had done. They were real tickled for them and told them that Tom could use their two wagons and that two of the boys could go and help him move it all. After they got moved, the boys wouldn't have anything to do for a while.

By the end of the week, the Ruckers had finished gathering the crop, had settled with Tom, and was moving out. Tom took his wagon and helped them move. With eleven of them, it didn't take long to load and unload the wagons. They had to make three trips each, the going and coming was what took so long, but they finished moving everything from the house in three days. On the last load, Dora and the girls went with them and they tied the two cows behind one of the wagons.

The next day, they came back, and they moved all of the outside things, including the hogs and chickens. John sold Tom his half of the bees, and he also bought a plow, a set of mules to plow with, and some farm tools.

Before they left, they helped Tom move all the things from the front porch into the house and John gave them the key. He and Dora told them how much they had enjoyed working for them and how much they had appreciated everything Tom had done for them through all these years. Tom told them it was the other way around, that he didn't know how he would have ever made it without them those first few years. After they got them moved, they decided to give the horses a rest before they went back after the rest of the furniture. It would take several days, and the horses had been working hard for the last two weeks. It was Thursday when they finished up, so they decided to wait and leave on Monday.

The next few days, Tom spent building taller sideboards to go on all three wagons. After moving the Ruckers, he saw real quick that he would need taller sideboards on the wagons with them moving furniture that far. He finished up on Saturday and was ready to leave on Monday.

They went to church on Sunday, and it was like they hadn't seen the Ruckers in no telling when. They all came around and told them hello. Dora and the girls hugged Ettie and told her how much they missed her already.

Martha had agreed to come and stay with Ettie while Tom, Jimmy, and Mark were gone. Billy decided they needed a man around, just in case one was needed, so he volunteered to stay also. He said Ettie would need someone to do the outside work. After church that afternoon, Tom and Ettie left with Martha, telling them they would see them bright and early in the morning.

Also, Tom and Ettie had talked it over and had agreed now was the time to send for Sallie. So he had written a letter for her to mail with money in it telling Sallie to come in three weeks. Ettie would see that it got put on the train when the three of them took the eggs in. In three weeks they would be in the house with a place for Sallie to stay.

Early the next morning, the boys were there with the two wagons. They had to put the taller sideboards on the wagon. Tom had been praying they would fit without him having to remake them, and sure enough they did. While they waited for them, Ettie had packed some food and made two cakes. She said one was for going up and one was for coming back. She had packed two sticks of sausage, bacon, eggs, potatoes, butter and jelly, and a gallon of milk. She said it was for the first day. She laughed and told Tom, "I don't want ya'll to get hungry." Without Ettie they could make better time. Tom thought they could make it in a little more than four days there and back. They left with all three of them waving and Ettie telling them, "Be careful and hurry back."

Billy hollered, "Tom, you don't have to worry about the womenfolks. I will take real good care of them."

Tom hollered back, "I know you will, and I appreciate it."

They made good time, and by noon they had covered over a third of the distant. They stopped by the creek where Ettie and Tom had stopped before. While he built a small fire and made a pot of coffee, the boys watered the horses and hobbled them so they could rest and also eat. They ate the cold biscuits, eggs, and sausage that Ettie had made that morning. The boys drank milk, but Tom had a cup of coffee, and he sure did need it for the last hour or so he had been so sleepy he had almost fell off the wagon several times. The boys were really enjoying it. They had never seen this part of the country and were taking in everything. Tom was so sleepy he told the boys they would rest for a while, then have their cake and coffee when they woke up. They had brought all the quilts back that they had the first load of furniture wrapped in. So they had enough for all three of them to have real soft pallets. They laid down and was so tired Tom thought they all fell asleep immediately.

They slept for about two hours. Again, that afternoon they made good time. Tom told the boys, "If we make as good of time tomorrow, we should be there late that afternoon. We could be loaded and, on our way, back early the following morning." They stopped just in time for them to get their supper fixed and over with before dark. Again, Tom built the fire and started supper while the boys took care of the horses. He made a big Dutch oven full of biscuits and fried some sausage and potatoes. While they fried, he made coffee, and when the sausage was done, he made a big skillet of gravy. Mark and Jimmy had never camped out, and they were really enjoying it. They both ate until Tom thought they were going to burst. After supper he told them he would clean up their mess while they checked the horses. Tom told them, "Make sure they are hobbled good.

We sure don't want to lose them during the night." By the time they had checked all six of the horses and got back, he had finished cleaning up everything. They sat around the fire and talked for a while. Then they all had a big piece of cake and a cup of coffee.

Jimmy told Tom, "I sure am enjoying camping out."

Jimmy said, "Camping out with Tom was what made me want to go to work on a ranch. I hope to have one of my own, like Tom's, one of these days."

Tom told him, "It is a lot of enjoyment, but it's a lot of hard work too. Especially in the winter and when the cattle began to calf. Then I stay busy day and night checking on them and circumcising the males so they will be ready at shipping time. They have to be checked every day to make sure blowflies don't find a cut place to get in and lay eggs. If that happens, it creates a big problem."

They talked awhile longer, but they had a busy and a hard day, so it wasn't too much longer until they all decided to turn in. They were like Ettie. They weren't too thrilled at the thought of sleeping out on the ground, so they all took their quilts and slept in their wagons.

They got up real early and ate breakfast, and as soon as they could see to hitch up the wagons, they were ready to go. They made real good time that morning. At noon they stopped and ate dinner and rested for about two hours or better. They had made a lot better time than Tom had thought they would.

He told the boys, "There is a creek and a place with plenty of grass just before we get to where we are going. We should get there around six, give or take a little. What do ya'll think about us stopping there and letting the horses rest and eat, until morning? We could go on, but there was no pasture for the horses to have water or grass. They needed plenty of food and rest before we start back with heavy loads like we will be carrying."

They both agreed that would be best, so it was settled. They would stay there and get up real early like they had this morning and be there before sunup. They got there by five thirty or so, and by dark they had hobbled the horses, ate supper, and were ready to go to bed. They didn't stay up and talk any that night; they were all tired and sleepy. As soon as they had checked the horses they all made their beds in the wagons and went to bed.

They got to the house the next morning just when the sun was coming up. It took a whole lot longer to load it all than Tom thought it would. They took all the drawers out of everything, and they were still heavy. Tom told Mark and Jimmy, "Back the wagon right up against the porch." With one of them holding the team to keep them from walking away from the porch and two trying to load the furniture, it was still too heavy. Tom decided they needed more help to load it all. So he walked up the road and got two men to come and help them load it, and even taking all the drawers out of everything, it still took the four of them to load them onto the wagons. The bedroom furniture and the dining room furniture were solid oak or pecan. The living room had two tables, two end tables, and a large coffee table. They all had marble tops and were oak. With the couch and two chairs, another small china cabinet, plus the kitchen stove, it all made a big load for three wagons to carry. With the help of the two men, they had it all loaded by one o'clock and was ready to pull out. They tried their best to distribute the weight evenly on all three wagons so it wouldn't be too hard on any of the horses. Even so, it still was big loads for them to pull that far. After they got it all loaded, Tom paid the men and thanked them for helping them. Then Tom made sure it was all tied down good and checked the house to make sure it was locked it up.

The trip back would take longer because they would have to stop and let the horses rest more often. They took their time, and about every three or four hours, they would stop and unhitch the horses and let them eat, drink, or just rest for an hour or better. By then the strain of driving such heavy loads, they were all ready to find a shade and rest too. It was real nerve-racking, driving a wagon loaded so heavy and having to be real careful with the furniture. He had told the boys, "Drive slow and watch your loads. We sure don't want the loads to shift and loose or scratch anything." Tom had made sure it was tied down good, but still, they didn't want to take any chances. The roads were dirt roads and weren't to smooth either, so they did drive pretty slow. And each time they stopped, they checked the ropes to make sure they were still tight. At night they would stop early to give the horses plenty of time to eat and rest for the next day.

The boys seemed to always enjoy fixing the meals and camping out. They asked, "Tom, is this the way you did when you were a real cowboy?" They would set around the campfire, and he would tell them stories about the things that had happened to him while he was on the ranch. Tom told them how he learned to shoot and why, how he learned to rope, and all the other things that had happened to him while he was there. Of course, it wouldn't be complete without telling them about Granny Heart and her great faith in him. They got a big kick out of her dance each time he accomplished something.

They laughed and said, "She must have been quite a woman."

Tom told them, "She was."

He was glad it was dark enough that they couldn't see the tears running down his face. Then he told them about the most wonderful man he had ever known and how Mr. Heart had picked him up and raised him as his very own son. He told them how he had waited too late to tell them both how much he loved them.

Tom told them, "Always tell those you love every day that you love them. Don't be afraid to tell them because tomorrow you might not get a chance."

While Tom was telling them these things, oh how they brought back memories and how he longed to go back just one more time. Again, he thought, *Oh, God, why did you have to let them die before I could go back?* Then Tom thought about J. B. *You have given me another precious friend, and I won't make that same mistake twice.*

He decided as soon as they got back and everything taken care of, Ettie, Sallie, and he would go see J. B. and tell him about the baby. They didn't have any trouble, and the trip went well. It was just long and nerve-racking. Both of the boys seem to look forward to their stops each time and especially the nights when they sat around the campfire, drinking coffee, eating cake, and talking. It took them almost three days to get back.

Chapter 19

THEY HAD DECIDED THAT THEY would just back the wagons up so they could unload them each on the porch. Mark said he thought it would be best that way and they would ride the horses home and come back the next day with some help to unload them.

It seemed Martha, Billy, and Ettie had really enjoyed themselves. They had been to town twice in the buggy to deliver the eggs. They had taken the whole day and looked around. Martha had found some pretty material for a dress, and Billy had found a knife that he just couldn't do without. So Ettie had paid them in advance for staying with her. After that, she and Martha would go up to the house and work some each day on it, playing dominos with Billy each night. Tom and the boys went down to the dugout shortly after they got the wagons backed up to the house and picked up Martha and Billy.

Billy told Tom, "The dugout was kinda crowded, but Ettie sure made real good chocolate candy and popped corn and that made up for it."

They all asked if they had any left, and Billy said, "Shoot no, we ate all of it."

Both boys asked him, "Was that fair?"

He seemed to think that it was, but Tom and the boys didn't agree with him. With them promising to see them the next day, Mark said, "We would like to get home before dark.

With us riding the horses bareback, we will be cutting it close already."

Tom and Ettie thanked them and waved at them until they were out of sight.

Tom asked Ettie, "Did you mail the letter to Sallie?"

She told him, "The next day after you left. Also, we have cleaned all the windows, took most of the canned goods up to the house, and have put them away."

He laughed and told her, "I thought you said ya'll played most of the time."

She said, "That was at night and when we rested, silly."

The Ruckers were back the next day before noon. Dora and the girls came with them; and between her, Ettie, and the two girls, they got the furniture all put in the right rooms and in the right places. Dora just had a fit over the furniture. It did look real pretty when they got it all arranged right and the lamps and everything in place.

Dora said, "Now all it needs were some curtains and the beds made."

Tom told her, "Coming right up," and went after the curtains and the quilts that were on each bed. "All the curtains need to be washed."

She looked at them real good and said, "Tom, I don't think they even need that. We could hang them on the line and let the wind blow through them awhile, and I think that would be all they need before we hang them. The girls and I will make the beds, then if Ettie will tell us what rooms she wants each set in, then we can hang each set with the quilt to match on the line."

Ettie agreed, "I think that is all they need too."

So Tom brought each set of curtains and quilts that was in each bedroom and laid them together. When he and Ettie had taken them down, he had folded them and the quilt together. Tom had thought, just in case they wanted them that way when they put them up. He put the dining room and living room curtains in the room they would go in. All the bedroom curtains and quilts he put on one bed in sets like he took them down. He told them, "Ettie can choose which group to put where." Tom thought they all decided together. They took each set from room to room before they finally decided on which set would look prettiest where.

When they had made up their mind, Dora and the girls took each set along with the quilt and hung it on the line to air good. Tom thought, boy was he glad he had been real careful folding them and had wrapped them good in several sheets. Dora had left her clotheslines, and she had quite a few lines, so they were able to get all the bedroom curtains and quilts hung out at one time. They hung the sets together so they would know what quilt went with what curtains.

While they were airing, Tom went after the sheets and pillowcases at the dugout. They made up all three beds while he brought in all the lamps, pictures, and trinkets that belonged in each room. Ettie had packed them in a tub for each room, but Tom hadn't kept them separated. But she said that didn't matter, that they would put them where they wanted them anyway. There were several nice hurricane lamps with glass shades. She had wrapped them really good and put them all in some long tin bath tubes. All these things Ettie and Tom had brought home first with her telling him over and over, "Those are glass. Be real careful with them." He had and they got there without breaking anything. They unpacked them all and hung pictures and put the trinkets around everywhere. After that they brought in one group of curtains and quilt. When they got the quilt put on the bed and the curtains hung, it sure was pretty. As they brought in one set, they would take out the dining room curtains and the living room curtains until they were all aired and hung when they got through.

Later Tom would bring all the glassware that they had gotten in their wedding shower that they still had packed in boxes and then put them in the china closet and the kitchen cabinet. They had gotten a small china cabinet and a small breakfast table and four chairs with all the furniture. With all they had got, they wouldn't have to move anything from the dugout except their good things that they had gotten in their shower and their clothes. John had built some clothes closets in the bedrooms to put clothes in with shelves up over them for quilts, and what have you.

With all the quilts J. B. and Jack had given Tom, the quilts they got in their showers, and now the quilts that came with the furniture, they sure did need the shelves to put them on. They had enough to last for years. By the time they got all the furniture in and everything Dora, Ettie, and the girls had done, it was dinnertime.

That morning, before they got there, Tom had fixed two Dutch ovens with deer roast, carrots, potatoes, and onions in them outside at the dugout. He had put plenty of hot coals around them so they would be done by noon. While Ettie and Dora made corn bread and opened some green beans, John and Tom went down in one of the wagons and brought the two Dutch ovens back. They had everything there at the house they needed in the way of pots, pans, dishes, knives, forks, and spoons so they didn't have to bring anything up right now to fix dinner. Ettie could decide what all she wanted to bring up later. Mary and Martha washed out the dishes and the silverware they would need. They found a tablecloth that was in the china cabinet drawers and set the dining table. After that they pumped water from the kitchen pump and filled the glasses. It came from a deep well and was ice cold. So the first meal in their new home was shared with their very dear friends. Tom asked John to honor them by asking God's blessing on the food and their home. He said he would be honored to, and he prayed such a beautiful prayer, until Tom thought they all would remember it for the rest of their lives. He knew he and Ettie would.

After dinner the woman did the dishes. They had filled up the reservoir on the stove, and while the bread cooked, it had heated so they had plenty of hot water. It didn't take them long, and after that they all went into the living room, sat down, and just visited. They had all worked hard that morning and needed a long rest. After that the Rockers went home. Tom tried to pay them, but they would have none of that and said they would see them Sunday. After they left, Tom went down and brought Lucky up. He was tickled to death to see Ettie. He wouldn't get an inch away from her all the rest of the day. Tom guessed he was afraid she would leave him again. The next day was a different story. He went from room to room examining everything.

That afternoon Tom told Ettie to choose the bedroom she wanted for their room, that he wanted her to lie down and rest for a while. Tom laughed and told her, "Make sure it has room enough for a baby bed because when I come back from cleaning the house, I am bringing one home."

She asked him, "What are you going to do while I rest?"

Tom told her, "I think I will bring all those boxes we had sitting on the shelves up here so we can put them away. Also tomorrow, I want to wash all the towels, cup towels, sheets, pillowcases, tablecloths, and what have you that we had gotten with the furniture." He wanted to get it all rounded up today. He told her, "I know it's all clean, but I thought we would feel better if it was washed before it was put away. I thought I would put it in the washpots and boil it and just rinse it good and hang it on the lines before we fold it and put it in the drawers."

It didn't take her long to go to sleep, and he let her sleep all afternoon with Lucky curled up right beside her. Tom hitched the horses up to the wagon and went down and got all the boxes from the dugout. He unpacked all the dishes and glassware and just put them on the dining room table so Ettie could put them where she wanted them in the next few days.

Ettie was so proud of the house and the furniture. She would go from room to room looking at it all. She was like a little girl at Christmas, she kept saying, "Oh, Tom, isn't it pretty, just look at this. Look at the lamps. Aren't they gorgeous, and didn't we all do a wonderful job of decorating everything?" Also, after living in the dugout for over three years, he knew it was to her a little bit of heaven come down to earth for her to enjoy.

The next day, he built a fire under two washpots and put some lye soap in with the water and just let it come to a boil, then he put some of the clothes in the pots and left them for about five minutes or better. Then he would take them out and put another load in and let it boil while he rinsed them several times and hung them on the lines. When he got through with it all, it looked like Dora's line on wash day. When they were dry, Tom brought them in smelling nice and fresh. Ettie ironed the tablecloths, folded them, as well as everything else that needed ironing, and put them all away in the drawers where she wanted them. It was a big job, but it was worth it, knowing everything was fresh and clean now.

It took them the most of three days to get everything washed, ironed, and put in place. Ettie washed all the dishes before she put them in the china cabinets. The dining room sure looked pretty when she got it finished. Also, they had put the breakfast table and chairs at one end of the kitchen with the small china cabinet on one side, close to it all. She had a set of dishes in each and pretty glasses and bowls. With a pretty tablecloth on the table and all the dishes put away in both rooms, everything sure looked pretty. That night Tom thought he would start moving all the outside stuff up the next day, starting with the pigs and chickens. The hogs weren't that hard to move. He just waited until feeding time and took a bucket of feed, and they followed him. John had followed his idea and dug a channel in and out of his pen, giving the hogs a place to wallow, like Tom had built. So he didn't have to do anything there. It was downstream and a good piece from the house.

The chickens were a different story. Tom would move them each night, but the next morning, they would just move themselves right back to their old home. He would take them back each night and feed them at the new place. This went on until Tom began to think the only way he was going to get them to stay was tear the chicken house down and bring it up too. Finally, they got the message that the only way they were going to get fed was at the new place, so some of them began to come up there. A few at a time would follow until finally they were all coming up there. The turkeys and guineas pretty well followed the chickens. But the geese were another big problem. Tom had to carry them up every night. The next morning they would look out, and they would be gone again.

He told Ettie, "Let's just hatch some more geese and leave those just where they are."

She said, "Now, Tom, you know we couldn't do that. They would be prey for anything that came along. They wouldn't last a week."

Tom told her, "It would serve them right for being so stubborn."

She always had the patience of Job. Every night she would go down and bring them up, and of course, Tom wouldn't let her go alone. He asked her, "Ettie, how long are we going to do this?" and she would say, "Tom, as long as it takes."

She made extra biscuits each day, and each night when they brought them home she would scatter bread all along the creek. They acted like they sure enjoyed it, but the next morning they would be gone again. She tried everything. She told Tom, "I don't think they like their new home."

Then one morning, when they woke up and looked out, there they still were. She was so tickled she ran out and took them some more bread. Each day she would feed them, but she didn't have any more trouble with them not staying. Everything seemed to love her. Tom said he thought he had mentioned that before, but they would come right up to her and she would pet them, bread or no bread.

Chapter 20

THAT FRIDAY, ETTIE WENT TO deliver her eggs, and when she came back, Sallie was with her. Sallie had written her and told her she would be in that Friday. She wanted to surprise Tom, so she hadn't told him she was coming that soon. She was tickled to death about the baby. They hadn't told her yet. Ettie had begun to show a little, so Ettie told her on the way home. She told Tom, "I am so glad to be here. I didn't think I could have stood that rat race for another week." Ettie showed her through the house and told her to take either bedroom she wanted. She was as tickled as Ettie was over everything and kept telling Ettie how pretty everything was. She told Ettie she wished she could have come earlier so she could have been here to help them all get moved. But she just had to give Mr. Tucker time to find someone to keep his children. After they had gone through the house twice, she chose the bedroom she wanted. So they worked in it, putting all her things away until time to get supper.

That Sunday, they went to church, and everyone was tickled to meet Sallie, especially the Ruckers. Sallie told them, "I feel like I know ya'll already. Tom and Ettie have told me so much about all of you. Also, I want to thank ya'll for helping Tom so much when he was trying to get started."

They said, "That worked both ways. He helped us as much as we did him, if not more."

Tom told her, "Oh, I don't know about that. I don't know what I would have done without them. They were my guardian angels, teaching me how to plant a garden, how to can the things after I had gotten them raised, how to kill a hog and dress it out, and so many other things. And oh yes, I almost forgot, I had a lot of helpers teaching me how to make lye soap."

All the Rucker kids and Tom burst out laughing. Sallie and all the other people around didn't see anything that funny about them making lye soap. But the Ruckers, Ettie, and Tom sure did. Tom didn't think they would ever let him live that boo-boo down. He told Ettie and Sallie that it was time to go see J. B. early in the week. So they had made plans to go on Monday. After church, he asked John if any of the boys would be free so he could hire them to stay and take care of the place while they went to see J. B. and ask if Dora and him would like to come along.

He said, "Dora and I can't, with me just getting started on the new job. Billy and Mike were the only boys left at home, and they would be glad to. With me working as foreman, the kids didn't have anything to do. So any time you need them, they are available. They get pretty bored with their new life."

When John told them, they were thrilled to death. They wanted to know if they could stay in the dugout.

Tom told them, "It would be fine with me, if it was all right with their parents."

John told the boys, "It would be fine with us, but ya'll had better take care of everything and not just play around. Remember Tom is putting his faith in you to take care of everything just as he does. So I had better not hear you let him down."

They told their dad, "We will make sure everything is okay every day and keep the outside work done up real good."

Their dad told them, "I know you will because that was the way you were taught."

They wanted to know if Tom needed them and could they stay on all week and help him. Tom told John, "It would be fine with me. We will probably be gone most of the week anyway." Tom told the boys, "There is plenty of meat in the smokehouse along with milk, eggs, and butter. Also, there is still plenty of canned goods in the dugout. There is lard, flour, and cornmeal under the bed still that we haven't had time to move yet. I will make sure there is some salt and baking powder there for you. Also, you know where the vegetable runs are in the gardens, so I don't think you will go hungry."

They were so excited they said to their father, "We will go over this afternoon so Tom can tell us if there is anything else he has forgotten to tell us."

They left right after that with them, promising they would be over as soon as they could get their things together.

Ettie was about as excited as they were. She said, "I want to get home and get J. B.'s chocolate cake made. I wouldn't dare go without it."

They had all their things packed and were ready, except the cakes. As soon as they got there, Ettie and Sallie, both, went into the kitchen and started on them. She always made three, one for them to eat going and coming and one to eat while they were there and for J. B. She always left him a whole one when they left. This time she made an extra one to put on the table in the dugout. By the time they made four cakes and iced them, it was late in the afternoon. When the boys came, Tom and the boys went down to the dugout and made the bed. He showed them where everything was and made sure about the salt, baking powder, and soda. After that they went out and did the night work. While they milked the cows and took care of the milk, Tom slipped up and got the cake and put it on the table. As soon as they went in the dugout, here they came. Both hugged Ettie and Sallie and thanked them for the cake. They told them, "Ya'll didn't have to do that." But Mike laughed and said, "But I sure was glad you did." They left right after that, telling Tom they would take care of the morning work so he wouldn't have to do anything but get up and go.

They got up real early, and before daylight they were on their way. They went in the wagon because they had Ettie's eggs to leave when they went through town and with all the extra food Ettie had packed to take along. The buggy wouldn't hold it and them too. She always took J. B. some sticks of sausage, eggs, butter, and some ham. Besides all the other things she wanted to cook him while they were there, he always told her he looked forward to them coming because he got some home-cooked meals. They always left real early so they could be there in time for her to fix supper for him on the second day.

They stopped at noon under a big shade tree. Tom made a small fire and went down and got some fresh water and made a pot of coffee. While it boiled he unhitched the horses and hobbled them so they could graze and rest awhile. Leaving so early that morning, the coffee sure tasted good. They ate the dinner that Ettie and Sallie had packed for them. It was so good they ate too much of the cake. Tom got the quilts out and had Ettie and Sallie lie down while he cleaned everything up and packed them back into the wagon. Before he had got started good, they were both sound to sleep. He let them sleep for a while because the horses needed to rest and needed to eat a little longer also. He made another pot of coffee, and when he woke them, they had their cake with another cup of coffee. Before they left Tom rinsed the pot out and poured water on the fire to make sure it was out. He finished packing the wagon, hitched up the horses, and was ready to go again. They stopped early that night. They had a hard day and were ready for some rest. After Tom had tended to the horses, he made a fire and got out the food. They still had enough left over from dinner for their supper. So he just made some coffee to go with it, and with the cake they had plenty. Tom made a fire on each side of the pallet, and it put out enough light to help Ettie and Sallie see good, and it helped keep them warm, but he didn't think either one of them slept good. The girls were afraid something might crawl on their bed, and it was a little chilly. Tom kept getting up all night to feed the fire so the girls would stay warm. They both finally took their quilts and went to the wagon to sleep.

They got there about three the second day. As usual J. B. came out and hugged Ettie first and asked, "How is my pretty girl?" Then he hugged Tom and asked him, "Who is this other pretty girl, you have brought with you?" Tom introduced Sallie, and he told her he was glad to meet her and that she sure had an ornery brother. Tom was supposed to bring Ettie to see him at least once a month, but somehow he never seemed to get around to it. Then he told Tom, "Now, young man, come over here and let's sit down so you can give account for yourself and let me know why you have stayed away so long this time. I had been looking for ya'll for a solid month. I have been waiting for my chocolate cake."

Tom told him, "Ettie hasn't forgot. It's in the wagon. Before I sit down, let me go get it. You old windbag, bet you haven't thought about us at all until you saw us pull up, and if you did, it was only because you got hungry for Ettie's chocolate cake."

J. B. laughed and told him, "Just every day, I don't know how many hours a day I sit thinking of all the good times that me, Jack, and you had restoring the dugout. Now let me help unload the wagon, so you can tell me what ya'll have been up to."

They unloaded the wagon; and he, as usual, was tickled to death over his chocolate cake.

Ettie told him, "Just to prove to you, I can make something besides chocolate. I brought a coconut cake to eat now." While they unloaded the wagon, she had made a pot of coffee.

She told him, "Now come in and set down at the table and let me cut you a great big piece."

They went in, and he told her, "Come and sit down and let Tom pour the coffee and cut the cake. I want you to tell me when the little one is due."

Ettie looked surprised and asked him, "Has Tom told you?"

He said, "No, but one look at you and I knew. A woman, when she is expecting has a special glow. She is prettier then, than she has ever been before." He took one look at her and thanked God that he was going to see his grandson at last before he died. "Now come and sit down and tell me all about it."

She hugged him with tears running down her face. She told him, "I had just about given up hope, but yes, I am expecting. I am going on four months, and he will be here in March or April."

They all kept saying "he," like it couldn't be anything but a boy. J. B. wanted to know had they decided on a name yet. Tom told him, "A little bird told me that your name was Boyd and Jack's real name was really Virgil. That way it would take care of naming him after two of the best friends I ever had."

He smiled and said, "Jack would like that. I know I do."

Ettie shooed them out to the front porch, telling them, "It is time for Sallie and me to get supper." She told Tom for him to tell him about the house and all of their pretty furniture while she and Sallie fixed their supper.

Tom and J. B. went out and sat down, and here came Ettie with another cup of coffee for them. J. B. thanked her for it and said to Tom, "Ain't that just like my girl." They sat and drank their coffee, and Tom told him about John getting a good job as foreman on this place and about John Junior and the two girls getting married, then about Jimmie's and Mark's good offer to go to work on a big ranch. With all them gone, John had said, the ones left couldn't work that much land. J. B. asked him what he had done with the land, was he going to work it all or find someone to rent it to again. Tom told him, there was no way he could work it by himself, and John had told him about a Mr. Yodel that wanted to rent just the land. Tom told him as of now he hadn't had the time to check with him. J. B. told Tom he didn't have to worry about him, he is a good honest man, that Tom could depend on him to do what he told him he would.

About that time Ettie called them for supper. She and Sallie had cooked a meal fit for any king. J. B. and Tom both ate two big helpings of everything. They told the girls they were to full for desert, but they would have some later. After supper the girls cleaned up everything, and then they played dominoes. The girls against J. B. and Tom. Of course, the girls beat them and J. B. told them they just let them beat them on purpose and Tom joined right along with him. They stayed up playing until about midnight. J. B. said he hadn't had any one to play with him in a long time and was sure enjoying it. The girls put sheets on the beds in the spare bedrooms, and they all just crashed.

Tom woke up to the smell of coffee. J. B. and Sallie had woke up and made coffee. They all sat around drinking coffee and talking until they ran out of coffee. Ettie and Sallie cooked a big breakfast and made another pot of coffee. They all sat at the table, talking and eating until about eleven. Tom told the girls they had better get up and get ready to go, as it was, they would have to sleep out at least two nights, that is if they were lucky.

J. B. said, "I envy ya'll. I haven't done that since we worked on the dugout."

Tom asked him, "Why don't you just come and go with us?"

He said, "Not now, but I will be up before the baby comes." He laughed. "I won't be going without a chocolate cake for that many months."

They left right after that with him hugging Ettie and telling her, "Now you take care of yourself and the little one. I want a healthy little bugger when it gets here." He told Tom, "You take good care of her, and don't let her work too hard."

Sallie told him, "Now that's what I am there for, and I will make sure that Ettie doesn't do anything that will hurt her."

Tom told him, "Take care of yourself and come to see us as soon as you can."

Ettie told him, "We will be looking for you soon."

He stood and waved until they were plum out of sight. They stopped about one, and the girls said they still weren't hungry, so Tom made a fire, and they just had some cake and coffee. Tom unhitched the horses and hobbled them so they could eat while he and the girls had their cake and coffee. Tom always remembered Mr. Heart telling him, "Now, Tom, you take good care of your horse and he will take care of you." So Tom tried to see that the team got plenty of rest and food while they were on any trip. He always took them down for water just right before he hitched them up to get started again. Today was no exception. Although they hadn't come very far, he took them down to see if they wanted to drink before he hitched them up again. They drove until about the middle of the afternoon, then Tom stopped under a nice shade tree, made a pallet for Ettie and Sallie, and made them lie down for a while. He took care of the horses and came back and laid down beside Ettie. They both were fast asleep, and it didn't take Tom long until he was too.

They stopped early for the night. Tom built them a nice fire; this time of the year it got a little cool at night. Tom told the girls he would take care of the horses, then he would fix their supper. Sallie told him, "You will do no such thing. I will fix it while you are gone." Ettie showed her how to make the bread in the Dutch oven, and by the time Tom got back they had it on. Sallie sliced the sausage and put them on to fry. While they were cooking, she made coffee. It wasn't long until they sat down to hot biscuits, sausage, and gravy with plenty of jelly and butter. "When you are traveling across country in a wagon, you don't have big fancy meals, but something simple and quick," he told Sallie. They ate, and he built another fire on both sides of the pallet. They had brought enough quilts to make them soft beds and plenty of cover to keep warm, with the fires going, but none of them slept good. Tom thought, they all were glad when it was light enough for them to get up and get breakfast and get to rolling again.

They stopped and let the horses rest about ten that morning. He made a pot of coffee and tried to rest for a while, but they were all anxious to get home. They had just barely finished their coffee, and Ettie said, "Tom, I don't need to rest. I am not tired, and I am ready to go again. I would like to get home tonight before it gets too late if it's possible."

They stopped about one and had dinner, and they all rested for about an hour or better.

Ettie said, "I'm still not tired."

But Tom told her, "The horses were and we have to let them rest."

The trip back always seemed longer than going, but they still got home, the second day before dark.

Tom stopped at the front of the house and told the girls to go on in and he would unload the wagon. They were both real tired, and it didn't take much coaching to get them to do it. He put everything on the back porch and took the horses and wagon on down to the barn. He just unhitched the horses and turned them into the pasture and went back to the house. By the time he got everything put away, the girls were already in bed. He was too tired to sleep, so he went out and sat on the porch. He needed to get back and finish taking care of the house, so if the people decided to come earlier, it would be clean. But after talking to J. B., he felt like he needed to go see Mr. Yodel and let him know he would rent the farm land to him. Tom decided, in the morning, right after breakfast, he would go down and tell Billy and Mark what he had planned on doing.

He wanted to make sure they could stay on until he got back. If so, he would go see Mr. Yodel. He could ride Jake and let the other horses rest all day. Then the next day he would go back to clean the house. With all his plans made, Tom went to bed and went to sleep right away.

The next morning, at the breakfast table, he told Ettie what he had planned. She agreed that it would be good to get the house cleaned just in case they did decide to come in earlier. She told Tom they sure wanted to keep their word and have it cleaned before they got there. So he went down and told the boys what he had decided. Tom just about knew it would be all right with them, but he wanted to make sure. They said it would be fine with them.

Tom told them, "Just tend to everything just like I do when I am here. Make sure and check with Ettie to see if she wants you all to take her eggs in each day." He left and went back to the house to tell Ettie, "Everything was settled. I told them to check with you about the eggs, and that they would be up as soon as they got the morning work finished."

She said, "I am glad you did, and yes, I think I will let them take them in today for me." She had barley finish saying that, until the boys were at the door.

Tom told them Ettie did want them to take the eggs in for her. He also told them, "Boys, I want ya'll to go and come without any playing around. Don't drive the buggy too fast and take your time. Now if I hear of you all doing otherwise, I won't let ya'll work for me anymore. Ya'll can eat at one of the cafes before you start back, just charge it to me." Tom asked Ettie,

"Do you need them to pick up anything for you or Sallie, while they are there."

She said, "No, but they will have time to look around for a while. It's no fun going to town and not be able to look around for a while, Tom, they are good boys, they won't get into any trouble." For Ettie's sake, Tom knew they wouldn't. If she had told them to see if they could hang another moon for her, Tom thought they would have tried to. Ettie asked them if they had any money, and they said no, they didn't, so Tom told them it wouldn't be any fun looking around without any money, so he gave them an advance on their salary. Ettie told the boys bye and told them, "Now, boys be careful." Tom told her, for her and Sallie to get some rest and he would see her as soon as he could get back from the Yodels. He saddled his horse while they loaded the eggs, and they all left at the same time. With them telling him, "Now, Tom, you don't have to worry. We won't ever do anything to hurt Ettie."

Tom told them, "I know ya'll won't, and I am proud of you both."

After that, for many years, they worked for him and he never had one complaint. They always said and did just what they said they would do.

Tom got to the Yodels and told him who he was and what he was there for. He said he would be glad to work it and told him what he wanted to plant and how he would work it. It wasn't as much as they got from the Ruckers, but without the house, Tom really didn't expect even that good. They shook hands on it, and Tom told him he would see him soon.

Tom was back home before noon. Ettie wanted to churn, but all the milk was at the dugout. Sallie shooed them out to the front porch, where the rockers were. It sure felt good just to sit in them and talk. Ettie asked, "Tom, what did you find out at the Yodels?"

Tom told her and on what terms. She was well pleased with it. Ettie was quite good with figuring money. In fact, a lot better than he was. Sallie brought some coffee out and joined them. Tom told them, "As soon as I drink my coffee, I will go down and get the milk. But I had promised you that I would get the smoke house fixed so you would have your milk and ever thing just like it was down there at the dugout."

She asked him, "Which one have you planed on fixing? There is two here, a small one, that the Ruckers smoked the meat in and a larger one that they hung their meat in after it was smoked. It is closer to the house and not too far from the creek at the back of the house. It has a spring like the one at the dugout and the water was just as cold."

Tom told Ettie, "I think I would fix the one closer to the house." It being closer to the house. It would be less digging and not as far for her to walk. "I think I will wait until tomorrow to go and finish cleaning the house. Right after dinner, I will dig a line where I want it to go from the creek to the smoke house and back to the creek, that way the boys can start digging on it while I go to get the rest of the things and clean the house."

Tom got started on it right after dinner, and he worked on it all afternoon. He just cut a trench for them to go by. He had just got through and had started doing the outside work when they got back. They helped him finish up, so he could show them what he wanted them to do while he was gone.

Tom showed them where he had dug and told them, "Dig it as wide and deep as the other one. If you should get both sides finished, before I get back. I don't think you will, but go ahead and do it like you had before. Just dig to the spring but don't open it until you get it all finished. Don't dig through the smokehouse. We will do that when I get back. With all the outside work and everything, I don't think ya'll will get that far anyway. Now I want you to take your time. I don't want ya'll to get out there and try to kill yourselves working on it. Make sure you stop and rest along. Also find out each day if Ettie has anything she needs you to do before you start on it."

By the time he finished showing them what they were going to do, it was getting dark.

They told Tom, "Don't worry, we will watch after the girls and do the outside work. Also we will do everything in the morning so you can get an early start. Now don't you worry, we will tend to everything, and after that, each day we will start the digging, and for you to be careful and hurry back."

Chapter 21

Tom left between three and four the next morning, He had packed all he needed, to take the night before. So he slipped out of bed and left without waking Ettie and Sallie. He would stop down the way, and while the horses rested, he would fix his breakfast. He made good time. About nine the horses begin to slow down, and Tom knew it was time to stop and let them rest. He found a big shade tree close to a small stream of water. He stopped and unhitched the horses and took them down to drink, then he hobbled them as usual and turned them loose to eat and rest for a while. He made a fire and cooked breakfast. Tom thought he was as tired as the horses. After he finished eating, he packed everything except the coffeepot and put them back in the wagon. He got a quilt and lay down. He was only going to rest for a while, but he went sound to sleep. He didn't know how long he slept, but at least an hour or so because the fire had pretty well burned down. The coffee was still warm enough to drink, so he drank a cup and then went for the horses. It didn't take him long until they were on their way again. Tom hoped the horses got enough rest until he could make up for the time he had lost. Tom didn't push them to fast, but he did keep a steady pace, until about one o'clock or after. Tom guessed he could have gone farther, but he had been using the horses quite a lot for the last few weeks, and he didn't want to break them down by pushing them to hard, neither one of them weren't spring chickens any more. They had served him well and would for some more years but at a slower pace. He got to the Scott's place on the third morning.

The first thing Tom did was go pick up the baby bed; it was still in the crate. So it wasn't any trouble to load. He had found an old chester drawers in the shed. It was in good shape; all it needed was sanding and varnishing. He wanted to surprise Ettie with it when he got it finished. Tom asked the man at the furniture store where he could get some sand paper and varnish. He told him where a lumber yard was, so he went down and the man helped Tom with the sandpaper and varnish. He told him he would probably need some stain if he wanted the bed and chester drawers to match. So they opened the end of the crate, and the man found a stain to match it. He asked Tom if he needed any paintbrushes. He helped Tom with them, and he bought three. He knew Mark and Billy would want to help him. He asked him, "Have you ever done any staining and varnishing before?"

Tom told him, "No, I haven't."

So the man told Tom how to sand it and wipe it off with some dry rags. He said, "Now you might want to go over it twice, to make sure you have all the dust off real good. After that, shake the can of stain real good and pour a little at a time on another clean rag, wipe it all over, always going with the grain until you have wiped it completely. Then let it dry overnight and then varnish it. It's best to put two coats on, letting it dry over night between the coats."

Tom laughed and told him, "I don't think this is going to be easy."

The man told him, "It is, it just sounds complicated. Just do it the way I told you, and it will be as easy as pie, nothing to it."

When Tom got back to the Scott's house, he backed the wagon right up to the porch. He unhitched the horses and put them in the lot and shut the gate. The rest of the day he gathered up everything from the barn and shed. He carried all of them around and put them on the front porch. He didn't load them on the wagon yet. Tom wanted to get everything out of the shed, barn, and house before he started loading them. That way he would be able to load it better if he could see what all he had to load. Tom had left a broom and mop in the house. So, when he got everything out of the barn and shed, he got the broom and swept out the shed good, the walls and all. Then he raked out the barns and made sure everything was out of them and they were both cleaned real good. By then it was getting dark.

He had stopped at the grocery store and got some cheese and some crackers so he wouldn't have to cook anything while he was there. As cool as it was, it would keep good so he had picked up a pretty good-sized hunk so he could take some back home for Ettie. Cheese was something they only had at Thanksgiving and Christmas, so it was quite a treat. Tom did make some coffee out in the chicken lot, so it wouldn't be any danger of getting anything on fire, then ate the cheese and crackers and drank his coffee. Tom could have done without the food, but by then he sure was wanting some coffee. After he finished eating, he poured the last of it in his cup. He drew some water from the well to pour on the fire to make sure it was out and took his coffee to the front porch. He had put a rocker out there earlier, so he sat down in it and finished drinking his coffee. Tomorrow he would clean the inside of the house, and if he was lucky, he would be able to leave the following day.

As soon as he drank the coffee, he made a pallet in the back of the wagon. He wanted to be up early in the morning, so he went to bed pretty early. It wasn't a very soft bed, but he was so tired, it didn't make any difference to him. He was asleep in no time and slept all night. Tom was up early and was in the house working before the sun was up. He washed all the windows and dusted all the walls and base boards. After that he mopped the whole house, there wasn't anything else he could do until it dried. So he started trying to figure out how he was going to get all the stuff on the wagon. Most of it was just hoes, racks, shovels, sharpshooters, tools, rolls of wire, and junk; but it all was good to have on a farm or ranch. Tom had to stack the longer lumber in the bed of the wagon first to be able to get it all in, even then it was hanging over the tail gate. On top of this, he put all of the short lumber.

The baby bed, the chester drawers, an old sewing machine, and the wooden rocker was about all the furniture left. He put all of them at the front of the wagon except the rocker, that he saved for the last. He was worried about the long lumber sticking so far out of the back of the wagon. He was hoping the furniture and the short lumber and everything else on top of it would hold it down and it wouldn't slide off the wagon. He placed the tools as straight as he could lay them on top of the lumber. He wanted to make sure he could get it all on. The stack of long lumber and the rolls of wire were the hardest things to get loaded. The rolls of wire he had to tie down over the lumber to hold both the lumber and wire in. He still had the rocker to do something with. He put some quilts at the front, next to the furniture. Then he turned the rocker upside down over the sideboards and tied it down real good to keep it from getting scratched and from falling off. When he got it all loaded, it was a big full-size load.

By then the floors were dry. Tom went in and waxed all the floors. While the wax dried, Tom went out and scattered the ashes where he had made a fire and checked again to make sure everything was cleaned good and that he hadn't forgotten to do anything. By the time he got through checking everything, he knew the wax had time to dry. So he went in and ran a dust mop over all the floors When he got through, it all looked real pretty and shiny, even if he did say so himself. When Tom finished with the floors, it was after four. He decided he had better take the key to the lady at the grocery store before she closed. He wanted to be long gone, a long time before she opened in the morning. He checked all around the house again and made sure he had locked all the doors. Tom didn't want to mess up anything, so he decided to grab something to eat at the café and close to the grocery store. All he liked was sweeping the porch and moping it. He did that real quick and then walked up to the grocery store. He gave the keys to the lady and told her, he had everything out and had cleaned it real good. Tom told her that Mr. Scott knew how to get in touch with him if he needed to. Then he went by the café and grabbed a bite to eat. He didn't stay long; he wanted to get back and make sure the porch was all right. He decided to spend the night where he and the boys had, when they came after the furniture, that way the horses could have plenty of good green grass to eat and plenty of water all night. He got there just before dark and hobbled the horses. He made a small fire to help keep the chill off him during the night and made his pallet next to it and laid down. He was dead tired, and it didn't take him long until he was sound to sleep.

 He was up and ready to leave at daylight. Tom had a long way to go, and he wanted to get home to check on Ettie as soon as he could. It took him two days and into the third day to get back. As soon as he got there, he backed the wagon up to the toolshed and turned the horses loose. The boys were already digging on the channel. Tom waved to them and went in to see about Ettie.

 She said, "Everything had gone just fine while you were gone. Did you get the baby bed?"

Tom told her, "It is in the front of the wagon just behind the seats, and I will have to unload everything before I can get to it."

Dora was there. She, Sallie, and Ettie were sewing on something. Ettie said, "Look, Tom, at what we are making," and held up a little baby gown.

Tom told her how cute it was and spoke to Sallie and Dora. Then he told them, "Guess I had better go see about the boys."

Dora said, "They are having the time of their life, getting to sleep in the dugout and cooking for their selves. Why, they even cooked dinner one day for the three of us in the dugout. They cooked a roast like you did. They told me, you had taught them to cook it that way, and it sure was good."

Tom told her, "That was the way we cooked them when we were camped out, checking fences and looking for strays."

Sallie said, "Yes, they told us all about it."

Tom told them, "Guess I had better leave ya'll to your sewing and go unload that wagon." He started on out. Then Tom happened to think about the sewing machine he had found in the storage room. He told them, "Oh, by the way, I found a Singer sewing machine in the storage room when I was cleaning everything out. I don't know how good it is, but the cabinet looks in pretty good shape."

Dora said, "Bring it in when you get time, and I will check it out. If the cabinet is in good shape more than likely the machine will be good also."

The boys and Tom unloaded the wagon and put everything where they thought it should go. After that they took the baby bed to the house. They uncrated it and put it together. Ettie showed them where to put it, and then they put the mattress in it. They went back and got the machine, then left, with the women putting sheets on the baby bed and fooling with the machine. Lucky was right at the middle of it all, at first inspecting the baby bed, then on top of the sewing machine.

Tom and the boys went back to the barn and inspected the chester drawers. Mark said, "I think it is called a highboy." It was about twenty-nine inches wide and between four or four and a half feet tall with a pretty mirror on the top of it.

Tom told the boys, "I want to do it first, but I guess the smokehouse should come first."

Mark told him, "I think we have more time to get the smokehouse done than we have for the chester drawers."

Billy said, "I think as much as they have been sewing, they will need a place to put the things in, pretty quick. Mama has been coming over here two or three times a week, and they either sew or go to town to take the eggs and spend the rest of the day looking for baby things. They all are having a picnic, sewing and looking for things for the baby. We better not be too long getting it done or they will be bringing one home." They all decided they had better work the rest of the day on it, and tomorrow they would dig the channel through the smokehouse. And after they got the big rocks and gravel down, they could pour the clay on it, then they would have to let it dry for several days, like they did before. While it was drying, they could work on the chester drawers again.

Mike said, "With all three of us, sanding on it, we ought to have it ready and the stain on it in a day or two. Then it can dry overnight, and we can put the first coat of varnish on it the next day."

Tom told them, "If we get it sanded, I will get the stain on it before I go to bed."

Billy told him, "Not just you but we. Mike and I will be right there, helping you until we get it stained."

They worked real hard that day, and by the time for them to do up the night work, they were pretty well on schedule.

They had all the drawers checked. Those that needed repairing finished and it cleaned good and was ready to start sanding on it. Tomorrow they would dig the hole under each side of the smokehouse and be ready to put the wire in, then the rock and clay. Then, as they had planned, they would be ready to start sanding on the chester drawers the following day.

They got up early and had already started digging when Sally hollered breakfast. She had fixed it for all of them. They went in and ate without too much talking. Sallie knew they were up to something and asked them, "What is so important that ya'll are rushing so fast?"

Both boys looked at Tom and grinned.

Tom told her, "We are just in a hurry to get the channel dug and ready to use so you can have the milk and everything right at the back door."

She told them, "That would be nice," and didn't ask any more questions.

Right after breakfast, Tom and the boys hauled the rocks and got them placed in the hole and that afternoon they went after the gravel and then the clay. By the time they got all the gravel in and the clay mixed and put in place, it was dusty dark and time to get the night work done. They were still on schedule, and tomorrow they would start on the chester drawers. Billy and Mike both knew more about sanding and varnishing than Tom did. They had helped their papa, and he had showed them how. Billy told Tom, "Like the man at the lumberyard said, now make sure you sand with the grain."

The first day they had the sanding done, and it wiped off not only two times, but three times. The boys said, "We want to make sure it is nice and clean with no dust on it." After that they put the stain on it so it could dry overnight. Mike and Billy slipped into the house with one of the small drawers that was up at the very top to make sure it was the right color while

Tom called Ettie and Sallie on the pretense of showing them the smokehouse. Ettie and Sally said, "It is perfect." So now they just had to wait until the next day so it would have time to dry.

    They couldn't work anymore on the smokehouse because it had to dry at least a day or two. So they just took off the rest of the day. They had worked hard, and all three of them needed some rest. The next morning the clay wasn't dry enough for them to work on. It would need that day and probably the next to dry real hard. So they decided to work on the chester drawers. By the time they stopped for dinner, they had the first coat of varnish on it. Boy, did it look pretty. Now they would have to let it dry for another day. The man at the lumberyard had sold Tom some real fine sandpaper and told him in between the varnishing to barely sand over it that would get any dust or runoff, if there was any. Then wipe it off real good before they varnished it and barely sanded it again, before they put the second varnish on. Tom knew Ettie and Sallie were wondering what they were doing with so many rags. Every time they wiped it, they used a clean rag. The next day they sanded it lightly like the man told them to do and wiped it down three times and put the second coat of varnish on it. They decided to let it dry for two days or longer before they took it to the house. Then it would depend on if it was sticky after the two days. That gave them the next two days to work on the smokehouse. They worked all day on the smokehouse, and by that night they had it ready to open the water flow the next day. They all decided they would finish it first so they could start using it while they worked on the shelves. The smokehouse wouldn't have any shelves in it at first, but they could still put the milk in the water channel while they were building on the shelves. They now had plenty of lumber to make all the shelves that they would need. By night they had the channel open, and the water was flowing through the smokehouse real good. They all were real proud of both jobs that they had almost completed.

On the third day, right after breakfast, Tom took Ettie and Sallie to the smokehouse on the pretense of showing them what they had accomplished. They were just going out when Dora came up, so she went with them. The boys were hiding, waiting for them to get inside the smokehouse so they could take the chester drawers in. Tom was to keep them in the smokehouse until they came out. Sallie said, "I am real proud of it, but would be prouder when you get the shelves build, so we can put both the butter and eggs, along with the milk, rather than having the boys take it down to the dugout." Ettie just told them how proud of it she was and how helpful it would be. She hugged each of them and thanked them for building it for her. Tom didn't know how they were going to get them into the bedroom, but Lucky took care of that. When they went into the house, he was making all kinds of noise. They all ran into the bedroom to see what he was up to. He was up on the top of the chester drawers looking in the mirror and talking to his image. He thought he was talking to another coon and he was really putting on a show. They all stood there laughing at Lucky until they were all out of breath. After they all got through laughing at Lucky, Ettie, Sallie, and Dora just had a fit over the chester drawers.

Ettie said, "So that is what you all have been so busy doing ever since Tom got back. It matches the baby bed just perfect." She hugged each of them and thanked them for fixing it for her.

Dora told Ettie, "Now you don't have to worry any more, about, where ya'll were going to find a chester drawers to put the baby's things in."

Billy laughed and said, "See, Tom, I was right, when I said we had better get it finished quick, fast and in a hurry or they would be coming in with one."

They had just got it finished in the nick of time. All three of the woman thanked them and just went on how pretty it was and how well it matched the bed.

Mike laughed and told Ettie, "While Tom took you and Sallie out to see the smokehouse, Billy and me slipped in and made sure it matched just perfect."

Ettie and Dora told them, "Ya'll sure did a good job, and I am real proud of all three of you."

Sallie told them, "We have been looking everywhere for one."

They all three told Tom how proud they were of the sewing machine, that it was a lifesaver. They were all dreading, hemming all those diapers on their fingers. "We would still be hemming on them when the baby came if he hadn't brought that machine to us."

Tom and the boys left them with Lucky still on the top of the chester drawers talking to his image, with the girls trying to decide what baby things needed to be put in each drawer.

Tom and the boys were anxious to get started back working on the shelves, and in a few days, they had them all built. Then they brought some of the meat that they had in the one down at the dugout and most of the honey. They left some of everything for Billy and Mike. They had taken over Jim's place of coon hunting with Tom. Also, Jim had left Scottie, his dog, with them. He said, "Skitter and Scottie hunted so good together, that it didn't seem right to separate them. Right now, I really don't have a place to keep him, after I got married." He had taken a job in town working for his wife's father. The boys and Tom hunted almost every night when the weather was good enough for them to hunt. Coon hides brought a good price, and they usually got several each night that they went out. Also, they still killed all the rabbits they could kill. Ettie and Sallie didn't like them, but the boys dressed them and either fixed them in the Dutch oven for themselves or took them to their parents. Dora had started cooking them in a Dutch oven also. So they didn't let any of the rabbits go to waste, and it sure helped to get rid of them, so they wouldn't eat the garden up.

Billy and Mike had stayed on in the dugout and helped Tom when he needed them or did odd jobs for other people in the church. There were always people there that needed someone to help them with some kind of work. With the odd jobs and helping him with the bees and the calves to brand and the shipping each year, plus the hides, they made enough to meet all their needs and still save some back for a rainy day. They raised their own hogs, chickens, and a garden, and, with Ettie and Sallie helping them, canned enough to do them all winter.

That year, right before August, Tom took all the cattle off that they had to sell. They were running later than they usually did, but with them going after the furniture and trying to get moved in and all the other things that had to be done, the time just crept up on them and it was time to ship them, but they just couldn't turn loose to take them right then. Tom and Billy took the cattle, and Mike stayed to help Ettie and Sallie. Ettie kept telling Tom he needed both of them, that she could take care of the things there but as hard as she tried she couldn't milk the cows. Tom told her, "Anyway the buckets are too heavy for you to lift to feed the hogs." They now had six sows that they kept year around for breading stock, and it took quite a few buckets of feed to feed that many.

They didn't have any trouble with the cattle; it just took time to take them. Tom thought, in his whole life, he would never have a third of the amount of cattle to ship as they had at the Heart ranch. With a smaller bunch, he didn't have to have as many men to drive them and because he had less cattle, they were more gentle. They took their time and drove them at a steady pace and didn't rush them. As Mr. Heart always said, "You don't want to run the weight off them while taking them in to ship, that you want to let them eat along and save as many pounds as you could, every pound you saved was money in your pocket." So Tom made the arrangement to ship them in advance and that way he had plenty of time without rushing them. When they got to the station, Billy helped Tom load them then he would go home and Tom would go on with the cattle. Someone had to go and make sure they sold and for a good price. That year they brought a real good price, and they needed it too. They had spent more than they had planned on, getting moved in, and buying Mr. Rucker's part of the bees and the extra farm equipment. They had used all the crop money, the money from the honey, and the hog money to make their payment on the note. They knew they would have the money from the cattle shipment to take care of everything that they would need for the coming year. With the good price they got, they would have more than enough.

Chapter 22

Tom was so pleased of how much they brought. He could hardly wait to tell Ettie how good they had done. She always knew just about when he would make it back and would always have plenty of hot water in the reservoir for him to take a hot bath. It was a long tiring trip. He would always take the first train back as soon as he got the cattle sold and the money for them. By the time he got home he was always dirty, tired, and hungry. She would always fix him something to eat while he took a good long hot bath. Then they would sit at the table, and Tom would tell her how much money the cattle had brought and how good they had done. Tom was so proud of the money they had got. He asked her to go get his billfold on the bed. He wanted to show her how much they had. When she came back, she said, "Tom, where did you say your billfold was?"

Tom told her, "On the bed, where I always put it."

She told him, "I looked there. But, Tom, it's not there."

Tom thought at first she was kidding him. She and Tom both went in and looked on the bed again. Tom thought it might have fallen out of his pants pocket, so he looked around the bed and even under the bed. Then he went in and looked in his dirty pants and took all the dirty clothes out of the dirty cloths box. They looked in every room that he had been in, but no billfold. Tom then went outside where he had unsaddled his horse and looked all around on the ground. With all the noise they were making, they woke Sallie and she got up to help them look.

She asked Tom, "Are you sure you had it when you got here?"

He told her, "Sis, I could have sworn I had it, but it might be I do the same thing every time and maybe I just thought I had it."

She asked, "Did any one sit beside you on the train and did you go to sleep?"

Tom told her, "No one sat beside me, and yes, I did go to sleep. But surely I would have felt someone if they had tried to pick my pockets."

"Not necessarily," she said, "There are people that are trained to do that, and you wouldn't even know they got that close to you." They looked and relooked, but still they didn't find it. The girls told Tom, "It either fell out of your pocket or someone would have had to take it, one way or the other, or it would be here. It couldn't have just walked off, and it's not in the house that's for sure."

Tom took a lamp and went back outside and looked again. It wasn't anywhere to be had. Tom was just beside himself, he asked Ettie, "What are we going to do? That was our money for the whole year. How can we make it for a year without any money?"

Ettie, bless her heart, was always the one to comfort and encourage you when you were down as far as you could go and couldn't see a way to turn to get out of it. She told Tom, "I know it looks bad, but it's not the end of the world. We still have some honey and eggs to sell. Plenty of milk, butter, and enough canned goods to do us until time to plant a garden again and a roof over our heads. Besides, we still have the coon hides and you all can still hunt. We will make it, and don't you worry. Do you remember telling me about the first year when you first came out here, you had a lot less. How many times have you told me how God had supplied your needs beyond any one's imagination? You did it once, and we will do it again." They went to bed with all of them feeling better because of what she said. But first they thanked God for all that they had left and for the roof over their heads.

Tom was too tired to sleep, so he went out and sat on the porch. He didn't know how; but he did know some way, somehow, with God's help, they would make it. He prayed, "God, it's in your hands." And after a little while, he went in and went to bed and went to sleep.

They had decided not to tell anyone about it. Tom told Ettie and Sallie, "If they knew about it they all, including the church, would want to help them, with money that they didn't have." He told Sallie, "That was the kind of neighbors and church we have. If one was in trouble, then all of them pitched in to help them."

J. B. came in November for Thanksgiving and to check on his grandson, he said. He also bought a high chair. Just in case he didn't get back, he said. He had written a letter telling them to pick him up at the café where Ettie delivered eggs. Dora, John, Mary, Martha, John Junior, Mark, and the ones they had married came for Thanksgiving, and, of course, Billy and Mike.

The day before Thanksgiving, late that afternoon, J. B. the boys and Tom killed a great big gobbler that Ettie had raised. She had saved one for Thanksgiving and one for Christmas. It was so big they had to scald it in the washpot. They all guessed it would weigh around thirty pounds. Late afternoon, they dressed and put the seasonings on it. They put it in a large roasting pan of Dora's and put the top on. They had built a fire earlier so they would have plenty of hot coals. J. B. took the hoe and dug out a place in the coals big enough to bury the pan and then covered it real good with some more hot coals. He was having the time of his life. He told them, "By early the next morning, it would be ready." Dora, Ettie, and Sallie had been making pies and cakes for days. The men told them, "We think ya'll have tried to make every one's favorite pie and cake." Also, Ettie had them eating chicken two or three times that month, so she would have plenty of chicken broth to make her dressing and dumplings with. She always made chicken dressing and dumplings. She said the turkey broth was to strong and she liked the chicken broth better. So, each year, the last of October or the first of November, they ate boiled chicken until she got all the broth she needed to make her dressing and dumplings.

Early the next morning, they put on a ham. It wasn't as big as the turkey, so it didn't have to cook as long. Dora was there bright and early, and all three of them were in the kitchen by daylight making pies. They stopped long enough to have cake and coffee for breakfast on the porch with everyone. They told the guys they didn't want them in the kitchen while they were trying to cook.

Dinnertime came, and Tom never saw such a meal! It was the traditional Thanksgiving dinner with a whole lot added to it. The table was completely full, and to top it off, Ettie had made her hot rolls. They all gathered around the dining room table, and Tom asked J. B. to ask the blessings. He said, "I would be honored to. But first, let's all hold hands, and I would like to ask each of you to tell something real special that God has done for you this year."

Ettie was sitting at his left, and he asked her to go first, and of course, she told about the baby, then said how they had just about given up hope and in God's own time he had blessed them. "Not only has He blessed us with the baby, but with all the precious family He has given to us. Tom came out here with nothing but the shirt on his back, all alone with no one to care whether he lived or died, but God cared and He gave him a new family. Then when Tom brought me out here, you all just opened your arms and took me in as one of the family and I want all of you to know how thankful Tom and I are that we have a family to spend Thanksgiving with."

One after another they told of something that God had blessed them with. Sallie told how at last she felt like she had a home again for the first time since Papa died. Then it was back to J. B., and he said, "You all know God gives you children that are born into your family and they become part of your life, then he gives you special children and they too become part of your life also. I am glad that God counted me worthy to have given me two of those special children, and now for the first time I am to be blessed by becoming a grandfather. Who could ask for more? Now let us bless this wonderful meal and eat before it gets cold."

Ettie and Tom shared many Thanksgiving meals together after that one, but he believed that one was the best one they ever had.

J. B. stayed on for two more weeks, and Tom had never seen anyone enjoy themselves as much as he did. He was up and out with Tom early each morning. He was right there helping him milk the cows, feeding the hogs, and everything else they had to do. At night when they went out coon hunting he had a blast. He hollered, "Sic-um," to the dogs. Every time they treed a coon, he was right there helping them skin the coons. When they started hunting rabbits, Tom gave him one of his guns and he shot as many as Tom did. When it was time to go get them, he was out and running for them as quick as the rest of them. When they started dressing them out, he grabbed one along with the rest of them. Tom told him, "Ettie and Sallie won't eat rabbit," so they invited themselves down the next day to eat with the boys; and of course, that tickled them to death. They got quite a few that night, and when they got through skinning the coons and dressing out the rabbits, he told the boys, "If ya'll are going to take them over to your folks, why don't you all go on and Tom and I will finish taking care of the coon hides?" So he and Tom took them in to the barn and finished stretching them, then nailed them to the barn to dry. They had a good year so far and had hides drying all around the barn. He said he had never seen so many coon hides in one place. When they finished, they went in the house to get warm. Ettie had a fire in the stove so they would have plenty of hot water. She and Sallie had brought in the bath tub so they could have a hot bath before they went to bed. She scolded Tom for having J. B. out in the cold for so long.

J. B. hugged her and said, "Now, honey, don't get on to him. I wouldn't have missed it for the world, and I don't know when I have enjoyed myself so much and had so much fun."

The next day the boys put some rabbits in the Dutch oven with potatoes, onions, and carrots with it and covered it with plenty of hot coals. They came up and told them that their papa might be over for dinner and to play dominoes. Billy said, "He told me to tell ya'll, that ya'll had better practice until he got here." So after they finished breakfast, they told Ettie they wouldn't be there for dinner that they all were having rabbit stew with the boys and spending the day with them playing dominoes.

The dugout was spotless, and Tom was glad because J. B. was so eager to go see it. He tried not to show it, but Tom could tell. The boys had made a pot of coffee, and they all sat down at the table and drank a cup. While they were drinking their coffee, J. B. told them, "You boys don't know it, but you all are wasting time. We could drink coffee while we are practicing, and we had better get started if you plan on beating us." So Mark got the dominoes out that Tom had bought for them. Billy and Tom were partners against J. B. and Mark. They gave them a pretty good run for their money. They would win one game, and then Billy and Tom would win one. This went on all morning. About noon John showed up, and they all stopped for dinner. The boys made some corn bread and opened some green beans to go with their stew and another pot of coffee. J. B. bragged and bragged on how good dinner was. When they got through, Mark said, "You guys let Papa take my place, and I will do the dishes while ya'll show Tom and Billy how to play dominoes."

Billy said, "We will see about that. We have been doing all right so far."

Mark laughed and started kidding them. Again, he told them, "Yes, but now you are going to play with experts, let's see how you all do now." He was right. They beat them every game. Mark took Billy's place, and they still beat them.

John really rubbed it in. He said, "I heard you all were real good coon hunters and fair at hunting rabbits. I'll tell you what J. B. and me will do since all three of you don't know how to play dominoes. I will stay over tonight and J. B. and me will see if you all are any good at hunting. We will take one dog, and Tom and the boys will take the other one, then we will see who gets the most coons and rabbits. Also, J. B. and I will let ya'll choose the two pastures ya'll want to hunt in, and we will take the other two."

Tom and the boys all agreed and told them they didn't have a chance. They all went out and did up the night work, and then they ate supper. By then it was getting dusty dark.

Billy and Mark were raring to go. Tom let them choose the pastures they wanted to hunt in. They all agreed they would hunt the rabbits first while it was light enough to see them, then they would dress them out. Then about nine or so they would hunt for coons. That would give the coons time to get settled down while they dressed the rabbits. They put the dogs in their doghouses as Tom sure didn't want them to start chasing rabbits, and besides, they wanted to save them fresh for the coon chase. J. B. and John wished them luck, and then they had to rub salt in the wound by saying, "You all will need it, if they couldn't hunt rabbits any better than they played dominoes."

The boys told them, "Just wait and see who is crowing when it's all over."

John told them, they would hunt until dark, then meet at the creek to skin and dress the kill.

J. B. hollered over his shoulders as they started off, "Now don't be late, we don't want to wait for ya'll all night."

Tom and the boys were closer to their hunting place, so they shot their first rabbits before they heard any shooting. Tom told the boys, "Count the shots each time, and we will know how many they get. J. B. is a perfect marksman, and every shot we hear will be a rabbit."

As they were going to their next water hole, they heard two shots real fast.

Billy told Tom and Mark, "Boys, we will have to do better next time. They are one ahead of us already."

Tom told them, "Maybe we will make up for it at the next water hole."

They had learned by experience that when they shot, they just as well leave that water hole and go to a new one because there wouldn't be any more rabbits come up for a while. So they hurried to the next one hoping to gain on them. Sure enough, they got two there. That put them one ahead of them. If they could make it to the next water hole, before they caught on to what they were doing, and if their luck held out, this time they might go at least two or three ahead. Right before they got to the next water hole, they heard them shoot. They all three tried to count the shots, but they were so fast. It was either two or three. Billy said two, but Mike and Tom thought it was three. Either way that put them ahead of them again by either one or two rabbits.

The rabbits were getting jittery. They were looking around to see where the sound was coming from and ready to run at a moment's notice. They all three slipped up to another water hole, trying not to make a sound. There were three rabbits, and Tom shot two. This put them either one ahead or two. Still to close for comfort. The next time they only heard one shot, if that was so, they were one ahead or even. It was time to head back. They hurried as fast as they could going back, hoping to find some rabbits at each place, but there wasn't any. When they got to the creek, John and J. B. were there already skinning their rabbits. They had only killed five, and that was what Tom and the boys had. They all three took a deep breath of relief. They all thought for sure it would be six or seven. This way they at least tied with them.

After they all skinned the rabbits and dressed them, they put them in some buckets and took them in to the smokehouse. This way they would stay cold until John took them home the next day. It was cold, so they all went in, and Billy and Mike made some hot cocoa and a pot of coffee. They sat around with J. B. and John kidding them.

John told them, "If ya'll hadn't got a head start J. B. and me would have won."

They said, "The next time that we get to hunt, we all will start off at the same time, one going one way and the others going the other way and see how this story ends."

They stayed in the dugout until about nine or nine thirty. It was cold, and Tom didn't think any of them were too eager to get out in it. Finally, John said, "Well, boys, the coons are waiting," so they all got up and put on all the layers of cloths they had. They walked up to the house to get the dogs.

Tom, J. B., and John had agreed to let Billy and Mark decide what dog went with what group. But they said it was only fair to put both dog's name in a hat and let each side draw for their dog, so that's what they did. J. B. and Tom did the drawing. J. B. went first and drew Scottie. He and John took the lower pastures. They hollered real loud at Scottie to sick-um, and they were gone. Tom and the boys took Skitter up toward the higher pasture and did the same. They had agreed to meet back at eleven or there about. Skitter was off, and it wasn't long until he was on the trail of a coon when they caught up. He was under a tree baying, and there was a big coon in the tree. They got that one down and hollered to him again, and away he went. This time they had no way of telling how many John and J. B. were getting. They had hunted the coons so long until they didn't always get a big amount like they used to, but they got three real nice big ones. By then it was eleven, and they all were cold and ready for something hot to drink. This time they got back before John and J. B. did and had started skinning their coons before they got there. They had only two. You never heard two boys holler so loud when they saw only two. All the time they were dressing them, they were kidding J. B. and their papa about they would be glad to teach them how to coon hunt. Of course, Tom joined right along with them. They blamed it on Scottie.

John said, "If he had been trained right, we would have got more."

J. B. told them, "Now of course it wasn't the poor dog's fault, that he wasn't trained right."

That's when the fat hit the fire, and they all three told them, "Ya'll were hunting with one of the best coon dogs in this part of the country. That Skitter and Scottie had treed more coons than any dog in this part of the country."

John and J.B. were laughing so hard at them, they were holding to each other to keep their balance. They both finally admitted that Skitter and Scottie were the finest coon dogs they had seen in a long time, but John said they do work better together. He had watch them together, and they seemed to know what each one was supposed to do and when. They are quite a pair. J. B. agreed and he said, "They work perfect together and not bad at all by their self."

They finished skinning the coons and stretched them on the barn and nailed them along with the rest of them. They would have a good amount to sell when time came. They were all cold and went down to the dugout for a hot cup of coffee and hot chocolate. They didn't want to wake Ettie and Sallie up, and they knew it would get quite noisy before they finished drinking their coffee and got to bed. Tom guessed it was close to two o'clock before they decided if they were going to be able to get the work done tomorrow they had better get to bed. So John, J. B., and Tom went to the house with the boys hollering at them, "Now when ya'll want to learn how to coon hunt, come back and we will teach ya'll."

John and J.B. hollered back, "Yeah and we will teach you how to play dominoes at the same time."

As usual, Ettie and Sallie had plenty of hot water for them to bathe, and the bathtub was inside for them. They tried to be real quiet and not wake them. When they all got through bathing and to bed, it was around two thirty or three.

Ettie and Sallie let them sleep until about seven. They put the coffeepot on around that time, and nothing will wake you up faster in the morning than a pot of coffee perking. While they were eating, Sallie and Ettie had to hear about the whole day. J. B. was so excited about it. John and Tom just backed off and let him do all the talking. He told about the dinner and what a meal they missed, then the domino game and how bad they had beat them, then about the challenges. Also, that they tied on the rabbit hunt, but he and John kind of thought that there might have been some hankie-pankie going on somewhere. That's when Tom put his two cents in and took up for them. Tom told about the coon hunt and for them blaming Scottie and what an uproar that caused. He and John were still laughing at the boys and how fast they defended the dogs. Of course, Ettie and Sallie were laughing along with them. Then J. B. said, "Ettie, I have never seen any two dogs work together like they did." John and he both were so amazed at how good they worked together. They both said they had never seen anything like it before.

About that time the boys came up to the back door, and when they saw that they all were awake, they started hollering, "What's wrong? Can't you oldies take a rough night out. We have been up and have gotten the morning work already done. Here is the milk to prove it."

Sallie told them, "I will take care of it, you come on in."

They asked Ettie, "What kind of tales have they been telling you all?"

Ettie said, "They sure have been telling some whoppers. They said yours and Tom's dog wasn't worth a hoot when it came to hunting coons."

And of course, that really got them started. They all started laughing and cutting up with them.

Sallie said, "You boys better come and sit down and let me fix ya'll some breakfast before you both blow a gasket. They are just jealous. They know you all have the best dog gone dogs in the country."

They all laughed, and J. B. told them, "I guess John and I will have to fess up. They are the best coon dogs either of us have ever seen."

Billy and Mark both laughed and said, "We knew all along that ya'll were only kidding us. But it wouldn't have been any fun if we hadn't fussed about it."

They sat around and talked until John said, "I guess I had better get home and go to work before I get fired. My boss just gave me one day off, not a week. Besides when I tell him what a good time we had, he might fire me anyway for not letting him come along." He told Ettie and Sallie bye and thanked them for everything.

J. B. and Tom walked down to the dugout with them. After John got his horse saddled and the boys got the rabbits for him, J. B. thanked him for coming over. They hugged each other, and John told them, "I wouldn't have missed it for the world. Boys, this old rascal and I go back a long, long way. We have been through thick and thin together."

J. B. said, "You bet we have. I was there for him each time he needed me. Also, he and Dora helped me take care of Martha all through her long illness, and they were at my side when Martha died. I guess I would have just curled up and died too if it wasn't for them."

John said, "Then when Dora had the next baby girl, we named it Martha for his Martha."

J. B. said, "They didn't know how much that meant to me. No man has ever had better friends than they were."

John left right after that, with him promising he would be back as soon as he could.

J. B. started talking about going home the next day, but Ettie talked him into staying on until Sunday and going to church with them and going home on Monday. It was the same church that he and Martha attended when they lived there, and he knew everyone there. Sunday, they all went to church, and everyone was so tickled to see J. B. again. Tom knew it was a sad day for him but a good day also because he saw that he still had many friends that remembered him and still cared for him. After the service, he went out to the little cemetery behind the church to see Martha's grave. After a while John went out there and stood beside him. It was only right, that again John was there beside him to comfort him in his sorrow. Everyone from the church waited to tell him bye before they left. Tom thought how wonderful it was to have a church home that showed so much love and compassion as was showed there that day. They all left right after he and John came back, with everyone telling him how glad they were to see him and for him to come again.

    The next morning, Tom and J. B. left right after breakfast. Tom took him to town in the buggy. With it having sides and a top, it made it warmer. As cold as it was, they needed all the warmth they could get. Ettie had a quilt in the buggy, and they wrapped up real good and stayed pretty warm. They got there early and went to the cafe and delivered the eggs for Ettie. They saved the oldest cafe that J. B. knew until last and went in and ordered some coffee. Ettie had made them some, but they had drank it on the way to help them stay warm, and they were good and ready for another cup. They stayed there waiting for the train, drinking coffee and talking.

    J. B. told Tom, "I have a mighty big request to ask of you."

    Tom told him, "J. B., you know I would do anything for you that I can."

    He told Tom, "I want you to promise me that when I die, you will see to it that I am buried next to Martha."

    Tom asked him, "Won't your son take care of that?"

    J. B. told him, "I don't know, but I would rest easier knowing that you would see to it."

    Tom told him, "Write out what you want done, then address it to me and put it in your Bible. Be sure you keep your Bible where it can be found. If I have that letter, nobody can stop me from carrying out your wishes. That way they will know that you had given me the authority to take you back and do what the letter told me to do."

Tom told him, "Then it is settled. Come hail or high water you will be buried next to Martha when that time comes."

About that time, they heard the train whistle, Tom took him down to the train station. They probably had plenty of time, but just in case the train left early, Tom and J. B. wanted to be there. Again, they tried to pay for their coffee, but the owner told him, "J. B., you know your money is no good here." She filled both of their thermos bottles with hot coffee. She told them they would need it before they got home. Sure enough, the men didn't have much to load on the train, so they hollered, "All aboard," not too long after Tom and J. B. got there.

Ettie had fixed him a lunch for Tom to give him when they got to the train station, and she had made him a chocolate cake for Tom to give him also. He was real tickled over both of them and told Tom to be sure and tell Ettie how much he appreciated it.

He said, "Tell her I didn't expect it, but I sure do appreciate it and especially my cake."

Tom told him, "She said you would say that and she told me to tell you that was an 'I love you' cake and to tell you that you don't think she would let you go home without your chocolate cake, do you?"

He told Tom again to "tell her thanks and tell her I was hoping she wouldn't. Tom, you don't know how God blessed me the day you came to my door. God saw how lonesome I was, and He gave me a son and later a precious daughter. Tell her I will see her Christmas."

They shook hands, and then he reached out and hugged Tom. He boarded the train and hollered, "Be happy, Tom, and take care of our baby."

Tom stood there and waved until the train was out of sight.

Chapter 23

THE NEXT WEEK, WHEN BILLY and Mark went to town to deliver the eggs and when they came back, they brought an unexpected guest with them. Bertha, Aunt Lou's daughter, was there. She had come in on the morning train and had asked the ticket agent where she could find someone she could hire to take her to their house. He had told her about the boys delivering eggs at the café, and she had got a ride to the cafe to see if she could catch them there. She had told the waitress that she was Tom's sister and what she wanted. The waitress told her usually the boys brought the eggs in and they hadn't got there yet, but she was welcome to stay there until they came. They were in the buggy, and it was crowded with two boys and an oversized woman. They couldn't get all her luggage in the buggy, and the boys had asked the waitress if she would keep it until they came back the following Monday. The boys told Tom she pitched a fit and told the waitress, "A week, my foot, Tom will be back after it tomorrow." She griped all the way back, about she probably wouldn't have any clothes left when Tom came to get them as it was and about being crowded. She wanted to know why Tom hadn't come himself and brought the wagon. He knew she would have luggage.

Billy said he tried to tell her, that as far as he knew that no one knew she was coming. She told them, that was not so, that she had written a week ago telling them she was coming and "the mail wasn't that slow, even in a godforsaken place like this." She went on to tell them, she didn't see why Tom had moved out to a place like this anyway. Mark told Tom after that remark that he told her if she wanted them to, they would be glad to turn around and take her back to the train station. She jumped all over him and told him he wasn't too big to have his mouth washed out with soap and she was the one that could do it too. Needless to say, by the time they got home, they were ready to turn around and take her back and they all wished they had.

She came in and barely said hello and wanted to know why Tom hadn't met her like he was supposed to and where was her room. Sallie and Ettie stood there dumbfounded, just like they didn't hear what they thought they had.

Ettie was the first one to speak and said she didn't think she had met her. She told her, "I am Ettie. I am Tom's wife, and this is our home." Ettie didn't think Bertha even caught the part where she had told her "And this is our home." If she did, she ignored it.

She stuck out her hand and said, "I am Bertha, Tom's sister."

Ettie ignored her hand and said, "You mean cousin, don't you?"

She told Ettie, "Well, nevertheless, I have come a long way and I am tired and would like to get some rest before suppertime. Where is my room?"

Ettie showed her to the extra bedroom and she did say thank you and went in and shut the door. Sallie and Ettie stood there not knowing what to say or do.

When Tom came in, they told him and Tom asked Sallie if she had asked her to come.

Sallie told him, "Now, Tom, you know better than that. I wouldn't ask anyone to come here without asking both of you if it was all right and I sure wouldn't have asked her anyway."

Tom guessed she had found out from Mary Ann that Sallie was living with them and thought she would just move in too.

Ettie asked, "Tom, what are we going to do? J. B. will be back for Christmas. Where will we put him?"

Sallie told them, "Now, Ettie, don't worry, if she is not gone by then, then I will move in with Bertha and you can give J. B. my room." She laughed. "But maybe we will luck out and she will leave before then."

Ettie laughed also and told her, "I don't think so. I think she plans on staying, permanently."

Supper wasn't any better. Bertha asked Sallie if she would fix her a cup of hot tea. She said she had a headache and she didn't drink coffee, also would they mind fixing her some soup, that she was sick at her stomach. She went back to her room as soon as she ate her soup, and they were all glad. Tom told the girls she was just tired and things would be better when she had a good night's sleep.

Sallie said, "Don't count on it."

The next morning, she was better and apologized for being so rude, she said, "Everything has gone wrong ever since I left home, and I have had a splitting headache and have been sick at my stomach."

Ettie told her, "That was all right and maybe things will go better from now on."

Lucky had always had the run of the house. He didn't meddle, but he was curious and would look at anything different that came into the house. Right after breakfast, Bertha said, "I think I will go, put up my clothes and get unpacked." Lucky, as usual, saw the door open and someone strange; and he went in to investigate. When she saw him, you would have thought she had seen a snake or something real dangerous, she started screaming at the top of her lungs. "Help, help, someone help me." They all ran in to see what was wrong. She was standing on the bed with a hairbrush drawn back for a weapon. Poor little Lucky was scared to death, he ran to Ettie making funny little sounds. Ettie picked him up, and he was shaking all over.

Bertha hollered out, "What is that creature doing in the house? I have never seen anything like it in my whole life, wild animals running everywhere."

Ettie always was real easygoing and was always good-natured, but this made her mad. She said, "This creature, as you called him, is my pet coon. This is his home. He lives here, and he has the run of the house. If you plan on visiting here, you better get used to him because he is not going anywhere."

Bertha said, "Not in my room, he won't."

Ettie was so mad, Tom thought she was going to throw Bertha out. She told Bertha real firm, "You are just a guest here. Lucky lives here. He is a member of our family, and no room is restricted from him. It never has been and never will be. If you plan on staying for a while, you better get used to him because he goes and comes as he pleases."

All day long Lucky didn't leave Ettie's side. He was either lying at her feet or, if she was sitting down, in her lap. When Bertha came into the room, he would try to hide under Ettie's arm. If he was in her lap or if she was standing, he would try to hide under her dress. Bertha didn't have to close her door. He made a wide circle around it and would never go near it. From that day on, he would bristle up as to fight if Bertha got near Ettie. He showed a hate toward her that they all noticed, and none of them had ever seen it in him before. He had always been real friendly with everyone and loved to have company come. Now if they were sitting down, he would go over and get in Ettie's lap and just lie there and stare at Bertha.

Tom told Bertha, "Don't get to close to Ettie, and don't try to touch her at all. He thinks you are a threat to her, and he will fight for her."

She told Tom, "That is stupid. No animal is that brave or smart. If I should offer to hit Ettie, he would run away to protect himself."

Tom told her, "Well, just don't you try anything that stupid anyway."

They all went to church Sunday, and she seemed like she enjoyed it. Everyone, as always, was real nice to her. The Ruckers all told them, "We will see ya'll Christmas." It seemed all the kids would be home for Christmas. Dora said, "I will be over to help a few days early" and told Ettie what kind of cakes she was making. They left with everyone in a real good mood, even Bertha. She even got in the kitchen and helped Sallie and Ettie fixed supper. It was mostly just to warm it and make coffee and bread. Sallie and Ettie had made most of it Saturday when they fixed the food to take to church.

Bertha said, "I will set the dining room table."

Ettie told her to set two extra plates for Mark and Billy.

She asked, "My goodness, do they eat up here all the time?"

Sallie didn't blink an eye and answered her, "As often as they want to, and they are always welcome."

On Monday it was a real pretty day. Sallie and Ettie decided to take the eggs in themselves. They said, "It is a nice day, and we have some things to get for our Christmas baking and no telling when we will find another pretty day." They asked Bertha, "Would you like to go along? And also we can pick up your other luggage."

Both cafes had sent word they needed some honey, and the grocery store was out of honey and had sent word to bring more eggs each time they came in so they would have plenty for Christmas. The boys loaded the eggs and two cases of honey. Tom told Ettie to tell both the grocery store and the cafe they would send some more cases of honey this coming week. Right after they loaded everything in the wagon, Ettie told them not to worry if they were late getting back as they had several things to do.

After they delivered their eggs, they ate their lunch as usual. Then went to the variety store and picked up some material to make the boys a shirt each before Christmas. They bought a pattern, thread, and buttons. Ettie and Sallie were both good seamstresses. So the shirts wouldn't be any trouble.

During the summer months every year, Ettie would start buying all the extra things she would need for Thanksgiving and Christmas. All summer when she went in to take her eggs, she would buy her raisins, cornstarch, brown sugar, extra flour, sugar, and anything else she could buy ahead of time so she would have it bought up by the time she needed it. Even though money was scarce, it hadn't affected their Thanksgiving and it wouldn't their Christmas. Ettie was real saving and always made money go farther than anyone Tom had ever known. Each year, long before she needed it, she had all her winter supplies bought up and stored away. She made sure they had plenty of everything that they had to buy and plenty of it so they wouldn't run out.

They had decided not to tell anyone about their missing money because they might not want to come if they knew how tight money really was right now at their house. Ettie could fix a meal fit for a king at any time but don't ask them for a dime because right now money was scarce and they didn't have any to loan. The only money they had was the egg money and the money they were getting from the honey. But they had everything bought up for winter, and the money they got each week would take care of anything they needed right now.

This would be the first year in their house for Christmas. Ettie and Sallie were both excited about it and eager to get home. That night they wanted to show Tom all they had bought. Ettie told Tom, "See, I told you everything would work out just fine.

God always takes care of his own. We have everything we need for our dinner." They had all decided not to exchange gifts a long time ago, so that was no problem. The shirts were a special something from Ettie and Sallie for the extra things that the boys were always doing for them and also because they needed them. Ettie and Sallie were looking forward to cutting them out the next day so they would have them before Christmas. Everyone was so happy that night. Even Bertha seemed to be in a better mood and wasn't complaining when the boys came up and brought the milk. They were going hunting right after supper, so they were going to eat there. They did most of the time when they all went hunting, that way they could leave faster, rather than the boys having to cook their supper first. They had gotten the wood in for Ettie and Sallie and had filled up the reservoir, so there would be plenty of hot water. There were no doors locked on the house, and most of the time they would just come in and bring wood or anything else before supper. If they didn't go hunting they would stay over and play games, make candy, popcorn, or just anything that struck their fancy. Bertha had griped about all the coming and going in their house, but that night she didn't even gripe about that. They helped put away the groceries, and they all fixed supper. The boys knew where everything was in the kitchen and would just come in and start helping Ettie like they lived there. Right after supper they left, and Bertha even helped clean up the kitchen. It seemed like she was going to accept their way of living and stop griping. Even the boys commented on it while they were out hunting with Tom.

They were dead wrong. The next day she was her usual old self. Nothing was right and everything was wrong. None of them could understand why she did it, as many times as Tom had cautioned her. Ettie and Sallie were working on the boys' shirts, and Lucky was up in Ettie's lap. Bertha was griping about the shirts would be dirty when they got them finished with that pesky coon all over them. Ettie told her, "You let Sallie and me worry about them" and went on about her sewing with Lucky looking at and handling every piece she worked on. Tom said later, he guessed it got on Bertha's nerves watching Lucky handling everything Ettie was trying to do. All of a sudden, she got up and went over to where Ettie was sitting and reached down like she was going to take Lucky out of Ettie's lap. Ettie stuck out her arm to stop her and said, "No, Bertha, leave him alone." Bertha hit at her arm not hard, but Lucky only saw her hit at her, and before anyone knew what was happening Lucky had leaped on her and was going for her throat. Bertha threw her arm up, and thank God she did. Lucky bit her arm in place of her throat. Tom said he didn't know what would have happened if he hadn't been in there because Lucky only saw that Ettie had been threatened and his wild instinct told him the only thing to do was to protect himself and that which was his. Tom grabbed him and threw him down on the floor before he bit him, but there was no talking to him to calm him down. He made another lunge at Bertha, and Tom had to take his foot and kick him away. Sallie ran over to help keep him away from Bertha, but Ettie got there first and started talking to him. She hollered for them to get back. She hollered at Bertha to get to her room and shut the door. She did as Ettie told her, and Sallie went with her to doctor the place on her arm where Lucky had bit her. Ettie picked up Lucky and started talking to him as if nothing had happened. He finally settled down, and Ettie took him over to her chair. She sat down and started rocking him. Lucky curled up as close as he could to her and started making little noises like he was crying. After Sallie doctored Bertha's arm and saw it wasn't as bad as she was trying to make them believe. Sallie came out to see how Lucky was doing. She went over and petted him. He looked up at her and began to make his little pitiful crying sound, like "What have I done wrong? Sallie petted him. She told him, "It's okay, Lucky. It's okay. You didn't do anything wrong."

Bertha stuck her head out the door and said, "If he had tried to kill you, you would have thought he had done something wrong."

Sallie told her, "Bertha, in the first place, I would have had more sense than to pull a stunt like that. Tom has told you over and over for you not to do that. Lucky didn't know you were just playing. He was just protecting Ettie."

Bertha said, "Well, nevertheless, I will not stay in a place where wild animals run everywhere and try to kill people. Tom will have to do something about it. I simply refuse to stay in this house with this creature another day, and I mean it. There is no telling when he will try to attack me again."

Tom told her, "Bertha, I don't blame you. I wouldn't stay in the house with any wild creature that hated me as much as Lucky hates you now either. And yes, you are right. There is no telling when he would try to attack you again. I will try to take care of it the only way I know how."

If a look could kill, Tom thought, both Ettie's and Sallie's look would have killed him.

Bertha stood there looking real smirk, like she guessed she took care of that problem.

Tom went on to say, "I will tell you what I will do. You go to your room and shut the door and don't come out all night. Then pack your suitcases, and first thing tomorrow I will take you in to catch the train."

You should have seen how quick that smirk look left her face. She wheeled around to go to her room and said, "Well, the very idea, choosing a creature like that over your own sister."

Before she slammed the door, Ettie hollered, "You mean cousin, don't you?"

Tom guessed she knew she had really overstepped her boundary because she was up and packed early the next morning. Ettie called her for breakfast; but she informed them, "I wouldn't eat a bite, with a bunch of hypocrites like ya'll are." Then she told Tom, "I am ready when you are," and slammed the door.

They all sat down and ate their breakfast while Tom drank a second cup of coffee. Ettie packed Bertha both a breakfast and a lunch. She told Tom, "It will be a long trip, and she will get mighty hungry before she gets back to her home." She made another pot of coffee and filled Tom's canteen with hot coffee and another one with hot tea. She told him, "Let Bertha take the canteen with her." Tom went out and harnessed the horses to the buggy and put the canteens and Bertha's food in the seat. Then he drove the buggy up to the house to get her and her luggage. When Tom hollered for her, she came out carrying both suitcases. He told her he would carry them.

She said, "No, I prefer to carry them myself."

Tom reached over and took them out of her hands, as if nothing had happened and said, "Don't be silly, you can't carry both of these by yourself."

She left about like she came. Sallie and Ettie were both standing there, and she walked right by them and never said a word.

They hadn't gone very far until she discovered the food and the extra canteen that Ettie had fixed and asked Tom what all that was. He told her, "Ettie had fixed you some breakfast, a lunch, and some tea. She said you would get mighty hungry before you got home."

She said, "Fat chance, she or Sallie either one would care if I did starve. Besides I would be afraid they poisoned it."

Before she could say another word, Tom stopped the buggy and said, "Now, Bertha, before we go another foot, we had better get something straight. Ettie is the most loving and caring person you will ever know. She would have bent over backward to help you and to make you feel welcome, but you came in with a chip on your shoulder and made life miserable for everyone. For some reason you were miserable and you wanted to make everyone the same. Poor little old Lucky had never given anything to anybody but love, and you started on him as soon as you got to our home and kept on until you made him for the first time in his little old life feel hate. You finally kept on until you turned him into a monster from which he may never recover. An animal is funny, when they accept you, they put their whole trust in you and they will love you with every ounce of their body. They would even die protecting you if they feel you are threatened. I found Lucky when he didn't even have his eyes opened and almost frozen to death. Something had killed his mama. She had fought until her last breath trying to protect her babies. When I found him, he was the only one left alive and he was almost dead. I took him to Ettie, and she fed and nourished him back to life. She got up day and night taking care of him. I told her, I didn't think Lucky would make it, but she never gave up. He became the baby that we had given up hope of ever having. Everyone loved him, and he loved everyone. I had to kick him to stop him from hurting you. You were a threat to Ettie, and he would have died protecting her. Now his trust in man has been destroyed, and he may never recover from it—all because of your hate and stupidly." When Tom got through she was crying.

She told him, "Tom, I was so miserable and sick of heart. I had left my husband and even before I got here, I was regretting coming and wanted to turn around and go right back. But I was afraid he wouldn't take me back. Tom, I'm still not sure he will. Pray for us that he will take me back and that we can get our life straightened up. Tell Ettie and Sallie how sorry I am, and I hope poor little Lucky will be all right."

Tom told her, "I will pray for you and your husband and Ettie and Sallie would too, but as far as Lucky, I doubt if he will ever be all right. It would just about break my heart to have to tell Ettie. We will keep him for a while and give him every chance we can, but I don't think he will ever get back to where he was before."

Now then Tom told her they had better get started if they were going to get to that train station on time. Tom gave her the breakfast Ettie had packed and told her, "Here, you better eat it so you will have enough strength to board the train when we get there." While she ate her breakfast, he drank his coffee and they drove along, talking. Tom actually enjoyed talking to her when she got over her hate, bitterness, and self-pity.

He told her, "Bertha, I am going to say this even if it makes you mad or not. If you and your husband don't work things out, don't fall back into that self-pity hole you were in when you came here. It will only ruin your life. People don't want to be around anyone filled with as much hate and self-pity as you showed when you came here."

She told Tom, "I have learned my lesson the hard way, and I promise I will never let that happen to me again. And by the way, I didn't write you as I said I did. I was so mad at Will that when I threatened to leave and he told me to go ahead, I just packed my bags and caught the train. If I had stopped to think, I never would have done it."

They got to the train station just barely on time. It was already there, and the whistle was blowing when they got there. Tom jumped out and handed her the reins and told her to hold them while he got them to wait. He boarded the train and told the conductor, "I have another passenger for you. Would you wait until we get the ticket?" He said, "No problem," so Tom ran back and tied up the horses and helped Bertha down and got her luggage. The conductor took her baggage and helped her on the train while Tom got her ticket. She hugged him and told him bye.

Tom told her, "Remember what you promised me and we will be praying for you."

She thanked him and told him, "Tom, thank you for the lecture. If it hadn't been for it, I would have left as bitter as I came. I will let you hear what happens."

Tom stood there waving until the train was out of sight and while he waved, he thanked God that He in his great mercy had straightened things out so there were no hard feelings.

Before Tom left the house, the boys had loaded the eggs and some honey for him so he stopped and delivered to each cafe and had a cup of coffee while he waited for the grocery store to open. He had the waitress to fill up his canteen so he would have some hot coffee to help him keep warm on his way back.

Chapter 24

When he got home, the boys had all the night work done and they were playing dominoes with Sallie and Ettie. Lucky was nowhere to be seen. Ettie said, "He had stayed hid all day. The only time he had come out was when Sallie had gone outside and no one was in the house except me. I am so worried about him. Do you think he will ever be all right again?"

Tom told her, "I don't know, Ettie. We will just have to wait and see."

She said, "He wouldn't even come out and say hello to the boys when they came up, and he always comes out regardless of where he was and was so proud to see them."

The boys wanted to know how the day went with the old dragon lady, and when he told them, they wouldn't believe it. Tom told them, "We had a long talk before we had got very far from home this morning and she told him she had left her husband and how miserable she was. She asked me to tell all of you how sorry she was and to ask you all to forgive her. She was really nice to be with after our talk, and I enjoyed her company. She asked us to pray for her and her husband that they could get everything worked out."

Billy said, "I sure will, because I sure don't want to have to pick her up and bring her here anymore."

They all got a big laugh out of that, and Mark said, "Next time, we will let Tom go get her by himself."

Billy said, "After all, she is his sister, or cousin, that I never did get that figured out, but anyway we will let him go next time."

Ettie and Sallie, both, had been acting like they couldn't wait to tell Tom something.

After the boys left he told them, "Okay, now out with it. What is so important that neither one of you could hardly wait for the boys to leave. What's going on?"

They both laughed and said, "Did it show that bad?"

Tom told them, "Both of you were acting like two teenagers that had been asked for their first date." He acted real concerned. "You haven't, have you? Who has been here today while I was gone?"

Sallie said, "Now, Tom, you don't think we would tell if someone had asked us, do you?"

"Well, someone tell me something," he told them. "What have you two girls been up to?"

Ettie said, "Tom, we have found our thief."

Then Tom laughed and asked them, "What's so funny about that, and what did he steal?"

Sallie said, "You wouldn't guess in a thousand years."

He saw they were having a big time out of this regardless of what it was, so he decided to go along with it. "Well, will one of you tell me something, or do you all want to play this game all night?"

Ettie told Sallie, "Guess we had better just show him."

They went into the spare bedroom where Bertha had been staying. On the bed laid a lot of things that they had missed.

"Well, what in the world?" he said.

Ettie told him, "Sallie and I had sat down at the machine to work on the shirts. Lucky came out, and any other time I wouldn't have paid any attention to him, but because he hadn't been coming out, I looked up just in time to see him get the buttons off the machine and slip out with them. Sallie and I waited a few minutes, and real quietly we followed him. That little dickens had climbed up over the window. See how the board at the top stands out from the window. He put our buttons down behind there. Sallie said, 'Let's wait until he goes in the other part of the house and gets busy with something else and we will see what that little mister has been up to.' So we tiptoed back without him seeing us and sat down and began to work on the shirts as if nothing had happened. He played around in there for a while and finally came out and got busy with something else. Sallie had washed the sheets from off the bed where Bertha slept, so in about an hour, she got the sheets off the line, and on the pretense of making up the bed, we went in and shut the door. We did that a lot of times to keep him off the bed while we made them up, so he didn't pay any attention to us. Sallie stood at the head of the bed and felt over behind the window facing and look at what all she found."

The little thief had been stealing them blind. She handed Tom some spools of thread, a thimble, some buttons, lot of change that no doubt he had stolen at different times when Tom had taken it out of his pockets and put it on the dresser, Sallie's ring that they had looked the house over for. Then Ettie said, "And look here what we found." She handed him his billfold. "And all your money is still in it."

Tom was so shocked. He didn't know what to say. He finally said, "I don't believe it. When did that little thief get it without us seeing him?"

They were all so happy they stood there not knowing whether to laugh or cry. They all three just bowed their heads and holding hands thanked God for another miracle. Tom didn't know how they were going to make it through the winter without any money, but they had just put their faith in God to help them, and He had. Not only did He see them through most of the winter without any money, but when winter was almost over, He gave them back the money.

Ettie said, "See, Tom, I told you it would be all right."

That night they all went to bed three happy people.

After that, things went real smooth. J. B. came a week early for Christmas as he had promised Ettie he would. Christmas was a repeat of Thanksgiving, except there was more of them and Lucky was missing. He wouldn't come out to see any of them. Always he acted like everyone was his company, and he was around greeting everyone. This year he stayed hidden all the time. When he did come out, he would sit at the window looking out as if he was longing to be out there and be free.

Dora had been coming over for several days. She, Sallie, and Ettie had cooked enough to last them all week. The boys and Tom, along with John and J. B. on Christmas Eve, had put the turkey and ham outside as they always did to cook overnight. The turkey was larger than the one for Thanksgiving, and they had a larger ham also.

All John and Dora's kids came Christmas Eve. They all brought snacks of one kind or another for supper and more cakes. Ettie, Dora, and Sallie had all kinds of pickles and had made plenty of punch, hot chocolate, and coffee. They all sat around until bedtime, eating, drinking, playing games, and singing carols. About eleven or twelve everyone decided it was time to go to bed. J. B. and Tom took the spare room, John and Dora took Sallie's, and Sallie slept with Ettie. All the kids made pallets—and you never saw so many pallets. There were pallets everywhere, and you never heard so much giggling and laughing in your whole life. The oldies just closed their doors and left it with them. Tom didn't know when they all ever went to sleep. They were really enjoying just being together. That was the first time for them since they had all left home.

Christmas morning, they were up early. The girls had all the pallets up and put away before Dora, Sallie, and Ettie had breakfast ready. They just had cake and coffee or hot chocolate for breakfast. Every one sat around talking and laughing and just enjoying themselves. "Those years all together with our friends and love ones has always been mine and Ettie's best Christmas memories." They didn't have much as far as earthly things, but the love and happiness that they shared with their love ones was something they all would cherished for the rest of all their life.

J. B. asked God's blessing on the food, but he didn't ask everyone to tell about a blessing they had. He said, "As many as are here, our food would be cold if we did. That would come while we eat our dessert." After they all got their dessert, he told them, "It is time for our show and tell."

Ettie and Sallie joined in together and told about Tom losing his billfold and how they had found it. Sallie said, "I have never seen so much love and happiness as I have seen since I have been here and how proud I am to be able to share in it." By the time every one told about something special, the evening was almost gone. J. B. ended by saying that he agreed with Sallie and he too felt really blessed that God had allowed him to become a part of all their family and share in such blessings. The rest of the day everyone just sort of did as they pleased. All the young folks played games, and the older ones sat around talking. Before they knew it, the day was gone. John, Dora, Sallie, J. B., Ettie, and Tom stood at the door and told everyone good-bye. It had started snowing, and to all the kiddoes the snow just finished making the perfect Christmas. As they all ran to get into their wagons to go home, they were throwing snowballs, laughing and hollering at every one "Merry Christmas." Tom and all the others just stood there watching them leave, and J. B. said, "It is a Merry Christmas. Who could ask for more!"

Dora and John stayed over. All the guys went outside and did all the outside work while the women took care of the kitchen. When they all came in, the girls had made some more coffee and hot chocolate for all of them. It was plenty cold, and something hot surely tasted good.

Christmas was a repeat of Thanksgiving. John and Dora had the week off, so with some persuasion they stayed over. Each day, after they got through with the outside work, the guys would go down to the dugout and play dominoes. With the heavy snow, it was easy to track the rabbits so they went rabbit hunting and the next day they made rabbit stew. Each night the guys would go coon hunting. They got several that week and hung them on the barn to cure out. Tom wasn't in real need of them as he had before Ettie and Sallie had found their money, but the boys still depended on them for their money to help them survive. John, J. B., and Tom would sleep at the house; but they would stay almost all the day at the dugout with the boys. On the third day, when they went out rabbit hunting, they saw a deer at the haystack. The boys had been telling Tom he was there, but they didn't need the meat right then, so Tom told them just let him alone until they needed him. He told them, "This is the perfect time. It is cold enough to keep the meat good, and we all could use it." He gave the guns to J. B. and John, and they crept up close enough to get a good shot. The boys and Tom stayed back with the dogs and kept them quiet. They were used to seeing the deer at the haystack until they didn't bark when they saw them anymore. Nevertheless, they wanted to give J. B. and John the chance to kill it. They never killed just for the pleasure of killing, but they killed the deer when they needed meat to help them get through the winter. John held back to let J. B. get the first shot. Tom knew he would for the memory of when J. B. use to have to hunt for their survival. He brought it down with one shot. Billy had gone to the dugout to get a rope and the team and wagon. Then they would load it into the wagon and take it to a tree to hang it so it would bleed out and then they would field dress it. After that they would take it to the house and finish dressing it out the next day.

J. B. was real tickled over it and said he could hardly wait for a big deer steak and a deer roast. He said, "I haven't had either since I was here Thanksgiving. You have your work cut out for you. I was hoping for a big steak right away and then a roast cooked in the Dutch oven later on before I go home."

This tickled the boys, and they told him, "How about tomorrow on the steaks."

He told them, "Then that sounds good to me."

Finding the deer took care of the rabbit hunting. By the time they got it to the smokehouse and skinned and hung the deer, it was late. J. B., John, and Tom were ready to call it a day. They told the boys good night and that they would see them tomorrow. The girls had coffee waiting for them, and they sure were ready for it. They didn't realize how cold they were until they got to the house and out of the snow. They sat around drinking coffee and told the girls about the deer hunt and everything that they had done that day.

The next day, they finished dressing out the deer, and sure enough the boys kept their word and they had deer steaks for dinner. They took some up to the girls to fix for their dinner, but the guys ate in the dugout. The next day it was too cold to get out for very long at a time. The boys took care of the outside chores and let the men stay inside. The boys stopped at the smokehouse and got some steaks and fixed them. J. B. told the boys, "Those are the best steaks I have eaten in a long time." He just bragged and bragged about them, and of course, that tickled the boys. After that, they played dominoes instead of forty-two so all seven of them could play.

The week passed real fast, and before they knew it, the week was gone. The boys did fix the deer roast that they had promised J. B., and J.B. made deer chili for them, and it surely was good. He made a huge pan, and what was left over they took to the smokehouse. It was still cold, so they didn't have to worry about it.

On the following Monday, John and Dora went home after telling them what a good time they had. Tom took J. B. to the train station at the same time. Again Ettie had a chocolate cake made for him to take with him. He told everyone what a good time he had. He told Ettie, "You will never know how happy ya'll have made an old man's Christmas."

The boys had come up for breakfast and to tell everyone bye. J.B. told them, "I will be back again before it gets too hot to hunt deer and ya'll need to have some spotted, so we all can have deer steak again."

They told him, "There was almost always some in the hay meadow, and if there aren't, we will have some spotted somewhere else."

Again, Ettie had made them two canteens of hot coffee, but as cold as it was, they had drained it a long time before they got to town. They went to the train station and got his ticket, then headed to the cafe to get some more hot coffee to warm them up and wait for the train. The conductor always blew the whistle a long time before they had to be there so they had plenty of time to drink coffee and for J. B. to shoot the breeze with some old cronies that just happened to be in the cafe. While he talked, Tom took the eggs in and also some honey. Finally, the whistle sounded and they tried to pay for their coffee, but the waitress said J. B.'s money wasn't any good in her cafe, so they thanked her and hurried out to make sure they got there on time. They got there just as the train was coming into the depot. They boarded the train, and Tom sat down with J. B.

until the conductor hollered, "All aboard." Then he hugged him bye and told him to come again soon. J. B. told Tom, "I will be back to see my first grandson." And with tears in his eyes, he told him again how happy they all had made his Christmas.

As soon as the train pulled out, Tom left and went by and delivered the rest of the eggs and honey at the other cafe and the grocery store. It was still plenty cold, and the waitress insisted on filling his canteen with some hot coffee before he left and again she wouldn't let him pay for it. People, there in their little town, were like that. Friends meant more than money did. After that Tom headed back home. He sure wanted to get there before dark, so he didn't fool around very long. It was late in the afternoon before he got home. The boys had finished the outside choirs and was Tom glad. He sure was glad they had. The only thing he wanted to do was go in, get warm, eat supper, and go to bed. The buggy's top and sides knocked off some of the wind, but it was still cold even with the blankets over him. When he got there, he was so cold and stiff he could hardly get out of the buggy. Ettie had a pot of coffee made waiting for him, and a warm quilt hung next to the stove to wrap around him to help him get warm. She helped him sit down and wrapped the quilt around him. She poured him a cup of coffee. Tom was so cold until he was shaking all over. While he drank the coffee, she and Sallie put supper on the table. They had made a big pot of soup and a pan of corn bread. The soup was steaming hot, and boy did it taste good. With it and the coffee, Tom finally got warm. Right after he finished eating, he went to bed. Ettie warmed another quilt and put on him, and it wasn't long until he was sound asleep.

At breakfast the next morning, Ettie told him, "Tom, I have to talk to you about Lucky. I have prayed and prayed that Lucky would get all right again, but yesterday when the boys brought the milk up, he tried to attack them. Billy got a little too close to me, Lucky sprang forward before we knew what was happening, and he would have bit him if I hadn't turned just in time to stop him. I scolded him, and he ran to the baby's bed and stayed there all day pouting. When any of us tried to talk to him, he would growl and make funny noises, like he was going to attack us. Not even I could calm him down. Tom, I hate to admit it, but we are going to have to do something with him. When the baby comes, I think he will resent it taking over the bed. Lucky thinks the bed is his and right now he is daring any of us to get close to it. The way he is acting now, I don't think I would trust him around the little one anyway. It's a shame because before Bertha came, I would have trusted him with the baby. I thought he would have enjoyed it as much as we will, but Bertha ruined all that." She started crying. "Oh, Tom, why did she have to come and spoil everything for us? It could have been such a joyful occasion for all of us. Lucky would have been so proud of it."

Tom took her in his arms and tried to comfort her. He knew how she felt. Lucky had taken the place of the baby that they thought they would never have for over two years and it was going to be hard to have to let him go. Later they were to learn that was the way all parents felt about their children when they grew up and it came time to let them go.

They knew the time had come to let Lucky go and they knew that they had to, but it didn't make it any easier. They decided to try and help him as much as they could before they turned him loose. His food had always been put out for him and also his water. He had never had to depend on himself to get his own food or water. So they decided from now on they would hide his food and water in different places in the house. This way he would have to depend on himself to find it or go hungry. The first day Tom killed a rabbit and dressed it out, and they hid it in the guest room under the bed and put his water there also. When he went to where his bowl used to be and found no food or water, they heard him fussing but neither Ettie nor Tom gave in to him. That night for the first time in his life he went hungry. By morning he was really complaining and came to Ettie begging for food, but Ettie paid him no mind except to tell him, "Go find your food yourself. You have to start taking care of yourself, if you are going to survive when we turn you lose. Now go find it or go hungry." That day he was one unhappy coon, but Ettie or Sallie, either one, didn't give in to him. Sallie wanted to at least show him the room where it was hidden so he could hunt for it there. But Ettie told her, "No, that he had to find it on his own." During the second night he found it. They heard him fussing when they went to bed. Tom told Ettie, "He smells it, but not enough to find it." All at once he stopped fussing. He and Ettie slipped out of bed and tiptoed to the door of the guest room, and sure enough he had found it. They couldn't tell whether he was more hungry or thirsty. He drank and drank before he started eating his food, then he gobbled it down like he was starved to death. Ettie commented on it and Tom told her, "If he don't learn to find it, he will be more hungry than that when he is out in the wild because the scent wouldn't be as strong as it is in the house. He will have to rely on his smell completely." After the first few days, he did real good. He seemed to think they were playing a game with him. Each morning he would go to where his bowl and water used to be and when he couldn't find it there, he would look at them as if to say, "Okay, if this is the kind of game you want to play, then I will go along with it, but I don't like it." Then he would turn around and go off looking for the place they had hidden his bowl. He got to where he could find it almost every day. The boys started hunting for some kind of food for him every day. Sometime it was a rabbit, a squirrel, or some kind of bird. They got to where they just took the intestines out and left the feathers and hide on them. This confused him again. It was harder for him to find, and he wasn't used to his meat this way, and he didn't like it at all. But if this was all he was going to get, then he would do the best he could with it. Then one day the boys brought some live fish in a pan of water. They didn't hide it. They just set it out in the room. Again, that night he went hungry. He drank some water and finely tried to catch the fish. They all hid and watched him try to catch them. He had never had to fish before and didn't have his mother to show him how. He fished and fished with no luck. Finally, he left the pan and went looking somewhere else for food. When he couldn't find any, he came back and again tried to catch some fish. It took him that day and into the night before he learned to catch some. They were small and wasn't enough to satisfy him, but he learned another lesson on how to survive on what he could catch. Before long he had learned how to fish real well and how to find his food.

It was getting close to mating season, and the boys and Tom decided it was time for them to turn him loose. They decided to wait until a warm day and take him to a large wooded area about a half day's journey from their place. As far as they knew, they didn't allow anyone to hunt there so he would be safe from hunters until he got used to living in the wild. About a week later they had a real nice day, so they decided today was a perfect day to take him. They had built a cage to put him in when the time came to take him. Before the trouble, he would have ridden up front with them and be perfectly happy, but not now. They brought the cage in. Luck was with them; it was one of his good days that he allowed Ettie to hold him. She picked him up and petted him and told him bye. She tried real hard not to cry or show any emotion to get him upset. After she told him bye and that she loved him, she walked over to the cage and put him in it and they closed the door real quick. He started growling and trying to get out. He was one unhappy coon and scared also. He had never been in a cage before. Ettie kept talking to him and told him no one was going to hurt him and he was going to be all right. He finally calmed down and acted like he was listening to her. She told him he was going away to live in the woods with other coons and it was for his own good, that she knew he wasn't happy with them anymore, so it was time he found him a mate so he could be happy. By then she was crying, and Tom looked around and saw everyone else was too. Again, she told him bye. "Now you be a good coon," she said. Then she turned and ran into the bedroom, and they could hear her crying her heart out. Lucky heard her too, and he began to try to get out to go to her. He was crying and growling and trying for all he was worth to break out. Tom told the boys to take him out and to be careful and don't let their fingers get anywhere he could reach them because he will bite them right now.

Then he went into Ettie to comfort her. He took her in his arms and told her how sorry he was and that she knew they had to do it now or latter. Between sobs she said, "I know, Tom, but why did it have to be this way. I know he will be happier now with his own kind, but why did it have to happen in the first place. Why did Bertha have to come and spoil everything?"

Tom tried to tell her everything had a reason, and God never let anything happen without a reason and for his children's own good. Right then he didn't know if she believed him or not because he was having a hard time believing it himself. He knew it was true. God never let anything happen to his children that wasn't for their own good, but right then he, like her, couldn't see God's purpose in letting this happen. Tom told her he would wait and see if he really wanted to leave before he came back home.

The boys had loaded the cage in the back of the wagon and were waiting for him. Ettie, bless her heart, had fixed them a lunch; and Sallie hollered at them and told them about it. Billy ran back to the porch to get it. Besides the lunch, she had fixed a canteen of milk for the boys, a canteen of coffee for Tom, and a jug of water.

It took them until about noon to get there. As soon as they got there, they opened the tailgate and pulled the cage right up to the edge and Mark got in the wagon. After Billy and Tom moved back to the front of the wagon, he opened it and Lucky leaped out. He didn't stop. As soon as his feet hit the ground, he was running toward the woods. Tom thought when he got to the edge of the woods he would turn and look back, but he didn't even stop. They sat there and ate their dinner waiting to see if he would come back. When they finished, they waited for about an hour or so and he still didn't come. The boys suggested they walk out into the woods to see if they could see him anywhere, but they never saw hide nor hair of him. They called and called to him. Always before he would come running as soon as he heard his name, but not this time. They found plenty of coon tracks but didn't see any coons. Billy said he would find them. It was getting close to mating season, and maybe he would find a female. They walked around a little longer calling for him, then they decided it was time for them to go home. Lucky had found his place. They all went back to the wagon knowing that they would never see Lucky again. They didn't talk much at first going home. They all had their memories of Lucky and the years he had lived with them.

Finally, Billy said, "Well, I hope Lucky finds a mate and has a big family of little coons. Boy, will he have plenty of stories to tell them."

They all laughed and started telling their own stories. The rest of the way home was spent with them talking about him.

They got home about dark. The boys told Tom to go in to Ettie, that she would be anxious to hear what happened. They said they would do up the night work. He told them to come up for supper, knowing Ettie she would have it ready for them. Ettie and Sallie both met Tom at the door. They both were real anxious to hear what happened. Tom told them, and both stood there with tears in their eyes. To cheer them up, Tom told them what Billy had said and they started laughing. Sallie said he will have plenty to tell, that is if coons tell their little ones stories.

Soon after that Billy brought the milk in to be strained and said, "Mark is getting the eggs." Sallie strained the milk, and Billy took it to the smokehouse. By that time Mark had put the eggs in the smokehouse, and they both came in for supper. All during supper the boys tried to keep a joyful conversation going for Ettie's sake. They told her how happy Lucky was to be free. Mark said, "It's mating season and the little scoundrel hit the ground running to go find himself a wife." They left shortly after supper. Sallie told Ettie and Tom, "Go on to bed and I will clean the kitchen. Ettie has had a hard day, and I know she is tired. We had taken everything off the baby bed and washed them and redone the bed."

Ettie started crying as soon as she got into bed. Tom tried to comfort her, and she told him, "Tom, I know all that Mark was saying is true, but I miss him so."

Tom told her, "It won't be long until the little one will be here, and you will have it to fill the gap in your heart that Lucky has left."

She said, "I know it, Tom, but it was so hard to see him go. He has been in my lap and around my feet for all these years, and all day I was either looking down to keep from stepping on him or every time I sat down, I was waiting for him to jump up on my lap."

Tom hugged her, trying his best to comfort her, and she finally cried herself to sleep.

A week later John and Dora came over and told Tom, J. B. had passed away and they were bringing him back to be buried next to Martha. Dora told Tom that she didn't think they ought to tell Ettie right now, that her time was getting to close for them to tell her news like that. That it could cause her to go into labor and they sure didn't want that to happen. So they all decided not to tell her until after the baby came. The day of the funeral, Sallie took his Sunday clothes out to the barn. He told Ettie the boys had asked for a day off so he would take the eggs in for her. If she thought anything about it, she didn't let on. He told her bye and went out and hitched the horse to the buggy, changed his clothes, and left.

All the family was there when Tom got there. J. B.'s son gave the letter that he had found in J. B.'s Bible addressed to Tom. He had fulfilled his daddy's request, just the way J. B. wanted it. So Tom just put the letter in his pocket and would destroy it later. At the end of the service, the preacher ended it by saying, "J. B. will be missed. He was a very special person to all of us. J. B. had so much love and compassion to give, and it took in every one he met. He was always there with hands reaching out to everyone he met that needed help. His passing will leave an empty place in all our hearts, but be happy for him because he is with his beloved Martha, where he has waited and longed to be ever since she passed away." The church had fixed dinner for everyone, but Tom didn't stay. He told them he had to get back to Ettie and why.

As soon as Tom got out of hearing distance, he started crying. He had held it back as long as he could. He had lost another precious friend. J. B. and Jack had been just like brothers to Tom. Tom thought back to the first year he has spent on the ranch. If it hadn't been for them, what would he have done? Tom thought of that first year and all the things they had given him and all the things they had helped him build. If it hadn't been for them, what would Tom have done? Tom stopped crying and said, "Lord, thank you for letting me meet them and have them as brothers as many years as You did. Forgive me for being so selfish. They are now where they want to be, and they are happy." Later on he would tell Ettie, and they would have their time of mourning. But right now he would just say, "Thank you for all the wonderful years You let me know them and all the wonderful memories You have given me."

Chapter 25

IN TWO WEEKS, SHE WENT into labor. Dora had come over during the week to be with her when the baby came. Now you must remember the doctor was several hours from them and most of the time a woman that had experience delivering babies, which they called midwives, would be there to deliver the babies. Dora had delivered plenty, as well as having so many herself.

Ettie had a long hard delivery. She was in labor all that day and into the night. They had kept Tom chased out of her room, but finally, Dora came in the living room and sat down. She said, "Tom, we are going to need your help. The little dickens got himself turned crossways."

Tom asked her, "Do you want me to go for the doctor?"

She said, "You go tell the boys to saddle the fastest horse you have and tell them to have it at the back door waiting. If I can't turn it, then we are in trouble. Then I want you to go, and I mean go fast. Right now I want you to come in and try to keep Ettie calm as much as you can. Talk to her and tell her to relax and calm down. Everything is going to be all right. And while you are doing it, pray that it will be."

They went into the kitchen. Dora washed her hands and arm, then she greased her right hand with Vaseline almost to her elbow. Tom opened the door for her, and when Sallie saw them, she went to the foot of the bed. Tom went to the head. Ettie looked so tired; but when he took her hand, she opened her eyes and said, "Tom, pray for our little one and that God will let me live to raise it."

Tom told her, "I will." So right then he just bowed his head and started asking God to spare her and their little one and give them back to him. When he got through praying, he told her, "Now I have asked God to spare you both. Now let's just relax and let Him take over, and believe me, He will."

She looked up, smiled slightly, and said that with him praying for her, she knew it will. Tom couldn't see what Dora and Sallie were doing. She told Ettie not to push anymore. "Just try to relax. Everything is going to be all right." Tom could hear the relief in Dora's voice. Ettie could also, because she said, "See, Tom, all I needed was for you to pray."

Tom told her, "I have been praying all day and night for you, sweetheart."

About that time Dora said, "Now, Ettie, push."

And it wasn't long until they heard a little cry, and Dora said, "It's here, Ettie, and it's a little boy."

He had coal-black hair like Ettie, and his eyes were as black as hers.

Dora said, "Well, look at his eyes."

This upset Ettie, and she said, "What's wrong with his eyes. Tell me what's wrong with my baby?"

Dora said, "Now calm down, there is nothing at all wrong with him. He is small but perfect. His eyes are black like yours, and most babies are born with blue eyes, and they change later."

Tom said out loud, "Thank you, God," because, like Ettie, he thought when Dora said, "Look at his eyes," that something was wrong also.

He was small. He only weighed a little more than four pounds. Dora and Sallie washed and dressed him. Then they brought him and put him in Tom's arms. He had never held a baby before, and he seemed so small and helpless, but he was perfect. Ettie had tried to stay awake so she could see him, but she was so tired that she had finally dozed off.

Tom woke her and said, "Look here, sweetheart, what we have," and held him over for her to see.

She looked and said, "Oh, Tom, isn't he beautiful," and was back to sleep.

Tom held him a few minutes, and Dora came in and said, "The baby and Ettie have both had a long hard day. Let's put him in his bed so he and Ettie both can get some rest. Sallie is fixing us something to eat."

It dawned on him that they all hadn't eaten all day. While she fixed the food, Tom hollered for the boys. They had just unsaddled the horse and put him in the pasture. He told them everything is just fine and "It's a boy." Tom thought people a mile away could have heard them hollering, "Yippee, yippee."

By then Sallie had supper. They all went in and ate some hot soup. Tom took some in to see if he could get Ettie to eat also, but she was still sleeping and so was the baby, so he tiptoed out and just let them sleep.

The next day Tom took the baby over to Ettie and asked her, "What are we going to name him?"

She said, "That was decided a long time ago, Virgil Boyd, after Jack Engles and J. B. Rogers."

So their precious son was named after two of the second best men Tom had ever known. He didn't know what he would have done without either one of them.

A few days later Dora dropped the bombshell that would change things for them for the rest of their whole life. She was bathing little Virgil on the kitchen table, close to the fire, so he would stay warm. Tom had just came into the house and poured him a cup of coffee and had sat down at the end of the table watching her bath him. She looked up with a strange look on her face and said, "Tom come over here a minute." He got up and walked around the table, and she said, "Look at his little legs. Does this one look shorter than the other one?" They laid him on his back and straightened his little legs out as straight as they could. Sure enough his left leg would only come to just above the ankle on his right leg. They tried to move him another way, but his left leg was still shorter. Every way they tried to turn him, it was shorter. Dora said, "Tom, his little left leg is a lot shorter than his little right one." Tom had already realized it but hearing her say it made it sound so much worse and so horrible. His beautiful little boy would be a crippled all his life. As hard as he tried not to, tears began to run down his cheeks. This little boy that they had dreamed and planned for so long. Tom had planned for the day he would be old enough for him to take hunting and fishing. He would be his buddy, and he would take him with him everywhere he went. He would teach him all the things that he had learned from Mr. Heart and the ranch hands. He would be the best at everything—roping, branding, and shooting. Now he had just learned he would never be able to do any of these things. Dora tried to tell him it wasn't the end of the world, that he still could do all the things that a normal boy could do. But Tom knew different, and he told her so. She jumped all over him and told him, "Now, Tom, you just listen to me. With that attitude, you would make a cripple out of him for sure. You have made a cripple out of him before he has got started. Give him a chance and encourage him. Tell him, he can do anything that any other boy can do, and he will do it. But he will be and will do exactly what his dad tells him he can do. If you teach him he can do anything he sets his head to do, then he will do it. He will be what you tell him he can be and don't you ever forget it." She turned and started dressing Virgil again, then she looked up and said, "I hope Ettie has more sense then you are showing right now."

Tom told her, "But, Dora, you don't understand."

Tom saw that this remark made Dora mad, and she told him, "No, Tom, it's you that don't understand. You could have lost both of them, and the baby could have had brain damage. You should thank God for saving both of them."

They decided not to tell Ettie until she was stronger. She was still real weak and tired from the ordeal of just bringing him into the world. Tom turned and went outside without saying another word, but he thought, *Yes, and she doesn't have a cripple son either. All her children had been perfect.* He went to the barn, and then he broke down completely. He started crying and asking God why. They had waited so long and prayed so hard, why did He make their baby a cripple? Then Tom stopped crying and said, "God, I won't have him a cripple. I will work with him until his leg grows the same length as the other one. He is a baby, and it will grow as long as the other one. I will make it."

At the end of the week, they told Ettie. She cried and blamed herself for him being that way. She said it was all her fault. Tom tried to tell her it was no one's fault, but she kept crying and telling him it was her fault but wouldn't tell him why she thought it was. He told her, "As soon as you get strong enough, we will take him to the doctor, and if we have to sell everything we have, we will find one that can help us make it grow as long as the other one."

As soon as his navel cord came off and it healed, Tom started working with him the next morning. When Sallie brought him in to bathe, he was there. They put him in the dish pan and while she held him, Tom rubbed his little leg. He started with five minutes at first. He would work up to more time, but right now he would do only five minutes every day. Then when Ettie got stronger, they would take him to the doctor and he would tell them what to do.

He was six weeks old when Ettie was strong enough and they found a pretty warm day to take Virgil in to see Dr. Renee.

He told them about the same thing that Dora told them. He told them now, "Tom, only God can create a miracle. Regardless to where you take him, there is not one of them that can start his leg to growing. They are not God. Now you can accept it and thank God you still have your wife and baby. From what they told me, you are lucky to have either one of them. As much trouble as she had, it was a miracle they both lived through it at all. You could spend everything you have running from doctor to doctor, and when you have spent everything, the verdict will still be the same. Or you can accept him as he is and not make him feel like he was a cripple. Also, you can work with him and he will be able to do everything that any other boy can do."

Tom thought, *Yeah, I could just see him riding a horse, roping a calf, and branding them like any other boy can do*. He told him, "But, Doctor, you don't understand, that we are ranchers."

He said, "Yes, I do, and Tom, you are the one that don't understand. He will learn to cope with his leg being shorter and will learn to do anything that any other boy can do, if ya'll don't make a cripple out of him to begin with. His leg is not that much shorter that he won't be able to walk and live a good life, if you all will let him. Now, Tom, I know you will go to see another doctor, and I don't blame ya'll. But when you see two more, then I want ya'll to promise me, ya'll will bring him back home and accept him as he is and don't spend all the money ya'll have and time running from one doctor to another, because as I told you, none of ya'll are God, and sooner or later you all will learn ya'll are not."

Tom left his office fighting mad. He would find someone else that would help his precious boy's leg to grow. A week later they left for Weatherford to see another doctor. About the only thing they accomplished was Ettie got to see her mother. Her mother got to see her grandchild, and Sallie and Tom got to see Mary Ann. They told Maw Cooker why they had come, and when she saw him, she told them the same thing the doctor and Dora told them. Tom told her, "We still want a second option," so she told them where the doctor lived and the next day they went to see him. When he examined Virgil, he told them the same thing that Dr. Renee had told them but made it plainer and stronger. He told them, "He is a beautiful and healthy little boy that one leg just happened to be a little shorter than the other one. For ya'll to accept him as he is and thank God for him or give him to some one that would be tickled to death to have him. We are not God, and we cannot create a miracle. Ya'll are holding one of God's miracles. Be proud of him and help him live a normal life and don't make a cripple out of him before he gets started."

Tom left his office as mad as an old wet hen. He would find someone to help their baby if it was the last thing he did. The next day Ettie and Tom left to take little Virgil to Dallas. They left Sallie to visit with Mary Ann until they came back. They spent that night in a hotel, and the next day inquired about a doctor. The hotel manager told them about a Dr. Thomas that might help them. He said he was a bone specialist, and if anyone could help he could. He called the doctor for them, and with high hopes, at two o'clock, they were in his office. He was real nice and seemed real concerned about their problem but told them the same thing as Dr. Renee had told them. Again, he told them, "Ya'll could spend every penny you have, taking him to doctors after doctors, and it wouldn't do any good. Ya'll have one of the best doctors that could be found, right there in your hometown. What did Dr. Renee tell ya'll?"

Tom told him, "Just what you and the other doctors told us. He told us that the problem was that we have to accept him just as he is and help him learn to do everything, that he would if both his legs were the same length. He told us, if we would learn to cope with it, he would."

Then he said, "Now I wasn't trying to be rude or cruel, but if you all think of him as a cripple, then he will be one. You both have got to be real firm with him and keep telling him he can do anything that any other boy can do and he will do it. Just remember, if he becomes a cripple, it will be mostly because you all make him one. Just take him home and thank God for him and love him enough to help him become the boy he can become. It won't be an easy job, but with God's help you all can do it, and it will be worth it in the end. He is a precious little boy that a lot of people would give anything for." Then he told them, and Tom would never forget what he said, "Just take him home and pray that God will make you both the kind of parents he needs to raise him. It takes special people to raise one of God's children that has a handicap, but he has chosen you two because He thought you were worthy, don't let Him down."

Tom thanked him and told him, "Pray for us that we can be the kind of parents he needs."

The doctor stood up and shook Tom's hand and said, "God bless you both, and tell Dr. Renee hello for me."

They left his office with both Ettie and Tom feeling so much better about it all. Dr. Thomas had given them both the peace of mind and the courage they needed. Now they were ready to take him home and do what all three of the doctors had told them to do. They caught the train and went back to Weatherford that afternoon. They stayed overnight with Mary Ann, and the next day they went to see Ettie's mother. She still lived and worked for Mr. Thompson. All the children, his and Maw's, seemed to think the world of him and they all seemed to be real happy. Of course, Mr. Thompson and Maw wanted to know what they had found out. They told them what the doctor had told them, and they had decided to do what he told them to do. Maw agreed with him. She told them, "You have to accept the gift that God had given you and be proud of it, that it could have been worse."

Mr. Thompson was as nice as he could be to Ettie and Tom. He tried to get them to stay longer, but they wanted to get back home as soon as they could. He thanked Tom again for the lesson and told him he would never forget it. He held Virgil almost the whole time they were there. He told them he was such a pretty baby and how proud he would have been to have one like him to carry on his name, that all his children were girls. He told Tom, "Be proud of him and thank God for such a wonderful gift. I know I would." They left that afternoon, with both of them telling them to come back as soon as they could.

They went by Mary Ann and Ross's to pick up Sallie. While the girls visited, Ross and Tom went to pick up their tickets. The train wouldn't be leaving until seven o'clock, so they would have a few hours to visit. Of course, they had to tell the story all over again. Mary Ann told Tom from what Sallie had said, he was real lucky to have Ettie or the baby either one. She told him, "Just thank God for them and be happy that God let them live." While Ross and Tom took care of Virgil, the girls fixed supper. They ate early so they would be ready to leave in time to catch the train by seven. By the time it was ready and they ate, it was just about time for them to go. They told them both bye and thanked them for everything and left to go to the train depot. By the time they got there it was almost time for the train to pull out. They made Virgil a bed in one of the seats, and it wasn't long until he was sound to sleep. They all three took turns watching him all night. That way they all could get a little sleep.

They got into Jacksboro about breakfast time the next day. Tom left Sallie, Ettie, and the baby at the station and went down and got the horse and buggy. No one was there. But Mr. Brown was use to him picking up his buggy or wagon when he came back and knew he would pay him for keeping them when he or the boys came in next time. Tom went back to the station and picked up the girls, then they went to the café and ordered breakfast. While they fixed breakfast, they all drank a cup of coffee but had little to say. They all three were hungry, sleepy, and tired, but mostly hungry. By the time they finished eating breakfast, the stores were beginning to open. Tom went up to pay for their meal, but the cashier said they had plenty of egg money there, that the boys had been delivering the eggs regularly. Tom had her fix them some food to take with them and had her fill the coffee canteens. He had coffee and a coffeepot, but Tom thought as cold as it was, they had better get home as fast as they could before night set in. He asked Ettie if they needed anything from the grocery store, and she said they didn't. So as soon as their lunch and coffee was ready, they headed for home. At the best they could do it, it would be around four before they could get home. Even though it looked like it would be a pretty nice day for this time of year, you never knew when a blizzard would blow in and Tom sure didn't want to be caught out at night in one with the girls and Virgil.

At noon, Tom knew he was going to have to stop and let the horse rest and graze for a while. They had only stopped long enough for Virgil to nurse and for them to have a cup of coffee, which really wasn't enough time for the horse to rest. Tom found a wooded area thick enough to knock off the wind. It was close to a creek, so they could get some fresh water and the horse would have a place to drink. This time Tom broke the first rule that Mr. Heart had taught him. He let the horse stand hitched up to the buggy while he built a fire. In this case he thought the girls and Virgil needed taking care of first. He built it close to the buggy so it would help keep what little wind was blowing off them. When it started burning real good and putting out some heat, he helped them out of the buggy and covered them up real good with the quilts that they always kept in the buggy. Then he took care of the horse and turned her loose to graze and go down and get a drink. By the time Tom finished taking care of the horse, Sallie had gotten the water jug and coffeepot out and made some coffee. When it was ready Tom got their lunch out. The fire was burning real good and was putting out plenty of heat to keep them warm. They ate their dinner and drank plenty of the hot coffee. When they had finished, Tom got the water jug and went down to get some fresh water. He made a fresh pot of coffee to fill up the canteens so they would have hot coffee to drink on the rest of the way home. Virgil woke up, and Ettie fed him while Sallie loaded the buggy. Tom went for the horse and hitched her up. He got some more water from the creek and put out the fire. Then they got in the buggy, and Tom covered Virgil and the girls up real good, and they were ready to go.

They got home around four thirty or five. It was beginning to get colder, and they all were worn out. Home sure looked good. The boys had done up all the night work and had a roaring fire going in the fireplace. They also had supper almost ready and boy, did it smell good. Mark and Tom unloaded the buggy and unhitched the horse while Billy finished supper. By then Ettie and Sallie had gotten Virgil's clothes changed and had him tucked in bed. He was worn out also, and it wasn't long until he was asleep. They all ate supper, and of course, the boys wanted to hear all about the trip and what they had found out about Virgil. Tom told them what the doctors had said, and both of them said, "We will teach him how to ride a horse and all the things he needs to know." No one could say they didn't keep their word. From that day on, they were up at the house all the time when they weren't busy helping Tom run the ranch. By the time Virgil began to crawl, they had him so spoiled that when they didn't show up to play with him he would fuss and cry until they finally got there that night.

When summer came, they had him down at the creek twice a day. They said, "The warm water will strengthen his leg and make it feel better." Tom didn't care how busy they were, one or the other never showed up until Virgil had his exercise. Although they knew nothing they did was going to help it grow and with all the exercises they did, it still was going to remain shorter than the other one but they said he enjoyed it and it would help to strengthen his legs. He didn't grow or put on weight like they thought he should. They took him back to Dr. Renee. He told them the same story as before. "Virgil is a healthy little baby. There are large babies, and they grow up to be large men, and there are small babies that grow up to be small men, and Virgil is one of them. He will probably be small all his life, and that don't mean he is unhealthy. He is a healthy small boy." He gave the same song and dance of not treating him any different from any other boy. He told them not to fail to come to see him if they needed him but to take their baby home and enjoy him.

Chapter 26

He was almost two when Ettie told Tom they were expecting another baby. As soon as she told him, he insisted that she go in to see Dr. Renee. Sallie kept Virgil while Tom took her in to see the doctor. Ettie and Tom were both scared that the same thing would happen again and this one would be born cripple also.

After Dr. Renee examined Ettie, he assured them, "It would be one chance in a million of it happening again. Ettie is in good health, and there is no reason the baby wouldn't be also. Go home and look forward to this wonderful blessing that God is giving you all."

They thanked him and went home with their mind somewhat relieved, but they decided when it was time for the baby to be born that Ettie and Tom would get a room in town so she would be closer to the doctor.

Time passed fast, and it wasn't long until it was time for the little one to be born. As they had planned, Ettie and Tom got a room in town and Sallie kept Virgil. One week after his second birthday, his little brother was born. Ettie had a pretty easy delivery when the baby came. Dr. Renee examined it from top to bottom and said with a great big smile, "He is a perfect little eight-pound boy."

They named him Monroe. Tom had found out from J. B. that Mr. Heart's name was Bill Monroe. So they named their son after the best man Tom had ever known. As Tom looked down at his son, he only wished that Mr. Heart was alive to know it. Tom thought back to the first time he saw Mr. Heart. A little eight-year-old boy, dirty, ragged, scared to death, feeling so alone, and not knowing what was to become of him. If it hadn't been for Mr. Heart, Tom often wondered what would have become of him.

Dr. Renee asked what they were going to name the baby, and when Tom told him, the doctor said, "My name is Monroe McGuire, and I sure would be pleased if you put that with the Monroe. I never had a son to carry on my name." So that was what they named him, the Monroe after the best man Tom had ever known and the McGuire after the doctor that delivered him.

He was three weeks old when they took him home. The boys had been by every week to see them when they brought the eggs and honey in. They always told them how everything was going at home. "Also, little Virgil is walking everywhere. We have stopped exercising Virgil's legs every day. With him walking, he exercises them aplenty. He runs all over the place, and it's all Sallie can do to keep up with him. He is trying to climb out of his bed but has not quite made it yet. We are sleeping at the house at night to watch him and let Sallie get some rest."

The day they left for home, Dr. Renee came by early and dismissed Ettie so they could get an early start. After he left, they went by and ate breakfast. This was the first day Ettie and the baby had been out. Tom had been going over and getting their meals three times a day and bringing them to their room.

Ettie was real excited about getting to show little Monroe off. Of course, everyone at the cafe had to see him, and they all agreed he looked like Tom. His hair was a reddish brown, and his eyes brown like Tom's. Virgil's hair and eyes were as black as coal, like Ettie's. After they ate breakfast and Maud, the owner of the café, fixed them a lunch and filled their canteens full of coffee, they left for home. They had a long drive ahead of them and they wanted to get home as early as possible. Tom did as they had when they brought Virgil in to the doctor that first time. They only stopped long enough for the baby to nurse and for them to have some hot coffee and let the horse rest. At noon they stopped, and Tom built a fire and made coffee, and they ate their dinner.

Tom let the horse rest longer this time because it wasn't cold like it was when they had taken Virgil to the doctors. They got home around three thirty or four. Billy came out to help Tom get Ettie and Monroe in the house while Mark watched Virgil. When they got to the door, here came Virgil running as fast as he could to his mama. He was so happy to see her. Then Ettie told him he had a little brother, and she had Tom to kneel down so he could see Monroe. At first he looked surprised, and Ettie told him to touch him. Then again she told him, "This is your little brother. He will grow up and play with you." The "play with him" did it. He grinned and touched him again. Then he bent over and kissed him. Ettie kept saying "Brother, brother," until he jabbered something; and Ettie said, "That's right, brother." It didn't sound like "brother" to Tom, but as long as they thought so, it was all right with him. They had been letting him sleep in the big bed with Sallie or the boys, so when Sallie took the baby in and put it in the baby bed, he didn't seem to mind. Ettie was real tired, so Sallie put her to bed also, and Virgil went over and tried to crawl up on the bed with her. Mark lifted him up on the bed, and he was perfectly willing to give the baby his bed.

While Sallie and the boys got supper, he lay beside his mama. She hugged him up, and he went sound to sleep. They both slept until supper was ready. When Sallie and the boys got it on the table, they woke them both. About that time Monroe woke up for his dinner also. Virgil was all right until

Ettie started feeding Monroe. Then he wanted to get up in her lap and nurse also. He didn't like it at all that his brother was getting his dinner and he had to eat from the table. He kept saying, "Mine, mine, mine," and wanted to get up in Ettie's lap so he could nurse too. Tom took him to the table, but he was real unhappy. He was crying and pointing at Ettie and saying over and over "Mine, mine." Tom felt so sorry for him. Sallie went over and got him and loved him to her and told him that's all right he could eat with Aunt Sallie. He was a happy little scoundrel after that, and it wasn't long until, with the boys picking at him and Sallie petting him that he was acting as if nothing had happened. But every time Ettie fed Monroe he would stand beside her chair and say, "Mine, mine" over and over. Ettie would pet him and tell him, "No, no, you are a big boy now." He would laugh and jabber something, and Ettie would say, "Yes, big boy now."

Tom didn't think he was completely convinced of this because each time he would be back when she fed Monroe and stand there while Monroe nursed. Tom laughed and told Ettie, "I don't think that you have quite convinced him that his brother is supposed to get his dinners. That is the only thing that he complains about, everything else, bed and all, he is perfectly willing for Monroe to have."

When Ettie would put Monroe on a pallet and if he started crying, Virgil would go over, lie down on his stomach, and jabber with him as if he was talking to him. And Tom guessed he was because Monroe would stop crying and look at him, as if to say, "Okay, I'm okay now. My big brother is here." Virgil was so proud of him. He was right there watching them regardless to what they were doing.

Needless to say, Monroe did everything quicker than Virgil had. When Monroe started trying to sit up, Virgil was right there trying to help him. When he started trying to crawl, it was so funny. Virgil stopped walking and started crawling with him. Then when Monroe started pulling up to things and standing, Virgil did to. It was so cute to see Virgil pulling up and waiting for Monroe to join him. Monroe was walking before he was a year old. Virgil acted like he was thrilled to death when Monroe started walking; and from then on, everywhere you saw Virgil, Monroe would be right behind him. Before Monroe was two, he was already larger than Virgil. But Virgil was the leader and the boss. He still protected Monroe. If he started to get in something that might hurt him, Virgil would make him leave it alone. But the two could still get into more mischief than a pack of rats. It took either Sallie or Ettie just to keep them out of trouble.

Billy and Mark would be up at the house playing with them every day when they didn't have something to do, and that helped a lot. The only thing about it was, now they had two spoiled babies instead of one.

When summer came, the boys kept them with them every day when they weren't working with Tom. They took them swimming, and when they were just checking the fences or cattle, the boys would have them on the front of the saddle with them. The days that they were working with the bees or doing things that they couldn't have them with them, they both would fuss and cry until the boys brought the milk in at night and then they were just as happy as they could be. They clung to the boys and didn't care whether Tom was around or not. Tom knew it was his fault because he let each boy take one every time they took them out. The boys seem to enjoy them so much, and that way it gave them one apiece. Tom couldn't take both of them at a time, so in place of them taking turns and switching the babies around, Tom just let the boys have one each. Tom didn't know what he was doing until it was too late. When they said "Boys" before they said "Daddy," he realized what he had done. But by then it was too late. When Tom and the boys came into the house, they would run to Billy and Mark instead of Tom, hollering, "Boys, boys" in place of "Daddy." It hurt Tom's feelings, but he realized it was his fault and not Virgil's, Monroe's, or the boys. Tom tried to make up for some of it. At night he would sit down with both boys in his lap and tell them stories about Granny Heart, Mr. Heart, and the ranch where he was raised. Tom wanted them to love Granny and Mr. Heart as he did and grow up remembering them.

When Monroe was almost nineteen months old, Ettie told Tom they were going to have another baby. Tom was determined that he wasn't going to make the same mistake with it as he had with them. This one would be his baby, and he would be the one to teach him everything he needed to know.

Ettie decided that since she hadn't had any trouble having Monroe that she would let it be born at home. She said, "It isn't fair on the boys, for her to be away from them that long." So it was settled. They would get Dora to come over when she needed her and Dora would deliver the baby at home. Everything went real good, and Ettie didn't have any trouble the whole time. When her time came, Dora had come over a few days early, and when Ettie's labor started, it wasn't long until the baby was born. Dora wrapped it in a baby blanket and said, "Tom, you have a beautiful little girl." When she said that, at first Tom was disappointed. He was wanting another boy, so he would have a sidekick like the two boys had. Dora handed her to him to take to Sallie to wash and dress. She said, "Tom look at her. Isn't she beautiful? And look, she has your auburn hair." Tom looked down to see the most beautiful little redheaded girl he had ever seen. She was the very picture of his mama. She was small like his mama and Ettie, and her hair and eyes were exactly like his mamas was. Also, her face features were exactly like his mama's. She caught hold of his finger and looked up as if to say, "That's all right, Daddy. I will still be your sidekick." Right then Tom wouldn't have traded her for ten little boys wrapped in gold blankets. He took her to the bed before he took her to Sallie and said, "Look, sweetheart, it's a little daughter and she is the spitting image of mama." By then tears were running down his face, and as hard as he tried, he couldn't stop from crying. It was like seeing his mama all over again. Sallie came around the bed to take her, and said, "Well, I do declare, she does look like our mama." And tears were running down her cheeks also. Sallie and Dora took the baby and went into the kitchen to bathe and dress her. Then Ettie told Tom, "Tom, I'm getting tired of living a lie. Do you remember when Virgil was born and was crippled and I blamed myself for it but I wouldn't tell you why. I was so scared that the same thing would happen to Monroe when he was born. It was because I was so young and I had lied to you about my age. Tom, I was just barely fourteen when we married. I was afraid that if I told you how old I was, you wouldn't have married me."

Tom took her in his arms and told her, "You are probably right. I would have most likely insisted that we wait until you got older, but look at all the happy years we had together." And with Tom always being such a cut up, he laughed and told her, "If we had waited until you grow up, you probably would have had more sense than to have married me."

Billy and Mark were waiting in the kitchen watching after the boys, and they could hardly wait to see the baby. Sallie told them, "It's a little girl." They held up Virgil and Monroe to see her and told them, "Ya'll have a little sister." Virgil was so tickled, he kept saying, "My sister, my sister," and clapping his hands. Monroe started clapping his hands, laughing and jabbering too. He didn't quite understand it all, but it made Virgil happy, so he was happy too.

They had always planned on naming their first daughter after Granny Heart. Ettie said, "Since she looks so much like your mother, it would be a shame not to name her part of her name." So they named her Leola after Granny Heart and Lorine after her grandmaw.

Whether she thought it or not, that first day, she kept her word of what Tom thought she was thinking. She was a daddy's girl from the very beginning. When she was a little older, when Tom came into the house, she would hold out her little arms for him to take her, regardless of who had her. The boys would always run to Billy and Mark, but she always wanted him.

By the time she was old enough to go with him, the boys had already started riding their own horses. Virgil could have had his own horse early, but he wouldn't leave Monroe. So, when Monroe was almost five, Tom gave them both their own horse. The horses were small like Hart was. They had worked with them until they were as gentle as little dogs. Tom didn't know which one was the proudest of them, him or Virgil. The boys had let them work with them while they were breaking them to ride. Virgil always wanted to know what they were doing and why. When Billy explained to him, "They have to be broke to ride," then he wanted to know, was Daddy going to sell them to someone. Billy told him, "Well, something like that." He would work with Billy, brushing the horse and leading him around. By the time he found out the horse was his, the horse was following him around like a little dog. Monroe was doing the same with his, but Tom got the feeling it was only because Virgil was doing it. He never seemed to be proud of his horse as Virgil was. When Tom told them that the horses were theirs, Virgil was so excited with his but Monroe didn't act as pleased over his. He never seemed to love animals or take to horses like Virgil did. He would do everything that Virgil did for his horse or any kind of animals, but it wasn't a chore of love like it was with Virgil. When Tom had given the horses to them, he told them the same thing Mr. Heart had told him that he would take them away from them if they didn't take care of them. Virgil assured him that he would never get his horse back, and Monroe followed suit, but not with the same enthusiasm as Virgil had. Tom asked them, as Mr. Heart had asked him, "Now what are you all going to name them?"

Virgil said, "Hart, after your Hart."

Tom told him, "That was a real nice thing for you to do, and I appreciate it. I hope she is as good a horse as my Hart was." He went on to tell him if he worked with her as much as he had Hart she would be. It surprised Tom that he had remembered some of the stories that he had told them. Monroe wanted to name his horse Hart also, but Tom told him, "You can't. Both horses can't be named Hart."

He got real upset with him and said, "I don't see why."

Tom told him, "Because the horses wouldn't know which one ya'll are calling when ya'll called them if both their names were the same. If we had named you and Virgil both Virgil, what would you do if I or your mama came to the back door and hollered, 'Virgil, come here.' Would you know which one we were calling or what to do?"

That satisfied him, but he still wanted to know what he was going to name his then. Virgil started trying to help him find a good name, but when their mama called them for supper they still hadn't come up with a name. Monroe was one unhappy little boy because Virgil's horse had a name and his didn't. His mama and Sallie both tried to help them come up with a name, but nothing seemed to be the right one. By bedtime, his horse still didn't have a name. This went on several days, and Monroe was getting more and more unhappy every day.

Then one day Tom heard Virgil tell Monroe, "I am going to teach my horse all kinds of tricks." Tom told Virgil, as Mr.

Heart told him, "She is a ranch working horse and not a circus horse. You need to teach her what she needs to know to be able to take care of you if it comes to that and not tricks. It's not as bad here as it was where I was raised because we don't have as many acres, but where I was raised, your horse knowing what to do might mean the difference in life or death. Suppose you fall off your horse and broke your leg and your horse didn't know to go for help, you would be in trouble." Then Tom told them how the wild pigs had him treed and Hart went for help.

Tom told them, "Ya'll need to teach your horse what to do to take care of you and don't worry about trying to make a trick horse out of her. You don't need any horses doing tricks here on the ranch."

Monroe grinned real big and hollered, "That's it! That's it! My horse's name will be Trixey."

Virgil agreed with him, "Trixey is a real good name for your horse."

Tom thought to make Monroe happy, it wouldn't have mattered what name he came up with, Virgil would have said it was all right. Monroe was as proud as punch when he went into the house that night and told his mama and Sallie that his horse finally had a name. They both agreed with him, that Trixey was a real nice name for his horse.

He would do everything that Virgil did for his horse, but Tom always thought it was more for Virgil than for the horse. It made Tom so sad every time he saw him with his horse. He would never feel that deep love for his horse as Tom or Virgil felt for theirs. Tom took him aside and told him, "A horse can sense how his master feels, and if he loves his horse, that the horse would love him back and would give his life for him if necessary." Tom told him how important it was that his horse learned to obey and love him. That if he was ever caught out in a storm, like Tom was, that his horse might mean whether he lived or died. Tom also told him about his horse taking him home when he got lost. He liked the stories, but Tom's message didn't seem to sink in.

The real change came when he was about six. Virgil wanted to go down and check the cattle for Tom while he and the boys were on roundup. They had been gone over a week, and Virgil got it in his head that they needed checking. Ettie thought that would give them something to do and there wasn't anything that could hurt them just down in the pasture. So she packed both of them a lunch and a canteen of water. She told them not to be gone too long and for them to be careful. They had been riding their horses all over the pastures with the boys several years now, and she knew they would be able to find their way home. They were laughing and, as Virgil said, just having fun.

When they came to the creek they weren't paying attention to what they were doing, and when the horses started to step down from the bank into the water, they weren't expecting the jar so both boys lost their balance and fell off. The water wasn't very deep, so they just waded out and neither one was hurt. Virgil's horse just stood and waited for him, but Monroe's horse spooked and ran for the house, taking his lunch and water with him. It was a warm day, so they ate Virgil's lunch and drank his water. Then waited for their clothes to dry some. After that they rode Virgil's horse and went on home in case Ettie saw Monroe's horse and got worried about them.

When Tom came home, Virgil was telling him about what Hart had done. He said, "Daddy, she just stood there and waited for me."

Tom asked Monroe, "What did your horse do?"

He reluctantly told him, "Trixey had spooked and ran for home."

Tom told him, "Son, this is what I have been trying to tell you. What if ya'll were way out, like I was, maybe a day or two from home and Trixey had left you with no food or water and you had to walk all the way back home. Where I was raised there were wolves, wild pigs, bobcats, and mountain lions. If you had to walk two days and a night, look at the danger you would have been in with no water or food. Can you imagine how thirsty and hungry you would have gotten? The nights get awfully cold after the sun goes down, and it gets dark. You think every noise you hear is a wild animal out looking for food and then you would try to find a tree to climb until it got daylight. With no horse to show you where to go, you would be on your own and would have to find your way home by yourself. Son, now do you see how important it is for you to train your horse to stay with you or come when you call her? You have to love your horse and train her, and she will love you and even give her life to save you if it necessary."

From that day on Monroe worked with his horse every day. By the end of the month, she was coming to him when Monroe called her and staying when he told her to. He would pretend he fell and lay there telling her to stay. When she learned to stay, then he would pretend to fall and tell her go get help. Of course, Virgil would be at the house waiting for her and follow her back to where Monroe was lying. He and Virgil both would pet her and tell her what a good horse she was. She got to where she did everything Monroe told her to do. He was so proud of her. He was outside as soon as he ate his breakfast working with her.

Ettie had to call him to come in for dinner and supper also. Of course, Virgil was right there with him. They were so close they should have been twins. Monroe was a lot larger than Virgil, but Virgil was still the boss and the one that was always getting them into trouble. It didn't matter what Virgil got himself into, Monroe was always there to help him get out of it.

By the time Leola was five, she had her own horse and was going everywhere with Tom. She didn't have any trouble managing her horse. When Tom gave it to her, she led it to the house, hollering for her mama and Aunt Sallie to come see her very own horse. Of course, they had seen it while Tom and the boys were breaking it for her, but she didn't know it.

When they came out, they both looked real surprised. Ettie told her, "It's your very own horse? Well, isn't she a cutie pie."

She was so excited she said, "Mama, you named my horse, you named my horse."

Ettie started laughing and said, "What?"

And she said again, "Mama, you named my horse. Her name will be Cutie Pie."

Both the boys and Virgil and Monroe were there, and they all started laughing. Virgil said, "That's no name for a horse. How would you like to be named Cutie Pie?"

She always was a spunky little thing, and no one ever got the best of her. She came back with, "Well, how would you like to be named Hart or Trixey. It is as good as your horses' names."

Her mama told her, "I think it is a pretty name."

So it was settled. Her horse's name would be Cutie Pie.

Tom told her as he had the boys, "Cutie Pie is your responsibility. You have to feed her and make sure she has water every day."

Virgil and Monroe volunteered to help her train her.

At first Leola told them, "I don't need your help."

But Ettie told her, "Oh yes, you do. See how good their horses do? They can help you, and it won't be no time until Cutie Pie will be doing as good as they are."

So she agreed, and Cutie Pie's training began. It wasn't long until she was doing everything that the boys' horses were doing and more. Leola was like her mama and Virgil. They just had a way with animals. Ettie told Tom, "That silly horse thinks she is human. She even tries to come in the house when Leola does."

When the boys were getting close to their teens, they began to drift away from Billy and Mark. As most boys do, they were beginning to think they were grown. They seemed to think they didn't need anyone except each other. They were still real close to each other, and where you saw one, the other one was somewhere close by. Neither one seemed to take too much interest in the ranch, and it just broke Tom's heart. He told them over and over that one day this would all belong to them and he wanted them to learn how to manage it when he was gone, but it went in one ear and out the other.

Tom complained to Ettie, and she told him, "Tom, both of them are their daddy's sons. You didn't train them to do the things that now you complain that they don't do. That you let Mark and Billy do everything because it was easier. They are slothful and lazy because you let them get away with it."

Anything they liked to do, they were real good at it. Each year, when roundup time came, they were really good help. Tom had taught them how to do everything that had to be done to get the cattle ready to ship. Monroe was a top-notch hand at everything while Virgil was good at everything except roping and getting them ready to brand. He could rope them, and he very seldom missed, but as small as he was, the calves were too large for him to handle. Everything else he did as good as any man or better. He never let his leg stop him from doing anything he wanted to do. Tom had got where he took them with them every year when they took the cattle to ship. They both loved every minute of it. Tom would go on with the cattle to see that they sold and that they got top dollar for them. Billy or Mark, Virgil and Monroe would go back home. It wasn't the fun and excitement as it was when Tom was a boy. They would be gone for weeks. With them, it only took two days and one night. On the second morning they would take them to the holding pen to wait for the train. The boys would stay and help Tom get them loaded on the train, then they would go on home. Mark or Billy would take turns staying home to do the outside work and make sure everything went all right. Ettie always took care of her chickens and gathered up the eggs, but as long as they were on the ranch, she never learned to milk, nor did Sallie.

Leola never drifted away from Tom at all. She was his sidekick until she got grown and married. With her, he had the boy he wanted. She was with him all the time. They hunted, fished, and skinned anything from coons to deer. She learned to stretch a coon hide on the barn as good as Tom. She could shoot and dress out a deer as good as any man.

Then one Sunday at church, their lives changed again. A young man had come to visit his aunt, and of course, he met Sallie. She fell head over heels in love with him, and it wasn't long until they were going steady.

Tom kept telling her he was no good, that he was just a bum and would never amount to anything, if he hadn't by now. He told her, "Why, Sallie, he doesn't even own his own horse and probably never would."

She just ignored him and went on seeing him. The boys really liked him because he was all play. That, Tom had to admit, he did well. He was always cutting up and everything was just a great big joke with him. Tom tried to make her see he was no good.

She told him, "Tom, I am getting almost past child-bearing age and I want a family of my own. How many men do you know around here that are my age?"

Tom tried to tell her, "Let me send you back to Mary Ann's, and maybe you can find someone there."

But she told him, "Tom, look how many years I was there, and I didn't find anyone."

He told her, "Well, sis, you haven't found anyone now. He is no good."

But he didn't do anything but make her mad. She told him, "Tom, I will never find anyone that would be good enough for me in your eyes. It's my life, and if and when he asks me to marry him, I am going to."

Tom tried and tried to tell her, "He don't have anything to offer you."

But she threw it back in his face, "What did you have to offer Ettie when she married you?"

Tom told her, "At least, I had a place to bring her to and a promise of having more in a few years, and he doesn't even have that."

The more Tom talked, the more she took up for him.

In a month, they ran off and got married. When they came back after her clothes, they didn't have a way to even get to town to catch the train to go back to his mother's house in a little town called Sherman. Ettie and Tom took them to town to catch the train. Tom was so mad he could hardly be civilized to either one of them. When they got to town, they went directly to the train station to get their tickets. He barely had enough money to pay for them. They were early, so Tom suggested they go eat before they left. Sallie and Ettie had made them a lunch for their dinner, and they had stopped and ate at noon and also rested the horses for a while. They went to eat, and sure enough, Tom knew that he would have to pay for it. Jeff didn't make any effort at all to at least pay for their part. Tom was so mad, but for Sallie's sake he tried not to show it. He and Ettie had agreed to give Sallie some money for a wedding present. When he hugged her bye at the train station, he slipped fifty dollars in her hand.

With tears in her eyes, she said, "Oh, Tom, be happy for me."

Tom told her, "I will try, but if you ever need us, just get in touch with us and you know you are always welcome to come back."

She whispered, "Tom, I know that," and thanked him for all he and Ettie had done for her. When she hugged Ettie, Ettie told her, "How will I ever get along without my sister?" And they both started crying. Ettie told her, "Tom knows you want your own home, but we sure wish that you could have found one around here."

About that time the conductor hollered, "All aboard" and they ran to get on the train. Tom stood there with his arm around Ettie, watching her go; and again, he asked, "God, why God? She is such a good woman. Why did He send someone like that to take her from us?" If it had been a good man, he could accepted it, but not a no-good scoundrel like that, she deserved more than that.

Ettie cried all the way home. Tom tried to comfort her, but he was almost in the same situation as she was, and it was hard for him to try to cheer her up. Sallie had been with them through all their good times and bad times for so long. They both wanted her to marry and have a home of her own, but both of them knew she wouldn't have one with this no-good scoundrel, that he would only break her heart.

The weeks stretched from weeks until months, and they still didn't hear from her. Ettie kept saying, "Tom, I know something is wrong or she would have written to us."

He kept telling her, "Give her time, they were probably moving around a lot and she just hasn't had time."

Finally, Tom told her, "As soon as we get caught up, we will make a trip to Sherman on the pretense of visiting her and see if everything was all right with them. We don't want to cause any trouble."

Chapter 27

BEFORE THEY COULD GO, TROUBLE broke out. Mr. Harper, the banker that had the note on the ranch and cattle, died. Mr. Harper's son took the bank over. He had never been as tolerant as his father, and for some reason he never liked Tom. He had never showed any mercy to anyone. His policy was you pay for what you owe or get out. Tom had never had any trouble with him because he had always dealt with his father. With Mr. Harper, Tom had always paid what he could. At the start, Mr. Harper had told Tom "just pay what you can each year." The first few years the payment was skimpy. He only had the crop money and very little more to pay on it. But Tom always paid more each year as the crops and cattle increased. By now he and Ettie were making real good payments. Mr. Harper would always ask Tom what was going on at the ranch and about his increase on his cattle, hogs, and horses. He always seemed so proud of what Tom had accomplished and always told him so.

Two weeks after Mr. Harper died, Tom's whole life fell completely apart. This strange man came to the door and asked for Mr. Brisco. He was down checking the bees, so Ettie called the kids to go with him and show him where their daddy was. It wasn't long until they came back. They talked awhile, then the man crawled back in his buggy and left. As soon as Ettie saw his face, she knew something was wrong. He was as pale as a ghost.

Ettie ran over to him and asked him, "What is wrong? Are you sick?" She got a chair for him, then she ran over to get a cold rag to wash his face.

He told her, "Worse than that. The man that was here came out to tell us that Mr. Harper's son was serving notice on us, that he was foreclosing on our ranch. He has given us two weeks to pay up or get out." Tom said he tried to tell him that they weren't behind on their payments, but he told him according to Jim they were and according to the papers he had showed him, they were.

After Tom sat in the chair for a while and got his bearings, he told Ettie, "Have the boys saddle my horse. I am going in and try to tell Jim we don't owe any thing, that we had already paid his father this year." He told Ettie after that for her to get all their receipts, showing they had never missed a payment. She hollered at the boys, and by the time Tom was ready, they had the horse ready and she had all the receipts.

Tom told Ettie he thought it was just a mistake, but knowing Jim and his crooked and scheming ways, pray that he can convince him. Tom told her, "Don't worry about me, but I don't know when I will be back."

Tom rode the horse as fast as he dared, but he wanted to get there as quick as he could. He got there about three that after noon and luck was with him. Jim was still there. He came around his desk and told Tom, well, guess he knew why he was there. He never offered to shake hands, but just said, "Well, let's get down to business," and walked around at his desk. Tom sat down in front of the desk and told him a Mr. White came out this morning to tell him that he was going to foreclose on him. Tom told him he was not behind, that he had already paid his payment for the year. Jim told him, "Not by my book you haven't. My books shows that very few times you have paid a full payment since you had bought the ranch."

Tom tried to tell him that he didn't have a regular set amount, that in the beginning, Mr. Harper had let him pay what he could afford until he was able to make bigger payments.

He told Tom, "I know Dad let you get by with about anything, but now you are not dealing with my dad. You will be dealing with me, and I expect a full payment each year. I have talked with my lawyer, and we have taken the amount that you had paid more regular as your regular yearly payment, and by my books, counting the back payment, you didn't pay and the interest, you are quite a lot of money behind. If you don't pay it within two weeks, I will be forced to foreclose on you and take the animals as well as the ranch."

Tom told him, "Man, be reasonable, you know we don't have that kind of money."

Jim told him that was his problem and he had two weeks to get it in or he would be coming out to enforce the notice. Tom tried to talk with him, but he wouldn't listen to anything Tom said. He kept telling him, "That's your problem, either pay it or get out." Tom asked him for more time to raise it, but he told him any court would tell him he has more than enough time to catch up already. He, finally told him, "Tom, I am not running a charity ward like my dad did, and I don't have time to talk to you all day." He got up and told Tom good day.

Tom didn't have the money to hire a lawyer to try and fight it, and besides there was only one lawyer in town, and it was the bank's lawyer anyway. Jim told him he would see him in two weeks. Tom followed him and asked him for more time to see if he could sell the cows and horses so he could pay it off. Jim told him he had better not sell them, that they belonged to the bank, animals, furniture, and all. Either pay or get out. He turned and walked out of the room, leaving Tom standing there.

There was no way Tom could raise that much money. His next best bet was to try to find a house and a job to take his family to. Tom went all over town asking if they knew any one that was hiring. Every one told him it was too late for any one that was hiring for crop sharing. If they did need someone, by now they had already hired them. He did talk to a man that did tell him they were needing families to pick fruit and berries in Lindale, Texas. Tom didn't know where that was, but he needed a job and a roof over his family's head, so what choice did he have.

For the first time in his whole life, he felt so helpless and so all alone. He had cried and prayed all the way home. By the time he got home, he had decided he would go to Lindale and see if he could find a job. Tom thought what choice did he have but to go and see if there was work there in Lindale. When he got there, Ettie was sound asleep. He decided he would wait and talk to her in the morning. The next morning Tom told her what he had found out and it didn't look good. He told her what a crocked stunt Jim was trying to pull. By the way he had worded it, by law it was legal and there was nothing they could do. "He is calling in the back money we are supposed to owe on our loan."

Ettie told him, "But we don't owe anything."

Tom told her, "The way he has presented it to the lawyer, we do. The papers show we are behind several years. Mr. Harper has written in his notes, 'Will pay more when he can.' So Jim is using that to make it appear that we were supposed to pay more on it each year to catch up."

Ettie told him, "But you know that is not right."

Tom told her, "You know that and I know it wasn't, but the paper says it is right, and Mr. Harper is the only one that could have told them different and Jim knows it."

Tom told her that Jim told him in no certain terms to pay or get out. "He has given us two weeks to pay up or get out."

She started crying and in between sobs told Tom, "What are we going to do? This is our home. We don't have any place to go. Where are we going to live?"

Tom told her, "I don't know, Ettie. We will just have to pray about it and depend on the Lord and have faith and He will see us through." At that time Tom didn't know how many years that was going to be, and how much faith it would take before they would be settled again.

He told her he had looked and asked for work all over Jacksboro and the only thing he had found was work in Lindale, Texas, and he wasn't certain of that. He said, "Ettie, a man told me they were hiring people to pick fruit there. I thought we could go there until we could do better. If it is all right with you?" She agreed as she had always done. Tom told her, "Now, Ettie, I don't know if he knew for sure what he was talking about, and I don't know where Lindale is, and if there will be any work when we get there, but we have to do something."

Ettie told him, "Tom, as long as we are all together. We will be all right."

Tom told her, "If we are going to take anything, we have to get it away from here before they come to appraise the place. After that everything will have to be left as they appraised it. So we have less than two weeks to get the wagon ready, loaded with what we will need, and moved from here. Knowing Jim, if he can, he won't let us have anything if he can get by with it. We have to have one of the wagons, a team of horses to pull it with, and I figured on taking two of our milk cows, and the kids' horses."

Ettie asked about her chickens, and he told her, "Well, maybe a dozen."

So it was settled. They would go to Lindale. So Tom began to get the wagon ready for them to travel in. He made a covering, like he remembered the chuck wagon on the ranch, insulating it so it wouldn't leak. Then he built a frame all around the inside of the wagon to form a false bottom to hold all their belongings. They put as many of their canned goods as they could under there. They loaded all their quilts on top of the canned goods. By spreading the quilts out flat they could get most of them under there. The rest they gave to the boys. Also, they were able to get some of their sheets, pillowcases, towels, and wash clothes under there also. On top of the false bottom, Tom built a lid with four strips of leather nailed on one side to make the hinges. On top of the lid he laid the mattresses. This was to be their bed. Tom didn't have very long to try and get it made and everything loaded and ready before Jim would send someone out to appraise it all and to serve the foreclosure notice on them. At the back of the wagon on the outside, he built a box effect to put what dishes they would need, the coffeepot, also the pots and pans that Ettie would need for cooking and two Dutch ovens. He made a table that folded down on the side of the wagon for her to use to set things on when she was cooking. It was all real crude, as fast as he had to build it, but it would have to do. Then they loaded it with their clothes, "that was as much as they could carry," which wasn't very much. They had to leave all their furniture and everything that they had accumulated all these years. It broke their hearts to do it, but they had no choice. When they got the wagon all loaded, they took it down in the woods on the next farm and hid it. They didn't know if Jim would try to take the wagon and horses or not.

    Tom took the two milk cows, the kid's ponies, and one of his cow ponies down into the woods and hid them along with the wagon and the two horses that they would need to pull the wagon with. Jim was taking all the cattle, the hogs, bees, chickens, and everything else; and Tom didn't know if he would try to take the little bit they were taking or not. So he told Ettie,

"Jim had been so mean and stubborn about it all. I don't want to take a chance of him taking the little bit we are carrying too." He had asked the neighbor about putting them down there until they were ready to go, and he said it would be fine. The last few days before Jim was supposed to come, John and Dora came over. What few things they wanted to keep, they agreed to keep for them until they could get settled again and had a place to put it. They all hauled some of Ettie's good dishes and some special gifts that Ettie had wanted to save and stored it at John's and Dora's house. It broke Ettie's and Tom's heart, but they had no choice. Everything they were taking was not on the bank note and had never been. Jim was getting more than enough to cover their loan as it was. Also, John took some of the chickens and a dozen for them. Tom made a crate to fit on the back of the wagon to put them in so they would have them when they got to where they were going. Tom had decided to take two of his best coon dogs in case he did get to hunt some. Coon hides were still selling, not for much, but every penny would help right now.

The last day of the month, they had everything moved. John suggested that the boys take the wagon and what few things they were taking over to their house. They could leave from there. That way Jim wouldn't know what they were taking and wouldn't try to keep it too. John said, "I know Jim. He would take the cows and horses if he saw them, and you wouldn't have anything left to pull the wagon with." So the boys took everything over to John's place for safekeeping. John, Dora, Ettie, Leola, and Tom slept at the house; and the boys stayed over at John's and Dora's house.

Sure enough, the next morning, which was the first day of the month, Jim came as he had said he would, bringing the papers to foreclose on them. Tom and John both tried again to talk to him about giving them more time, but he wouldn't talk to either of them at all.

John tried to tell him, "Tom has enough cattle to pay if you would allow him to sell them."

He told John, "Now this is not any of your affair, and I would appreciate it if you would mind your own business and stay out of mine." He had brought several men to take inventory again to make sure the animals and everything was all still there. When they got through checking everything, he told him, "Now, Tom, everything had better be here that's on the list when I come back to check it or I will send the law after you."

Tom knew it was wrong, but he told him, "What's wrong, Jim? Are you afraid I will steal it from you like you're doing me."

That made him mad, and he told Tom, "I think all our business is taken care of, and I think it's time for all of you to leave."

Jim had made arrangements for Mark and Billy to stay on in the dugout and take care of the animals until he could do something with them. The boys at first told Tom they would let them starve first, but Tom told them, "Ya'll are like I am. You have no place to go, and here, at least, ya'll will be drawing a salary and have a roof over your heads." So they had agreed to stay. With tears in all their eyes, they all told the boys good-bye. Then they all got in the Rucker's wagon and left as if they were going to stay with them.

Tom was glad that they had taken what they did over to the Ruckers because he knew the way Jim acted, that if the wagon and horses and all the other things they had taken were there, he would have taken it also. They didn't talk much going to John and Dora's house, Ettie and Tom was so brokenhearted they could hardly keep from crying. The tears would come later when they were all alone. Everything they had worked for all their life was gone. The few things they had managed to save at the Ruckers were all they had left in this world. They spent the night at the Ruckers, and early the next morning they loaded the chickens in the crate, tied the two cows and Tom's horse to the back of the wagon, hitched the horses to the wagon, and was ready to go before sunup. The kids had saddled their horses and were ready by the time Tom was. They told the Ruckers goodbye and told them how much they thanked them for helping them all these years that they couldn't have made it without them. Ettie and Dora had made it real good until they told each other good-bye, then they both broke down and began to cry. It was all that John and Tom could do to keep from following suit. They walked away from them to keep from breaking down. Also John and Tom hugged each other bye, and Tom promised him, "If it is the Lord's will, we will see you all again someday."

John told Tom, "I don't have a brother that I think more of than I do you, and that ya'll have helped our family more than any of our own brothers or sisters had, or anyone else has, as far as that goes. We will never forget ya'll." By that time tears were running down both of their cheeks. Ettie and Tom climbed on the wagon with their last words ringing in their ears, "God bless you all, and good luck."

They would make a big circle out of their way to keep from going through town. Tom didn't want to take a chance of Jim seeing them and causing trouble. They didn't know exactly where Lindale was, but the guy said there was work there picking fruit and berries so that was where they would go. Tom stopped along to let the horses rest. He always tried to stop by a creek where they could have fresh water for them and a place for the animals to drink and grass to eat. At noon they stopped at a real shady place for Ettie to cook dinner. Bless her heart, she fried some meat and potatoes and made some gravy and hot biscuits. They were all so sad. Tom guessed she thought that would help them to feel better. While she and Leola were doing that, the boys and Tom hobbled the stock so they could graze and wouldn't wander too far. The dogs were tired and, after they had gone to the creek for water, came back and lay in the shade waiting for their dinner. They ate, and after they all cleaned up their mess. They laid down and rested. They were all tired and sick at heart.

It took them almost three weeks to get to Lindale. It was a long, hard trip. The boys griped and complained all the way. Ettie and Leola never complained one time. Tom finally heard Ettie tell the boys when she thought he had gone to take care of the livestock. "Now, boys, I have put up with your complaining and gripping at your daddy as long as I am going to. Can't you see how all this has broke his heart? Do you think this is easy on him, to lose everything he had worked for all his life? You boys have never had to go hungry or do without anything yet. But I am afraid before this is over. We will see how lucky we all have always been. In place of gripping and complaining all the time, you could pitch in and help him some. I don't want to hear either of you gripe or complain again. If you can't help him and realize how hard this is on him, then keep your mouth shut."

Tom slipped away without them knowing he had heard anything and went to the creek, and then the tears came. He asked, "God, why God? Why God did this have to happen?"

Now before you judge the boys, remember they had never had to do anything they didn't want to or any real hard work. Yes, they did help with the branding at roundup and did go with him on the drive to take the cows to be shipped. But those few days were more play than work. They had always had full range of the ranch and went and came as they pleased with little responsibility. Both Ettie and Tom wanted their children to have an easier life than they had. Now they were good boys and minded Tom and Ettie real good. They never had any trouble with either one of them. They always did everything Tom asked them to do. The trouble was he never asked them to do much, and now all of a sudden everything had been taken away from them, and they were confused and hurt. They, like the rest of them, didn't know which way to turn or go.

The trip was long and hard. They traveled from early to late, and when they stopped at night, they were all bone tired. They stopped along to let the horses rest and also them but traveling for three whole weeks was hard. The days were hot, and the nights were cold. Tom tried to camp each night in wooded areas where there was a creek with plenty of water to bathe and for the animals to drink and plenty of grass for them. Each night they turned the chicken coup upside down with the lid open so the chickens could have some grass to scratch in. Also, Tom tried to find a wooded area where there might be some coons to hunt.

After they got everything done at night and had eaten supper, Tom and Leola would take the dogs out to see if they could find some. Coon hides were still selling good, and every little bit of money they could get helped. The boys stayed with their mother. They both were expert marksmen, and Ettie could shoot as well as any man and better than most, so Tom wasn't afraid to leave them. Most of the time Leola and Tom would get some coons. She and Tom would dress them and stretch them on boards to dry, then put them in the trees round about the camp until they were ready to go the next day. The meat they feed to the dogs, and they were always glad to get it. Ettie, Leola, and Tom slept in the wagon; but the boys slept under the wagon on a pallet. They had plenty of quilts to cover with, so they didn't get cold. The dogs slept under the wagon at Virgil's and Monroe's feet. They heard every little sound and would go to the head of the pallet, one on each side, and nudge Virgil and Monroe to wake them if anything came around. It didn't matter if it was man or beast, they didn't hang around long after they alerted the boys. They were out as fast as a bullet at the side of the wagon, growling at ever what it was, and believe you me, nothing would stay long and face two angry dogs of their size.

The first night it happened, the boys were real amazed at how they did and told Tom the next morning. They told him, "We don't have to be afraid about anything or anybody surprising us at night while we are sleeping" and they told him what the dogs did.

Virgil said, "Why, Dad, they didn't make a sound until they nudged us awake, then they were out before we knew what was happening, growling at whatever it was."

Monroe said, "We didn't get awake well enough to see what it was, but you better believe, it didn't stay around long enough to say hello, man or beast."

On Sunday, they stopped all day to rest and have a devotional. Tom always thanked God for keeping them safe and for bringing them this far. Then they took the washpot down to the creek bank and filled it with water, then built a fire under it to heat the water so they could wash their clothes. Ettie had plenty of lye soap that she had made, so they didn't have to worry about soap for washing their clothes or bathing.

Ettie reminded him so much of Granny. She told the boys, "Now, you boys go down and take a real good bath and change your clothes, just because we are traveling in a wagon across country, we don't have to go dirty and look like a bunch of heathens."

Again, Tom's mind wondered back to when he was a little boy and he heard Granny say the same thing, and again he thought, *Oh, God, if only I could have gone back just one time before they died.*

Chapter 28

WHEN THEY GOT TO LINDALE, Tom camped in a wooded area close to a creek. Ettie, Leola, and the boys washed their clothes while he went to town to see if he could find out about a place that was looking for pickers. He went in to the first cafe he came to and luck was with him. Tom asked if they knew anyone that needed pickers, and they told him about a Mr. Tompkins that had come in that very morning looking for someone. They told him how to get to his house and wished him luck. He didn't have any trouble finding his place and was there by ten o'clock. Tom told him what he wanted, and Mr. Tompkins asked him, "How many do you have to pick."

Tom told him, "Three kids, my wife, and myself." Because at the cafe, they had told him, all places are looking for a whole family to pick.

He told him, "I want someone to get in there and pick and not fool around before the fruit gets overripe, because overripe fruit means loss of money for me. Have ya'll ever picked fruit before?"

Tom told him, "Only our own on the ranch."

He didn't ask any questions about that, but he said, "That would do. I will show you which ones to pick for shipping." He told him how much he would pay them for each lug and said he would furnish them a house to live in while they were there. He took Tom down and showed him the berries, then the house. It was a little more than a shack, but it was a roof over their head, and they had a job.

He asked Tom, "When can ya'll start?"

Tom told him, "We can be here this afternoon. We are camped just on the other side of Lindale."

Then Mr. Tompkins let the bomb fall. He told him, "I can't pay you until the fruit is gathered and sold. I can give you all kind of references of people who will tell you that I am good at my word and will pay you as soon as the fruit is sold. I am like everyone else raising fruit. I work from year to year on what I make each year. Last year I didn't have as good of a crop as I was expecting, and I am running a little short of cash. After buying the crates we needed to put the fruit in, it left me pretty well depending on the fruit crop that's coming on to make it."

Tom told him, "I know what you mean. The bank had foreclosed on us, and took all we had. I will accept the deal that you have offered me, at least we will have a roof over our heads and would be working."

He told Tom, "It will be a few days before the fruit will be ripe, but that will give you time to get moved in and settled before you have to start."

Tom went back and told Ettie and the kids what he had found. "We all will have to work. They want the whole family to pick the fruit, and that is the only way I could get the job and the house. We will have a roof over our heads, but no money until we gather all the berries and they are sold. It is going to be tough going until we get the berries gathered." Tom tried to prepare them for the shack that they would be living in.

Ettie told him, "Tom, you never promised me a mansion when you married me. You only promised me a roof over my head and plenty to eat and to love me, and you haven't broken your word yet."

As hard as he tried to tell the kids, they weren't prepared for what they saw. Ettie must have been talking to them all morning about not saying a word, regardless to what it was. Tom could see the expression on their faces, but neither one of them said anything. The house had a kitchen with a stove, an old table, two benches, an old built-in cabinet with some shelves over it, and three small bedrooms with an old iron bed in each room. Ettie never batted an eye. She told the kids, "Now let's all get started so we can get moved in before we have to go to work." She told Virgil and Monroe, "Go get some wood for a fire, so we can heat some water. Leola and I will get the beds, table, and benches outside to scrub while ya'll are gone." She told Tom, "There is a chicken house behind the house. Could you see if it needs anything done to it before we put the chickens in it. The poor things need to be gotten out of that crate as soon as possible and watered."

They all pitched in, and by late that afternoon the table, benches, and beds had all been scrubbed with lye soap and scalding hot water that they had heated in the washpot. The stove had been cleaned, the windows had been washed, and the floors and cabinets had been scrubbed in scalding water also. When everything had dried, Ettie told the boys, "It is time to put the beds and furniture back in the house." They did all that and began to unload the wagon. They brought the mattresses in first, then found the sheets so Ettie and Leola could make the beds. By night they had the beds ready to sleep in, and Ettie and Leola cooked supper on the stove in the kitchen. They all sat down to eat; and Tom thanked God for at last they had a roof over their heads, a bed to sleep in, and a job. There were no cloths closets, so the next day the boys and Tom stretched some wire across the corners in each bed room to hang their clothes on. Also, they didn't have a place to put the sheets and towels or their folded clothes, so the boys and Tom found some old lumber, and by the next day, they had built some shelves to put in all three of the rooms so they would have a place to put them.

Ettie and Leola again washed them down good with lye soap and hot water. The boys and Tom brought in all the sheets, pillowcases, towels, washcloths, and clothes that had to be folded. Ettie put some sheets, towels, washcloths, and their clothes in each room. The quilts they just had to put under the mattress, some under each bed. By the time they got through, all the house was neat and clean.

By the time the berries were ready to pick, they were all settled in. It was long hot work, from sunup to sundown, bending over and picking the berries. They took very few breaks. Mr. Tompkins wanted the berries out as soon as possible. They took their lunch to the field and didn't take very long to eat it. Tom saw his sweet dear wife and children's skin turn brown and dry from the hot sun and their hands bleed from the thorns. It broke Tom's heart, but they had to make enough money to last them through the winter if they were going to survive. Tom's wife and kids that had never worked hard in their life, now were working right along with him, grubbing for just a mere living. Tom, for the first time in his life, became bitter and pushed them as hard as he could, to make as much as they could, so they could get a house and have food for the winter.

With no money coming in, it didn't take long until they were out of flour, cornmeal, and coffee. Tom found out from Mr. Tompkins, there was a trade day every first Monday at a little town not far from where they were. He told Ettie, "I will take one of the cows and my horse and go in and see if I can either sell them or do some trading to get the groceries we need." He told Mr. Tompkins Saturday night what he planned to do on Monday. Mr. Tompkins told him, "It will be all right, and I wish you good luck." Tom asked him if he could get just enough money to buy a sack of feed and a sack of salt. He didn't ask any questions, but told Tom, "I have some feed in the barn and some salt I had left over from hog killing time, and you are welcome to it." After supper the boys and Tom went after the feed and salt. Sunday night Tom mixed the feed with some of the salt and fed the cow and his horse all the feed they could eat. Tom brushed them both down real good until their coats were so pretty, it just glistened. Monday morning Tom was up and ready to go before daylight. He wanted to get over to the trade ground as soon as he could. He left the last of the flour for Ettie and the kids to have for breakfast. Ettie did have enough coffee left to make him a pot of coffee. He drank one cup and filled the canteen for later.

The kids were still asleep, but they would be up before long and ready to go to the berry patch. Tom kissed Ettie bye and told her not to worry he would bring some food home for supper. Bless her heart, she told him, "Tom, I know you will, you have never failed us yet." She took her ring off her finger and handed it to him and said, "Tom, take this and sell it, in case you need some money for boot, if you find a good deal on something."

That just broke Tom's heart. He told her, "No, absolutely no," but she insisted. He finally took it and stuck it in his pocket. He knew they had to have money for groceries, but he thought, *God help me, I will beg, borrow, or steal before I sell her ring.*

She kissed him and said, "Good luck and hurry back to us."

Tom kissed her again and told her, "With a wife like you, how can I fail?" Tom rode off on his last cow pony leading the cow. He intended to sell the horse and saddle. Without the horse, he didn't have any use for the saddle.

He turned around once before he got out of sight, and Ettie was still standing there waving. Somehow, he knew she would be. Tom waved to her, and the next time he looked, she was out of sight. Tom knew she must have shed many tears, but if she did no one ever knew it. She was always their strength and their backbone. She was always the one that held the family together. It just broke Tom's heart because they were in such a predicament. He prayed all the way to the trade grounds. "Lord, help me and show me the way and give me the knowhow to be able to take back the groceries we need to my family for tonight."

When he got there, it was already full of people and all kind of animals, chickens, geese, and turkeys. Tom found a place and unsaddled the horse, hobbled the cow and the horse, and put the saddle out in front of the horse. It wasn't long until a man came by and asked if the cow was for sale. Tom told him it was and quoted him a price.

He looked her all over and asked him, "Is she in good shape?"

Tom told him, "Now, mister, you feel free to examine her all you want to, and if you find anything wrong with her, then don't buy her."

He told Tom, "I don't have that much money, but I have a good horse. I will give you and ten dollars to boot."

Tom asked him, "Where is the horse?"

He told him he was just a few spots down.

Tom asked the man next to him, "Would you watch the cow and horse while I go down to look at the horse?"

And that's how Tom met Benjamin Brown. He and his family were traveling in a covered wagon on their way to West Texas. He said, "We haven't been able to find any work, and I was just making each trade day along the way. Doing anything I can do for a little money or anything I could buy to resell. I will be glad to keep an eye on things until you get back."

Tom went down and saw the skinniest horse and cow he had ever seen.

The man told Tom, "I know the horse is in poor shape, but he is young, was in good health, and was of good stock."

Tom told him, "He might be, but I have two hours to get back to where I am living, and it wasn't guaranteed that the horse or that skinny cow, either one, would get there alive."

He told Tom, "I know they are in bad shape, but right now I need a milk cow for my baby."

Tom told him, "No cow will give milk long if it is treated like these animals have been. Man, you had better make up your mind, to either buy milk or buy feed to feed a cow before you buy another one. I just can't sell my cow to you with you thinking she was as fat as mud. We have been traveling from the hill country down here to pick fruit, and she hasn't had any feed but grass until Sunday night, and I had fed her good so she would look good to sell. She was giving milk, but not a lot because of that, but if she got some sweet feed and grass, she would probably start giving more milk. I had raised her from a calf, and she has always been a good milk cow. But any cow, regardless to how good or poor, has to have feed and plenty of water and grass to make a good milk cow. Now if you are not going to see to that, then I wouldn't let you have her at any price."

He assured Tom that he would take good care of her. He said, "I usually take good care of my stock, but my wife had died, and there for a while I haven't cared for them or myself. It took the law, threatening to take my baby away from me to make me see that I had to straighten up and live for her. I have another cow that is expecting a calf, and by the time the calf comes, I will have her in good shape. Then I can let this cow go dry and breed her. I have a good pasture to keep them in."

Tom told him, "I can't trade her for just the cow and ten dollars, but I will trade her for the cow and horse and fifteen dollars to boot." He offered Tom ten; but Tom told him, "Now, mister, it took me two hours to get here riding a good horse and leading a good cow. I will have to go as slow as a snail to get home with them, and then I won't be sure they will make it. I might end up with only the fifteen dollars for my cow and two dead animals. Besides I need the money to buy a bill of groceries for my family, or I wouldn't trade at all. If you don't want her at that price, then I will have to wait for a better deal."

Tom turned to walk off, but the man stopped him and told him, "All right, it's a deal." He gave him the money, and they led the horse and cow back down to where Tom's horse and cow was. He thanked him and shook hands. Tom wished him good luck, and he said the same thing to him. He left leading his cow. Tom began to saddle his horse. God had blessed him. He had enough money to buy some groceries and didn't have to sell Ettie's ring or his horse and saddle. Benjamin Brown laughed and said, "Man, what do you have there? You didn't trade that good cow for those two creatures that looks like they are ready for the soap factory, did you?"

Tom laughed and told him, "I got some boot, and if I am lucky enough to get them home, you won't recognize them in a month."

Tom told him good-bye, and as soon as fruit picking time was over, they would be coming to West Texas, maybe they would run into him again.

Ben laughed and said, "I hope so. I would like to know if your two bag of bones made it home."

They shook hands and each wished the other one good luck. Tom left, leading the poorest critters he had ever seen. He was ashamed for anyone to see him with them. As he was leaving the trade grounds, people looked at the poor animals and just shook their heads. Tom pulled his hat down as low as he could, he didn't want anyone to recognize him if they ever saw him again. It took Tom almost four hours to get back to Lindale. He had to stop several times and let the cow and horse rest. Tom tried to find a creek each time so they could drink, graze, or just plain rest. He would hobble them each time so they wouldn't wonder too far, but he didn't think he had to worry about that anyway. Tom thought each time they stopped, they were too tired to go any further. Each time they stopped, Tom was wondering if they were going to make it home. When they got to Lindale, Tom debated whether he should take them on home and come back after groceries. He was tired and hungry, so he decided to stop and get what he could carry in two tow sacks. Tom thought he could tie the sacks on his horse and walk. His horse was in good shape and had gone a lot farther than that day and had carried more weight than the groceries would weigh.

At the grocery store, there was a vacant lot behind it. Tom went in and asked the woman that was running the store if he could tie his two horses and a cow there while he got some groceries. She told him it was just fine, that people always tied their wagon and horses there while they came in to shop. Tom went back and tied them in the shade. There was some grass there, so they could eat while he got his groceries. Then he went back into the store. The lady again asked him if she could help him. Ettie had made out a list so Tom gave it to her and told her she sure could, that he wasn't very good at shopping. He told her he had fifteen dollars to spend. She told him she thought that would buy that much and more. Ettie had written down, ten pounds of flour, five pounds of cornmeal, and one bag of coffee. Tom told her he wanted to spend the whole fifteen and asked if he would he have enough money to cover it. She told him and then some. He added baking powder and soda. When she got through adding it up, Tom still had money left so he got a sack of sweet feed. After that the lady told him he still had two dollars. So he got some baloney, a pound of steak, and some cans of pork and beans. Tom thought the baloney and pork and bean would be their dinner to carry to the field with them. After he paid for it all he still had ten cents left, so he bought two plugs of tobacco to crumble into the sweet feed for the horse and cow. The woman helped Tom put all the groceries into tow sacks. Tom tied the tops with the rope that he had been using to hobble the cow and horses. Then he hung them over his horse's saddle, some on each side and the sweet feed he tied in the saddle. He would have to walk, but that was all right. It beat having to come back. Tom thought as he was walking home, *Thank you, Lord, that we still had some can goods, that Ettie had canned and some salt pork and plenty of dried beans.*

When he got home, he stopped at the back door to unload the groceries. As soon as they heard him, they all came out to help him. He was hoping he could get the groceries unloaded and the cow and horse to the pasture before Ettie or the kids saw them. Tom actually was ashamed for anyone to see them. Ettie and the kids took the groceries, and he started to take the animals to the pasture and he heard Virgil and Monroe laughing.

Monroe said, "Can you believe he traded that perfectly good cow for those bag of bones."

Tom pretended that he didn't hear them, but it hurt. He heard Ettie say, "Shut your mouth, both of you. That bag of bones, as you called them, will buy another bill of groceries next month to keep you from going hungry. You could have offered to go and take them to the pasture and unsaddle his horse. When he left this morning, he left without any breakfast, because he left what little we had for Leola, me, and you ungrateful boys. Couldn't you all see he was just barely able to put one food in front of the other one because he is so dead tired? He hasn't had a bite to eat all day and walked all the way from town to bring home food for ya'll. I am getting real mad at you two ungrateful brats, criticizing him, when he is doing the best he can. If you two would listen to him and pay attention to what he tells you, one of these days you might be as smart as he is. People all over the world are dying from starvation, and you have never missed a meal, thanks to him. Now don't you ever let me hear you say one word against him again when he is doing the best he can."

Tom couldn't resist turning around and looking at them. They stood there looking dumbfounded. Their mama had never talked that way to them before. From that day forward, Tom thought they began to understand the situation that they were in. They came out to where he was and said, "Dad, let us put the animals away and you go rest until supper is ready." Tom told them thanks but "I want to feed the two skinny ones some sweet feed with some salt and chewing tobacco in it before I turn them loose."

They told him, "Show us how much, and we will do it."

They led them down and unsaddled Tom's horse and turned him loose in the pasture. The horse went on toward the creek, and Tom showed the boys how much salt to put in the feed, then they crumbled a little tobacco in it and fed them. They wanted to know why the tobacco. Tom told them, "It will give them an appetite and get rid of any parasites, if they have any. As poor as they are, I don't want to take a chance on whether or not they have some."

After that they went to the house, and Ettie and Leola had the steak and potatoes on for supper. They had made biscuits, and when the steak and potatoes was done, they made a large skillet of gravy to go with it. After they had thanked God for the food they all sat down to eat.

That night after all the kids went to bed, Tom gave Ettie back her ring. He kissed her and thanked her for her being willing to sacrifice the one thing that had meant so much to her all these years so their kids could eat. Tom didn't think the kids ever knew what a sacrifice their mother had been willing to make to feed them.

From that day on, when they came in at night, the boys helped Tom with the outside work while Ettie and Leola got supper. The chickens had begun to lay good, and the cow was giving plenty of milk for them. Every night from then on Monroe would milk the cow and Virgil gathered the eggs and saw that the hens were in the henhouse with the door locked. Tom would feed the skinny horse and cow. They both had begun to fill out some.

One night Monroe said, "Dad, they sure are filling out and looking better, aren't they?"

It made Tom so proud that he had noticed. He told him, "They sure are, son, and by trade day, they will be looking real good." Always after supper Tom would take the dogs and go coon hunting. He found out the colored folks would buy the dressed coons to eat, so rather than feeding all of them to the dogs, after that, each night he would dress them out and put them in buckets and then in the creek to keep cold. The creek was spring feed, so it stayed ice cold. Twice a week he would take them to town and sell them. Finally, he had one man that offered to come to the house and pick them all up and asked, "Have you ever got any rabbits?"

Tom told him, "I have seen plenty, but I haven't killed any of them."

He told Tom, "I will take all the coons and rabbits you have."

So from then on, Tom hunted both rabbits and coons. He and the boys would dress them and put them in buckets. They would put them in the creek, and the man would come and get them each night after they got home from work. They didn't bring very much, but every dime helped.

The next month, Tom had coon hides ready to sell, so he took them to town and sold them. They brought enough to get a few groceries for the month. On first Monday, Tom took the cow and horse back to the trade ground. They were as fat as mud. Tom and the boys had brushed them until they just shined. Again, he left early. He told Ettie, "The sooner I get there, the better spot I will be able to get." Tom wasn't a bit ashamed to be seen leading them back. They looked real pretty and fat. A far cry from what he took home a month age. That month Ettie persuaded him to take Virgil with him. She told him, "Tom, how will he ever learn if you don't take him and teach him."

When they got there, they found a real good spot to set up and it wasn't long until they had men stopping to inquire about both of them. The cow sold for twenty-five dollars, right off, which was a good price for her. One man came by leading a beautiful roan. He said she was as gentle as a little dog, that she loved kids, and would make a good pony for kids to ride. He told Tom, "Let my boy put your saddle on her and ride her." The boy must have been eight or nine years old. He saddled her and rode off as pretty as you please. Then Virgil rode her and agreed she was gentle and handled real good. She was a beautiful mare but was as poor as mud, but Tom knew with some feed and care it wouldn't take long to get her in good shape. The man wanted to trade for the horse and some boot. Tom told him, "I will trade, but I am the one that will have to have boot. Your mare is in bad shape."

He said, "I know she is, but with some rest and feed she would be all right."

Tom told him, "The feed would cost money, which I don't have." They talked for a while, and finally, he asked Tom, would he trade for five dollars. Tom saw he was really wanting to trade, so Tom told him no but he would take ten dollars. After a while of the man hem-hawing around, Tom ended up with the mare and ten dollars to boot. After that they were ready to go home. Tom told Virgil, "With the poor mare, we will have to go slow.

Take the saddle off her and get my horse saddled." Tom thought something was kind of funny when the man said, while they close the deal, "Why don't you let the boys tie her behind you son's horse and they would be ready to go." Tom thought it was strange that he never got close to her, but at the time he didn't think too much about it. The poor old horse led just fine, and they didn't have a bit of trouble getting her home. They stopped at the grocery store and picked up the groceries on Ettie's list and some sweet feed, salt, and tobacco plugs.

When they got home in place of Monroe making fun of her, he asked, "Dad, how did ya'll do today?"

Tom told him, "Real good, we got thirty-five dollars for the two of them plus the mare." Ettie and Leola came out with Monroe to see the mare, and he told them, "She is poor, but by next month she will be in real good shape to take back." Monroe asking him about how they did sure tickled Tom. He told Ettie later about it and told her, "I think both the boys have finally realized how hard the times are, not only for us, but they are others like us also."

Tom told the boys, "Take her down and put her in the pasture, and I will start doing the night work."

Monroe informed them, "I have got it all done." He told his dad, "Now I know how much feed, salt, and tobacco to mix for her feed, so let me feed her while you and Virgil go in and rest until suppertime." When he came in, he sure was bragging on her and said, "Dad, you sure made a good trade. This time, she is beautiful and is gentle."

The next morning Tom went down to check on her. He walked out into the pasture where she was grazing. She raised her head up when she saw him and came toward him with her teeth barred. Tom knew she meant business, so he turned to run. She was nipping at the seat of his pants every time his foot hit the ground and was barely missing. The boys heard him hollering and came running to see what was wrong. By the time they got there, they were bent over laughing. Tom hollered, "Open the gate," and he just barely made it through without getting the seat bit out of his pants. They shut the gate, and both said, "Dad, what did you do to her, to make her that mad?" They walked up to her, and she just laid her head over on Monroe's shoulder and did all put purr. Tom told them he didn't do anything to her. She just saw him and got mad. Ettie and Leola came out and saw her with her head on Monroe's shoulder and asked him the same thing.

He told them, "I am getting tired of ya'll asking, what I did to her. Not one of you have asked me what she was about to do to me, and I will tell you anyway, she was about to bite the whole seat out of my britches and she hadn't planned on stopping there."

They all started laughing until tears were running down their faces. Boy was they getting a bang out of kidding Tom. Ettie didn't make it any easier.

She said, "Now, Tom, you would have had to do something to make her that mad. Look at her now."

Leola walked up to her and asked him, "Now, Dad, what did you do to make her that mad? You would have had to do something. Look how calm she is."

That stupid horse just stood there looking so innocent like she was trying to say, "Yes, just look at me. Tell them what you did to me, Dad."

Tom was mad at all of them, including the horse. He said, "Yes, just look at her now. She is another Delilah, so pretty but so deceiving." He turned to go into the house, calling back, "Is breakfast ready?" Everyone ran to catch up with him, still just barely able to get their breath from laughing.

Leola said, "I know what made her mad. She didn't like his red hair." Everyone began to laugh again and said, "I bet that's right."

Tom told them, "Okay, now they had their fun, but from now on, ya'll can just take care of her."

As long as they had her, she never got to where Tom could get around her. The kids and Ettie could do anything with her, but she hated Tom and didn't make any bones about letting him know it. Every time he got in the pasture, here she came with all the hate she had for him showing and that was plenty. Tom told Ettie, "She must have been beaten and mistreated by a man, and now she is taking all her hate out on me."

That day, when they got to the house, they all ate breakfast real fast so they wouldn't be late and in just a little while they were on their way to the berry patch. The day went faster and easier with Ettie and the kids kidding him all day about Delilah as they named her.

As long as they stayed there, Tom always made first Monday's trade day. Most of the time, he came back with some cows, horses, goats, donkeys, or just anything he could fatten up to take back to sell or trade. On one of the trips, he traded for twelve hens and a rooster. When Ettie saw them, you would have thought he had brought her a diamond ring. She told him, "Oh, Tom, I am so proud of them." It wouldn't be long until she could have some eggs to hatch and they could have pullets to eat later on. Sure enough, it wasn't but a few weeks until she had hens sitting. When they began to hatch, she was so proud of them. After they hatched from six to eight weeks, they began to have fryers to eat.

They finished the berries, and the peach trees were easier to pick and was shadier and not so hot, but still they had to work from sunup to sundown. They picked peaches, plums, apricots, and cherries. Mr. Tompkins gave them some of the fruit that was too ripe to ship. Ettie and Leola would can it each night. They didn't have sugar to put in it, but it would made real good cobblers and preserves later on when they had sugar. Also Mr. Tompkins had acres of corn and potatoes with all that, they had enough work to last them from early spring to late summer. When they had finished with the fruit trees, Mr. Tompkins paid them, as he had promised to do. It wasn't much, but it would buy groceries and help get them through part of the winter.

Chapter 29

TOM HEARD THEY WERE HIRING families to pick cotton in Childress, Texas. Promising Mr. Tompkins they would be back for berry picking this coming year. Again, they loaded everything they owned on the wagon. The boys and Tom had to make Ettie another large crate to put the increase of chickens she had accumulated. They tied the chicken crates on the back of the wagon, all the livestock they tied behind the back, and headed toward West Texas. They didn't know exactly where Childress was, all they knew was it was in West Texas and they were going there to find work.

They hadn't heard from Sallie since they had left the ranch and found out they would go through Sherman going to Childress. So they planned on trying to find her. It took over a week to get there, and they were all worn out including the animals. Tom knew it was time to let the animals rest more than just overnight. When they got just outside of Sherman they found a real shady place. It had a creek running right next to a big tree where it looked like someone had camped before. Tom asked the man that owned the land if they could camp there for a few days and told him their plans. He said, "It is all right to stay as long as ya'll want to." After they all bathed and dressed in their best clothes, they went to look for Sallie. At the address they had, no one seemed to know anything about her. Tom went to the police station, and it didn't take him long to find out that Jeff had been in and out of jail for years and they told him where Sallie lived. They found the place, but the neighbors told them she was at work and would be home about five. They left telling them, "We will be back after supper time." Tom stressed, "Be sure and tell her after suppertime." From the looks of things, he didn't think she could have fixed a meal if her life depended upon it.

They went back to the wagon, changed cloths, and just rested. They were all tired after the long trip. They had come almost two hundred miles, give or take a few. The horses were beginning to feel the strain also. Although they had stopped along the way and let them rest and stopped early each night, it had been a long hard trip, both on them and the animals. They had hobbled the livestock before they left to go to Sallie's so they could eat and get to the water. The dogs, they never tied so they would have free range to watch the livestock and the wagon. The chickens, they had watered, opened the lid on their cage, and turned it upside down so they could scratch around in the grass. About five, they all got up and Ettie and Leola fixed supper while the boys and Tom checked on the livestock and milked the cow and checked to see if the hens had laid any eggs. They had only one cow giving milk now and not much of that. The trip had been extra hard on the cows. They weren't used to walking that far each day, and it affected the milk she gave. It really didn't matter that much about the milk because they didn't have a way to keep it all day anyway. At night they put it in the creek to stay cold. They drank the cold milk for breakfast, and Ettie made bread for the day and the rest of it the dogs got. After they ate supper, they all put back on their good clothes again and headed back to Sallie's.

She was home when they got there, but Jeff was no place to be seen. After they had all greeted her, the boys asked about him. She said, "I don't know. He hasn't been home in several months." After that the boys asked if they could go to town and look around for a while. They had never been to Sherman and like all kids wanted to see it. Tom told them they could and for them to be careful and not to stay long. Leola wanted to go with them. They promised to watch after her, so away they went. The house where Sallie lived was behind an old laundry. It was a three-room house (or I should say a three-room shack). It was one of several of the same kind of houses built right next door to the side of the laundry fence. They were built down the side and across the back, then down the other side. At the back of the laundry, on the other side of the fence, was a pond where the hot dirty water ran into from the laundry. The tall fence was made of boards and cut off most of the breeze to the houses and what there was, was coming off the hot water, so it was hot and humid.

After the kids left, Sallie told Tom, "You were right. He has never made me a living, and half of the time, I never know where he is. We lived with his mother until she told us she couldn't keep us anymore and told Jeff he had to get out and get a job. We found this place and moved in it. Right after that he left. His mother helped me find a job keeping house and doing the washing and ironing for a judge, his wife, and two sons. They were in high school and dirtied a lot of clothes, along with the judge. I don't make very much, but it pays the rent and buys the groceries I need. Also, I get one meal a day."

Tom told her about them losing the ranch and where they were going and for what, and she was welcome to come along. She told him, "Brother, I married him for better or worse, and I won't leave him."

Tom tried to tell her, "He has already left you," but she told them, "He will be back and I have to be here waiting for him." Tom tried not to show how angry he was. She had already been hurt enough without him adding to it. They stayed there a week trying to pressure her to go with them. Finally, Tom told her, "Sis, we can't stay here any longer if we want to get to Childress in time to pick cotton. So we can make enough to make it through the winter. Ettie and I have talked it over, and we will be back and spend the winter here in Sherman."

They left the next day for a long hard trip to Childress. It took them almost three weeks to get there. The animals were beginning to show the strain of the long trip, and Tom knew he had to let them rest more or lose them. He knew he couldn't afford to lose them, so they would stop earlier and stay longer so the animals could rest, and also them. When they got there, it didn't take them long to find a place to work. Benjamin Brown had told him to hire out to pick a bale a day and he could get a house and job a lot quicker. So that's what he told the people. Tom told them there were five of them and they could pick a bail a day. Tom had no idea what he was getting them into, but he did know they had to have a job and a house to live in. A man by the name of Sam Jones finally came into the café where Tom was inquiring about pickers and told Tom he was looking for help.

He asked him, "Have you ever picked cotton before?"

Tom couldn't lie to him, and he told him, "No, but if anyone else can do it, we can too. We need the money to make it through the winter. We have come all the way from Sherman to work."

He hired them and they followed him home. He took them down to where the house was. Again it wasn't much, but it was a roof over their heads and they had a job. It was Friday when they got there, and he told them, "Get settled in, and then on Monday I will show ya'll how to pick cotton."

There was a pasture close to the house with a windmill. It had a crude tank for a watering trough to water the stock. A stream of cold water ran out of a pipe into the tank. Sam told them, "Always keep a bucket or two of water filled because if the wind don't blow, the windmill don't turn and you won't have any water." Boy was he right. They learned not only to have two buckets of water filled, but the washpot also so they would have water each night to bath in. The house was just about like the one they had in East Texas. It was four rooms and was as dirty as the other one was. Again, it had three iron beds, a table, a stove, some crude cabinets built on the wall and two benches one on each side of the table. They brought water from the windmill and began to heat it in the washpot. Tom went up and asked Sam, "Do you have any lumber and nails so we can build some shelves for our cloths."

He told him, "Send the boys up to the house and I have some they can have." While the water heated in the pot, they went for the lumber. Sam told them, "Load it on my wagon and I will bring it down for you." When the water was hot, Ettie and Leola started washing the cabinets, stove, and floors down with the hot water and lye soap. Tom took the table, benches, and beds outside and began the job of cleaning them up. When Sam and the boys got there with the lumber, the boys unloaded it while Sam and Tom talked for a while. When he started to leave, Tom thanked him for the lumber and nails. Then he and the boys started working on the shelves. They didn't get them finished that night. The house did get dry enough to bring the mattress in. They made up the beds and cooked supper on the stove, and again Tom thanked God they had a roof over their heads and beds to sleep in. The next day they finished the shelves and washed them down real good with scalding water and lye soap. When they were good and dry, they nailed one set to the wall in each bedroom. As they finished them, Ettie and Leola put some sheets, pillowcases, towels, washrags, and their folded clothes in each room. On Sunday, they all just rested. They were all worn out. That night Tom told them, what they were in for. He told them, "I have told the man we could pick a bale a day to get the job and house. He is anxious to get his cotton out before it rains, and we have to do it."

The next morning they got up early and by daylight were at Mr. Jones's house, waiting for him to take them down to show them how to pick cotton. It was a hard, back-breaking job. He gave them each a long narrow sack made of heavy duckin material. It had a strap that went across his shoulder, leaving the mouth of the sack open, making it easier to put the cotton in. He told them to put their heads through the strap opening with the sack to their left side. Then he showed them how to pull it along behind them and how to pull the white cotton out of the burrs. Before the cotton opened up, it was in a green ball that was called bowels. Then when it ripened, it opened up; and the cotton balls, or bowels as they called them, began to turn a brownish color, and then it was called burrs after they got ripe. They would fall down like petals. There were several petals to a bowel, and they had sharp points on the top of each petal. It didn't take long to learn to get the white cotton from the center to keep from getting stuck by the sharp points on the burrs. He gave each of them cloth gloves and told them they would keep them from getting their fingers stuck by the burs. They helped, but by night their fingers were stuck over and over by the burrs and were sore and some bleeding. The cotton was put in the sack and pulled along behind them. By the time they got halfway of the field, they would have a full sack of cotton. It was heavy and hard to pull. Sam had a wagon with real high sideboards, set up halfway of the field. On the back of it was two one-by-two's, one nailed on each side of a two- by-four that was part of the corner of the sideboards on the wagon. About halfway to the center of these boards, where they came together were two more boards nailed to form a brace. On each side of these, they went back and were nailed on each side of the first one by two at the wagon. On the end of the first boards were some scales with a hook hanging down to weigh the cotton on. It was fastened to the end of the boards with wire. Mary, Sam's wife, would weigh the sack of cotton and write the amount down in a book under each name. Then they emptied the sack in the wagon, got a cold drink of water, and started back to work.

At noon they stopped for dinner. They were all so tired. They didn't feel like eating. They got a cold cup of water and just propped back against the wagon wheels and rested in the shade beside the wagon. It wasn't long until the kids and Ettie were fast asleep.

Sam and his wife went home for dinner. He had told Tom, "We always take an hour off for dinner." Tom let everyone rest for thirty minutes, then woke them and told them, "Ya'll had better eat, so we will be ready to go back to work at one." Ettie had packed a lunch in a lard bucket so the insects couldn't get into it. Tom had bought some cans of pork and beans. While he opened them, Ettie got out some fried meat and bread. Leola peeled an onion, and the boys filled their glasses with some more cold water. They were all hungry by then, and everyone ate like they were starved to death. By the time they finished eating, Sam and his wife were back and it was time to go back to work. They worked until dusty dark. They were still 250 pounds short of their thousand pounds. Monroe and Tom had pulled 200 each, Leola 150, and Ettie and Virgil 100 each.

Sam said, "That was real good. I didn't expect you to get the bail the first day. Even seasoned pickers, when they started each year, never get their full amount the first week." That made all of them feel better. He gave them some cream to rub on their hands and told them that would toughen them. It looked like axle grease, but it did make them feel better. He told Ettie to put some more on before they went to bed.

When they got home, they were so tired. While Ettie and Leola fixed supper, Tom and the boys took care of the outside chores. After Tom had milked, he took it in to be strained. Ettie strained it in a lard bucket, and Tom took it to the tank to put it in the cold water so it would stay cold. The boys brought fresh water from the windmill for supper. It was ice cold. Then they filled up the washpot and built a fire under it. That way they would have plenty of hot water for their bathes. They were all not only dirty, but filthy from the sweat and dirt (that had blown all day). But the wind blowing did help to keep them a little cooler.

Each night it was the same routine. Tom and the boys did the night chores. By the time they were through and had a fire going under the washpot, Ettie and Leola had supper ready. They would eat without too much talking, and right after supper they took their baths. There was a little shed built on to the back of the house for a place to take a bath. It was a little larger than the toilet that was behind the house, close to the pasture. Each night when they had all bathe, the boys would refill the washpot with fresh water and make sure the fire was out from under it. Ettie and Leola would clean the kitchen. Then they would go to bed. By then they were all dog tired, and daylight would be there before they knew it. As Sam told them, they would work from can do to can't do. If you are wondering what that meant, it was from the time you could see until you couldn't see

Each morning they were up again before daylight. The boys and Tom opened the chicken door to the chicken house and milked the cow; and while Tom took the milk to the house, the boys checked on the other livestock. After Tom's run-in with Delilah, they always checked the livestock.

By the time they got to the house, breakfast was ready and Leola and Ettie had their lunch packed for the day. They were in the field at daybreak before Sam got there. Mary didn't come until much later. Their hands were sore, and their backs ached, but they did better each day. By the end of the first week they were getting their bale a day. Monroe, Leola, and Tom were getting 250 each. Ettie and Virgil were getting the rest to make their bale. If they didn't get it by quitting time, Monroe, Leola and Tom would stay and pick what they lacked while Virgil and Ettie would go in and do the night work and get supper. Virgil would have plenty of hot water when they came in. Not too many times did they have to go back, they decided they had rather work a little harder than to have to stay over. They had Saturday and Sunday off. Of course, the kids wanted to go to town. They all pitched in and did the washing. They didn't have too many clothes to wash; and it wasn't long until they were all bathed, dressed, and headed for town. Tom told the boys to meet them back at a little cafe that had a sign in their window "Five hamburgers for a dollar and also a milkshake for a nickel." At noon they were back, ready for dinner. They all went in and got a milkshake and the five hamburgers. Boy, were they good. The kids told Tom and Ettie they had seen a picture show down the street that was showing a cowboy movie. They said it cost a nickel. Tom told Ettie as hard as they had worked, they deserved to get to go see it, so he gave them the money to go.

Tom asked Ettie, "Would you want to go?"

But she said, "I had rather just go home and rest."

The kids said, "We will walk home as soon as the show is over. It isn't that far and can we stay and see it twice. We heard a boy say, you can stay and see it twice if you want to and it don't cost anymore."

Tom told them they could, and they left hurrying so they wouldn't miss any of it.

Ettie and Tom got what groceries they needed and headed for home. That became their Saturday routine. They would get up early and get the clothes washed, then head out for town for a hamburger, a milkshake, and then later the movies. Sometimes Ettie and Tom would go, but they only stayed for one show. Leola and the boys always stayed for two and would walk home later. It was cool in the show, and besides, they had met some kids their age that were out here pulling cotton also. All the kids started meeting at the cafe, and all eating together, then all going to the show together. Leola had met a girl her age from Post, Texas, that she chummed with, and she told her mother later was crazy about Virgil. There were several in the group, and as they walked home, some left at each farm along the way. They all were in the same fix as Tom's family was, some was even worse off than they were.

Monroe told Tom, "Most of them went back Saturday morning and picked cotton to buy their hamburger, milkshake, and their show ticket. Can we go back and do that?"

Tom told him, "We can afford the quarter that I give each of you, but if you want more, you can go back."

So they started going back each Saturday morning.

Monroe saved what he made and always had money in his pocket, but Virgil spent his as fast as he got it. He would buy popped corn, candy, and cold drinks for the girls. Monroe told Virgil, "Let them buy their own, they pick cotton the same as we do and get just as much as we get for picking it. Money is too hard to come by to blow it in on girls." Leola saved hers also. They never made a lot, but as Monroe said, "Every penny counts toward having a dollar."

They finished the cotton-picking season and again loaded all their belongings in the wagon and left for Sherman. They had decided to spend the winter there. That way they would be a little more than halfway between Childress and Lindale. It took them a little over two weeks of hard going to get to Sherman. They stopped early each day to let the horses and cows rest and started later in the mornings. Also, they stopped on Saturday and stayed put for the weekend. That gave the stock longer to rest and graze and gave them more time to rest also.

Chapter 30

By the time they got to Sherman, they all were dead tired, including the animals. They camped in the same spot where they had camped before. Tom asked the man again if it would be all right and told him, "We will be looking for a house to rent. We will be spending the winter here." Also, Tom asked him, "Could we leave our stock there in your pasture until we find a place. We will pay you rent." He told Tom that it would be all right and told him about a man by the name of Hill that had a house for rent. He said it had a big backyard that was fenced in and told Tom where the house was. They went down and got the wagon set up. Tom and the boys took care of the stock, and watered the chickens, and turned their cages upside down in the shade so they could have grass to peck in. Then they all dressed and went in to see Mr. Hill. After they saw him, they would go check on Sallie, but first they must see about the house. Luck was with them. They found the place without any trouble, and he was there, working on the house. It wasn't much. It had three large rooms with a little room at the back big enough for a bed and a chester draws. The kitchen was in front of the little room with one room to the left of the kitchen. The second room was at the front of the kitchen, and both rooms had a door leading out to a big front porch. It had water at the back of the house. Also it had a small chicken house and a small barn. All the backyard was fenced in. Tom told him they only wanted it for the winter months, that they would be leaving for Lindale in the early spring to pick fruit and then to West Texas to pick cotton. Then back again for the winter each year. He agreed to let them have it for six dollars a month. There was no bathroom, but they weren't used to one anyway. It did have a toilet at the back of the lot from the alley. Mr. Hill told them some men came by every other day and emptied the buckets under the toilet seats. It was called the honey wagon. But they wouldn't need it because their toilet had a commode in it and a water tank that flush the commode. The boys told him, "It is a big improvement over what we did have." The house was on the highway that ran through Sherman to Whitesboro. Across the street from the house was the main cemetery of Sherman. Mr. Hill told Tom, "There is a pasture at the end of the cemetery that you could probably rent for the horses. It is a large pasture and has plenty of good grass and a creek runs through it that has plenty of water in it all year around." He gave Tom the man's name that had it and where he lived. Tom thanked him for the information and told him he would be needing it as he also had some cows.

Mr. Hill told him, "Speaking of information, do you know where you have to go to put up your water deposit."

Tom told him, "We have always lived in the country, and we didn't even know there was a place like that to have put up a deposit to get water."

Mr. Hill told him, "Ya'll have to go down and put up the deposit before they will turn on the water."

Tom paid him the six dollars, and he said, "I will be around to collect the rent each month." After he left the boys went down to put the deposit up for the water and to see about getting it turned on while Tom went to see about renting the pasture. Ettie and Leola stayed at the house. Mr. Hill was right. It was a large pasture and had plenty of grass and water. After

Tom saw the pasture he went looking for the house where the man lived that owned it. It wasn't hard to find his house. Mr. Hill had told him, "Coming back from the pasture, it will be two blocks up and one block left, back toward the house that ya'll have rented." The man was sitting at the back of the house when Tom got there. Tom told him what he wanted, and the man asked, "How many livestock are you talking about?"

Tom told him, "I have two cows and eight horses right now, but I will be getting rid of two, come first Monday. We came from Childress, and I traded for them along the way. I will never have more than that at any time."

He told Tom he didn't need all that room for one cow, so he agreed to rent it to him. Tom paid him and told him where they were moving, that they would be putting their cows and horses in there tomorrow. By the time he got back, the boys were back and said, "They would have the water on tomorrow after ten." Without water, they couldn't do too much cleaning, so they went back to where they were camped. The boys and Tom took care of the livestock and got some fresh cold water from the creek. By then Ettie and Leola had supper ready. They ate, and after supper they went back to see about Sallie. She was still living in the same house, and Jeff was still gone. They told her where they would be living and that they would be there all winter. She said, "I know exactly where it is. I come by it every morning, going to work, I work on Binkley Street, almost right behind the hospital." They didn't stay long. They told her, "We have been all morning getting here and have spent the afternoon finding the house and pasture. We are tired and want to get some rest so we can get moved in tomorrow." When they got back to where they were camped, they all went right straight to bed. They were all worn out.

The next morning, they got up early, ate breakfast, loaded all the chickens and coups, and tied the cattle behind the wagon.

Tom wanted to be there before the man came to turn on the water. He and the boys set the chicken coups off at the house, then took the livestock to the pasture. Ettie and Leola opened the crates and let the chickens out. There was some grass in the backyard, so they went right out and started scratching in it for something to eat. Then Ettie and Leola went in to wait for the man to come to turn on the water. They didn't have anything to worry about; the man didn't show up until almost eleven.

After the water was turned on, they heated water in the washpot, and while Ettie and Leola scrubbed everything down, the boys and Tom went looking for a place to buy some furniture. When they got to the house that morning, they all realized they didn't have any furniture. They had always had the beds, stove, table, and benches at each house. They found a second-hand store without any trouble and bought three iron beds, three chester drawers, a stove, a table, and some chairs, also an icebox to keep the milk and butter in. The man said, "We will deliver it all about noon." The house had a built-in cabinet on the east side, from the door going to the small room around the corner and to the door leading to the room at the left. So they didn't have to worry about places to put the dishes and groceries. Around one o'clock, their furniture arrived. By then the floors were dry. They were able to put everything in the house and in place. By four all the mattresses were unloaded with everything in the house and put away. Again, they were settled into a house, but this time for the winter. Ettie and Tom went to town to get the groceries they needed, and the boys asked if they could go to town and look around. Of course, Leola wanted to go with them. Going to Kresses' and McClellan's was a big thing with them. In the little towns they had been staying, they didn't have one, let alone one of each. They promised to be home before suppertime. Ettie and Tom found a large grocery store and got a big bill of groceries. They were back and had them put away before Sallie came by. Sallie and Ettie fixed supper, and before they finished putting it on the table, the kids were back. That became their regular routine each night. Sallie would come by, and most of the time she stayed for supper. Always she would leave in time to get home before dark.

Then one night when she came by, she looked so happy. Before Tom could say anything, she said, "Oh, Tom, Jeff is back. Tom, be happy for me. I know you don't like him, but this time he promised he would stay and get a job."

Tom wanted to tell her, "Sis, you know he is only lying to you. If there were any jobs to be had, he would have one." But she looked so happy, Tom just couldn't spoil it for her. He hugged her and told her, "Sis, I am happy for you, and I hope everything works out all right. You deserve all the happiness you can get."

She hugged him and told him how glad she was because she thought he would be mad.

The boys and Tom found a place to cut wood. The man that owned the wooded area wanted it cleared and said, "I will give ya'll the wood if you will clear the land and burn the brush as you go." They would stop about four and haul it in so they could find someone to buy it. It wasn't long until they had a regular route of customers that they took wood to every week. The small wood that wouldn't sell, they took home for them to burn in the kitchen stove. When winter came they realized they didn't have a heater. So they had to go back to the used furniture store and buy a heater so they could keep one room warm. His and Ettie's bedroom was the only room that had a chimney. It and the kitchen stove shared the same chimney. They all sat around it so they could all keep warm during the day. The boys and Tom brought in all the smaller limbs, each night to burn in both stoves just to keep warm. They cut and sold wood all winter. By the time they were ready to leave for Lindale, they had cleared the land, burned all the brush that wasn't big enough to sell, and took the horses, and pulled all the stumps out of the field and burned them also.

Tom always made the trade day, regardless to where they were. One month he told Ettie, "I need to look for some more horses. That ours are getting older and tired. If we made another trip to Lindale and to West Texas, I think we are going to have to have some younger horses to pull the wagon." So on trade day, the boys and Tom took their horses and went up to the sale. During the winter months, Ettie insisted the boys go with him so he could teach them how to buy and sell. They found a place to tie their horses, then went looking for some horses to trade for.

Tom told the boys, "When ya'll find some, now don't act to enthused, if they think we really want them, they will jack the price up. Now one of you ask, 'What do you think?' and the other say, 'Well, I've seen better.' Don't ever let them know what you really think about them when you are trying to trade for something. Try to find everything you can, wrong with them. Remember the man that is trading or selling them is trying to hide everything that's wrong with them, and if you are lucky, you might get the best end of the deal. But you can't know it all, regardless of how long you buy and sell. Remember one of these days, there will be someone out there that will skin you good, you can't win them all!"

They walked around looking, and finally Monroe said, "Dad, look at that pair of horses. Aren't they beautiful? They match completely."

Virgil said, "They look like they could pull anything, and they look young."

They were poor as dirt but otherwise looked in good shape.

Tom told them, "Now remember what I told you. Don't act too anxious." He asked the man, "Are they for sell or trade?"

He told them, "I had rather sell them, but would trade."

Tom told him, "I have a pair of horses that is a real good team, but they had come all the way from Childress and were going on to Lindale. They are tired and need some rest. As soon as they get rest, they will be okay." Tom didn't tell him how long it had been since they came from Childress, or how old they were. He told the boys later, "That's another thing in trading. You don't tell the man everything you know. Some things are none of their business."

The boys walked up to where the horses were and started discussing them, like they knew it all, about horses. The man asked, "Where are your horses?" and Tom told him. They all walked down to see them while the man's boys took care of his horses. He began to do the same thing that Tom had told the boys to do. Tom winked at them, and they both grinned. Monroe said to Virgil, "There is nothing wrong with our horses except they are just tired from the long trip." Virgil said, like he was whispering and didn't want them to hear, "I don't see why Dad wants to trade anyway. If they can rest all winter, then they will be as good as ever."

The man continued looking Tom's horses over and finally said, "Well, I will tell you what I will do. I will trade with you for twenty dollars to boot."

Tom told him, "I was sorter thinking about asking for the twenty dollars myself." They talked for a while, neither one wanting the other to think he was anxious to trade or in a hurry. Finally, the man said, "I will trade even, my team for yours."

Tom saw the look in Virgil and Monroe's eyes, and he could read their thoughts, saying, *Dad, take it, take it*. He looked the man square in the eyes and said, "Man, there is nothing wrong with these horses, but they are just tired. Yours are dirt poor. I will tell you what I will do. For the twenty dollars you had mentioned for boot, I will trade with you. With a little rest, these horses will be as good as new. Yours will have to have a bunch of feed to get them strong enough to pull a wagon. That would cost money, which I don't have."

He thought for a minute as if he wasn't sure and was waiting to see if Tom would change his mind. Then he finally said, "I will trade and split the difference with you." Tom knew he was wanting to trade and if he held his ground he would come across.

Tom told him, "It will take more feed than that and that is as low as I can go."

The man stood around for a while longer, then turned to walk off. When he saw Tom wasn't going to stop him, he came back and said, "You got yourself a deal." He paid Tom and asked him, "Where is this pasture?"

He said, "The boys and I will be heading out past it, and why don't me and the boys just ride along with them. I will hitch your horses up to my wagon and tie the other ones behind the wagon. That way when we get to the pasture, we could just drop you and the horses off. That way you and the boys won't have to walk and lead them."

The boys and Tom thought that was a great idea, so they took their horses. Virgil and Monroe helped his boys hitch them to the wagon and tied the new ones behind the wagon. They all climbed into the wagon. The man suggested that the boys drive and he and Tom ride at the back of the wagon.

When they got to the pasture, while the boys put the new horses in the pasture, the man and Tom exchanged a few words. Then Tom told him thanks, and he told Tom good luck, and they started home. When they were out of sight, the boys began to laugh.

Monroe said, "Dad, you sure got the best of that deal, didn't you?"

Virgil said, "Dad, how did you know he would pay boot?"

Tom told them, like he had told them before, "Watch their face. Don't ever let them know you are anxious to trade. I saw he was really wanting to trade, so I played along with him until I got the best deal I could."

By then they were home, and the boys told Ettie what a beautiful team of horses they had traded for and told her, "And, Mom, Dad even got twenty dollars to boot."

Ettie told them that would buy a lot of groceries for the winter. They had no reason to hitch the horses up to the wagon the rest of the winter so they just let them stay in the pasture and eat and get in good shape for the spring.

As Tom had said they were on the highway going to Whitesboro. There wasn't a lot of traffic, but there were a lot of hobos traveling through the country, most of them kids. Tom told Ettie he saw himself in the eyes of every one of them that comes to the door asking for something to eat and a place to sleep for the night. Tom thought each one he saw could have been him if Mr. Heart hadn't taken him in. So they never turned any of them away. Ettie always fixed some food for them regardless to what time of day it was. They always had plenty of milk, butter, and eggs. Tom had traded for two hogs, and they had fattened them up. And the first cold spell, they had killed them and cured the meat so they had plenty of ham, bacon, or sausage. They had put an extra bed in the front bedroom, and Leola and the boys had changed rooms. That way when they came by, they could get a good meal and at least one good warm night of rest. If it was real bad, they would ask if they could stay longer and most of them would go out with the boys and Tom and help cut wood, or if it was too bad to cut wood, they would always help get the wood in and the night work done. Most of them were good boys that were looking for work, a roof over their heads, and three meals a day. Most of them were headed to West Texas to be there to hoe cotton or corn when it was time.

The winter passed real fast, and it wasn't long before it was time for them to go to Lindale if they were to be there in time to get settled in before berry picking time. Ettie had been feeling bad for some time, and Tom hated to go. He asked her if he could get Sallie to come and stay with her if she would stay there for a while.

She told him, "Now, Tom, you know we can't afford for me to stay here and let them all go. Besides I wouldn't be happy that way. I would be so miserable without ya'll, then I would sure enough be sick. I will just take it easy for a while, then I will be all right."

They decided to leave the following Monday. On Saturday morning the boys and Tom pulled the wagon out of the barn and cleaned it up real good. That afternoon, while the kids went to the show, Ettie and Tom went to town and got a big bill of groceries. Food was cheaper here than it was in Lindale. With the boys and him cutting wood and selling it and with his trading, they had some money left over and would be all right until they collected the berry-and-fruit-picking money. So they decided to stock up before they left. They splurged and bought a case of green beans, English peas, corn, canned milk, tomatoes, also some macaroni. Then they got dried beans, flour, cornmeal, coffee, sugar, baking powder, and salt. They had lived barely on the necessaries so long that it was good to be able to go to town and buy a big bill of groceries. They had plenty of lard, cured meat, sausage, and ham. Leola and Ettie had made lye soap when they killed the hogs, so there were plenty to do them while they were gone.

On Sunday, they loaded everything in the wagon that they could. All the groceries they had bought and everything else they could spare. The mattresses, table, and stove they had to wait until the next day. There was a little shed at the back of the barn. Tom had made arrangements with Mr. Hill to store their furniture there and pay him rent on it. He said for them to get a lock and be sure it was locked up good and he would check it every month when he came to collect the people's rent. They wanted to get an early start, so Monday morning they didn't build a fire in the stoves. They wanted to make sure they were good and cold before they put them in the shed.

That night, the boys went down to the pasture and brought the horses and cows up and put them in the backyard. When they got back, Tom milked the cow and gave it to the neighbors the second house down. They had a bunch of kids and were real proud to get it. Tom told them, "Give me something to put it in, and ya'll can have the morning milk also." They gave him a big bucket, and Tom told them they would put it on the porch as they were going to leave by daylight. The neighbor man said, "We are always up early because I have to be at work by six so that will be just fine." He thanked and thanked Tom for it and wished them good luck.

Monday morning they were up and had everything in the shed. Before they put the stoves in there, they emptied the ashes out of each of them and made sure they were cold. They locked the door with two locks on it. The boys decided when they went after the locks that they wouldn't take a chance on one, if one was good two would be better. Before daylight they had milked the cow, had put it on the neighbor's front porch, and were ready to pull out. Tom made a quick look through the house to make sure they hadn't forgotten anything, and it was all clean. The boys had checked the backyard and pulled the wagon to the front yard and locked the gate. All the hens were in crates, and all the animals were tied behind the wagon. Ettie and Tom got upon the seat of the wagon, and he told the kids they were ready to go. Tom took the reins and shook them a little and told the horses to get up. They turned and looked at him and didn't move a muscle. Again, Tom hollered, "Get up" a little louder. Still they just stood there. He took the end of the reins and popped it over their heads and hollered get up again. But still they took one look at him and just stood there as if to say, "You make us." The kids began to laugh and said, "Dad they have been in the pasture all winter with Delilah, do you think she has been talking to them?" By then Tom had just about lost his patience. He told the kids, "Talk or no talk, I bet I will make them move." This time he got the whip and cracked it over their heads. With no results at all. Those crazy horses just stood there and bowed their back like, "We know what's coming next." Tom gave it to them right across their backs. This made Ettie mad, and she said, "Now, Tom, you are not going to beat them. If you can't drive them, get down and let one of the boys drive them or Leola. They all have driven horses before."

Tom told her, "Now, Ettie, it's not that I can't drive them. The stupid beast won't let me drive them."

He got down and Leola must have felt sorry for him because she got off her horse and said, "Here, Dad, you can ride Cutie Pie and I will drive the team for you." She crawled upon the seat and took the reins. The horses looked back and saw Tom standing there and walked off as pretty as you please.

Those crazy boys were laughing their heads off, and Ettie joined along with them. When they stopped for breakfast and to let the horses rest, the boys said, "We will unharness the team and hobble them." Ettie still wasn't feeling good, so they all pitched in and cooked breakfast. Ettie ate very little. They cleaned up their mess, then they rested for a while. Tom tied the sides of the wagon up and told Ettie, "Why don't you lie down in it and see if you can get some rest." It wasn't long until she was fast asleep.

They let her sleep for about an hour before they woke her. She said, "I am feeling better." Tom went down and filled the canteens with fresh cold water and brought her a drink. Then he wet a wash rag and told her, "Wash your face with it, and maybe that would help you feel better. Why don't you just stay laying down in the back of the wagon, and I will leave the sides up so you can get plenty of air."

She said, "I think I will feel better sitting up, and besides whoever drives the wagon will need company to stay wake." The horses did just fine as long as they could see Tom. It didn't matter whether he was riding on a horse or walking, the minute they couldn't see him, they stopped and wouldn't take a step until they could see where he was. This went on all the way to Lindale. Tom was so mad at those crazy horses, he could about kill them by the time they got there. He had to walk or ride a horse all the way. The boys or Leola could ride in the wagon any time, but if Tom tried to slip into the back of it and they couldn't see him they stopped and wouldn't move a muscle until they saw him again. They stopped every Saturday and Sunday to let Ettie and the livestock rest. They would camp in a good shady place, close to a creek, so the rest of them could do the washing while Ettie rested. On one of those Sunday afternoons, Tom told the boys he thought he had an idea of how he could work with those stupid horses and get them to pull the wagon with him in it, that he was going to get them to pull that wagon with him in it or die trying. While Ettie and Leola were resting, Tom took a small bunch of brush and leaves and put it in two piles in front of the wagon. The horses would let him harness them; but after that, when he got up into the wagon, they wouldn't pull the wagon one inch.

Tom thought if he could get them to pull it just a short distance they would get the message of what he wanted them to do. The boys kept telling him, "Dad, they know what to do. They are just not going to do it for you."

"Anyway," he told the boys, "they will move one way or the other. I am getting tired of their nonsense. You boys get some hot coals and put them on the brush pile that I have built under their bellies. I bet when it gets hot enough they will move."

The boys kept telling him, "It isn't going to work," but Tom told them, "Just do as I say. It will work, just hide and watch." So they put the hot coals on each of the brush piles. When it started getting hot, the horses did move. They began to pull as pretty as you please, but as soon as they got the fire under the wagon, they stopped and wouldn't move another step. Tom hollered at the boys, "Come and help me." Leola ran over and unhitched them from the wagon and drove them out of the way. The boys and Tom pulled the wagon off the brush piles before the wagon caught on fire. Those crazy horses just stood there looking back as if to say, "Guess you know that trick has been pulled on us before." The kids were laughing so hard, tears were running down their faces.

Tom told them, "If I didn't need those stupid horses to pull the wagon, I would just shoot them both and leave them for the buzzards to eat."

Leola said, "Now, Dad, burning them up, wagon and all, is not going to make them pull."

The boys joined right in kidding him and said, "Sis, he said he was going to make them pull the wagon if it killed him. Guess he is going to take them along so he could keep trying."

Ettie got up and came over and joined in with the kids, but Tom didn't think she was kidding. She said, "Now, Tom, what in the world did you think you were doing. Didn't you realize everything we own is on that wagon. If it had caught on fire and burned up, what do you think we would do?"

The boys said, "Now, Mama, don't be too hard on him. He was only trying to get those stupid horses moving. The only thing, they had that little trick figured out before he did."

They were laughing so hard, Tom couldn't spoil their fun so he started funning along with them. He told them, "Mr. Heart told me once in training a dog, the first step was, you had to have more sense than the dog. I guess that applies to horses too."

Leola said, "Now, Dad, I will take up for you. It's not that the horses are smarter than you are. It's that Delilah has been talking to them about your red hair, and they don't like it either."

The boys said, "Well, in that case, why do they let you drive the wagon?"

She came back with, "Well, they said they like me in spite of my red hair."

That was all the boys needed, they started kidding their sister. Monroe said to Virgil, "Our sister not only talks to horses, but they talk back to her."

Virgil said, "While she was talking to them, why didn't she try to persuade them to let Dad drive the wagon. It sure would improve his temper if they would and all our lives too."

She grabbed a stick and started toward them, and of course, they ran off just dying laughing and shouting back at her.

The next morning they loaded everything on the wagon and were ready to pull out. Monroe and Virgil came up to Tom and real serious like said, "Dad, do you have any more smart ideas you want to try to get those stupid horses going before one of us drives them?"

Ettie, Leola, and the boys were just dying laughing.

Ettie said, "Well, I will tell you one thing, you better not build any more fires."

They finally got to Lindale. They were later than usual, but Mr. Tompkins said the berries weren't ripe yet so that would give them a few days to get settled in. He asked Tom, "Would you pick and I pay later like you had been doing?"

Tom told him, "It is just fine."

Mr. Tompkins told them, "Go on down then, and I will let you know when they are ready. From the looks of them, it will probably be in three or four days."

They had the house to clean as usual. The kids and Tom told Ettie to rest and they would get it cleaned. By late that afternoon, they had everything washed, scrubbed, dried, and everything moved in and in place. Again, they had a roof over their heads for the next several months.

By Saturday, the berries still weren't ready, so the kids asked if they could go to town. Lindale didn't have a show, but the kids said, "It did have a five-and-dime store that we can go and look around in."

Chapter 31

AFTER THEY LEFT, TOM AND Ettie sat down at the table, and Ettie dropped the bombshell. Just out of the cold blue sky, she said, "Tom, I'm pregnant."

He almost dropped his coffee cup. He told her, "Ettie, you couldn't be."

She told him, "Tom, I could be, and I am." She went on to tell him, she thought she was around three months.

Tom sat there just plain dumbfounded. He finally asked, "How long have you known?"

Ettie told him, "I had begun to suspect it when I started getting sick at my stomach."

Tom told her, "You have known all this time, and you didn't tell me."

"Now, Tom," she said, "I knew you wouldn't have come down here if you had known."

He told her, "You better believe I wouldn't."

She told Tom, "You know we had to make enough to do us all winter, and besides what difference does it make if I have the baby here or in Sherman."

At first, Tom was real aggravated at her because she hadn't told him, but how could he stay mad at her when he knew she was right. Tom went around and took her in his arms, and she had tears running down her face. She said, "Tom be glad that God is giving us another baby."

He told her, "I am glad, but I am worried about you. What would I do if anything happened to you?"

The next day at the dinner table, Tom told the kids that they were going to have a new addition to their family, that mama was going to have a baby.

Leola was tickled to death. She said, "I do hope you have a little girl so she can help me hold our own with these ornery boys." Then she asked her mama, "Mama, you wouldn't do that to me and have another boy would you?"

They all laughed, and Virgil said, "Well, just to spite you, I hope it is."

Monroe didn't have anything to say. He just got up and went outside.

That afternoon Mr. Tompkins came down and told them the berries would be ready to start gathering on Monday. Tom told him that Ettie wouldn't be able to work this year and told him why.

Tom told him, "I would have told you sooner, but I didn't know it myself until yesterday. Don't you worry, we will get your berries gathered, and on time, even if we have to work all day and half the nights."

He thanked Tom and said, "Congratulations and I will see you tomorrow."

Tom asked him about a doctor, and he told him, "There is one in Lindale. He practices out of his home and will be there Saturdays."

That Saturday, they were up and the kids were in the patch as usual. Tom had everything done, and Ettie and he were in town by ten o'clock and trying to find the doctors house. Mr. Tompkins had told him where he lived, and it wasn't hard to find. When they knocked at the door, a man opened the door and spoke to them. "I am Dr. Baker, what can I do for ya'll?" Tom introduced them and told him why they were there. They went into his office. It was a large room with some bookshelves on the wall, three chairs, a desk, and an examining table. He told them to sit down, and first he would get the information he needed before he examined Ettie. He asked about each child's birth.

Ettie told him, "Virgil was breach. The baby and I almost died, and he was born with one leg longer than the other and was real small. He is still small. The other two were normal, and their birth wasn't any harder than normal."

Then he asked, "And how are they?"

She told him, "Normal healthy children." After that she told him she had been sick and tired all the time.

He examined her, then he told them, "You are anemic. I will give you some iron pills, and if we are real lucky, it will build your blood back up before the baby gets here. Now you are going to have to get plenty of rest and eat three good meals a day. Also, no more moving across the country until this little one comes."

Tom told him, "We will be here until the fruit season is over and then some if she needs to stay longer."

He told Tom, "You see to it that she gets three good meals a day and plenty of rest. I don't want her out picking anything until we get her built up and she gets over being sick at her stomach. The baby should be born the last of July or the first part of August." He also wanted to know if she had seen a doctor before today.

Ettie told him no, and he asked, "Why?"

Tom told him, "She hadn't told me until this last Saturday."

And again he asked her, "Why?"

She told him, "Doctor, if I had told him, he wouldn't have come down here to pick fruit. And we have to have the money to make it through the winter. We were lucky. We have this job to come to and then to Childress each year, and the money we make on both jobs will carry us through the winter."

Tom asked, "How much do we owe you?"

He said, "Don't worry about that right now. You have from now until I deliver the baby to get it paid for. I want to see Ettie in a month to see how the iron pills are working." He gave them some pills and told Tom, "Now you make sure she takes one of these a day and that she gets plenty of rest."

When they left his office, they went by the five-and-dime store. They didn't have any place to buy material, but there and Ettie was real anxious to get started making some baby clothes. She got some soft white material for baby dresses and some outing material for gowns, slips, and whatever else she needed. She could hardly wait until that night to show Leola. Leola was excited over the material as Ettie was and asked her mother if she could help her make them. Ettie told her she could help her on Sundays when they didn't have to work. Every Sunday they weren't in the field, she would help on them in place of going to town with the boys. She said, "There isn't anything to see except the five and dime, and I had seen everything they had in it."

The boys and Tom would go to town the Sundays they had off and get the groceries they needed. When the fruit was ready, they would work seven days a week until they got it gathered. One Sunday, they had off they found a chester drawers for sale in a person's yard. They stopped and looked at it. It needed some work done on it, but that wouldn't be a problem if they could find some small nails at the five and dime and all the other stuff they would need. The boys assured Tom they had seen nails and paint there. Sure enough they did have everything they would need. They took it home and began to work on it. It reminded Tom of the first chester drawers that he redone for Ettie before Virgil was born and what fun Billy, Mark, and he had redoing it. This one wouldn't be a surprise because they didn't have a barn to work in and would have to work on it on the back porch. When they got home with it, Ettie and Leola both were real proud of it.

Tom told Ettie, "It don't look like much now, but it will when we finish with it."

She said, "Tom, I know it will. Remember the first one."

The kids wanted to know about the first one, so they all sat down on the back porch and Tom told them all about the very first one and how surprised Ettie was when they brought it to the house. The boys helped him with it each Sunday they were off. They had to nail it together and sand it before they could start painting it. They had to paint it because it wasn't good enough to varnish. The boys seemed like they really enjoyed working on it with Tom. Then one weekend they put the last coat of paint on it, and on Monday it was dry enough to bring in. Ettie was so proud of it. She kept thanking and thanking them for it. Tom laughed and told the boys, "The way she is caring on, you would think it was brand-new."

She said, "It was better than brand-new because my boys and you made it for me." She showed them where to put it, and she and Leola started putting the things they had made in it. It seemed like she started showing overnight. She began to feel better, and when they took her back to the doctor, he said her blood was better.

"It's not up to where it belongs but is better than it was when you came in the first time. Now you will get in touch with me when ya'll need me. Also remember come as soon as her labor starts. I don't want any surprises."

Tom assured him, "I will," and he gave Ettie some more pills and said, "I will see you then."

Tom still made first Monday every month. He wanted to make sure he had enough money to pay the doctor. He always bought or traded for poor rundown stock and brought them home and the following month took them back fat and in good shape. Most of the time, he sold them or traded for more, always with so much to boot. By the time they needed the money, he had enough to pay the doctor and with several head of cows and horses to boot.

July was here before they knew it. Leola stayed each day at the house with her mother. They didn't leave her by herself at all. Tom had stopped going coon hunting at night because he didn't want to take any chances of not being there when she needed him.

Then early one Sunday morning, she woke Tom up and said, "Tom, I think it is time to get the doctor." He woke Monroe and told him to saddle his horse and go for the doctor as fast as he could. Monroe woke Virgil and sent him out to saddle the horse in his underpants while he got dressed. He was gone before Tom knew it, and now there wasn't anything to do but wait for the doctor and hope he made it on time. Before, Tom had Sallie and Dora, but this time he was alone. He began to break out in a cold sweat. What would he do if the doctor didn't get there in time? Tom didn't mind telling you, he was scared to death.

Every time Ettie had a sharp pain, he would hold her hand and pray, "Lord, let the doctor get here in time." After it was over, he would rush to the window and look out to see if he could see them coming. He never saw anything so pretty as when he saw Monroe coming up the road. He rushed in and said the doctor is right behind him, and sure enough, it wasn't long until Tom saw his buggy.

He wasn't there to long until Tom heard him say, "Okay, you are doing good, just one more big push, and it will be over with." Tom was standing at the head of the bed holding her hand when he heard a little cry, and Dr. Baker said, "You have another little daughter." He handed her to Tom, and he took her into the kitchen. Tom had already told Virgil to build a fire in the stove and heat some water. He told Leola to put a quilt with a sheet over it on the table so they would be ready to bath the baby when it got there. That much Tom did know to do.

The kids were all waiting to know what it was; and when Tom told them they had a little sister, Leola hollered, "Yippee, yippee, now we are even." Tom didn't think it mattered too much with the boys anyway. They were just glad it was over with. They pretended to be disappointed more or less just to torment Leola. Leola and Tom bathed and dressed her while the boys stood and watched them. She had blond hair and blue eyes. She didn't look at all like any of the other kids. They all were dark eyed and dark haired and had darker complexion.

After they had bathed her, they took her in to Ettie. The doctor examined her, then told Ettie, "She is a perfect little girl." He wanted to know where the blond hair and blue eyes came from, because they all had dark eyes and hair. Ettie told him, "She favored my mother and Tom's sister."

Shortly after that the doctor and Tom sat down at the kitchen table and had a well-deserved cup of coffee. Tom told him how much he thanked him and that he didn't know what he would have done without him. He assured Tom, "If it had been necessary, you would have done all right. It looked like you had everything under control when I got here."

After they had their coffee, Tom paid him. After that the doctor went in and checked on Ettie and the baby again. He asked her, "Now what name do I write down on this birth certificate."

Ettie looked at Tom and said, "What do we want to name her?" They had thought about naming her Elizabeth after Sallie, but that was as far as they had gotten. The doctor said, "My wife's name was Ethel Elizabeth, and I think Ethel Elizabeth is a real pretty name."

All three kids said, "We think so too." So Ethel Elizabeth was what he wrote down on the certificate. He asked, "Is everyone satisfied with that name?" and everyone said, "Yes, we are." He said, "In that case, let's all get out of here and let both mama and Ethel Elizabeth get some rest." He told Ettie, "Let me know if you or Ethel need me."

Tom followed him out to his buggy, and he told him, "Take good care of Ettie and the baby, they both need plenty of rest. If you need me, be sure and let me know."

Tom told him, "I will and thank you again." Tom went back in the house to Ettie and the baby. The kids were all gathered around the bed, acting real tickled over their little sister. Tom told them, "I think it's time for you to get some breakfast and let your mama and sister rest."

They all went into the kitchen and got breakfast. They took some in to Ettie, but she and the baby were both fast asleep, so they decided to let her sleep until she woke up, then fix her some breakfast. The boys and Tom went outside to tend to the stock, and Leola cleaned the kitchen and listened for her mother to wake up.

By Monday Ettie was feeling all right, so the boys and Tom went to work. Leola stayed at the house to take care of Ettie and little Ethel. She told Tom, "Now, Daddy, don't worry about Mama and the baby. I will take real good care of them." Bless her heart, she had to grow up so fast after they had lost the ranch. At ten years old she was already cooking as well as any woman.

Tom hated to leave her to take care of them, but what choice did he have. Mr. Tompkins had hired them to pick his fruit, and that was his livelihood for winter. If they didn't get it picked when it was ready, it would ruin and he wouldn't have enough money to make it through the winter. Also, he couldn't pay them if they didn't get the fruit picked and ready for him to sell. They worked seven days a week to get it in. With just three of them picking, it took them longer. They worked from daylight to dark. Leola did the night work, so they could work longer. She tended to her mama and sister, did the outside chores, morning and night, and had supper ready when they came home.

After two weeks Ettie was up and able to stay by herself and take care of the little one. Leola was able to go back to the orchard and start helping them. It sure did help, and they were able to get the fruit picked and on time.

Chapter 32

ON ONE OF THE WEEKENDS that they were waiting for the next fruit trees to ripen, the boys went to town after they all had finished the washing. They weren't gone long until they came back real excited. They rushed in, and both began to talk at once. It seemed they had found a truck for sale cheap. In fact, if they would give the man the money he owed on it, they could have it.

Monroe told him, "Dad, it will go over twenty miles an hour. That way we can get to Sherman in a little over a day. Look at the time that it would save us, and it wouldn't be near as hard on Mama and the baby, also on us too, and we will have more time to get to Childress and could hoe cotton in place of spending all that time traveling."

Tom wasn't at all impressed and told them, "What would we do with a truck? None of us know how to drive it."

Virgil spoke up real quick and said, "The man said he would teach us how to drive it before we have to leave."

Tom still wasn't at all impressed and had no intentions of buying a truck, but they were so excited about it, he just couldn't disappoint them by refusing to go look at it. So into town they went to see a truck that he didn't even have the money to buy it with and had no intentions of buying it anyway.

Monroe said, "Dad, we could sell the cattle and buy the truck, and we could pay the money back with the cotton chopping, and we could do extra. It would be so much easier on all of us and we could be all the way to Childress in four days or five at the most and look at the time we could save."

Virgil said, "Dad, he took us for a ride and the motor sounds real good."

When they got to the man's house, sure enough, a truck was sitting out in front of the house with a big bold sign on it, reading "For Sale." The man introduced himself as Jim Rogers. He said, "Just call me Jim. The bank is going to foreclose on me the following Monday. I have lost my job and am behind with my payment." He told Tom what the boys had said and that he could let them have it real cheap if he could come up with the cash money by Monday. He took them for a ride, and the boys were right. The motor sounded real good as far as Tom knew. He had never ridden in a truck and didn't know how one was exactly supposed to sound. But it wasn't missing a beat and the man said it was purring like a kitten. Tom told him he would have to leave that up to him, that he didn't know anything about trucks.

Jim told him he wouldn't sell it at all if he could make the payment, that it got good gas mileage, didn't use much oil, and the tires were in good shape. He told Tom, "I am a Christian man and wouldn't lie about it to sell it. I'm selling it only because the bank is going to take it back Monday anyway. The only thing it will do is save my credit if I can pay it off."

When they got back from their ride, Tom was as impressed as the boys were. He told him, "I could pay for it in a week or so. I would need time to sell my horses and wagon, if the bank would extend the time until then."

Jim told him, "We could ask, but I don't think they will."

They left with Tom promising him that he would meet him at the bank Monday morning as soon as it opened.

All the way home the boys and Tom talked about the truck. Tom told them, "We have enough money saved to buy it with, but that would break us until the horses and wagon sold."

Monroe said, "Dad, "We have been broke before, and come first Monday, you will be able to go to trade day and sell the wagon and horses. I am pretty sure we can make it until then. You have always come through for us, and I know you will again."

Virgil agreed with him.

Well, that made Tom feel ten feet tall. He didn't think they would ever completely forgive him for losing the ranch, but he thought they were beginning to realize that they weren't the only ones that had lost their home and all that they had. They were a lot better off than most of them because Tom had been able to buy, hunt, and trade. It had been hard on all of them, and looking back, Tom could see he was awfully hard on them. But he had to make enough money to feed and clothe them all winter and he couldn't do it by himself as low as wages were. It took all of them working like dogs just to make it each year.

When they got back to the house, the boys told Ettie and Leola. They were both proud to hear about the truck, and Leola said, "I can't wait until Monday to see it." She wanted to know if she and the boys could go back in to see it before then.

Tom told her, "No, do you all remember me telling ya'll, when you are on a trade, not to appear to anxious. You don't want him to see how bad you want it or he will raise the price on you ever time. So you will just have to wait until Monday, and if the boys or me can drive it by that afternoon, we will take you all riding."

Ettie started laughing and said, "You beat all I ever saw, buying a truck and can't even drive one."

All three of the kids burst out laughing. The boys said, "That's our dad, all right. How many dads do you know that would buy a truck and not even be able to drive it?"

Leola joined in with them and said, "Not any, but how many dads would trade for a horse that wouldn't even let him in the same pasture with him or a team of horses that wouldn't even let him ride in the wagon?"

By then they were dying laughing. Virgil said, "Not many."

Leola came back with, "What do you mean not many?"

Monroe couldn't let them get the best of him, and he came back with, "What do you mean not many? Now answer me this, have any of you seen anyone that has pulled any of these stunts?" He turned to his mama. "Mama, have you ever seen anyone like that before?"

She too was getting a big kick out of them kidding Tom and joined along with the fun. She said, "Now let me think." She put her hand under her chin like she sure enough was thinking, then said, "Come to think about it, no. I don't think I have ever seen anyone quite like your dad before."

Then the boys went on and told them, "The man said he would teach us all three how to drive it and what we needed to know about the truck before we leave for Sherman."

The boys could hardly wait until Monday morning. Tom told them, "I will go and meet the man at the bank and you boys can go check with Mr. Tompkins, and if the fruit wasn't ready, ya'll could come in later and meet us at Jim's house."

When they got to the bank, Tom asked the banker if he would give him two weeks and told him his plans. He told Tom he wouldn't give him even one day, that he had to have the money today or the truck. Tom told him that was just fine. It did Tom's heart good to tell him, "I have the money to pay it off, but it would have made it easier on me if you could have worked with us." Tom gave him the money. "I would like a receipt, showing it has been paid." They finished up their business at the bank. They both thanked him.

When they got to Jim's house, all three of the children were already there waiting for them. Leola could hardly keep from jumping up and down. She was so proud of it. Jim told the boys, "Well, boys, it's yours now, let's teach you all how to drive it." The first thing he showed them was how to put the gas in and where to put the water, then he showed them all about adding oil and completely changing it and how often. He told them, "Now it's real important to make sure you have plenty of oil and water in it at all times. If it runs out, it will ruin your motor." After that they all piled into the truck, and he drove out to a well-deserted road. Then he got out and held out the keys and said, "Which one of you brave boys want to be first."

Monroe said, "Let Virgil be first because he is the oldest."

Virgil was so eager, it didn't take him a second to take the keys. Jim showed them how to put the key in the switch, then said, "Now let's get out and I will show ya'll how to start it. It's not much more than saying 'get up' to a horse." Then he started kidding them and asked Tom, "Ya'll do know how to do that, don't you"?

All three told him, "We sure do." He acted surprised and asked Leola, "Young lady, do you mean you know how to drive a wagon too."

She told him, "I sure do and better than either one of them too." That started an argument, but they were so excited about driving, it didn't last long.

He told them, "This is the crank, and you be careful with it and never lose or misplace it or you will be up salt creek without a paddle." He showed them how to put it in and how to turn it. Then he told Monroe, "Go around and choke it when I turned the crank to start it." He showed them all where the choke was and how to pull it out a little bit to give it extra gas so it would start. "Also be careful and don't turn loose of the crank before it starts, or it could turn back real quick, and before you could get your arm out of the way, it could break it."

They all took turns cranking it and choking it until he was satisfied that they all knew how to do both jobs. Then he told them, "Get in the car all, except Monroe." Virgil got under the steering wheel, then turned the key on. He was ready for Monroe to crank it and tell him when to choke it. After they got it started, Jim got in next to Virgil and turned off the key. Then he told them all they needed to know about shifting gears. "There is a first, second, third, and reverse gear. You need to always have it out of gear when you start it, or it will run away from you before you have time to get in the car." He showed them the clutch, the brake, and the gas pedal. "You put it in first to start off in, then you shift up to second. That's the pulling gear. And when you get it to running good, you shift down to third." As he told them this, he shifted the gears. Then he told Virgil, "I want you to pretend you are shifting it and it is running. Now, don't take your eyes off the road, or you will end up in a ditch. Always keep your eyes on the road. Just reach down and put it in first, and when you are going good, then bring it up to second, then back down to third." He went over and over this with each of them until they could do it without taking their eyes off the road. Then he said, "Now, let's see what ya'll can do with it running. Now I am not going to say a word until you both show me how to start it." They started it just fine, then Monroe got in and put the crank under the seat and Virgil put it in first gear and they started rolling. He shifted it up into second, and when they were rolling real good, he shifted it down to third.

He had driven about a mile when Jim told him, "Stop and let Monroe drive awhile. Virgil has done real good." Monroe got under the wheel and Virgil did the cranking. They didn't have any trouble with that part, but Monroe had trouble keeping his eyes on the road while he shifted gears. Jim kept telling him, "Now just feel, don't look down." He hadn't driven very long until he started shifting real good. Jim let him drive about a mile and told him, "Stop. Now it is Tom's turn, and don't let them tell you it's easier to drive a car than a wagon." Tom thought he had a harder time than either one of them. Jim finally told him, "Stop." He asked Leola, "Do you want to try?"

She said, "No, I will wait until they all learn first. I want to be sure they all know how real good, so they can get us to Sherman okay. I don't want to walk."

Jim laughed and told her, "You are a smart girl."

Next, Jim showed them how to put it in reverse and to back up. That was hard for all of them. They practiced every day on backing up. Then one night, Mr. Tompkins came up and told them, "The fruit was ready to start picking tomorrow." They still hadn't learned to back very good. Jim still hadn't let them take it home, he said, "I had rather make good and sure ya'll can all drive it and back it up good before ya'll take it home." When they got the orchard all gathered, they were right back again practicing, but this time they didn't have very long until another orchard was ready. They kept doing this until one day Jim told them, "I think it's time to take it home. Come back if you think ya'll need me for anything. I sure am going to miss ya'll."

Virgil caught on the fastest, and most of the time he drove and Monroe cranked it. Tom just let them take over driving and cranking it most of the time. They got such a big kick out of it. When they had time, they worked on the truck, making the sideboards taller and putting the canvas on it. Also, they made a dog pen to fasten on the back of the truck for the dogs to ride in. They had always run along the side of the wagon, but the boys said, "Dad, we don't think the dogs can keep up with the truck." Tom told them, "I don't think they could either."

A BOY CALLED KID

So they suggested making a doghouse. They had gotten real creative since they left the ranch and had to depend on themselves. Also, they had made a larger pen for Ettie's chickens. She had increased her flock quite a lot, and they were getting plenty of eggs. And she was selling quite a few. Also, with plenty of eggs for them and with the milk and butter, it sure did help on their grocery bill. Along with all that, she had hatched quite a few chickens this year, and they were having plenty of young roosters to fry for fried chicken. Times were hard, but they had a job and plenty to eat. Like Ettie kept telling them, "We had to work hard, but God had blessed us with a roof over our heads and plenty to eat every day. Grant you, it wasn't as good as we used to have, but it was a lot better than a lot of other people had these days. We haven't missed a meal yet. While some were going hungry and others were just about starving. We have a roof over our heads, a bed to sleep in, and plenty to eat."

The boys and Tom had decided they didn't have to be in a hurry to sell the animals. So they decided they could take some of them on each first Monday until they got rid of them. That way they would probably get a better price for them. The boys said, "We think it would be better to take the wagon and team first in case we need more time to sell them." Luck was with them, and the next first Monday fell on one of the times before the next orchard was ready to pick. So both boys and Tom were able to go. Since both boys could go, they took the wagon and team and also Delilah.

Monroe said, "I will take care of the team," and Virgil said, "I will handle Delilah." They said, "Now, Dad, just make sure you take care of our horses and saddles so we will have a ride home if we sell the wagon and horses." They told Ettie and Leola bye, and they wished them good luck. They turned to go and Leola couldn't pass up one last dig about Delilah. She ran out to where they were, and real serious like she said, "Now, boys, I know it will be hard knowing how crazy Dad is about Delilah, but don't let him talk ya'll into letting him keep her." Ettie and the boys got a big kick out of that. All three started laughing and kidding Tom about his favorite horse. Tom acted like he was mad and said, "That will be the day. She has chased me her last day. If I can't sell her for a nickel, then I will give her to the glue factory."

The boys said, "I know she is the most favorite horse he has ever had, but we promise we will make him sell her or ride her all the way to Sherman."

After that they waved again; and with both Ettie, Leola, and the boys hollering remarks about Delilah, they left.

They stopped to rest, and Tom told the boys, "Now, boys, I have been thinking. Ever since we left home, just what are we going to do with Delilah? She's not even a descent horse to sell to my worst enemy. Suppose she hurts someone real bad."

Monroe told him, "Now, Dad, what can we do with her? She is a beautiful horse and look how good she is with children. She doesn't seem to mind Virgil and me, and she lets us ride her and take care of her, and she will do the same with any other children if they grow up with her. But for some reason she just don't like you. We can't take her, and we dog gone sure can't leave her in the pasture or turn her loose. She sure would hurt someone, and they would come looking for us with ropes. I don't know about ya'll, but I sure ain't hankering to get hung."

Virgil agreed with him and asked him, "Dad, what could we do?"

Tom told them, "We could tell the truth and try to find someone that will take her off our hands. In all the time we have had her, we have never even taken her to a trade's day."

When they got there, they had just barely found a place and got settled in when this man came by and walked up to Delilah as pretty as you please. He started petting her and said,

"So there you are old girl, Molly. Where have you been all this time? I have looked everywhere for you." He saw how shocked they were and started laughing. He said, "I bet you have been having trouble with her."

Tom told him, "I have, but the boys could do anything they wanted to do with her. With them, she was as gentle as a little dog."

He introduced himself and told them, "I am a clown in a rodeo. Molly was the star performer in one of my acts. I had trained her that when I put my red wig on, she would chase me around the arena like she was going to tear me up. I would scream and holler and hide behind a post, then a little kid would come out and Molly would put her head on his shoulder and almost purr, then the kid would lead her out, leaving the crowd roaring with laugher. The owner of the rodeo died, and Molly was accidentally sold by mistake one day when I was gone, and I have been looking for her ever since. Mister, I don't have an act without her. I will be glad to pay you for her, plus her keep, and for all the trouble she has caused you." Then he laughed. "With all that red hair, I bet it was plenty." They ended up with him paying him what she cost him, plus he insisted on paying for her board all this time they had her. He said, "I have gone to every trade day everywhere and couldn't find anyone that knew anything about her. I kept hoping that maybe, somewhere, some way, she would run into a redheaded man that would have trouble with her and could tell me where she was. I had just about given up hope, I was afraid someone had killed her."

After they settled up and he thanked Tom over and over for not mistreating her because as he said, "She was only doing what she was taught to do." He left leading Molly just as gentle and loving as a little dog you ever saw. The boys just roared with laughter as soon as he got out of sight.

Virgil said, "So it was your red hair after all, just wait until we tell sis and mama."

Now their next great problem was getting rid of the team and wagon. They stayed there all day. Several men came by and looked at the horses. Some of them wanted to know if they were for sale or trade. It was hard for Tom to turn down a trade, but they had to have a way to get the wagon home. So late that afternoon they left, taking the team and wagon with them.

When they got home, it was late. Leola had all the night work done, and she and her mother had supper ready.

Ettie told them, "We have been so worried about ya'll. What took you so long?"

Before Tom could tell her anything, the boys butted in with their story about Delilah. They told them, "Mama, Dad started making excuses as soon as we got there, about not getting rid of Delilah. We thought we were never going to get Daddy to sell her. You know he almost cried when we made him let her go." After they all had finally got through kidding him, they told them the truth. That really tickled them.

Ettie said, "That beats all I have ever heard of."

Leola said, "See, Daddy, I told you all along, that it was your red hair." Then real serious she said, "I am so glad she has a good home."

The boys went out and put the horses and wagon away while Leola and Ettie finished putting supper on the table. Needless to say Delilah was the sole conversation all during supper and for days to come.

They sold all the other horses and all the cows, except two of their real good cows. Those they had planned on keeping until closer to time for them to go. They still had the team and wagon. Tom had started getting a little worried about it not selling.

One night, Ettie told them when they came in, "A man came by today to look at the horses and wagon. He acted like he liked them and said he would be back later tonight." Sure enough, they had just barely got through with supper when they heard someone holler. Tom went to the door, and it was him. He told Tom, "Your wife had showed me the horses and wagon. I liked what I saw. I want to know how much cash on the barrel head you will take for them." They went out to the pasture, and Tom told him, if he sold them, what he would have to have for them. Tom saw he wasn't much of a trader. He didn't even ask him to come down any. He just told Tom he would take them. He went on to tell Tom, he had lost his job and he couldn't find anything to do anywhere. Jim had told him about Tom and his family, how they came out here and picked berries and fruit in the spring and summer, then went to West Texas in the fall. So they thought they would try it also. He went on to say they had to do something to make a living and there was nothing around here except fruit and berries to gather.

Tom told him, "Mister, "I don't think I could sell the wagon and team to you."

The man said, "What did you say?"

Tom repeated what he had said, and the man wanted to know why, that he had the cash money to pay him for them and he understood the wagon and horses were for sale. He told Tom he was not asking for charity. He went on to say, "Mister, we have to get started right away if we are going to get there in time to find work, and we can't walk."

Tom told him, "Look here, mister, I did want to sell them in the worst way. In fact, I have to sell them before we leave. But if I sell them to you, that's exactly what you would do, is walk and I mean all the way to West Texas." Then he told him about the horses. "They are fine horses and are strong and young and gentle. They would pull all day for my kids and wife, but for a man they wouldn't do anything. Those ornery horses wouldn't even go unless they could see me walking along beside the side of the wagon. They won't even let me ride in the wagon."

The man laughed and said, "I don't believe they are that bad. I have trained horses all my life, and I have never found any that with a whole lot of love, patience, and training that I couldn't get them to do whatever I wanted them to do. Mister, I need the wagon and horses bad. If I don't get them, then we can't go, and if we don't go, we will be going hungry this winter. I am willing to gamble on them if you will."

Tom told him, "Mister, the wagon is in good shape and is ready to go, but I just can't sell those horses to you with a free conscience, seeing I know what they were and what they will do."

He told Tom, "Now you let me be the judge of that and forget about your conscience. Another thing I will have to ask you if I could leave them here until we get ready to go. Then I would need to take the wagon home so we could pack it and I will come back each day and work with the horses until we are ready to go."

Tom got the kids to harness them to the wagon and go with him to bring them back, and he left being the proud owner of the horses and wagon. He kept his word. Ettie said, "He was out each day working with them." In two weeks he told Tom, "I am ready to go," and the horses were too. "I want to leave the next day. I will be taking the horses, so they will be there in the morning. I am at Jim's house if you want to check later to clear your conscience, but they are doing fine."

Tom told him, "I will and good luck. Maybe we will see ya'll out there, and may God bless you and keep you safe."

Chapter 33

EVERY SUNDAY, THE BOYS HAD off, which was far and few between. They would take the truck and go riding. Sometimes Ettie and Tom would go with them, but most of the time just the kids went. Tom told Ettie, "They need to drive as much as they can to get used to driving before we leave." They had one more field to gather, and then they would be through.

On one of those outings, the kids came back early. Monroe told Tom, "We have something to show you." Monroe was the one that always figured out most of their problems, to make things easier on them. He said, "I have found a horse trailer."

Tom asked him, "What do we need with a horse trailer? We have sold all the horses."

Monroe told him, "But, Dad, we still have two cows. And if we have the trailer, we could take them with us. With just three or four days, or less, from here to Childress, we could take them and wouldn't have to worry about milk and butter. The cows are real good milk cows, and it would be hard to replace them when we get out there. It was more or less just a frame with a bottom on it, but the lumber on the bottom was good and we could build sideboards for it. The man needs the money and will sell it cheap. It is real small, but it's long enough to haul the two cows in, and that's all we need."

Sure enough, he was right. It was small, but as he said it was barely big enough and that's all they needed. The man quoted a price, and Tom told him, "We couldn't pay that. We are only getting a frame, and we will have to be out a lot of money to finish building it."

The man told Tom, "Mister, that's all I was selling, is the frame."

But Tom held his ground, and he finally came down to what Tom thought was a fair price for both of them, and he bought it. They took it home first, then went after some lumber. The man had told them where a lumberyard was in the next town as he said, "Just up the road."

With all three of them working on it, they had something that resembled sideboards together in the next few days. As Monroe said, "It's not perfect, but it would keep the cows from falling out and that's all we needed." Then they got some ducking and made ducking tops for the trailer and also the truck bed. They were tall enough so the air could blow under it to keep the cows cool and anyone riding in the truck bed.

By the time they got the last field gathered, they were ready to go. They were up before daylight, had everything loaded in the truck, and made sure the chicken pen and dog pen were wired good onto the frame that they had built to hold them. Then they loaded them all. They put the cows into the trailer, and they were ready to go. Boy, it sure was a lot easier than it usually was. Virgil started out driving. Monroe did the cranking, and Leola rode in front with them.

Ettie and Tom had made them a place to sit and lean back against the back of the truck bed. Ettie had fixed a bed close to them where she could lay Ethel. It was good and cool in the back, and it wasn't long until they all three were laying back, fast asleep. Always before, they had driven around the towns, but this time they went through them. There weren't a lot of gas stations like there is today, so they didn't take a chance of running out of gas. They stopped and filled up when they were a half tank low and each time checked the oil. By noon they had come a good ways. They stopped and bought some baloney, cheese, onion, and bread. They stopped right outside of town where they always camped and spent the night when they were in the wagon. They let the cows out of the trailer so they could water them and let them graze for a while. They also let the dogs out and unwired the chicken coop and turned it upside down on the grass so they could water them and they could find grass seed to eat. Then they sat down and ate their dinner. Ettie had made a big chocolate cake the day before. With that and what they bought, they thought they had a meal good enough for anyone. The boys talked about how much easier it had been than being in the wagon and said, "Just think, Dad, we are almost halfway there. With good luck we will be in Sherman by eight or nine o'clock at the very most."

Leola said, "And we are all not just worn out."

They rested for an hour or better, mostly for the cow's sake. Then loaded the cows, chickens, and dogs and were on their way again. They got to the place in Sherman where they usually parked by nine that night and had stopped several times to let the cows and dogs out to rest and water them. Each time they would water the chickens and check them too. All the animals seem to be standing the trip just fine. The boys said, "Better than behind the wagon walking." They decided to get the camp set up, fix their supper, and eat. After that they would take a bath and go to bed early. They would rest tomorrow, then go in to see about Sallie that night when she got off from work. They had no reason to stay more than a day, so they could be on their way the next day. That way, maybe they could get out to Childress in time to help chop the cotton also. Like the boys said, "The quicker they got out there, the more money they could make for the winter."

The next night, they ate supper and were ready and there before Sallie got home from work. Just as Tom had expected Jeff was gone again. Sallie said, "He was off looking for work." Again, he tried to get her to go with them, but she said, "Tom, I just can't leave him. He will be back in due time. He always is, and I have to be here when he comes." She was real surprised to see the little one and was real pleased that Ettie had named her Elizabeth after her. She commented, "Guess your kids will be all the children I ever have." They stayed for a while, and Tom gave her some money that they all had agreed to set aside for her. They left telling her, "We want to get an early start in the morning. We will be in the same place as before if you need us for anything."

The next morning, they were ready to pull out by four o'clock. They all decided to get up and drive for a while, then stop and eat breakfast when it got hot. That way they could let the cows, dogs, and chickens out at the same time and save time stopping for them. They drove until about ten o'clock, or at least Monroe and Virgil did. Leola and the rest of them lay in the back and went sound to sleep. They stopped at one of the camping places that they had been camping at along the way each year. Leola and Ettie fixed breakfast while the boys and Tom let the cows out and hobbled them so they could get water and also graze. They turned the dogs out and watered the chickens. By then breakfast was ready. They ate, and the boys rested awhile, but they said, "With both of us taking turns driving and with our pesk in the front seat pestering us, we aren't tired and had rather drive on, so we can get there."

Leola answered them back, "Oh, yes, if it wasn't for me, you all would have been lost before you ever got started."

With that remark, all the animals were loaded in the truck. Tom, Ettie, and little Ethel crawled in the back with Leola in the front seat with the boys and drove off. They didn't stop a lot, only to let the animals rest for a while and water them. They did decide they would stop at night and let the animals rest and eat, also that would get them there early the next day and not at night.

When they got there, they just went on out to Mr. Jones's place and asked him, "Can we help hoe cotton as well as pick it?"

He acted like he was real proud to have them. He asked, "Have you ever hoed cotton?"

Of course, they told him no.

"It don't matter, I sure am glad to have you and I will show you how on Monday, that will give ya'll time to get settled in and rest for a while." They went on down to their same house that they had been staying in for years. As always, the first thing they did was find some wood and build a fire under the washpot. Tom and the boys filled it up with water. While the water heated, Leola and Ettie swept the house and the boys let the dogs out and put the chickens in the henhouse. And Tom took the livestock and turned them loose in the pasture.

By then the water was hot, and with all of them working, they had the house and furniture scrubbed with hot water, cleaned, and dried before dark. Ettie and Leola got supper, and Tom milked the cow. By the time supper was ready, they were too tired to do anything else, so they just put the mattress on the floor and said, "We will do the rest tomorrow." It would be Saturday, but they could finish unloading everything in no time flat and have the rest of Saturday and all day Sunday to rest before they had to start working.

On Monday they were up and ready to go by daylight. Tom and the kids walked up to Sam's house and were waiting for him when he came out. He told them, "I sure am glad to get ya'll. I haven't found enough people to hoe all my cotton and was beginning to get worried. I pay a dollar a day and that is from sunup to dust." He laughed. "As the workers say, they work from can to can't." He showed them how to hoe. Then he told them, "You only have to hoe the rows. I will come back later and plow the middles. One of you will be the leader, and I expect the rest to keep up with him. I don't expect you to kill yourself, but I don't want you to drag your feet either. I will make a few rounds with you, that way you can see how fast I expect you to go. Some places will be grassier than others, but all in all I expect you to keep up."

They had all hoed in the garden on the ranch, so they didn't have too much trouble keeping up with him. After several rounds, he asked, "Are you all sure you all have never hoed cotton before? You all are doing great." Tom told him about hoeing in the garden. He told Tom, "I know I won't have any trouble out of ya'll, but some will spend more time at the water wagon and sharpening their hoes than working if I didn't tell them that I expect each man to make so many rounds a day." So if any one asks, tell them he told them how many. Tom said later, for the life of him, right then he couldn't remember how many, but at that time, it sure sounded like a lot. Mr. Jones said, "Now I will be by every so often to leave ya'll sharp hoes. When you get to the water wagon for a drink and there are some hoes there under the wagon, get one and leave your old one propped up against the wagon with the hoe on the ground. That way I will know you have got them each time. I will sharpen the old ones and put them back under the wagon. I will move the wagon periodically so ya'll won't have too far to walk, to change hoes, and get a drink. Also, be sure and drink plenty of water. I always try to keep plenty of cold well water out for my workers at all times."

He went from field to field, moving the water wagon and sharpening hoes. His wife would go from field to field keeping fresh cold water in the jugs, and as picking cotton, they take an hour off for lunch. He told Tom, "You will be the leader. Just chop like you have been with me, and you all won't have any trouble making your rounds each day."

Tom told him, "If we do, we will make up for them on Saturday and Sunday. We cheat no man."

He told Tom, "I know you don't, and I am glad to have you working for me."

Chopping cotton was a lot easier than picking it and wasn't as crucial as picking berries. Mr. Jones had told them early that they didn't work on weekends, so they would have Saturdays and Sundays off. That is, he went on to say, at least most weekends. At noon they stopped for dinner. They were tired, but they had all been used to hard work, so they weren't as tired as they were the first year that they came here. Ettie had fixed them a good dinner, bless her heart. She had made a cake Sunday, and she had put some of it in their bucket, also baked chicken from yesterday, bread, pork and beans, and onion. Also Sam's wife had just left some cold water. They all ate and then laid down to rest.

Tom told the kids, "Four dollars is not much for a whole day's work."

But Monroe said, "Well, Dad, look at it this way. It beats nothing, and that's what we made on our long trip out here when we had to come by wagon."

Virgil said, "Dad, that's twenty dollars a week for all of us and a house to live in."

Tom knew they were trying to make him feel good because Leola said, "Dad, that's almost a hundred dollars a month, and that will buy a lot of groceries this winter."

There was no my money and your money. It was all put up to save for winter, and they used it for what they needed it for all winter, whether it was for shoes, clothes, or food.

Chapter 34

THEY WEREN'T THERE LONG WHEN out of the clear blue, Tom began to have spells breathing. No one knows what it's like until they can't get their breath. Ettie made him go to the doctor, and he told Tom he had asthma and that something in this vicinity was causing it and he was going to have to find a place to live where he wouldn't have it.

Tom told Ettie, "I can't afford to try to find a different place. We have a place to work and a place to stay and I am not going to give it up and start out looking for another place, as hard as it is to find jobs." Tom was sick most of the time and had to be off a lot because of his breathing, but they finished hoeing the cotton and had time to rest some before they had to start picking it.

Outside of that, life went on about the same as each year passed. The Moon family came back later on to pick cotton, and all the young folks would go back each Saturday and pick extra cotton for spending money. Monroe would still save his, and Virgil still spent his showing the girls a good time especially Leola's friend that they called Lacey.

Leola told her mother, "I think they are getting serious about each other."

Ettie told Tom that night what Leola told her. "Tom, he is too young for such nonsense and besides, as bad as things are now days, how would he support her?"

Tom told her, "Ettie, you are borrowing trouble. Surely he has more sense than that."

Tom really thought he had, but as the fall passed and it was time for them to go back to Sherman, he was head over heels in love with her. That was just about all he could talk about.

Ettie told Tom, "Now, Tom, you are going to have to have a serious talk with that young man before it's too late."

Tom tried, but he thought it was already too late. He told Ettie, "I don't think Virgil heard a thing I said."

He told Tom, "Dad, the depression can't last forever, then I can get a job."

They finally left for Sherman, but he was one unhappy boy. When they got to Sherman, they went directly to see Mr. Hill and were able to get their old house back. Tom's asthma seemed to be better all winter, but by the time they reached Lindale, he was one sick little puppy. Again, Ettie made him go to the doctor, and he told them the same thing as the other doctor had said. Tom told the doctor, "I don't have that choice. We have to work so we will have money to make it through the winter. It's either stay and work or go hungry this winter. That's the only choice we have."

He told Tom, "If you don't find a place you can breathe, you won't have to worry about this winter because you won't be around to see it."

For the next year, they went from place to place trying to find a place to work and a place where he could breathe. They ended up at a little place called Leon Junction.

They went to work on another place picking fruit, but the kids and Ettie were doing most of the work. Tom would have days when he could hardly get his breath, let alone work. Again, God blessed them as an Indian family was working in the same field where they were. One day when Tom was down again, one of the old men asked Ettie, "What's wrong with the mister? Is he down again?"

Ettie told him, "Yes, he is down most of the time because he can't breathe." She told him what both of the doctors had said.

He told Ettie, "I can cure him if he will let me."

Ettie told him, "Mister, we would be tickled to death if you would."

After work that night he came to the house and talked to Tom. Tom told him the same thing that Ettie had. Also he told him, "Mister, I can't go on like this. I am getting worse all the time."

The old Indian told Tom, "You don't have to, if you will take my medicine. Now it is bad tasting, but if you will take it, it will drive the poison from out of your body and you will be all right."

Tom told him, "I will take anything that will make me well." Tom didn't tell him, but he had got to the point where he didn't think he was going to make it. He thought, *What have I got to lose? It will either kill or cure.* The old man took the boys out in the pasture and showed them what wild roots he wanted them to dig and told Ettie to wash them and then scrape them real good. After that put them in some water and boil them until he got back. He left, and it wasn't over an hour until he was back with a sack of stuff along with some honey and whiskey. He strained the concoction that Ettie had been boiling and mixed it with the honey and whiskey. Tom didn't know what all he put in it, but he showed Ettie. Then told her when he wanted water to make him take a sip of that. He was right, it was as bitter as quinine. Then he told her to make him take a hot bath every day, as hot as he could stand it, and put some ice cream salt in the water each time. Then he gave her a big bag of ice cream salt.

He told Tom, "Now it won't cure you in the bottle. If you want to get well, then you take it and also the hot bath to drive the poison out."

Tom told him, "I want to get well, and I will do just like you have told me to do."

Ettie paid him for what he had spent, and he left with very little else to say. Tom did exactly what he told him to. At least now he had hope of getting better. A lot of people would have laughed at him for trusting in an Indian remedy, but he was willing to try anything. And in a month, Tom was a lot better. His asthma was better, and he was breathing a lot better. By the end of the season, he told Ettie and the kids that he thought he could go down and help them finish up. They all told him to take care of himself and maybe he would be able to go back to Childress when time came. Sure enough, Tom was feeling a lot better by then and was able to travel just fine. A few days before they left, the boys went down in the pasture and dug the roots Ettie needed to make him a good supply of his medicine. She got the Indian man to get the whiskey, honey, and everything else she needed to make it. He seemed real pleased that Tom was doing so good.

Tom asked him, "How long should I take the medicine?"

He told Tom, "You will know when you should stop it."

They went by and checked on Sallie as usual. Again, she used the excuse Jeff was gone looking for work. They didn't stay long. She looked like she was dead tired. She had lost a lot of weight and looked like warmed over death. Ettie and the boys gave her some more money. She thanked them and told them she sure could use it to pay her rent, that she had been sick and hadn't been able to work for a while. Again, Tom asked her to come with them, but again she said she had to be there when Jeff came back.

Tom told her, "You know where you can get in touch with us if you need us." He always checked in with the police as soon as they got to where they would be staying and let them know where they would be if they got any messages. So, if she needed them, she could just call the police station and they would come and let Tom know. They spent the night where they always camped. They still had the cows, the chickens, and the dogs; and this gave them a chance to rest before they started out tomorrow. They got up at four o'clock again and were on the road a long time before it began to get daylight. When it got breakfast time, they stopped and had breakfast.

Again, they got to Childress in the middle of the afternoon. They checked in with Jim and went on down to get settled before dark. It was already cotton-chopping time, so he said, "Ya'll can start on Monday. How are you doing, Tom?"

Tom told him, "Much better and I hope I can hold up to a full day of chopping."

Jim told Tom, "Do what you can, but don't overdo it. Just keep up with the hours you work and we will figure them together to make the days."

Tom was able to work a half day, each day for most of the chopping time. Just before they got through, he had gained enough strength to hoe all day. The Indian had told him he would know when it was time for him to stop the medicine, but Tom still wasn't ready to stop it for fear the asthma would come back.

That fall went just as they always went, except the kids started having parties on Saturday night. Some of the men and boys sang and played instruments. So they would meet in different homes each week. The women would take turns baking cakes for refreshments. That way it gave the young people something to do and also the parents. After a hard week of working, they all looked forward to go to the get together on

Saturday night each week. They would all sing and also square dance and just having a good time in general. It was good for all of them, and they got acquainted with some of the parents. That was where Tom met Benjamin Brown again. At first he didn't recognize him, but Benjamin reminded Tom, because of the skinny cow and horse he traded for. He had to tell everyone about Tom trading a good fat milk cow for two bags of bones.

He said, "I had often wondered if you got home with them still alive."

Monroe was standing there listening, and he had to finish the story. "Not only did he get home with the poorest and awful-looking cow and horse he had ever seen but with a big bill of groceries and a sack of sweet feed to feed them with. By the next trade day, they were as fat as mud and in good shape. He took them back and traded them for some more skinny ones, almost as bad as the first ones and enough money to buy another big bill of groceries to do them another month. He did that the whole time we were there, and by the time we left from there, he had several cows and horses to boot all from that skinny cow and horse and we have never missed a meal."

They all laughed, but it made Tom so proud of his son. At last Tom began to see that they were growing up to be good men that faced the burdens of life as it was dished out to them.

By late in the fall, Tom was able to pick cotton most of the days. He was beginning to get his strength back, but it was slow. By the end of the season he was working all day, every day. He told Ettie, "It is time for me to stop my medicine, but I think I will wait until we get to Sherman and not take any chances."

When the season was over, they went back to Sherman. Their house wasn't empty, but Mr. Hill had one they could have until and if their old one came available. The new one was larger, but it also cost more to rent it. They stayed there a month and the second month when Mr. Hill told them the people were moving and they could have their house if they wanted it. So again they moved into it. It was closer to the pasture Tom rented each year and wasn't as far to go after the milk cow each night and made it easier on them. Mr. Hill got to where if it was about time for them to come in, he would just hold it for them. He knew each year when they would be there and how long they would stay. It got old, going from fruit picking to cotton picking each year, but there was still no jobs to be had and at least it made them a living. After the first year of going to Leon Junction they went back there each year. It paid more, and they got more time in to work. Also, the kids liked to go there better because they could go to town when they had time off. It wasn't real close, but with the truck it didn't matter that much.

Chapter 35

ON ONE OF THE KID'S trips to town, Ettie and Tom were home alone, except for Ethel. Ettie told Tom, "Come sit down, I have something to tell you." The only place they had to sit was at the kitchen table or the front porch on a bench. When they were traveling from place to place, they didn't have the luxury of having living rooms with chairs and couches in it. So they sat down at the table. She poured Tom a cup of coffee, and they had just barely sat down when she blurted out, "Tom, I think I am pregnant again." Tom sure was glad she gave him time to sit down or he probably would have fallen flat on his face.

Tom asked her, "Ettie, are you sure? I don't see how you could be."

She answered him with, "If I'm not, then something is wrong. Smelling food makes me sick, and each morning I am getting up sick at my stomach." With tears running down her face she said, "Tom, what will we do? We just can't afford another baby."

Tom went over and put his arms around her and told her, "Honey, don't worry about it. If God sees fit to give us another baby, then He will make a way for us to support it. Just be proud that God is giving us another blessing. When we were on the ranch, we used to talk about having a large family, and each month you fretted because we weren't going to have one. Now we are having a large family, and you are fretting." Then

Tom started teasing her. He told her, "I bet the Lord is thinking, He can't please that woman regardless to what He does. First, she wants one, now she don't. Wish she would make up her mind."

She laughed and said, "Tom, I want it, but how can we afford it. We are barely able to take care of what we had already. You and the kids work so hard just keeping a roof over our heads and food to eat." Then she started crying. "What are we going to tell the children?"

Tom told her, "The only way I know is the truth, that God was going to bless us with another precious addition to our family."

They decided to wait awhile before they told them, as Tom told Ettie until they knew for sure anyway. She told Tom they would do as he says, but as for her, she was almost positive that she was.

The weeks passed, and each week, she was still sick, so sick until she had to spend most of the days in bed. Tom left Leola with her each day to take care of Ethel. Then one night when she felt strong enough to come to the supper table, Leola out of the clear asked, "Mama, are you pregnant?"

Ettie looked at Tom for the words to say, and she told him later she remembered him saying, just tell the truth. She told them, "Yes, I am. Tom and I are going to the doctor Saturday. Your dad wants me to see a doctor and make sure before we told you, but for me, I am already sure that I am." It just about broke Ettie's heart. Monroe didn't say a word; he just got up and walked out. Virgil sat there for a while and, then like Monroe, got up and walked out. Ettie started crying. Leola went over and put her arms around her mother and said, "It's all right, Mama. We both will love it, whether anyone else does or not."

Tom went over and put his arms around both of them and told them, "That makes three of us."

She still continued to cry. At that moment Tom wanted to go out and beat them two boys half to death for hurting their mother so much. He told her so, but she said, "They are entitled to their own opinions. And, Tom, they work so hard helping us, just barely make a living. Don't be mad at them."

On Saturday, they went to the doctor, and he confirmed Ettie's opinions. She was sure enough pregnant, and that the baby would be here the last of February or early March. He also told them, "Ettie is a really bad anemic." He asked her if she had ever been on any kind of iron medicine.

Tom told him, "Yes, she was, before our last daughter was born."

He wanted to know why she stopped it. "Did a doctor tell her to?"

She told him, "No, I didn't think I needed it after the baby came."

He told her, "You should have continued it until your blood was all right again."

When they got up to leave, he told his nurse to take Ettie to the front and get her some iron medicine. Then he told Tom, "Mr. Brisco, she is in a bad shape, and it is going to be hard to save her. I want to see her every week until the baby comes, and I don't want her to miss one week. We have got to get her blood built up before time for the baby to come or we will be in serious trouble. Also, she is to get plenty of rest with three meals a day and plenty of vegetables."

Tom left his office for the first time feeling a resentment for this little one she was carrying. Tom was so afraid it was going to take Ettie from him. He prayed all the way home. "God, remove this resentment that I have in my heart."

When they got home, Tom put Ettie to bed and told her, "You need to sleep and get some rest. The kids and I will get supper and take care of Ethel." He sat by her bed until she was asleep. She looked so frail and tired. Tom cursed himself for not realizing how tired she looked a long time ago. The doctor also told him, "Traveling back to Sherman was out of the question unless you want to take a chance of killing both her and the baby." He sat there by her bed and silently prayed, "God don't take her from me. Please God, don't do this to me. What would the kids and I do without her. God she is our strength and our backbone. She is the one that has held us together through all the losing of our ranch and all the bad times we have had." He sat there without breaking down as long as he could. He didn't want the kids to hear or see him crying. So he tiptoed out of her room and told the kids to call him if she woke up, that he had to go down and check on the cows and he would milk them while he was there. Both boys offered to go, but he told them, "No, I will do it." They must have known something was wrong because they didn't insist. There was a creek at the back of the pasture, and Tom walked all the way there before he broke down. Then he knelt there on the ground crying and praying until he was completely exhausted. It was over an hour before he got up, washed his face, and went to the house to see about Ettie. As soon as he walked in, the kids saw something was wrong because he had forgotten to milk the cows. They did ask where the milk was, and he told them he had gotten busy and had completely forgotten to milk them.

The boys said, "Don't worry about it, Dad. We will do it later, and besides, it's a little early to milk them anyway."

Leola said, "Dad, Mama is still resting. She woke up once. We gave her a cold glass of water, and she went right back to sleep."

Tom went in and sat by her bed, feeling a calm that had come over him that he didn't have before. He sat there until suppertime, thinking she will be all right. He knew she would.

Tom heard the kids stirring around and realized it was suppertime. Leola and Tom finished fixing supper while the boys went down to milk and check everything. After they got supper on, Leola took Ethel with her to go feed the chickens and gather up the eggs while Tom watched supper. Ethel had taken a nap earlier but had woke up crying for her mama. The boys and Leola had taken turns walking her outside to keep her from waking their mama, but she was still real unhappy, because they wouldn't let her go to her mama. They had made a pot of vegetable soup and a pan of corn bread. While they ate, Tom fed Ethel and ate also. He woke Ettie and coaxed her into eating some by telling her, "You know what the doctor said about you eating for yourself and also the little one." She finally ate about a half bowl of the soup and very little of the corn bread. While he fed her, the kids watched Ethel and cleaned up the kitchen. She was back to sleep almost before he got out of the room.

Leola asked him, "Is Mama going to be all right?"

Tom told them, "I hope so. The doctor said she would need plenty of rest and some good fresh vegetables and meat, that she was anemic again like she was before."

They wanted to know what kind of meat and fresh vegetables.

Tom told them, "Anything that would build blood."

After that, they played forty-two and sat around the table talking until bedtime. Tom bathed Ethel and put her to bed. It wasn't long until she was fast asleep. Tom told the kids, "Good night and be sure and pray for your mama."

Monroe had never said a word about the baby or anything about the way he acted, but the next day he asked, "If Virgil and I can use the truck, I need to go somewhere."

Tom told him, "That would be fine," and he didn't ask any questions. Tom thought if he wanted me to know, he would have told me.

They left right after breakfast. Leola wouldn't go. She said, "I need to stay and help Daddy with Mama and Ethel."

They were gone all morning. About one o'clock, here they came, bringing in all kinds of fresh vegetables, a roast, and some liver, also several bottles of grape juice.

Tom asked them, "Boys, where in the world did you get all this stuff?"

They told Tom, "You said Mama needed plenty of fresh vegetables. We didn't know what kind, so we went and talked to the doctor. He told us what to get, so we got it. He said she needed liver at least once a week and plenty of red meat. Also, he said, a little wine with her meals wouldn't hurt. So we knew she wouldn't drink wine, so we bought grape juice."

Leola and Tom fixed the liver that night for supper and smothered it in onions. They made a big bowl of gravy, fixed fresh green beans, and creamed some potatoes. Ettie felt stronger and came to the table to eat her supper. Tom told her, "Look here, what your boys have done" and told her what all they had bought for her. She, like Tom, wanted to know how they knew what to buy and they told her about going to the doctor.

Then they told her, "You know he wouldn't charge us for the visit. When we asked him what we owed for the visit, he said not a dime, just take that money and buy more fruit and vegetables for your mama. He said she needed liver at least once a week, so from now on we will have to have liver on Saturday or Sunday ever week." Then they told her about the grape juice and told her what they had told Tom. She got a big kick out of it. From then on, they saw she had a bottle of grape juice in the well cooling for her meal. Tom didn't think she liked it very much, but for her boys she drank a glass with dinner and supper every day, just like they told her to. She did start getting better. After they knew what to get her, they went around to gardens and bought vegetables. Monroe, like his dad, being a trader, asked some of the ladies if they could use some milk and butter. From then on, he traded milk and butter for vegetables. After supper each night, regardless to how tired they were, he and Virgil would deliver the milk and butter to his customers. Some asked about buttermilk, so he started taking it with him too. He came home every night with a big sack of vegetables for dinner the next day. Anything from cantaloupes, watermelons, okra, black-eyed peas, green beans, corn, or anything else they had gathered for that day. Ettie loved cantaloupe, so usually they brought some in every day. As she told them, "Because of you boys, we are eating like kings every day." They also saw she had liver each week.

At the end of the month, the doctor told them, "I am surprised that she is so much better. And I see the boys kept their word." Then he told them about their nice visit and what a kick he got out of it. He said, "You both must be awful proud of them. One don't see boys like that very often."

Ettie had to tell him about them going around to gardens where they lived and asking them if they would trade vegetables for milk and butter. She told him they were getting more fresh vegetables and fruit than they could eat. She told him, "Our daughter and I were canning all the leftover fruit."

He told her, "That is just fine, but don't overdo it. They are remarkable boys. I wish my boys had been more like that." He gave her some more medicine. "Now don't miss a dose. And, Tom, you see to it that she doesn't, regardless to how much better she gets. If anything at all goes wrong, send for me immediately, whether you think it's bad enough or not. With her anything can be bad."

When they left his office, she started crying. She told Tom, "I don't think he thinks I would carry this little tike long enough for it to live. Bless its little heart, no one really wants it except Leola and me. And bless its heart, it's trying so hard to live."

Tom tried to tell her, "Yes, the boys and me all want it. In the beginning they were all so shocked that they didn't know what to say. Look how the boys are getting fresh food for you? Don't that prove they want it?"

She said, "No, I appreciate it, but they are doing it to save my life and not the little one."

Tom tried to tell her, "The little one is part of you now, and we are all trying to save you and the little one too."

That night when the boys and Tom went out to milk the cows he told them what their mama said.

They both said, "It's not that, Dad. But it's just another mouth to feed. We can't hardly afford to feed the ones we have, let alone another one."

That made him fighting mad. He asked them, "Well, boys, which one of us would you all like to get rid of to make it easier on us. I will get the gun and ya'll can tell me, which one of them, you and Virgil would like me to shoot and get rid of? That way it will be a lot easier for the rest. Without so many mouths to feed, ya'll wouldn't have to work so hard."

Monroe said, "Now, Dad, don't be ridiculous, you know you don't want to get rid of any of them. They are all family."

Tom asked them, "You mean this little one that is trying so hard to be born is not going to be part of our family? God is giving us another child, and Ettie is just as proud of it as she was over any of you. She is fighting just as hard to bring it into the world as she did you and Virgil, Leola, or Ethel. She almost died bringing Virgil into the world, but when she found out she was expecting Monroe, do you think she said, 'I almost died having Virgil, so I don't want this one, let's just kill it.' You bet your boots she didn't. I remember her saying with a great big smile on her face, 'Tom, God is going to bless us with another baby.' That's how she feels about this little one. Whether it lives or dies will be God's decision, but whether your mama lives or dies will depend a lot on you all and how ya'll accept this situation as a family and not make her feel like she has to be ashamed for putting another burden on us to have to take care of, and as you all said another mouth to feed."

After that talk, they acted much happier over the little one, or at least for their mama's sake, pretended to be. Then started asking their mama questions about what she was going to name it and when it would be here. She had got where she was doing a lot better. She and Leola would fix supper for them each night and have it on the table as soon as they got home. The kids and Tom were beginning to breathe a little easier thinking everything was going to be all right. They would eat, and then Monroe would deliver his milk and butter and then pick up his vegetables for the next day. They laughed and kidded him that they never knew what they would have the next day until he came back that night. But it didn't matter it was all good. He had accumulated some extra money that the milk, buttermilk, and butter had brought over the price of the vegetables. He just told them to keep it for later. He had also started delivering some eggs to them each week. The eggs they didn't take he would take them to town on Saturday and trade for meat at the grocery store. Monroe took after his dad and was quite a trader. Like Ettie said, they were eating like kings.

They finished gathering the fruit crop. Usually about now they would be heading for West Texas, but this year Tom had talked to the owner about staying there through the fall and winter. Tom told him their situation and asked him if he would have any work they could do in the fall and winter to pay for their rent. He told him he always had the trees to spray and lay by for the winter, also there was always some plowing and cleaning the orchards to do and a lot of odd and end jobs. All that he paid for by the day, if they were interested. Tom told him they would be glad to get it. He said, "In that case the house is furnished with the job. So they could stay there all winter and until the next fall." They had plenty to keep them busy all fall and all the pretty days. They had work to do all winter.

On December 17, it started snowing about midmorning. By noon, it was snowing so hard they could barely see in front of them. Ettie started feeling bad and cramping around that time. She told them, she thought they had better go for the doctor. When she said that, Tom as well as the kids were all dumfounded.

He said, "But, Ettie, it's not time yet."

She said, "Tom, I know that and you all know that, but I think we all had forgotten to tell the little one that."

That brought all four of them to their feet. Monroe and Virgil grabbed their coats and headed toward the door with Tom shouting orders at them like, "Now it's bad out there and the roads will be bad, and for you to drive slow, so ya'll won't slide off in a ditch and watch ahead of you for other cars. Go slow so you will make it." All that time he was grabbing his coat and running right behind them. They had filled some sacks up with sand earlier and stacked them by the side of the house in case it was bad when she went into labor and they would need them. Tom told the boys it was better to be safe than sorry. Monroe and Tom began to grab the sacks and pitch them in the truck bed, and Virgil began to clean the windows so they could see out. By the time they got the sand loaded, Virgil was in the driver's seat waiting for them to crank the truck. Tom was afraid it wouldn't start, but a few turns and it started. Tom hollered more orders at them like, "Now, Virgil, you drive slow and be careful. Monroe you help him watch the road." But they were gone before they heard all his orders. Tom went back in the house. Leola had put Ettie to bed and helped her get on her gown. Then she had put pans of water on the stove to get hot.

Tom laughed and asked her, "What are you going to do with all that water when it gets hot?"

She said, "I don't know, Daddy, but in the movies, they always say put some water on to get hot. And I know with Ethel we had water on the stove, but I couldn't remember how much. So I wanted to be sure we had enough."

Ethel was asleep already. Tom told Leola, "Sister, you take care of Ethel when she wakes up, and I will see to Mama."

She told him, "Now you don't worry about Ethel. I will take care of her. You just take care of Mama."

Then they both went in to tell Ettie that the boys had gone after the doctor. Her first statement was, "Tom, my boys shouldn't be out in weather like this. I am so afraid they will get hurt."

Tom told her, "Try to stop them if you can. They were gone before any of us thought of anything except getting help for you."

Now the waiting game started, Tom thought they would never get back. Every time Ettie had a sharp pain he would hold her hand and tell Leola to go look out and see if they were coming. Of course, she couldn't see anything. By then the snow was falling so fast until they couldn't see out the window or the door even with it opened. It was almost four hours before they heard them coming. Leola had three hot toddies in cups all except the hot water waiting for them, she said, "I knew they would be half frozen when they get here." When Tom saw them, his heart almost stopped beating there was only the truck. Leola said, "Daddy, where is the doctor? We need the doctor." Then they heard a voice and knew it wasn't the boys' voices. The doctor had come with them. Leola and Tom both took a long breath of just plain relief. They were out of the truck and in the house immediately. The doctor headed right to the bedroom with Tom behind him and his nurse behind him. Tom heard the doctor talking to her, but most of all, he heard Ettie say, "Oh, Doctor, it's not time yet. I'm going to lose my baby." Then she started crying.

He said, "Now, now, let's don't give up so soon and besides with your fretting, it will only make it worse. Now you dry your eyes and be a brave girl and pray every time you have a pain that God will make everything be all right."

By then the nurse was there at his side, talking to her also. Leola finished fixing her hot toddies and brought two in for the doctor and his nurse, who was also his wife. They were both nearly frozen and thanked Leola for being so thoughtful and having it ready for them. He checked Ettie and said, "The baby is ready to be born. It will be only a matter of time if everything goes well."

But everything didn't go well, Ettie continued to have sharp pains, but the baby didn't come. The doctor then said, "Maybe we could stop the pains if we can. That will give the baby some extra growing time. It is so small right now." He gave her some medicine. "Now let's hope this works and her pains will stop." They slowed down, but they didn't stop. In between the pains, he told them what a hard time they had, getting there. He said, "When I saw who it was at the door, I hollered at my wife to grab her coat and come on, that I might need her. I told the boys for them to follow me, just in case I had trouble or slide off in the ditch. Sure enough we hadn't gone far until I slid off into the ditch. The boys pushed the car out of the ditch, but they hadn't gone but a few miles until I slid off again. After the third time, the boys suggested that we just come on in the truck that it seemed to hold to the road better. Then they could take us back afterward. Frankly, I was glad that the boys suggested that. I was worried how I was going to make it here and worse still how I was going to make it back without the boys to help me. So we piled into the front seat with my wife in my lap. We were crowded, but it did help keep the warmth in."

Time just seemed to drag on. Ettie started having real hard pains that seemed to just take her breath. After one of them, the doctor told Tom, "I think the baby has got itself turned crossways and now it can't get out. I am going to have to go up and turn it before it suffocates. Now you go up and hold her shoulders and talk to her while my wife and I see if we can turn it."

Ettie was almost out of her head. She had hurt so badly. The doctor was able to turn it, and it wasn't but a few seconds until they heard a very weak cry. It sounded like a little baby cat meowing in place of a baby. He handed his wife a little baby that wasn't as big as a baby doll and told her to go take care of it, that he had to take care of the mama. She took it into the kitchen and began to try to save its life. He could hear Leola and her talking. Leola had gotten a quilt, folded it halfway, and laid it on the table, then laid a baby blanket over it. She asked the nurse, "What else can I do?"

The nurse told her "You might make some strong coffee for the doctor and your dad. They need it badly."

Tom heard her say, "I already have some made for them."

It wasn't long until here she came carrying two cups of steaming coffee. The doctor took a cup and said, "Thank you, young lady, we sure can use that."

She said, "I had it made for a long time, but I didn't know whether to bring it in or not."

He told her, "Now was the perfect time for it."

She asked him, "Is Mama going to be all right?"

He told her, "We hope so. It will take a lot of praying, but you all can do that, can't you?"

She told him, "The boys and I have done that all night."

He looked at her real funny and said, "You mean they all have been up all night?"

"As long as you all have," she told him. Then she turned to go and said, "I have to get back and help the nurse with the little baby. Call if you need some more coffee."

The doctor looked at Tom and said, "Tom, you are a lucky man to have three wonderful kids like these. I have done all I can do for her, and I won't lie to you. Only a miracle will save her and the baby. It will be all those prayers that are being offered up that will turn the tide, so along with the kids, I suggest you pray with them and pray hard."

It wasn't long until Leola came in and told them, "The nurse told me to get some warm clothes for the baby and tell you it is breathing all right now." She and the nurse had bathed the baby and wrapped it in a blanket, then they put it in a shoebox and set it behind the stove. The boys had been out doing the outside work. They brought the milk in and strained it and took it out to the well and brought in some cold milk. The three of them started breakfast. They told the nurse to sit down and rest that she had a hard night and they would get breakfast.

She told Tom later that she just sat down and watched them. It just amazed her the way they worked. Leola made the biscuits, Virgil made a fresh pot of coffee, while Monroe started frying bacon and making gravy. Virgil scrambled the eggs. When Leola got her biscuits in the oven, she set the table and put the jelly, butter, and a big pitcher of cold milk on it. It wasn't long until they had a breakfast on the table good enough for any one. She told Tom she had never seen three kids work so fast and so good together.

They all went in, and Virgil and Monroe stayed in with Ettie. Before the doctor and Tom sat down, they went behind the stove and looked at the little one. He checked it and said, "It looks like it's breathing just fine. She and her mother both had a rough time of it, and both are dog tired."

Tom told him, "You said she." He didn't know until then that it was a girl. She had red auburn hair and looked just like Leola did when she was born, but just a whole lot smaller. Tom commented on how small it was and asked the doctor, how much did he think she weighed.

The doctor told Tom, "I figure between two and a half and three pounds, not over three, if that."

They ate breakfast with the doctor and his wife bragging all the time on how good it was. He asked who made the biscuits, and Leola told him she did. He told her, "Young lady, I believe these are the best biscuits I have ever eaten."

Of course that pleased her, and she told him, "Mama taught me how to make them."

Virgil said, "If you think those were good, you should eat some of Mama's."

Monroe said, "Doctor, she will be all right, won't she? We have prayed all night that God will let her be all right. He will, won't he?"

The doctor said, "Son, do you mean ya'll had been up praying all night?" He acted like he just couldn't believe it.

Monroe answered him with, "As long as ya'll have. Did ya'll think we could go to bed with our mama in there fighting for her life?"

The doctor told him, "Son, I won't lie to you. She is real bad, but with the kind of faith as you three kids have showed, I don't see how God could do anything else but make her well. For ya'll just keep praying. I have done everything I know how to do. Now it's in God's hands. It's up to Him to perform a miracle." He went in to check on Ettie again, and when he came back, he said, "She is breathing good and her heart seemed to be beating good and strong. She just needs plenty of rest and liquid. You try to feed her some broth a little later. She needs some liquid off and on all day to help her gain her strength." Then he checked the baby and told them, "Just keep it comfortable and warm. Only a miracle from God will save it. First of all, it is premature and next it is so small. That's about all ya'll can really do is keep it warm and comfortable, then wait for God and His miracle. Without it, there is no hope. Ya'll could try to get it to drink some milk, but only a little at a time."

Leola spoke up and said, "I will take care of it, and how often do I try?"

He told her, "As small as she is, it wouldn't hurt to try to get some down her every few hours."

The snow had let up, and the sun was trying to come out. The boys cleaned off the snow from the car windows, and it wasn't long until they had it started and ready to take the doctor and his wife home.

The doctor told Tom, "Be sure to send for me if you need me. If there is any change, be sure and come for me." Then he told Leola, "You help your dad and to take good care of your mama and little sister and I will see ya'll Saturday."

Leola told him, "Oh, I will."

And he told her, "I know you will, young lady."

The boys were gone all morning. When they came back, they told Tom they had to stop and pull the doctors car out of the ditch. Then they had to go real slow to keep from sliding off in the ditch. The doctor did and they had to pull him out the second time. They said, "We have never seen it so cold and bad. It is awful out there. Oh"—they both laughed—"the doctor said he would like to hire Virgil to drive for him in this kind of weather, that we did great."

Ettie hung on between life and death. She didn't seem to get any better, but as far as they could tell she didn't get any worse. Tom sat up with her day and night. The boys finally told him, "Dad, you can't keep this up. Let us take care of her in the daytime, and you take care of her at night. And we will call you if there is any change."

Leola said, "And, Daddy, you don't have to worry about the little one and Ethel. I am taking good care of them both."

Tom thanked them. Then with tears running down his face, he told them, "How could I make it without all of you. God has really blessed me with children like ya'll."

By then they all had tears running down their faces. Monroe said, "Dad, she will be all right. I know she will. God couldn't do that to us as bad as we need her."

Tom went to bed in the boys' room, and he just died off. He didn't know he was so tired. Leola woke him up around eight or nine and asked him, "Do you want to get up and eat some supper. I have made some soup for ya'll, and the boys has fed some to mama off and on all afternoon."

Tom asked her, "How is Mama?"

She said, "The boys said she was better. I have had my hands full tending to the little one and Ethel. Ethel had cried and cried for Mama. Also, I had cooked supper. Monroe did the night work while Virgil watched Mama."

This went on for the next several days. Tom stayed with her all night, and the boys did the outside work and watched her all day. Also, they helped Leola do the cooking. Leola took care of the baby and Ethel. As of yet the boys hadn't looked at the baby. They just pretended it didn't exist. Leola got up day and night if it cried and tended to it. At night she took it and it's little shoebox to bed with her, and in the morning, she would bathe and feed it. Then she would put it back in the shoebox and set it behind the stove to keep it warm. She told Tom, "It is so small. I am afraid I might hurt it if it wasn't in the shoebox." After she feed and bathe Ettie, she would take it and Ethel both back to bed and try to sleep some more. Tom didn't think she got much sleep, day or night, because it would wake her every few hours for something to eat. He was so worried about Ettie, he never even thought to ask her what she was feeding it. It was doing a lot better than Ettie.

On the third day, Ettie opened her eyes and looked around. The boys called him. He didn't think she recognize any of them. She kept saying, "My baby, my baby."

Tom told the boys, "Maybe if we got the baby and she saw it was all right, she would settle down."

He hollered for Leola to bring the baby. They laid it in her arms, and she did settle down for a little while. But all of a sudden, she picked up the baby, and if Tom hadn't been right there, she would have thrown it off the bed. Tom grabbed it, and when they got her settled down, he told the boys, "I think it is time to go get the doctor. Something is wrong with her."

They were out of the house and on their way before he could tell them to drive careful and not to go too fast. Leola came running in, and Tom told her, "Sister, you take care of the baby and Ethel while I take care of Mama." Tom really thought Ettie was dying, so he didn't want her in there when she did. He had to hold her down. She was fighting, trying to get up, mumbling something like, "My baby, my baby," and she was as hot as she could be.

The snow had melted, and the boys made good time. They brought the doctor and nurse back in the truck. The doctor said, "Virgil didn't even kill the motor. Monroe ran up to the door, hollering every step he took. I heard them before Monroe got to the door and ran to it. Monroe hollered, 'Come quick, Mama needs you.' He told me to come and go in the truck. We can make better time in it." The doctor's wife was there by the time he got to the door with his bag. They ran down the steps, and before they slammed the car doors, Virgil was pulling off. He drove fast but good. He told Tom, "It was the fastest thirty miles I had ever made."

When he had given Ettie something to settle her down, he examined her. He said, "She has blood poison. I won't lie to ya'll, she doesn't have much of a chance. A strong healthy woman would have less than a fifty-fifty chance. Ettie is not strong or healthy." So they knew what her chances were. He went on to say, "I think you, Tom, should go prepare the children for it. My wife and I will stay here with her while you go to the children."

His wife said, "Tom is in no shape to tell them. You go with him and I will stay with Ettie until ya'll get back. She has calmed down, and they need ya'll both right now more than she does."

Tom and the doctor went in to the kitchen. All three jumped up at once and asked the doctor, "She will be all right, won't she?"

He told them, "Let's sit down over here at the table, and I sure could use a cup of that hot coffee." He and Tom walked over to the table. The doctor was just as calm as he could be, but his wife was right, Tom couldn't say a word. He was thinking over and over, *God, don't let her die. We need her so much. Please, God, give her back to us.*

The kids brought two cups over and poured the coffee, then sat down. The doctor told them, "I know ya'll know that your mama is critical." He told them just what he had told Tom.

Tom couldn't say anything. All he could do was sit there with tears running down his checks.

Monroe jumped up and almost shouted at him, "No, she's not. We won't let her die. God knows how much we need her. He won't take her from us. I know He won't. I know He won't." He turned to Virgil and Leola and said, "Come on, as long as there is life, there is still hope. As long as she is breathing, we will be in the bedroom on our knees praying." And they started to walk out.

The doctor hollered at them, "Just a moment, I have something else to say. While ya'll are at it, you might pray for the little one also. It is critical too, and your mama is fighting for it as much as she would for the two of you. She thinks it is dead or dying, and that is why she was struggling so hard to get up when I came in. Mothers are funny little creatures. God put so much love into their hearts until it almost destroys them. Regardless of how many children she has, she still has a full complete unconditional love for each of them. She doesn't have to divide her one big love between how many children she has, but she has a complete love for every one of them. She will fight until her death for each and every one that God chooses to give her. She is right there fighting day and night for the one that needs her most at that time, with you all trying to keep that little one alive, it will play a big part on how she recovers."

Monroe and Virgil both had tears running down their faces by then. They told the doctor, "Oh we will, Doctor, we will." They all three went into the other room. Leola looked so pathetic carrying the little shoebox with the precious little bundle in it and leading Ethel. They didn't hear another word from them until suppertime. They came out of the bedroom, and all three begin to fix supper. When it was ready, Monroe and Virgil came in and told them, "Supper is ready. We will sit with Mama while the rest of you go eat." They all went in and ate. The doctor and his wife just bragged and bragged on what a good meal they had cooked.

The nurse tried to get Leola to let her take care of the little one. Leola asked her if she was doing all right taking care of her. The nurse told her no one could do better. She told the nurse, "Then I am going to take care of her." With tears rolling down her cheeks, she said, "I promised Mama I would. If you and the doctor will just take care of Mama, I will take good care of it."

The nurse hugged her and told her, "I know you will. No one can do better."

Ettie hovered between life and death all night and the next day. The doctor and his wife stayed right there with them. He told Tom later, "There is no way we would have gone and left those precious children in that other room praying for their mama. They kept bathing her with alcohol diluted with water all night to try to get her fever down. It was sky high."

Tom knew it was because she was so hot. On the second night, she seemed to be doing better, and by midnight, they all could tell that she had improved a whole lot.

On the third morning her fever broke. She opened her eyes. The first word she said was, "My baby, did it live?" The nurse called the children, and Leola showed her the baby, but Tom didn't think she still was coherent enough to understand anything. She was back to sleep before Leola could tell her more than yes. She went on to say "And, Mama, I am taking real good care of it."

The doctor told the kids, "Borrowing no more trouble, I think she is going to make it, if it's God's will. Her fever has broken, and she is resting."

Monroe said, "Doctor, I know it's God's will." The other two just shook their heads.

Right after breakfast he told them, "My wife and I had better go home. Everyone will be wondering what has happened to us. Continue giving her the medicine and doing what you have been doing. And for some of you to stay with her day and night and don't leave her by herself for any reason."

Before Virgil took them back home, they all promised the doctor they would come for him if she needed him. Also thanking both of them for all they had done. Monroe told them, "I will stay here and make Dad get some rest while Virgil takes you home. Dad looks like he is about to pass out also."

The doctor agreed with him and said, "Now, Tom, you get some rest today, so you can take care of her tonight."

Leola and Tom cleaned the kitchen while Monroe went in to sit with his mother. After that Leola said, "Now, Dad, you get some sleep while I bathe and feed the little one and Ethel." As yet they hadn't given the baby a name.

Ettie seemed to get better every day. They fed her soup broth several times a day. And by the end of the week, she was eating regular food. She was still weak and still slept a lot, but she seemed to know what was going on. She kept asking about the baby but didn't ask to see it.

Then one day she kept calling for Leola. When Leola came in, she asked her, "Sister, did my baby live?" Then they all took a long deep breath because they knew she was going to be all right.

Leola told her, "Yes, Mama, it's a little girl. She is small, but it's doing just fine now. I have been taking real good care of her."

Then Ettie asked if she could see it. Leola took it out of the shoebox and laid it beside her. Ettie was still so weak she couldn't hold it. She said, "Sister, it's the spitting image of you. It has bright auburn hair and big brown eyes."

Leola looked so proud when Ettie told her that. She told her, "Yes, Mama, Daddy said it looked just like me and his mother."

The following week she could sit up in bed but still wasn't strong enough to walk. Leola would bathe and dress the little one and take it to the bed for her to hold. One day Tom was standing there beside the bed when Leola brought it in. She asked her mama, "What are we going to name it? We can't just call it the little one the rest of its life."

Ettie looked surprised and said, "Bless its heart, you mean it doesn't have a name yet?"

Leola said, "No, we were waiting for you to get all right so we could all name it together, like we did Ethel."

She told her, "Then tonight, after the boys get in the house, we will pick out a name for it. It's small, but it looks healthy. What have you been feeding it."

She told her mama, "I didn't know exactly what to give it besides milk. She would get cold a lot and turn blue. I didn't have time to warm the milk, so I would put a little of daddy's hot coffee in it. When there was no coffee, I would make some hot tea with sugar and put it in the milk. She really seemed to like that. I didn't have a baby bottle so I have been spooning it into its little mouth. And, Mama, now it's eating like a little pig. At first, it didn't take me no time to feed her, but now it's eating real good. This week I have started putting just a little cream potatoes in its milk and coffee. The milk and coffee didn't seem to satisfy her any more. I remember you putting a little potatoes in Ethel's milk, so I did it for her."

Ettie said, "Sister, you could kill her giving her that. She is too small to feed yet."

Leola told her, "But, Mama, she sure does like it. And she is growing like a little pig."

After supper they all went into Mama's room. Leola brought the little one. She was still carrying it around in the shoebox.

Ettie said, "I heard today that this precious little thing doesn't have a name yet. We need to take care of that tonight. So what are we going to name her?"

Virgil said, "The doctor's wife's name was Thelma. They were so good to stay here and take care of you, Mama, that I don't know what we would have done without them. So I think we ought to name it Thelma after her, to show how much we appreciated them for helping us."

Ettie said, "I think that is a very good idea. What do the rest of you think?"

They all agreed that they thought that was fine.

Leola said, "Well, now she has a first name. What about a middle name?"

Ettie said, "If it had been a boy, I had thought about naming him Thomas Joshua after your daddy, so why not try to find a name that starts with a *J*. Then she will have at least his initials."

They thought and thought, and they couldn't think of anything that they thought was suitable. Finally, Leola said, "Oh, I know, what about Jewel?" Everyone agreed with her.

Ettie said, "There our baby has a name. Thelma Jewel. Little T. J. after its daddy."

Leola said, "Well, I hope we don't intend to call it little T. J."

Everyone laughed, and the boys just for pure old cursedness said, "We think that would be just fine." And they went around calling it T. J. until their mama put a stop to it.

It took Ettie quite a while to get where she was strong enough to take care of both Ethel and the baby, so Leola kept taking care of little Thelma. She would tell her mama that while she bathed and fed Ethel she would also bathe and feed Thelma. By the time Ettie was really strong enough to start tending to Thelma, she was so attached to Leola, until she wouldn't let anyone care for her except Leola.

When Thelma was two months old, Tom insisted that Ettie go to the doctor for a checkup. Ettie was still weak and tired most of the time. They took her on Saturday because the boys and Tom were working most of the time in and around the orchards, getting everything in shape for the fruit harvest.

Both the doctor and his wife were at the door almost by the time they knocked. The doctor said, "Well, look who is here. Young lady, you sure gave us a scare. I didn't think you would make it there for a while."

His wife said, "The only reason she did was those precious children praying all the time that God would let you live. It was a miracle that God performed for them because they prayed so hard and ask for one."

Virgil told them, "The Bible says, ask and you shall receive, and that's all we did."

The doctor said, "And look here at another miracle. My how she has gown. I didn't think she had a chance at all of making it." Then he asked Leola, "Young lady, what have you been feeding her to make her so pretty and healthy? I knew your mama didn't have any milk for her."

Leola looked at her mama as if to say, "Oh my goodness, what am I supposed to tell him?"

Ettie said, "Tell him, sister."

Leola said, "Well, Doctor, at first she would turn real blue like she was cold. I didn't have time to warm some milk to give her, so I warmed it with a little coffee. I guess it worked because each time she would warm back up and turn back just as pretty and pink as she was before."

The doctor said, "That's amazing, young lady. Each time you did that, you were actually saving your little sister's life. Her heart was trying to stop, and each time you gave her the coffee, it stimulated the heart and it started beating right again. If your mama had been able to take care of her, she probably would have died because you wouldn't have given her the coffee."

Ettie told him, "No, I wouldn't have. In fact when I came to, I asked her what she had been feeding her. When she told me, I told her, 'Sister, that will kill my baby.' She told me, 'Mama I don't think it will. She is eating like a little pig and growing like a weed.'"

The doctor just shook his head, then he told Leola, "Young lady, God preformed another miracle through you. None of us adults would have known to do that." Then he asked, "What name am I going to put on the birth certificate?"

Leola told them, "Thelma, after your wife, because ya'll had been so good to stay with us and take care of our mama, and Jewel, because Mama had planned on naming it Thomas Joshua if it had been a boy, so we named it daddy's initials."

The doctor and his wife both acted real pleased over the baby's name, and she kept on thanking them for naming the baby after her. Both told them how proud they were, but they were only doing what any other good nurse and doctor would have done, that it was God that preformed the miracle and that it was God that deserved all the credit.

After that he told Ettie, "Continue the iron medicine and eat like you did before the baby was born. Your blood is still low, and that is why you are so tired."

They all thanked them, and Tom asked, "What do we owe you?"

His wife spoke up. "Not a dime, meeting such wonderful children and you all naming the baby after me is payment enough."

Tom tried to tell them that wasn't right, but they kept insisting it was more than enough. They left with the boys still telling them how much they appreciated them being there with them.

The doctor told them, "Now you make your mama come back before you leave this fall."

They promised they would.

Spring harvest came, and they picked fruit every day. Each night the boys would bring a bag of culls from ever what they were picking. So they always had plenty of fruit. Also, the boys had continued delivering milk, eggs, and butter to their customers as long as they had it to spare. They had told the ladies just put the leftover money on their account. So they had quite a lot saved for their vegetables. So again, each night, they would go pick up fresh vegetables and deliver whatever they had to spare. So they never hurt for fresh fruit and vegetables. The leftovers Leola and Ettie canned.

Chapter 36

FALL CAME AND THEY WERE through gathering the fruit. The boys were ready to go back to Childress. They kept their word and took Ettie and the baby back to see the doctor on Saturday before they left on Monday.

The doctor said, "She is doing just fine but is still not completely recovered yet. And she is to continue taking her medicine. Little Thelma is doing just fine. She is still small but is healthy as she can be."

Leola was still caring for her. Thelma would cry if she left her for anything. So Ettie was caring for Ethel and Leola for Thelma. Ettie was still weak and tired most of the time, so it made it easier that way.

He told Leola, "You are doing a real good job taking care of little Thelma. You continue helping your mama."

As for any little girl, this made Leola as proud as could be. She told him, "Oh, I will. I will take care of little Thelma as long as Mama needs me to. I promise you, I will."

He smiled and said "I know you will." He turned to Ettie and Tom and told them, "You know, Tom, you two people are the richest people I have ever known. You all might not have a lot of money, but God has blessed you all with these wonderful children and that is worth more than all the money He could have given you. I wish He had blessed us that way. We gave our children everything, and in return they have given us nothing but trouble. We wanted to give them all the things we didn't have. But we forgot, giving them love and companionship was the most important thing we could have given them. We didn't realize that until we met you all. Now it's too late. We can't go back and raise them again. But after meeting you all, if we could, I guarantee you, they would be raised differently."

They both thanked him for the nice compliment and told him, "Ours was pretty well spoiled, until we lost all we had and had to change our whole lifestyle. It was hard on us all at first, but we had learned to accept what God had given us and to be thankful for it."

They left right after that with him telling them to be careful and take good care of Ettie and little Thelma and for them to bring them back as soon as they came back in the spring. They all promised him that they would, and again they all thanked him and his wife for being there with them and that if they hadn't been there to take care of Ettie, she wouldn't be here now.

He thanked them but said, "No, if you kids hadn't prayed all the time we were helping her, she wouldn't be here today. It wasn't what we did that saved her, but what you all did."

On Monday they had everything loaded and left real early so they could be in Sherman before dark. As usual they parked in the same place so they would have a place for the cows, chickens, and dogs to stay.

After they got set up, they went by to see Sallie. Nothing had changed. Jeff still came and went as he pleased. Again, Tom asked her to come and go with them, and again she refused. Tom gave her a little money. They all had talked it over, and as usual they all agreed that they just had to help her a little. They couldn't help her much, but back then every little bit helped.

They left the next morning and were in Childress before six o'clock. Sam was real proud to see them and asked what had happened to them last year. Tom told him, and he said, "That same house was empty if ya'll want it."

Tom also told him, "It will only be three or four of us picking from now on and most of the time three as Ettie won't be able to at all and Leola, only when her mother don't need her. But we will work as hard as we can, but I'm afraid we won't be able to get a bail a day at cotton picking time or chop as much as we have been."

He told them, "I will appreciate all ya'll can do. Help is getting harder and harder to get."

Tom told him, "We are ready to start as soon as we get moved in."

But he told them, "Take your time and get moved in and rest a day or two before ya'll get started."

Tom thanked him and told him they would see him Wednesday.

The house was as dirty as it was the first time they cleaned it. You could tell no one had lived in it since they left. The boys unloaded the cows and put them in the pasture. Then put the hens in the chicken house and turned the dogs loose while Leola and Tom got the washpot out of the truck and filled it up with water, then built a fire under it. Then the boys took all the furniture outside to wash while the water was heating. Leola and Tom swept the dust out of the house. When they all finished their jobs, the water was hot enough for them to start cleaning. The boys cleaned the furniture, and Leola and Tom washed down the walls and scrubbed the floor. It didn't take them long, and before very long the floors were ready to move the furniture in. The girls were beginning to get cranky and tired, so they moved the beds in first and Ettie and both girls laid down and it wasn't long until all three were fast asleep. All four of them unloaded the truck and put everything in each room and made the beds. By then it was late in the afternoon and almost time to milk the cows and get supper.

The next few years went the same. They spent the winters in Sherman, went to Leon Junction for berry and fruit picking, then back to Childress for cotton chopping and picking.

Ettie stayed at the house. She fussed about her having to stay. They all told her, they had rather have her stay there and have supper ready for them and keep the girls. She tried to keep them, but Thelma fussed and cried all the time for Leola. Finally, Leola asked her mama if she could just take her with her. At first Ettie would have none of it. She told Leola, "Sister, she will burn up, and she has to have milk regular."

Leola told her mama, "I have that figured out. I will put it in a fruit jar, then put it in our ice water to stay cold, and when we stop to weigh each time, I will feed her and change her clothes. Thelma can lie on my cotton sack, and I can pull her. I have seen other mamas with their babies riding on their sacks, and she can too. Let me try it for a day, then if it don't work out, then I can leave her at the house with you."

Ettie finally agreed, so the next morning Thelma went with them.

She was walking everywhere by then. Tom told Leola, "I don't think it is going to work," but she was determined that it would. When they got to the field, she put her milk in the water barrel, hung her diapers on the end of the wagon so nothing could get in them. Then she put her little bonnet on her, gave her a cold drink, and sat her on her cotton sack. She put the sides of the cotton sack in each of her hands and told her to hold on real good. At first, she kept falling off, but when she finally learned she had to hold to stay on, she did just fine, and by night she was riding as if she had done it always. While the boys weighed Leola's cotton, she would give her some cold milk and change her diaper; and just before they left the wagon, when they all got a drink of cold water, Leola would give her one also. She never cried and acted like she was really enjoying the ride. At noon, Leola fed her while they all ate, and when they all laid down for an hour, she went to sleep just like the rest of them.

By the end of the week, she was riding on the sack without holding. Only when Leola started shaking the sack, to try and shake her off, would she grab the cotton sack. Then she would grab it and hold on for dear life and just die laughing. She would play with the cotton bolls and try to grab them while Leola picked the cotton, then when she got tired she would just lie back and go to sleep. The wagon, being in the middle of the field, they would stop, weigh their cotton, empty the sacks, and get a cold drink each time. Leola would give her a cold drink, change her, and before they left, offer her some milk. She would give her a piece of a biscuit to suck on, but most of the time she would just sat on the sack and play with it while Leola pulled cotton. She was a lot of enjoyment to all of them. The boys would pick at her and try to push her off the sack. When she saw them coming, she would grab the sack and hold on as tight as she could. By night she would be like the rest of them, hungry, tired, and filthy. Ettie would have a fire build under the washpot with plenty of hot water, and they would all take a bath and eat supper. The boys would always fill the pot back up, so it would be full for the next night. So Ettie wouldn't have to do it. They would put the wood back around it so she would only have to start a fire each night. She always had everything done outside but the cows milked. As long as they had cows, she never did learn to milk. She just didn't have enough strength in her hands to milk.

Each night, no one had to tell them to go to bed, they were all so tired, including Thelma. As soon as they bathed and ate supper, they all went to bed. Most of the time, Thelma was asleep before they finished supper, but the next morning she was ready to go again. Ethel never wanted to go, she was perfectly happy staying with her mother at the house. She was afraid of bugs and worms, and there were plenty of them in the cotton field. Thelma got to where she would throw them off the cotton sack when they got on it. She acted like that was her place to play and they didn't have any business being on it. She would crawl over to where they were, pick them up, and throw them as hard as she could. Of course, they all got a big kick out of watching her. As soon as she could walk well enough to keep up with them, she would run all over the field to each of them, trying to pick cotton too. She would ride on the boy's sack, and they got a big kick out of trying to shake her off their sacks. She would hold on and laugh but very seldom could they shake her off.

She was closer to Leola than she ever was. She would come over to any of them as long as she could still see Leola, but she wouldn't let her out of her sight. If she was riding on one of their sacks, she was fine as long as she could see her, but if Leola got behind or ahead of them and she couldn't see her, she would roll off the sack and here she would go looking for her. She never would cry, but she had learned how to say "sitter." They figured out that was supposed to mean "sister." Here she would go hollering, "Sitter, sitter" over and over until she located her, and always when she got tired and sleepy, she would go to her sack to go to sleep. On Saturday, when the kids went back to make their extra money, she was right with them.

When Thelma was around four years old, they came through Sherman going to Childress and Sallie was real upset. Jeff was in trouble and was in jail. He and some more men had set the court house on fire to get a colored man out. The colored man had been accused of raping a white woman. They had drug him all over colored town and had killed him. All the men were in jail and waiting their trial. As usual, Sallie was taking up for him and wanted Tom to loan her the money to get him out of jail. Tom hated to turn her down, but he didn't have the kind of money she was asking for.

She told him, "Tom, I will go with you and pick cotton and pay you back."

Tom told her, "We don't have that kind of money and besides, if we got him out, the very first chance he got, he would skip out and leave us holding the bag for the whole amount."

She told him, "Tom, I think he has learned his lesson this time, and he has promised me he will go to work and help me pay ya'll back."

Tom told her, "Sis, we don't have that kind of money, and even if we did, I couldn't take it away from my family for something like this. We all work hard so we can have a mere living, and if I did what you asked, we would go hungry this winter."

She told him, "Tom, some way, somehow, I have to raise it" and asked him to stay around a few days, so if she did get it, she could go with them and pick cotton to pay it back.

Tom told her they would stay until the end of the week but after that they would have to go. Tom didn't know how she did it, but she got the judge that she worked for to loan her the money. Tom found out later that he made Jeff sign the note.

The judge told him, "Jeff, you will be responsible for every dime of it, and if you try to skip out, I will put every cop I can find on your trail, and when you are caught, you will be tried for murder. I am getting sick and tired of the way you treat Sallie. This time you will go to work and pay it back not her." He put him in the custody of Sallie, and somehow, she got the judge in charge of the case to let them go to Childress with Tom to pick cotton. Promising him they would get in touch with the police as soon as they got there. She just paid the rent on her house to hold it and they just took their clothes, mattress, pillows, and a few things for their own house. It was crowded with all of them in the truck, but thank the Lord they didn't have that long to have to stay in it. They left real early so they could get there early enough to get settled in before night. Sallie helped Ettie take care of the two girls, and she was a lot of help

When they got there, they stopped at Sam's house to see if he could use Sallie and Jeff for both chopping and picking. He told them he would be real glad to have them, but told Tom, "I don't have another house empty for them. All the houses are full."

There was nothing Tom could do but say, "If it's okay with you, I guess we could share ours with them, until and if one comes available."

So they all went down to their little house. First thing they did was unload the cows, turn the dogs loose, and put the chickens in the henhouse. Sallie and Jeff both jumped in and helped clean the house. They had everything cleaned and drying when Sam brought another iron bed down. Tom sure was proud of it.

He told Sam, "I didn't know what we were going to do. We have four mattresses but only three beds." They gave Leola's room to Sallie and Jeff and put her and Thelma's bed in Tom and Ettie's room. They asked Sam if he had any more old lumber that they could get to build another set of shelves with. He told them he did, and Jeff and the boys went back with him to get it while Sallie and Tom washed the bed he had brought. Tom was surprised at Jeff. He just pitched in and worked as hard as the rest of them, getting the house in shape. By suppertime, Sallie and Ettie were able to cook supper on the stove, and they ate in the house at the table. Jeff and the boys didn't get the shelves finished, but they were far enough along, that they would finish them the next day. After supper the womenfolk bathed the girls, put them to bed, and took their baths while the men cleaned the kitchen up and milked the cows. Again, Tom was surprised at Jeff. He pitched in and helped them just like he had done it all his life.

The next day they finished the shelf and washed them down. While they were drying, they had enough lumber that they built a bench to go on the front porch for them to sit on. When the shelves were dry, they took them into Tom and Ettie's room and nailed them to the wall. Then Ettie and Leola put her and Thelma's things in it and their towels and sheets. With nine people in four rooms, it was crowded. But as Ettie always said they had a roof over their heads, a bed to sleep in, and plenty to eat. Monroe continued trading their spare milk, eggs, and butter for vegetables; so they always had plenty to eat.

On Monday, after they got there, they all went to the field, except Ettie and Ethel. The boys insisted on their mother staying home. "We almost lost her once, and we are not going to take another chance on losing her." Again, Jeff surprised them all. He worked just as hard as the rest of them. Both he and Sallie made good hands. On Saturday, after they all got paid on Friday. They rode in to town with Leola and the boys. They mailed a payment to Judge Sneed on the loan, and every Saturday after that they would mail a payment to him.

Into the second month they were there, they all were in about the middle of the field when a big black car drove up to the end of the rows and just sat there as if waiting for them. When they got to the end of the row, a well-dressed woman got out leading a child and came out to where they were. She went right to Jeff and said, "Jeff, if you are not going to stay home and help support your child, then you can just have her. I can't support her by myself." She left the child and just turned around went back to the car. She got into the car and drove off without even a backward glance. They all just stood there dumbfounded, looking after the car.

A BOY CALLED KID

Sallie was the first one to speak. She turned to Jeff, her face as white as snow, and asked him, "What did she mean, by your child?"

Jeff looked around as if looking for a hole to crawl in and said, "Yes, Sallie, she is my child. I have wanted to tell you for several years, but I just couldn't find the words to tell you."

Sallie didn't bat an eye and said, "Jeff, the truth is always the best way."

The poor little child was just standing there with tears running down her cheeks. Sallie dropped her hoe and went over and picked her up and started talking to her. They all heard her saying to the little girl, "Now, now, it's all right, don't cry. I want you, and I will take care of you."

The little girl started crying harder, and the more she cried the more Sallie talked to her, telling her over and over, "I will take care of you. I will love you and be your mama." After a while she stopped crying and put her arms around Sallie's neck and just hung on to her. Sallie finally put her down and took her hand. She told her, "Now you come and follow me while I finish working, then we will go home." Not another word did she say to anyone, but the little girl stayed right beside her all the rest of the afternoon. Thelma must have sensed her need because she went over and stayed there with her all afternoon and that was unusual because she didn't get that far from Leola very long at a time. Leola must have realized it too because she let Thelma stay with her. There was very little said the rest of the day. Tom was so mad at Jeff until he could have taken his hoe and chopped his head off for hurting Sallie like he had and he thought all the rest felt just like he did. They finished the day and went home. The little girl clung to Sallie all the way home.

Jeff told them, "Her name is Eula, and she is going on four years old."

When they got to the house, Sallie took her in her arms and brought her into the house. She told Ettie, "Sister, this is mine and Jeff's little daughter," and that was all that was said.

As always, Ettie had supper ready when they came in and hot water for all their baths. The eggs were gathered up, and all the night work was done except the milking. Right after supper Virgil and Monroe left to deliver their eggs, milk, and butter while Jeff and Tom milked the cows. The girls all cleaned up the kitchen. After that Sallie, Eula, Leola, and Thelma went out to bathe. Sallie borrowed a gown of Thelma's and dressed Eula while Leola dressed Thelma, and again Thelma went in to Sallie's room and laid down with Eula. She had never done that before. Sallie told her, "Now you go to bed with Thelma and I will be in shortly." The girls laid down together, and it wasn't long until they were fast asleep. Both were dead tired from walking the rows all evening.

Ettie and Ethel always took their baths before they came in. So after Jeff and Tom did the night work, they took theirs. Then they put more water in the pot for Virgil and Monroe. They had worked out a routine for them to follow and it wasn't hard on any of them. Jeff didn't say a word to explain what had happened, and Tom didn't push the matter. Tom thought he and Sallie would tell them when they were ready.

The next morning Sallie got up and dressed Eula, as if she had done it all her life and went to the cotton field as usual. Nothing more was said about the situation. For a few days Thelma stayed most of the time with Eula. Some of the time, they would be with Leola, but most of the time, they would be with Sallie. Eula wouldn't get far from Sallie at any time. So Leola and Sallie started working next to each other. That way the girls could play between the rows and be close to both Sallie and Leola. At noon they were always dead tired, and soon as they ate their dinner, they went sound asleep with the rest of them. This went on all week. Sallie and Jeff acted as if nothing had happened. They both acted real proud of Eula. You would think she belonged to both of them.

Saturday, while they were eating breakfast, Jeff announced he was going back to the cotton field with the kids to pick for a half day, that he wanted to make some extra money so Sallie could buy material to make some things for Eula, that she only had one dress and one pair panties. Sallie was borrowing a set of clothes and a gown from Thelma until she could make her some clothes of her own.

While they were gone, Sallie said, "Bud, I want to talk to you two. I know you think it strange the way I have accepted Eula, knowing that she is Jeff's child by another woman. That night Jeff and I talked long after all of ya'll had gone to sleep. He told me he would take Eula and leave if I wanted him to. I asked him what kind of life would that be for Eula. That she wasn't responsible for his or the other woman's sins. That she didn't have anything to do with what they did. I told him, she was just an innocent little baby, so why should she have to suffer for what they did. We agreed that we would try to raise her together. As soon as we can get enough money, we will adopt her, so her mama can't ever take her from me. Tom, I have prayed and prayed for a child, When Ethel was born, I cried and prayed for weeks, asking God why He didn't give me a child. Again, when I saw Thelma, it broke my heart. She looked so much like mama. I cried and prayed again for weeks, begging God for a child. When I saw this little child, she looked so lost, so lonely, and scared. I took her in my arms and begin to comfort her, and it was as if God spoke to me and said here is a child for you. I know that sounds crazy to you all, but I just can't abandon her, like her daddy and mama has, and the only way I can have her is if Jeff stays. He has made it clear, if he goes, she goes also, and I won't give her up."

Tom went over and put his arms around her and told her, "Sis, it takes a mighty big woman to do what you are doing, and I am proud of you."

At noon, they all came in from the field. They ate their dinner and bathed. Sallie had Eula dressed and ready. She said, "Jeff wouldn't know what to buy for Eula, and besides, we have to mail the payment to the judge and let him know everything was going all right so we're going with them." And they all were gone in no time.

On Sunday, Sallie, Ettie, and Leola all sat around sewing on the material that she had bought, making Eula some clothes. She acted like she was real proud of them. Fall came, and again Jeff picked cotton just as fast and hard as they did. Sallie took Eula and went along each day and picked with the rest of them. Eula and Thelma would play until they got tired, then they would crawl upon Leola and Sallie's cotton sacks and go to sleep. Jeff had done real good. Outside of the money they sent the judge and paying his and Sallie's share of the grocery bill, they had saved all the rest for them to have to live on during the winter. Also they were saving some for the adoption papers. They said they wanted to get it as soon as they could to make sure her mama didn't change her mind and try to take Eula back. They spent the winter in Sherman, and as usual they were able to get their house back

Sallie and Jeff went back to their own house behind the laundry. Sallie started working for the judge and his family. Ettie kept Eula while she worked. So Sallie would drop her off when she came by and then pick her up when she finished her day of work.

When spring came, Sallie and Jeff went with them to pick berries and fruit. Again, they couldn't get a house, so they stayed all together in one house. Jeff and Sallie both worked real hard. Mr. Tompkins was real proud to get them and told them so.

Thelma and Eula went to the field with Leola and Sallie each day. They never gave them any trouble. They just played wherever Leola and Sallie were working.

They finished gathering the berries and fruit and went back to Sherman and on to Childress. Jeff and Sallie went with them, and they finished another year of work. That fall, just before they left to come back to Sherman, Virgil and Lacey Lee came in one night and told them, "We are married. We have been married ever since we got here." It wasn't a shock because Tom and Ettie knew sooner or later it would happen. When they left for Sherman, Lacey Lee went with them. Again, they got their same house, and Jeff and Sallie still had their things in the one behind the laundry, so they stayed there. The little four-room house was crowded. Again, Monroe moved into the small room. Virgil and Lacey Lee took Leola's and Thelma's room. They had to put another bed in Tom and Ettie's room for Leola and Thelma.

That winter Monroe got a job at a dairy and left home. He got his room and board and so much salary. He told them it was long hard hours but he was used to hard work. They hardly got to see him anymore. He milked the cows twice a day starting at four in the morning and four in the evening. They took the milk to the plant every morning, then cleaned the barn twice a day and the room where the milk separators were cleaned every morning. By the time they did all that, it didn't leave much time for sleeping.

Leola and Thelma moved back in the little back room, and Tom thought, it did make it a lot better. Five people in one bedroom was quite crowded. But as Ettie said, "You do what you have to do." Bless her heart, she never complained about anything. She just took everything as it came and thanked the Lord for what they had.

That spring Jeff, Sallie, and Eula went with them again to Leon Junction along with Lacey Lee, Virgil, Ettie, the two little girls, and Leola. Again, they couldn't get two houses, so they all had to stay in one house that they had been staying in. They had to put two beds in Tom and Ettie's room, and again, they all five stayed in it. That year when they got to Childress, Virgil and Lacey Lee stayed with her mother. So it made it a lot easier.

That was the year of 1929. Tom wondered if times were ever going to get any better. They had traveled all these years back and forth from Leon Junction to Childress living in shacks and just barely making a living, thinking every year, *Lord, it's got to get better.* But that year was one of the saddest years of Tom's life. Leola ran off and got married. She had met this boy, and before the fall was up, she had run off and married him. She was Tom's sidekick from the time she was big enough to walk around good. The two boys stayed all the time with their mother and were mama's boys. When Leola was born, he was bound and determined not to make the same mistake three times so he took her with him everywhere. They hunted together, skinned coons together, and rode horses together. She helped him train coon dogs. She pulled many a coon hide around the house, to leave the scent for the dogs to find. While the boys and Ethel stayed with their mother, Leola and Thelma would be with Tom. Thelma became his sidekick and buddy also because she was always with Leola. Leola was his right hand, his sidekick, and his buddy. He hated her husband because he took her away from him, and he didn't pretend otherwise.

Looking back, Tom guessed, if she had married anyone else he would have felt the same. But at that time, he could only see all his bad points, and in his eyes, he had plenty. Because Tom made it so obvious how he felt about him, he disliked Tom as much as Tom did him. Because of that, shortly after they married, they moved to East Texas. Ettie always accused Tom of driving them away because of the way he felt toward him, and Tom guessed he did. He couldn't see anything good about him. Only that he had taken something precious that had belonged to him.

Ettie kept telling him, "We raised them to grow up and have their own life. We don't own them. They were a precious gift loaned to us for a short time from God."

Tom knew what she said was true, but it didn't make it any easier. He told her, "Ettie, he wasn't even man enough to come and ask for her."

That made Ettie real mad, and she told him, "Tom, if he had, would you have let them get married? Would you have been man enough to let her go? You know and she knew that you wouldn't have."

Leola wanted to take Thelma with her and told Tom flat footed that he had given Thelma to her to raise when she was three days old and she had raised her as if she was her own. Her husband didn't help matters. He joined right in with Leola and told Tom how selfish he was taking Thelma away from them. The rest of them stayed on in Childress and finished picking cotton until the season was over. Then Tom, Ettie, Sallie, Jeff, and the three girls went back to Sherman; and they were able to get their little house again. Sallie and Jeff went back to their own house behind the laundry. As always, they spent the winter in Sherman.

Virgil and Lace went to Post, Texas, to spend the winter with Lace's mother, but he couldn't find any work there, so they were back with Tom and Ettie in just a few weeks. Tom didn't know it but that was to be their last trip to Childress. At the end of October, Tom got another great shock.

Virgil had been out all day looking for work. When he came home, he was really upset. He told his dad, "A depression has started. Banks were closing. People everywhere were being laid off. Businesses were closing down. The wealthy people were losing all their money, and some had even committed suicide. It's awful. People are in a panic. They are rushing to the banks to try to get their money out before they close. Dad, what will we do if we can't find fruit to pick or cotton? The radio says factories after factories have been forced to shut down and thousands of people have lost their jobs. That there is no money to buy or sell anything. Dad, I know it's been hard but at least we have had a job and a roof over our heads, but without fruit and cotton to pick, what in the world are we going to do?"

Tom told him, "Son, I don't know. We came through one time when we didn't have anything but the few things we had in our wagon, going to a place we didn't know where it was, hoping to find work that we didn't know whether it would be there when we got there We was just trusting in God to take care of us and that's what we have to do now."

That night, Virgil and Lace told them they were expecting a baby, their first grandchild. Ettie was thrilled to death. At first Tom didn't know whether to be happy or cry. Like Monroe said about Thelma, it was just another mouth to feed and how were they going to feed it. Virgil and Lace could hardly make enough to take care of themselves. Although they had always taught Virgil he could do anything he set his head to do, he still had a crippled leg. Men that didn't have any handicap couldn't find work. It made it twice as hard on him.

Ettie again was his support. She kept telling him, "Tom, be proud of what God has given us. He has given us another daughter and now our first grandchild. Just thank God and pray it's a healthy normal child. Tom, you are so filled with hate because of what you thought you have lost, you can't see what God has given us." Tom knew he had a lot to be thankful for. Lace had been just like another daughter to them and was all their life. Like Ettie said, he couldn't see what God had given him for what he had lost.

The following week Monroe came by and told him about a job he had been offered at the cemetery that was right across the street from the house they had been renting each year. He told him, "Now, Dad, its hard work, but it's a steady job all year long and ya'll wouldn't have to run all over the country anymore." That night Ettie and Tom prayed that God would lead him in doing the right thing. Also, if it was His will for them to stay there in Sherman, that He would help him get the job. The next morning, they prayed again at the breakfast table. Monroe told him they went to work at eight o'clock, so at eight, he was down there waiting for them to show up.

When they got there, Tom asked which one was the boss, a little man about the size of Virgil said he was. He said his name was Mr. Crags. Tom told him what he was there for. He told Tom what the job consisted of, that it was a hard, dirty work.

"We dig the graves, take care of the funeral, then fill them up later on. It is a hard, dirty, and heartbreaking job. Also, we keep the cemetery clean, water the grass all summer, and anything else that comes up. In the summer it's hot, and in the winter it's cold, and we are out digging graves and working regardless to whether it's cold, hot, raining, snowing, or what. We are off on Sunday if we don't have a funeral. If we do, then two men work until we are finished, regardless of what time it is. Holidays are the same. In other words, we work anytime we are needed. We get off at five if we are through. If not, we work until we get through. Believe me, a lot of nights we are not through by then. It pays two fifty a day, six days a week, whether we work on Saturday or not." Then he asked Tom, "Do you think you will be up to that kind of hard work, and do you still want the job?"

Tom told him, "It's not whether I want the job or not, that it's whether you want me. I am use to hard work and long hours."

"In that case," Mr. Crags told him, "you are hired. When can you start?"

Tom told him, "Whenever you want me to. I am ready."

He told Tom, "I have to clear it with the city."

So they went in to his office, and he filled out all the papers that they would need, then he told Tom to report for work the next morning at eight.

Tom went home and told Ettie that he had the job and it paid two fifty a day. Tom told her, "It's not as much as we all were making, but it is just the two of us left to work now, and the job is all year long. Also, we don't have to be moving all the time. You and the children don't have to work, and we could put the two children in school and settle down to one place again. At last we would have a permanent place to stay and a roof over our head."

That afternoon they went over to see Mr. Hill and told him they would be staying all year long each year from now on. Also, Tom took some of their winter money and bought Ettie two-bedroom suits. They didn't have a place for a living room. They knew Virgil and Lace would be there for the winter, and they had to have the front room for them.

Mr. Crags was right. It was hard work. The first day they had two graves to dig for the next day. They had to dig them with a sharpshooter and a shovel. Mr. Crags showed Tom how to dig it the right size and how deep. When he got it dug and all the loose dirt taken out, they lined the sides with white material that they called grave lining material. The people that could afford it had real nice material. All the other people had a thin cheaper grade. Mr. Crags showed him how to line the wall so none of the dirt would show. After that they put a large pine box in the grave. When they finished all that, he showed Tom how to cover the pile of dirt he had taken out of the grave with a green rug that looked like grass. Mr. Crags told Tom, "We either bring clean clothes to change into for the funeral, or as close as you are, you could go home and change, as long as you are back on time." Tom told Ettie at noon. The only trouble with that was he didn't have any good clothes to change in to.

She told him, "Now, don't you worry. They will be here when you need them tomorrow."

Tom ate his dinner and went back to work. He worried all afternoon about not having any good clothes for the funeral.

That afternoon, Ettie went to town, to a men's clothing store, and told them her husband had a job and where and told them what she needed and that she didn't have enough money to pay cash, but she could pay some on them every other week until she paid them out. She also got him a good pair of shoes. When she got home she laid them on the bed. They would be there when Tom got home that night.

Mr. Crags showed Tom how to put the frame over the grave that the casket would sit on. The frame had two heavy green straps that locked each side of the frame that was for the casket to sit on. The pallbearers would set the casket on the heavy green straps. The men would stand by and wait until the funeral was over. Then two of them would go to the foot and the other two to the head of the grave. Everything was done by hand. They would undo the straps from the frame and gently lower it into the ground.

Most of the time, the people would leave while they covered it and put the flowers on the grave, but sometimes they would stay and watch them cover it up. If so, they would uncover the dirt and lower the lid on the box as gently as they could, then cover it. They always tried to shovel the dirt in real easy so it wouldn't make a lot of noise when it hit the lid. Sometimes the family would place the flowers on the grave, but most of the time the men did it. They would put the shovels and everything else back on the dirt pile behind the grave and cover them back with the green rug again. After that, if the family had stayed, the men would pay their respect to the family, then they would leave and the family could stay as long as they wanted to. It was a hard sad job, but as Mr. Crags said someone had to do it.

The next day, they would go back with a wagon drawn by two horses and remove the leftover dirt and all the other equipment. They worked from daylight to dark, a lot of the time getting everything ready for the funeral. Everything had to be ready, especially if the funeral was early in the morning. They had to get it ready before they left regardless to what time it was. Tom always went home for dinner unless they had a funeral that kept him from going.

One month, Mr. Hill came to collect his rent at noon. He apologized for being there just at noon. Ettie told him it was all right and told him to come in, and as usual, she asked him to have dinner with them. He told her if they would let him pay for it, that he could smell those red beans all the way out in the yard and he hadn't had any since his wife died. Ettie told him they would be more than glad to have him eat with them but paying was out of the question. All he wanted was red beans, corn bread, and a great big onion. Ettie had also made a bread pudding.

When they had finished eating, she told him, "You do want some bread pudding, don't you?"

You would have thought she had asked him if he wanted a million dollars.

He said, "Bread pudding, you did say bread pudding, didn't you? My wife always made me bread pudding because that was my favorite dessert." Tears came into his eyes. "I haven't had a bread pudding since she died either."

Ettie gave him a big bowl, and he just raved over it. He said, "It is just like my wife used to make for me. You know, these young people just don't know how to make bread pudding."

Ettie told him, "Well, it won't be the last one you get. I will have one made for you when you come next month to collect rent."

He asked her, "Red beans and corn bread too?"

She told him, "If that's what you want."

So it was settled. He would come next month at noon for his rent and eat dinner with them. Somehow, it got to where he would always come at noon, and Ettie would have red beans, corn bread, onion, and a bread pudding waiting for him. He acted like she had fixed him a Christmas dinner. He was so proud to get it.

Winter came and went. This was the first spring in many a year that they didn't pack and head for East Texas. It was so nice to know that they were settled down for the summer and that his family didn't have to work all summer and fall, just so they could have food for the winter. The girls were in school, and Ettie was doing a lot better. Tom thanked God again for the job and that they had a place to call home at last.

The summer was hot and dry, and the work was long and hard, but at least Tom had a job and his family didn't have to be out in the hot sun working. One month when Mr. Hill came to collect his rent, he could hardly talk. Tom could tell he was having an asthma attack. When you have gone through just one spell, it don't take you long to recognize what's going on later. He ate very little for dinner because he was having so much trouble just trying to breath.

After dinner, Tom asked him how long had he had asthma, and he told him, "For years." Then Tom told him, "Ettie can cure you of it, if you will let her and do what she tells you to do."

He told her, "If you can, I will do anything you tell me to. I have been to doctor after doctor and no one seems to know what to do."

Tom told him about the old Indian that had taught her how to make the medicine and how to take it. He said, "I will try anything, if it would cure me of it."

She told him what she would need to make it. He left promising to be back as soon as he could. Tom had to go back to work, but she sent Virgil down to the pasture to walk the creek bank for the poke roots and broomweed roots. When he got back, she scrapped it and put it on to boil.

She said, "When Mr. Hill gets back, it would have boiled enough for her to finish it."

When he got there, she had it ready to put all the other things in it, and when it was cool enough to take up, she strained it into some fruit jars. She showed him how much to put in a quart of water and told him, as the old Indian told her, "Now, when you get thirsty, drink some of this. As the old Indian said, it won't cure you in the jars. It is real bitter and don't taste a bit good, but if you will drink it, it will cure you of the asthma. The salt is for you to put in your bath water and soak each night."

By the time he came back to collect rent, he was a lot better. He brought the makings for her to make him some more medicine. By the time summer was over, he didn't have a trace of asthma at all. He was still taking the medicine. He said he was afraid to stop because he was afraid it would come back. She told him, "The old Indian said, you will know when to stop taking it."

By late fall, he told her, "I think I am ready to stop taking it, but I want you to make me a batch, for just in case." He left with his precious medicine, and all winter he told them he didn't have to take any of it. He told Tom, "I dread summer because those are my worse months."

But summer came and all summer he didn't have to take any of the medicine. He tried and tried to pay Ettie for the medicine and also for coming each month for dinner. He would tell them it's not right for him to come each month for free. He didn't want to miss his red beans and bread pudding, but he wanted to pay for it. Tom would always tell him, "Mr. Hill, God has blessed us with plenty of food, and we are always glad to share it with someone else. Now let us get another blessing by sharing it with you."

One month, he told Ettie and Tom, "Tom, why don't I just sell the house to ya'll." He told them he would take six hundred dollars for it, and he would carry the loan without any interest and the payment would still remain six dollars a month.

Tom was shocked. He told him, "Mr. Hill, you know the house is worth more than that, and you are getting the six dollars a month now. What would you gain by selling it to us?"

He told them, "The pleasure of knowing ya'll would have a roof over your heads long after I am gone. Besides I am so grateful to Ettie for the medicine and curing me of my asthma."

Ettie and Tom both told him, "We could in no way do that. The house is worth a lot more than that, and we would be cheating you, and as far as the medicine, you don't owe us anything for that."

He told them, "Think about it and we can discuss it later."

Then one Monday, when he got to work, Mr. Crags told him that "Japan had bombed Pearl Harbor and we were in war." Tom, like everyone else, was shocked. He, like everyone, was asking, "Why Lord, why?" No one thought it would last long, but America wasn't ready for a war, and it went on and on. It, like the depression, affected all of them. Nearly every family had sons to go into the services and a lot didn't come home. All America was grieving over the loss of their boys.

Factories began to open up everywhere, making different kinds of materials, guns of all kinds, and ammunition, and also training camps. People were able to find jobs again, but what a great price it was costing them in the loss of their love ones to have them.

Chapter 37

Then another disaster happened in Tom's life. He thought all the other ones were bad, but this was the worst one yet. Tom said he wish he could say that Jeff and Sallie lived happily for ever after, and Jeff did try. But somehow, he always went back to drinking. Again, he was staying gone for weeks at a time, using the excuse he was looking for work. Sallie went back to work for Mrs. Sneed. She would come by each day, but this time, she would leave to be home when Eula got out of school. She had got a larger house, one street over from the laundry. It had a big yard and some trees to shade the house, making it a lot cooler. Most of the time she would leave before Tom got home, so he didn't get to see her a whole lot.

Ettie told him, "Sallie wasn't feeling very good. It seemed like it was all she could do, just to keep going." Finely Ettie talked her into going to the doctor. That day she went. That evening, when Tom got off from work, she and Eula were at the house.

She told them, "I am going to have to have surgery. I have a tumor in my stomach, and the doctor said it had to come out. He has made the arrangements for me to go into the hospital the next afternoon, and I will have surgery the following day. My biggest concern is over Eula. I want to know if ya'll would keep her until I get out of the hospital."

Tom told her, "Sister, you know you didn't even have to ask. You know we would. Also, Ettie and I will be right there with you at the hospital."

She told him, "Tom, I knew you would. No one could have a better brother than you have been." They stayed for supper, but right after they finished she left. She said, "I have a lot of things to get done, before I go into the hospital tomorrow."

The next day she was there when Tom came home at noon and ate dinner with them. She talked all during dinner, telling them things to do just in case.

Tom told her, "Nothing is going to happen to you, and you're going to be as good as new when the doctor gets through with you."

She smiled and said, "Well, just in case, you need to know what to do."

Right after dinner, Tom walked her almost to the hospital. She kept insisting she could go by herself and that if he didn't go on to work he would be late. Finally, to please her, Tom handed her the suitcase, then kissed her on the cheek. Tom laughed and told her, "Okay, if you are going to fuss all the way, I will."

She kidded him about being a worrisome big brother, that she was a big girl now. She took the suitcase and waved. Tom told her he would bring Eula out to see her later that afternoon. As she turned to leave, she hollered back over her shoulder that she would be looking for them.

The next day the doctor operated on her. Ettie and Tom was able to stay with her until they took her in for surgery. It wasn't long before the doctor came out and told them everything had gone wrong. That it wasn't a tumor, but she was pregnant and the baby had died in the tubes. He said gangrene had set in and it had spread all over her insides and that he couldn't do anything to help her and it was just a matter of time.

He said the nurses were moving her to a room and they could stay with her until she passed away. He told them he was so sorry. He said she had come to him for years wanting to get pregnant and over and over he had told her she probably never would if she hadn't in all these years. Now the thing she had wanted so bad is what killed her. A nurse came out about that time and told them she would take them to her room. The doctor said again he was so sorry, that he did all he could but she was too far gone when they operated. "Sometimes all you can do is not enough when God is ready for us."

They went to her room and stayed there with her. Tom held her hand until she drew her last breath. She just took a deep breath and was gone. Ettie called the nurse, and they called the funeral home for them. They stayed until they got there. Mr. D., the man that owned the funeral home, came with them in his own car. He took Ettie and Tom home.

The girls had left a note telling them they had gone with Eula over to her house to get something she had forgotten. Mr. D. drove Tom on over to Sallie's house. The girls were about halfway home when they saw them. They stopped and picked up Eula. Tom told Ethel and Thelma they would meet them at the house.

The hardest thing Tom ever did was tell Eula her mother was gone. If Mr. D. hadn't been with him, he didn't know what he would have done. Tom choked up and couldn't say a word. He just took over and finished telling her. She started crying. "No, I don't believe you. She can't be gone. She was all right this morning." She clung to Tom and said, "Oh, Uncle Tom, tell me he is lying. I know that God wouldn't take her from us. We need her so."

When they got to the house, Ettie came running out and she and Mr. D. helped both Eula and Tom into the house.

Tom told Mr. D., "We will be up in a little while to make the arrangements."

He told Tom, "Tomorrow would be soon enough, around nine, if that is all right with ya'll, it would be fine with us."

Tom told him, "That was fine with us."

He told them how sorry he was and if he could do anything for them, just let him know. He left shortly after that.

Tom told Ettie and Eula that he had to go to the cemetery and let Mr. Crag know what had happened and they would need to buy a lot. Tom wanted more than one space so they all could be buried together. Mr. Crag was real kind and told Tom to take off as long as he needed to. Tom told him he needed to buy a lot with about eight grave spaces and he would need to pay it out. He told Tom that wouldn't be any problem. He showed Tom some, about two blocks west of their house, close to the street. They were in a good location, so Tom told him he would take them. They went to the office and filled out the papers.

Tom told him, "I don't know when the funeral will be. We have to go up at nine tomorrow and make the arrangements."

Mr. Crag said, "The funeral home will let me know when to dig the grave."

They went down to the lots again, and Tom showed him on which one to dig the grave.

Tom left, telling him, "I will be back to work as soon as I can."

Again Mr. Crag told him again, "Take all the time you need."

They didn't know where Jeff was. Tom told Ettie, "The only thing I know to do is go to the police station and see if they can locate him." He went and they told him they would do their best to locate him, to show their respect to Eula and Sallie and that Sallie was well respected and liked at the police station.

The police came out early the next morning before they had to go to the funeral home and told them they had found him and he would be in before that night.

They all went to the funeral home and made all the arrangements for the funeral. Tom told Ettie, "Thank God, I had taken out an insurance policy on Sallie, along with all our family, about a year ago."

Tom had seen so many people lose love ones without anything to bury them with. Ettie and Tom had talked it over and decided on the insurance policies. They had taken one out on Sallie and Eula because they knew if anything happened to them, it would be up to Tom and Ettie to see to everything. They had to pay out the cemetery lots, but thank God, the policy paid for all the funeral expense.

That afternoon Jeff came home as drunk as a skunk. They tried to sober him up, then put him to bed, hoping he would be sober and stay sober for the next day. The next morning he was sober enough to know what was going on. After breakfast Tom took him outside and gave him a good talking to. He told him, "Eula needs you now more than she ever would. How ashamed she would be if you showed up drunk for the funeral. I hope you will remember that and think of someone else rather than yourself."

He promised, "I won't drink another drop until after the funeral." If he gave his word, he would keep it, and he did stay sober for the funeral. He left right after the funeral, and they didn't see him until the next day and he had been drinking, but he was not drunk. He asked Tom, "What am I going to do? You know I am not fit to raise Eula."

Tom told him, "It is time for you to get fit, as you call it, and start being a daddy to her. Jeff, you have never thought of anyone but yourself and that bottle you swig on. She could stay with us until you make up your mind what you are going to do."

So Eula came to live with them.

Jeff didn't show up for two weeks, and he was drunk. It really upset Eula. She just cried and cried and asked, "Uncle Tom, what am I going to do? What's going to become of me?"

Tom put his arm around her and told her, "As long as we have a home, you have one as long as you want it."

She and Tom put Jeff to bed, hoping he would sober up by the next day. He was still sleeping when the girls left for school. After they left, Tom woke him up and he really bawled him out. Tom told him, "You are welcomed anytime you come to see us, sober, but do not to ever show up at our house drunk again. You know I don't approve of it, and I am not going to have it."

He started crying and said, "Tom, I never thought you would ever talk that way to me. For crying out loud I have just lost my wife."

That made Tom mad. He told him, "It's high time someone did. Eula has just lost her mother, and I have just lost my sister. We both are not drowning our self in a bottle. I don't feel any pity for you. You never were home to take care of them anyway. When things got hard, you just left. The only thing that is wrong is you are feeling guilty for not staying home and taking care of them. That it is time you thought of Eula and not of yourself."

Right after that he left, but he didn't come to see Eula drunk any more. Always from then on, when he came, he was sober. Eula continued staying with them. Tom and Ettie had Virgil, Lace, and their three children Ethel, Thelma, and Eula living in four rooms. It was crowded, but as Ettie said "We are a lot better off than a lot of people. We have a roof over our heads and plenty to eat. None of us ever went to bed hungry."

Then one week Jeff came to tell Eula good-bye. He said, "I have a job on a ranch. It is close to Comanche, Texas, and I will be leaving tomorrow. I will write you as soon as I get settled."

Eula didn't say anything, but Tom knew it broke her heart. Tom though she was hoping that he would straighten up and they could have a home again. As far as Tom knew she never heard from him. He just dropped out of sight. The years passed, and the depression went on. Everyone thought it would be over by now. Virgil couldn't find a job, he and his family tried to go back to Childress and pick cotton, but with his leg being shorter than the other, he never could pick very much. They tried but would always be back, sooner or later. Lace never once complained. She was as good to them as if she was their own daughter.

Tom still went to trades day on the first Monday of each month when he got off from work. He always had a few cows or horses to trade to make a little extra money. It never was much, but it helped them get by. On one trade day, Tom got to talking to a man and he told Tom he had several hogs he raised but they had come down with what he thought was the cholera and was all dying. That he didn't have the money to pay a veterinarian to come out and look at them.

Tom told him, "I have raised hogs and would be glad to go out and look at them."

He told Tom, "I couldn't pay you. I don't have one dime to pay you."

Tom told him, "I don't expect pay."

So they went out to his place to see them. The pens were filthy, and the water smelled to high heaven. Tom knew they didn't have cholera but were just sick from the water and filth. He told him he needed to move his pens to a cleaner place and dig another wallowing hole for them and give them some clean fresh water to drink. The man didn't like Tom telling him that and told him he wasn't going to be out one more dime on them or work either. He said, "I think the best thing is just to kill them and get them out of their misery."

Tom told him not to do that, if he was going to just kill them, to sell them to him. He told Tom, "Man, you are crazy, wanting to buy sick hogs that are half dead already. But it's your money, if you've got it to blow in, I will be glad to take it and it will save me the time and work of burying them."

So Tom bought twenty sows and two males for almost nothing. Most of them couldn't even walk. Also, he had an old wagon, and Tom bought it to haul them home in. The trade was if he would help Virgil and Tom load them.

They went back to town to get Virgil and a neighbor man to help load them. They stopped by the pasture and got two horses to pull the wagon with. When they got back to where the hogs were, the neighbor said, "You mean to bury them, not haul them, don't you? Most of them won't last until morning."

The owner said, "That's what I told him, but he bought them anyway."

Tom told him, "Now you let me worry about that."

Virgil said, "If they can be saved, Dad will save them."

The two men just laughed but didn't say another word. They got the first ones loaded and brought in. They put them close to the creek that ran through the pasture. Tom didn't have to worry about a pen right now because as weak as they were, they weren't going anywhere. While the fellows went back for another load, Tom went to town to get some medicine to give them. By the time they got back with another load, he had almost finished doctoring the first load. Being summer it didn't get dark until late, and before dark, they had them all moved and doctored. The ones that was able, went to the creek and drank and began to wallow in a shallow place just below where they had drank. The other ones, Virgil and Tom brought water up for them to drink. After that they carried water up to wash the filth off them and to cool their bodies. The next morning Virgil and Tom were up early and went down to check on them.

The worse ones were covered with sores. Virgil and Tom made a paste of sulfur and lard and rubbed all of them down real good. For two purposes, one to heal them and the other to keep the blowflies off them. Before eight, they had them all doctored and Tom was ready to go to work. Virgil went after some material and started building a pen to hold them in. Tom told him, "We have to get one built fast because it won't be long until they will be strong enough to start wondering around."

The man Tom bought them from told him, "I have been picking up garbage from the hotel there in Sherman," so Tom bought his barrels that he used. At noon Tom went to see them. He told them I have bought the hogs and would like to continue hauling off all your garbage. We will put a fresh clean barrel there every day when we pick it up and guarantee to keep it clean." Tom had a hunch by the looks of the hogs and the barrels he bought that the barrels there wouldn't look any better. They showed him where it was, and he was right. Tom told them, "From now on the barrels will be cleaned every day and they will have lids on them." The man was well pleased with what Tom said. And also Tom told them, "My son will be after the barrel before two o'clock every day and replace it with a clean barrel each time." Then Tom thanked him and left hurrying so he could get back to the house and tell Virgil what he had found out and what Virgil needed to do. Tom also told him to come back by the house and to borrow Ettie's largest washpot. For now he could take it down there to cook the scrap food in. Tom told him to make sure there wasn't any paper in it and to let it come to a good boil and boil for a while. Then put it in a clean barrel and covered. That it would be cooled when Tom got home so they could feed them each day when he got off from work. Tom also told him to make sure the barrel he took to the hotel was washed out with lye soap and hot water and then rinsed good before he took them back each day.

Tom didn't get to eat lunch, but he did get back in plenty of time to go back to work at one. After work that day, he went directly back to the pasture. Virgil had the garbage cooked off, and it was warm but still cool enough to feed them. Tom had told Virgil to pick up a sack of shorts (a hog feed) at the feed store when he came by, and they mixed some with the cooked food. They had to bucket it down the bank to the hogs. Most of them were up and hungry, so they put their medicine in the hog trough that they made by nailing two wide boards together in a V shape and nailing a board at both ends of it. They then drove two-by-fours in the ground on each end and on each side of it to keep the hogs from rooting it over. Only four of the hogs were still lying on the ground. Tom put their medicine in some of the food that he had made into a liquid and fed it to them. He had to straddle them and hold their heads up and, real slow, pour a little in their mouth at a time; but he did get each one of them to eat some.

By morning, they were still down but much better. They checked all of them, and the ones that still had sores (which was most of them) they doctored with the sulfur again. This they did every day until the sores were healed, and by then all the hogs were on their feet eating good. They had twenty good sows and two males that were looking real good and had cost them practically nothing but some hard work and patience. By the following spring, they had baby pigs running everywhere. Virgil had to make more pens for birthing pens and for the mothers and babies until they were old enough to be put in the regular pens. They had gotten some more restaurants to pick up their garbage each day. They also had built a funnel from the bank down to the hog troughs so they didn't have to carry the food down the bank. That fall they had young sholts (a young hog) plenty to carry to Fort Worth to sell. They brought a good price, and Virgil and Tom halved the profit. That gave Virgil a well-needed job and Tom some extra money to help them survive.

Virgil and his family found them an apartment just down the street from Tom and Ettie and moved. Also, that year he finally found a job. It was working pouring concrete. It paid good, but he only got to work when they had jobs to do.

He still picked up the garbage and helped take care of the hogs. Every year, the hogs brought a good price, and with his half, he and his family were able to keep their apartment. That gave Tom and Ettie more room for the girls and Ettie and him. But not for long at a time, it seemed like their house was always full of children that had lost one or the other of their parents and needed a place to stay until the remaining parent was able to take them back or put them in foster homes. Ettie never knew how many would be there for supper or how many beds she would need that night.

There were always people that needed a helping hand until they could get on their feet. One of those times, it was a man and his wife that were traveling in a covered wagon. They had asked Tom if they could camp at the side of his pasture and put their two horses in the pasture. The horses were just plain worn out and needed some rest. The man told Tom, "Mister, I don't have any money to pay you, but we need help bad. I lost my job, and we are trying to make it down to the valley where our kids are. They told us if we could make it down there, we could find a job picking fruit and vegetables. When we get down there and get a job, I will send you the money for the rent on the pasture, but right now, I have a few dollars for some groceries to get us there."

Tom, as always, told him, "Just go ahead and put the horses in the pasture and don't worry about the rent. What little they eat won't break me." He also told Thelma, "Let the man milk a half gallon of milk at night and leave it with them before you bring the cow up to the house." Thelma always brought the cow to the house at night so Tom could milk and feed her.

Then in the morning after Tom milked and before Thelma went to school, she would take the cow to the pasture.

They were there about a week when it came a real bad ice storm. It rained and sleeted all day, and all that night, everything was frozen. When Virgil went down to feed the hogs. He came back by and told his dad that the people were about frozen, that their wagon was leaking, and they didn't have a place to even build a fire to stay warm.

Tom told Ettie, "I am going down to see about them. They must not only be cold but hungry."

Ettie told him, "Tom, I don't know where we could put anyone else in this house, all the beds are full."

They sat down to eat supper, but neither Ettie nor Tom could eat. They kept thinking of those poor cold hungry souls. Finally, Ettie pushed away from the table and said, "Tom, go get them. I've been thinking where I could put them. I can put a bed in the kitchen for them. It's not much, but at least it will be dry and warm. While you go get them, I will fix supper for them. I can't eat knowing they are down there cold and hungry."

Tom went down, and sure enough, their wagon had leaked and they were almost frozen. Tom brought them back, and Ettie had supper ready for them. They were cold as well as starving. Virgil was right. They hadn't been able to build a fire because all the wood they had was so wet it wouldn't burn and besides with it raining they had no place to get out of the rain to build it. After they had eaten, with tears in his eyes the man told them, "We had been praying for a miracle. And that we had almost given up hope of surviving." When Tom got there, they knew God had answered their prayer. As long as they were there, she helped Ettie do all the cooking and cleaning the house. He took over tending to the hogs, milking the cow, cutting the wood, and doing up all the night work. They stayed until the weather broke, and it got warm enough to go on. They were both so grateful. They kept thanking them over and over again. They said if it hadn't been for them they would have frozen to death. Tom tried to tell them, it wasn't much of a place to offer them. But the man said, "Let me tell you this, Tom. When you are cold, hungry, and thinking you won't make it another day, then what you offered us looked like a little piece of heaven that God had sent down to us."

There were many other times that they were called upon to go farther than they thought they could go, but God always provided a way and the means for them to do them. No one was ever turned down or out. Tom said, he guessed the funniest one was when another covered wagon came by the pasture and the man asked if they could stay there a few days and rest their horses, and of course, Tom told them they could. It was a man and his wife and several children.

He then said, "Sir, I hate to ask another favor of you, but would you please let us put our dog down on the creek, close to the water, and in a shady place. You see we are from the north, and the dog is not used to hot weather. If we don't get him to a cool place, I think we are going to lose him."

They walked around to where the dog was lying, and Tom could see he was in real bad shape. He was panting real hard, just trying to breath. He had real thick fur, and the hot weather was too much for him. Tom told him they could, and the kids pulled him on a cardboard box all the way down to the creek right next to the water and into a good shady spot. The kids told Tom the dog's name was Butch. Tom told the kids, "Butch would make it a lot better if ya'll would cut all that shaggy wool off him."

They said, "Mister, we know he would, but we don't have any scissors to cut it off with."

So one of the older boys followed Tom up to the house to borrow a pair of scissors. The next day they had sheared him, and he was breathing a lot better. Tom told the boys, "Get some of the pig food and feed him." He ate like he was starved to death. The people stayed for about two weeks, and the dog continued to get better, but only because he was in a cool place and where he could get into the cool water when he got hot.

Then one night when Tom went to get the cow, they told him that they had to move on. But they just couldn't take the dog. The man asked Tom if he would let him stay there until winter and if they were able to come back through here, they would pick him up again. With those little kids standing there begging him to keep him so he wouldn't die, Tom as usual just couldn't say no. So now he had a dog, which he didn't need, along with the hogs.

Butch didn't bother the hogs, unless one got out, then he would put it back in to the pen in no time flat. He turned out to be a lot of help. They didn't have to worry about anyone trying to steal any of them. If anyone he didn't know came close to the pigpens, he would chase them out in no time flat. He hadn't been there very long when they learned how protective he really was with them.

Virgil hadn't been down to the pasture in a long time. A boy had come by one day that had been whipped really badly by his father. He told them, "My daddy would get drunk and would beat me. I decided I was not going to take another one of his beatings, so I ran off." He asked if he could stay there and work for just his room and board until he got old enough to join the service in a year or two. So, naturally, Tom took him in. Virgil was working steady now, so Tom let him start going after the garbage and feeding the hogs. Butch took up with the boy and ran to the wagon to meet him and hung around with him all the time he was getting the feed ready for the hogs. The boy's name was Dick, and he would always pick out special food for the dog. They had created a special bond between the two of them, both needing someone to love. Always after Dick finished his jobs he would wave to Butch. Butch would go back to the hogs as if that was his job to take care of them.

One night, Dick didn't get back to go get the garbage and tend to the hogs. He had told them that he was going that day to see about signing up for the army, but he would be back as soon as possible. Virgil had come over and had agreed to go in his place. He got the garbage, and when he got to the pasture, he got off the wagon and started unloading the garbage and here came Butch to welcome the boy. When he saw someone strange there at the wagon, for a second he just stood there with his head turned to one side, as if trying to figure out what he was doing there. Finally, he started growling, as if he had figured out the problem that he didn't know what this strange man was there for, but in any case, he didn't belong there. He started barking and growling. Virgil started talking to him, but he saw right away that the dog wasn't going to buy any part of that. Virgil started backing up toward the closest tree, just in case he needed it, and it didn't take him long to decide he would need it. Butch kept coming toward him, backing him up. When he got to the tree, Virgil grabbed for the lower branch and the dog made a lunge for him. Virgil just barely managed to get high enough to keep the dog from grabbing his leg. The dog stayed there, keeping him treed. Every time Virgil made a sound, Butch was up growling and lunging at the tree to make him climb a little higher.

When Tom came home, Ettie told him she was worried about Virgil, that he had come by the house with the garbage and had stopped to pick up what garbage she had about an hour and a half ago. Tom told her usually it took a little over an hour and with him not tending to them in a while it would probably take him a little longer but that if he wasn't back by the time they ate supper he would go look for him. Well, he wasn't back, and Ettie told him she was going with him that she knew something was wrong or he would have been back by now. Tom tried to talk her out of it, but she would have no part in it. She told him, "Now, Tom, I am going and I mean right now. I just know something is wrong, or he would be back by now." She grabbed a washcloth, a towel, some bandages, her coat; and out the door she went. Tom had to almost run to keep up with her.

When they got there, Butch came running over to them and sat down in front of them and started whining as if to say, "I got the scoundrel, and he didn't get any of our hogs either. Now what are you going to do with him?"

Tom, always kidding, hollered at Virgil, "What are you doing up in that tree, boy? You are supposed to be tending to the hogs."

Virgil hollered back, "I would have but that dad blasted dog won't let me down. You didn't tell me you had a watch dog down here now. You at least could have told me the password to get by him. He has kept me treed ever since I got here, and I am about frozen. He wouldn't let me stop long enough to get my coat before he put me up here."

Tom looked at Ettie and winked and said, "I 'swaney,' Ettie, I have forgot the password to make Butch let him down. Oh well, I will think of it before I get the hogs fed, if not I know I will before tomorrow," and he turned to leave. He looked back and said, "You will be all right until I think of the password, won't you?"

Virgil shouted back at him, "Now look here, Dad, I am cold, aggravated, and hungry. And I am in no mood for your monkey play. Now you call that dad blasted dog off me so I can get down."

Ettie as usual said, "Now, Tom, you stop your foolishness and call Butch over here so Virgil can get down."

Tom had to get the last word in. He said, "Oh, all right, but I didn't have anything to do with putting him up there." He called Butch and talked to him and told him, nice dog and that it was all right for him to let the thief down now. Virgil came down grumbling. Tom brought Butch over and patted Virgil on the shoulder and kept talking to Butch about Virgil. It wasn't long until Butch was wagging his tail and was just as friendly as a puppy with two tails toward Virgil. They went on feeding the hogs, and Tom told Virgil, "You feed him his supper now so he will remember you." Virgil did, and it wasn't long until Butch and Virgil was close bosom buddies. Before they were through feeding the hogs, Butch was following him everywhere and Virgil took a liking to him also.

Dick did get into the service that day, and in a few days, he was gone. Virgil took back over feeding the hogs. Butch was always waiting for him when he got there. In the weeks that followed the two of them had developed a special bond between them. Butch stayed right with him all the time he was there and rode in the wagon to the gate with Virgil every time. When Virgil got out to open the gate, Butch would jump out of the wagon and wait until Virgil got back on the wagon and started toward the house, Virgil would always holler, "Bye, Butch, see you tomorrow. Now you go back and watch the hogs." He would turn and go back to the hogs, but he would always be waiting upon the bank the next day when Virgil got there

The weather began to turn bad, and Virgil was worried about Butch being down there in the cold. Tom tried to tell him that Butch was used to cold weather, but Virgil kept wanting to bring him up to the house. He told his dad, "Butch could stay there in the backyard, and besides, we had someone to come into the house just this week and had almost stole my pants with my billfold in them." Virgil woke up while the thief was trying to get them and hollered. The thief dropped the pants in the kitchen and fled before anyone could get awake to see him good. Virgil and his family had moved back into the front bedroom and the girls were back in the little bedroom at the back of the house. The thief ran through that bedroom and out the back door to the backyard. Virgil argued, "Butch was needed worse up here than he was watching the hogs." So Tom agreed, and that night, Virgil brought Butch home with him. Virgil fixed him a little swinging door so he could get into the house or out in the yard either one. That put a stop to their thief coming in the backyard or house either. After that Virgil and Butch would go pick up the garbage and then go down to feed the hogs. Butch was as happy as he could be with the arrangement as long as he was with Virgil.

Then one month, Mr. Hill didn't show up for his rent. A few days later a man came out and told Ettie he was Roy Grant. He was Mr. Hill's lawyer and that Mr. Hill had died and he needed to see both Mr. and Mrs. Brisco in his office that afternoon if possible.

When Tom came home for dinner, Ettie told him. They weren't busy, so he told Mr. Crags and asked him for the afternoon off. When they got there, the lawyer told him Mr. Hill had left the house to them and they were to pay his niece five hundred dollars if they wanted it. There were no houses to rent anywhere since the Air Force field had opened up in Sherman, so they went to the bank to see if they could get a loan to buy it. The house would bring twice that much or more. So they loaned them the whole amount. So the thing Mr. Hill had wanted all these years had been completed. Tom and Ettie at last owned the little house on Lamar.

Everything was going real good until another problem occurred. One morning Tom went out to milk the cow and there was one of Ettie's hens out. He checked the henhouse and the door was still locked. When he took the milk in to Ettie to strain and put in the ice box, he made mention to her that one of her hens was left out of the henhouse last night. Nothing more was said about it, but the next morning he noticed another hen in the yard that was left out. Again, he told Ettie, and this time she told him that she had put them in the henhouse herself and made sure the door was locked. Also, she was real careful to make sure she got them all in. They both went out to see what was going on.

When she saw the hen, she said, "Tom, that is not my hen."

Tom laughed at her and said, "Now come on and admit you left her out. How do you think she would have opened the door and got out, then shut it back by herself?"

Ettie told him, "I don't know, but don't you know I would know my own hens, for goodness sake. I have raised them all from baby chickens myself."

Tom laughed at her, but all day he worried about it. As much as Ettie babied her chickens, he was pretty certain she would know each one of them. He wondered all day if the person who tried to steal Virgil's pants could have gotten mad because they had brought up a watch dog and had decided to get even with them.

That night, he stayed up until after midnight but saw nothing unusual. The next morning when he went out to milk the cow, sure enough there was another hen. When he took the milk in, he told Ettie she had another hen. He told her, "I think someone is trying to get us in trouble for stealing chickens."

She told him, "But, Tom, we are not stealing them."

He said, "I know that and you know that, but can we prove it. The chickens are here in our yard. If we are not real busy today, I will ask to get off and go to the police station and report it."

When he told his boss what was happening, he told him, "Go ahead and report it. It does sound like someone is trying to get you in trouble. The sooner you report it, the better it will be. With you not knowing, when they plan on trying to report it, the sooner the police hear your side of the story the better off you will be."

So he took off and went to the police station and told them what was happening. They wrote all the information down, then told him, "Mr. Brisco, we agree with you. It seems like someone is trying to get you in trouble. You did the smart thing in coming to us. Now when they try their little scheme, we will be ready for them and it won't be you but them that get into trouble. You go ahead about your business, and don't worry about it. You let us take care of this."

Tom went on back to work and told his boss what they had said and that they told him to let them handle it and for him not to worry.

But he did worry. The next morning there was another chicken out in the yard. He told Ettie but tried not to let on that he was worried. He worried all day about it. Who hated him enough to pull a stunt like this? When he got off from work, he went back to the police station and again reported the stolen chicken.

The police chief said, "We will send out some men to watch the yard and see if they can catch them. They will slip in after dark. Now if you hear anything, don't pay any attention. We will try to slip in without making any noise, but you know how that is, so you all just go about your business as if nothing had happened."

They stayed that night and several more and nothing happened. Each morning when Tom went out to milk, there were no strange chickens running around. Finally, the police chief came out and told them that undoubtedly whoever who was doing it knew they were watching. He told them, "More than likely they wouldn't have any more trouble since he knew we were on to him. Just let us know if anything else happened."

The next morning when Tom went out to milk, sure enough there was another strange chicken. Tom was beginning to really get upset. Who would keep doing this thing? Who would dislike them that much?

Again, when he got off from work, he went to the police station. The police chief told him, "We are as baffled as you are. We have no clue to what's going on. I will assign a patrol car to check on that area all night and see if we can catch him as he brings the chicken in. He has got to be walking, or you all would have heard him. So maybe we will catch him with the chicken."

Again, they watched the house all night, and again, they reported they saw nothing strange and there was no chicken either. But the next morning, after they stopped patrolling, there was a chicken. This went on for several weeks. When they patrolled it, there was no chickens. When they didn't, there would always be a chicken the next morning. It was about to drive all of them crazy. Tom decided to take the matters into his own hands and stay up all night. He would watch from the window to see if he could catch them. About midnight he must have dozed off. All of a sudden something woke him. He looked out, just in time to see Butch clear the fence with a chicken in his mouth. He set the chicken down, ran off, and never made a sound. Tom went outside, and Butch came running to him wagging his tail and looking like he was trying to say, "Look, I brought your dinner to you again." Tom rubbed his neck and said, "Well, I declare, you old rascal. No wonder your owner was so sad to leave you, they taught you to steal chickens for them."

When Ettie got up, he told her he had caught the thief. She was as shocked as he was and asked Tom, "What are we going to tell the police?" Tom as usual had that figured out already and told her, "The truth, we will tell them the truth." That night Tom went to the police station, the chief saw him coming and met him at the door. He opened the door for him and said, "Well, Tom, what's wrong now?" Tom, always being a cut up, thought he would have a little fun. He said, "You won't believe it, but last night I caught the thief." All the police force that had been assigned to the case had been so worried and upset. The chief said, "Wait a minute" and he told his secretary to have, and he called several names, to come into his office right now. When they got there, he told them, "Tom has caught the thief."

Several started talking at once. They said, "We don't believe it. We have tried everything in the book, and we couldn't find a clue."

The chief told Tom, "Now you tell us how you did it."

As always, Tom, being a cut up, made it sound more elaborate than it really was; and by the time he got through, the chief, as well as all the men, were just about rolling in the floor with laughter.

The chief said, "Now, Tom, what are you going to do with all those chickens you have?"

Tom didn't crack a smile. He looked at the chief and said, "Well, sir, when your boys solve a crime, you confiscate the stolen goods, right? Well, I thought since I solved the crime for them, the least your boys could do is to confiscate the stolen goods and find out who they belong to."

All the boys began to holler, "Not on your life. Can you just see us going all over town asking at every house has any one stolen any chickens from them?"

The chief said, "Tom, you just keep them, and if any one complains about losing that many chickens, and if they find out who did it, we will do our dead level best to keep them from hanging you and the dog too."

The next day Virgil took Butch back to the pasture, thus ending the case of the stolen chickens. Tom never did learn how the chief wrote out his report on it and how it was solved, but he kind of thought that was one case that was never put into the files.

It was several years before Leola forgave him enough to come back, and her husband never did forgive him. When they did come, Tom got the impression it was to see Ettie and Thelma and not him. There was always that dislike between her husband and Tom, and neither one could do anything right in each other's eyes.

They stayed a few weeks, and it was hard for her husband and Tom to stay under the same roof together. Everything Tom did was wrong in his eyes, and everything he did was wrong in Tom's eyes. They were like two small boys fighting over a toy that one had taken from the other that both clamed, and neither one was willing to give it up. Leola and Ettie were hoping after all this time they would be able to solve their problems and both learn how to forget and forgive. It seemed one was just as stubborn as the other one. Neither one would give an inch. Leola left with a broken heart.

Not too many years later the police again came out to Tom's house. This time they brought news about Jeff. They told Eula he had been working on a ranch in Comanche, Texas. The people on the ranch told the police, he had been working for them several years, then one payday he collected his money and went to town.

He didn't say one word about quitting, but Monday morning he didn't show up for work. They said they hadn't thought anything about it because they had men to do that before. But right after the spring thaw, a man found him in a ditch where he had fallen and frozen to death. The police told Eula, they had checked him for foul play but he didn't have a bruise on him and he still had his billfold on him. They said the week he disappeared, they had a real bad snowstorm. They just figured he had started home and fell in the ditch and couldn't get up. They told Eula as for as they knew he hadn't been drinking and wasn't drunk. Tom thought they told them that because of Eula, to keep from hurting her any more than she was already hurt. They had already buried him out there. The police told them he was so decomposed that they buried him as soon as they were through with the autopsy.

Tom was determined he wasn't going to make the same mistake with Ethel, Eula, and Thelma as he did with the first three. This time he would take time to be with them. As tired as he was, when he got home at night, he would take them to different things that were going on. In the summertime there was always something to do. On Friday and Saturday night, there were baseball games in the park, and every month band concerts going on in different parks. People would take their quilts and sit on the ground, listening to different bands play. People didn't have any money to pay to go to anything, and all this was free.

Thelma and Tom really enjoyed the ball games, but Eula and Ethel didn't care too much for them. On those nights, they told Tom they would just walk around to see who was there that they knew. They were teenagers, and they thought they had Tom fooled. He remembered he was a teenager once and knew they were looking at the boys they didn't know and were hoping to get acquainted with some of them and not those they already knew. So Tom just played dumb, like he believed them, and let them walk with all the other boys and girls that were hoping to meet someone also.

They did seem to enjoy the band concert. Tom thought it was mostly because there were plenty of good-looking boys playing in it and not the music. Also, in the summer there was always swimming. Ethel and Eula did go with Tom and Thelma some, but they didn't like it because it got their hair wet. It mostly was Virgil's girls, Thelma and Tom. In the cool months Tom and Thelma would go coon hunting and horseback riding. Thelma had taken Leola's place of helping Tom train coon dogs and going with him coon hunting. Leola could skin a coon as fast as Tom and just as good. But Thelma never did learn to skin them. She would stretch them on the frames and help hang them on the side of the shed to dry but skinning them was another thing.

She was Tom's sidekick just like Leola had been. The days Tom had to take the dead flowers off the graves, he let her go with him and she would drive the wagon for him while he went from grave to grave picking up the flowers and throwing them in the back of the wagon. They would go from street to street with Tom walking, picking up all the trash and Thelma driving, telling the horses to get up and whoa. It was years later before Thelma learned the horses were trained for that job and would have gone whether she was on the wagon or not. But it was fun being with Tom, and he always told her how much help she was. Years later she would laugh and tell him, well, she guessed she was a lot of help and they would laugh and kid each other. She guessed it was better than just going along all day saying "Get up" and "Whoa."

Not too many weeks after that, things changed again. Eula was prowling through Sallie's trunk and found some papers that Sallie had hid. It was at the back of the top of the trunk. Eula thought it was a place in the lining that had come loose and her mother had sewed it up. Eula ran her hand over it remembering the love her mama showed when she made things for her. She felt something in the lining and noticed it had been whipped together so it could be taken out. She pulled the thread out and saw there were some papers tucked inside. She took them out and discovered it was the adoption papers that Sallie had worked so hard and saved money for until she got enough saved to get them, making Eula her very own daughter. Sallie was so proud of them. They were what made Eula her lawful daughter. She took the papers to Ettie and asked her, "What do they mean? Am I really not my mama's child and only an adopted child?"

Ettie tried to explain to her and told her, "Sallie couldn't have loved you any more if she had given birth to you." Ettie told her the story that Sallie told her, about when she first saw Eula standing there with tears running down her cheeks and how lost she seemed to be. How it was like God had spoken to her and told her, "You have been praying for a baby, well, I am giving you this little one and she needs you so badly." She wanted to hear all about the story and why her real mama had abandoned her. Ettie told her the whole story as Sallie had told her. She finally told her how proud of these papers she was. Ettie told her, "I remember how she had brought them over and showed them to me. She said, 'Look, sister, now Eula is my very own little girl and no one can ever take her from me.'"

She asked Ettie, "Then Jeff is my real father, but Mama just took me and raised me as her very own daughter?"

Ettie told her, "And no one could have loved you more. She loved you as if you were her very own, that she had given birth to you."

She didn't ask any more questions, but it seemed from then on she had changed toward them. Then one day when Tom came in, she told him she wanted to talk to him. She told him, "Mrs. Sneed and another lady that Mama had worked for had helped me fill out the papers to go into an orphanage home. It is not right for you to work so hard to support me with all the other ones that you have to take care of. Uncle Tom, you work so hard supporting all of us, and with me gone, it will be one less for you to have to take care of. I have wanted to continue with my voice and music lessons, and this will give me that chance. Mrs. Sneed thought I would have more time, but she found out I have to go before my birthday or I can't get in as I would be too old. Even now, if it wasn't for Judge Sneed and his wife, they wouldn't have taken me." She told him she would be going right away. With tears running down her cheeks, she told him, "Now, Uncle Tom, you know I love you just as if you were my real uncle, but it's not fair for you to have to work so hard to support me when you need that money for your own family."

Tom told her, "Now you know you have a home here as long as you want it."

She told him, "Yes, I do know, but I think I need to try to make it on my own, and this is a good opportunity for me. That it was only because of the Sneed's helping the home that they will take me anyway. You know I appreciate all you and Aunt Ettie have done for me, and I will never forget it. I will always love you both, but you and Aunt Ettie both have to work so hard, and this way it will be one less mouth for you all to have to feed."

Mrs. Sneed and the other lady had agreed to sponsor her. So one day Mrs. Sneed and the other lady came over and took Eula shopping for the clothes she would need, and in a few days, they came to get her and took her to the orphan's home. At first she wrote regularly and told all about the home. She told them they raised their own food and had their own milk cows and hens. The boys did the outside work, and the girls did the inside work. They helped do the cooking, canning, washing the dishes, cleaning the kitchen, churning the milk, and helping to take care of the younger children. Each week they were assigned to the job they would do all week. "Oh, and by the way, Aunt Ettie, we churn our milk in a washing machine that they bought just for that purpose." She told her, she sure was glad that they would have never gotten it all churned without it.

Then school started, and the letters got fewer and farther apart. She said she was sorry, but with her schoolwork, her music, and choir practice, she stayed so busy that she didn't have much time to write. Once in a while she got to come and see them in the summer months, but mostly she traveled with the choir going from church to church, singing. She had a beautiful voice, and she wrote. She was doing really good with her music and voice lessons.

The years passed. She and Ethel finished school, and shortly afterward, Ethel got married and the letters stopped coming from Eula.

Several years passed then one day Tom got a letter from her telling him she was coming to Sherman and wanted him to see if he could help her get her birth certificate. A few days later she came. She told them, "I have signed up to go into the service if I can get my birth certificate." She told them, "I married a boy that was in the home right after we finished collage. We were doing good until he started drinking. I told him, I watched my daddy work my mother to death with very little to eat or wear and finally caused her death with his drinking all the time and that I was not going to put up with it. I gave him a choice. It was either me or the bottle. I gave him three chances, and the third time I left him and divorced him. Now I am going to start a new life for myself without him. I know divorcing him wasn't right. But, Uncle Tom, every time he came in drunk, I saw my mother and what she went through and I just couldn't take it."

Tom helped her get her birth certificate, and shortly after that she left again. Tom and Ettie didn't hear from her any more until years later. She came by to see them and told them she had married again. They were both schoolteachers and had a family and was real happy.

Tom always had a way of telling you something or teaching you a lesson that you needed to know without anyone else knowing what was going on. One of those times, Thelma said she would never forget that all her life when things came up that she had to make an important decision, she would always think of it. She was about seventeen when Jim, a boy that had been raised in the neighborhood, started coming over to the house. Ettie and Lace wanted to go see Leola real badly, and Tom got him to drive their car and take them to see her. He was a truck driver, and Tom trusted his driving. Of course, Thelma went along as she always did each summer when she got a chance to go see Leola. They stayed almost a week, with Leola's boys, Jim, and Thelma roaming the woods. The boys hunted for squirrels or anything else they could kill to eat. Leola had taught both of them how to shoot, how to hunt and fish, and how to swim; and they were good at it all. Besides that, they would roam the woods looking for sweet gum trees that was about all the gum they ever had. It was bitter and not at all good, but after a while you got use to the bitter taste.

At the end of the week and by the time they came home, Jim was head over heels in love with Thelma. He came over after work almost every day and kept asking her to marry him. Each time she would tell him no, that she was too young to get married and besides she didn't love him. That didn't stop him. He told her he loved her enough for both of them and she would learn to love him later. After a while, he started telling her if she didn't marry him, he was going to kill himself, that he didn't want to live without her. She tried to reason with him, but the more she tried, the worse it got. And finally, he told her he would give her until the following Sunday to make up her mind. School had started, and Thelma told her best girlfriend Liz what a mess she had gotten herself in. They talked about it each day walking back and forth to school. They agreed it wouldn't be right to let him kill himself but neither one knew what to do. Liz came over on Sunday afternoon to see if Thelma had made up her mind on what she was going to do. Of course, Liz thought it was real romantic, having a boy saying he was going to kill himself if she didn't marry him and told Thelma so. They were sitting out on the front porch discussing it with no one else around. Liz said that was the only decent thing she could do as she sure didn't want him to kill himself.

Before they could say anything else, Tom appeared at the front door and hollered, "How would you all like to go swimming?" It was a really hot day, and Thelma didn't know too many teenagers that would turn down a chance like that. So she and Liz jumped up and ran into the house, changed clothes, and were ready to go. The swimming place was the creek that ran through Tom's pasture, up above the hogpens. It was deep and always cool but not ice cold like the one at Leola's. By the time they got to Tom's pasture, they had several more kids that had joined them. When they got there, they all jumped in including Tom. He swam out to the middle of the creek where it was real deep and hollered for Thelma to come to him. She could swim but not a long distance because she would get out of breath. Tom had always warned her never swim out where she couldn't touch the bottom because of this. She thought it was funny because he had always scolded her before if she got out far enough that she started getting short of breath. And today, he told her to come to him, that he would hold her until she got her breath, so she could swim back. She swam out, and sure enough by the time she got there, she had begun to get short of breath. In place of him reaching out and holding her like he said he would, he just swam off and left her struggling. He just swam on to the bank and sat there, watching her struggling for her life. She would start to go under and would stop and dog paddle for a while until she got her breath and then go on.

By the time she got to the bank, she was so mad at her daddy and hurt because he had told her he would catch her. By the time she got there she was almost crying because her feelings were so hurt. She sat down beside him and was almost yelling at him. She told him, "Why didn't you catch me? You told me you would. You left me out there struggling for my life, and you knew I couldn't make it." He told her, and as long as she lives she would never forget it, he looked up with that serious look that he had and said, "Thelma, let this be a lesson to you. Don't let anyone ever persuade you to do anything that you know is wrong or that will mess up your own life. Just remember your life is the most precious thing you have, guard it and protect it and don't let anyone ever tell you or threaten you to do anything to mess it up. Always remember you can't replace your life. It is a precious gift from God, so always protect and treasure it. As everyone else should do, but you can't make their decisions for them. Their life is theirs. If they have the sense that God gave a goose, they will protect it as you do yours."

She knew he had overheard what was going on and knew he was helping her to make the right decision without saying a word about it. That night when Jim came, she told him her answer was no, that her life was the most precious gift she had and she was not going to let him or anyone else threaten her in doing anything to mess it up. She told him she didn't want him to kill himself, "but just remember that will be your own decision, that the life God gave to you is also the most precious gift you have also and you can't replace it. I am not and will not ever be responsible for what you do with your life, so don't blame me if you don't have sense enough to know it is the only life you will ever have, and you should guard and protect it." He left with tears running down his cheeks, and he never came back again, but he didn't kill himself either. Years later she heard he had married and had a real nice family.

The next few years of Tom's and Ettie's life made a drastic change. Their last daughter got married. Tom knew she and the boy she was going with was getting serious, but he wasn't prepared for what happened. One Sunday the boy came to the house and asked her where her daddy was. She told him her daddy was in the backyard, and he went on out to where he was. He spoke to Tom and started hem hawing around. Tom knew something was up. After a while he blurted out, "Mr. Brisco, I am planning on getting married." This just about floored Tom. He knew what he was getting around to, but Tom as usual couldn't pass up a chance like this. So he thought he would play along with him for a while. He told him that was real nice, that every boy ought to find him a good girl and marry and settle down some time. He asked him, "Who is the lucky girl?"

After much hem hawing around, he blurted out, "Well, sir, I was hoping to marry Thelma. I haven't asked her yet. I wanted to ask you first."

Tom looked at him and grinned and said, "Well, son, I think you had better ask her then." He turned real fast and headed for the house. Tom, laughing, told Ettie about it later; and she got all over him and told him, "Tom, you ought to be ashamed of yourself. Don't you remember how scared we were when we were going to tell maw."

Tom thought back with tears in his eyes and told Ettie, "Where have all these years gone? It seems like that was only yesterday that I was taking you home to the ranch as my bride."

That Friday afternoon Thelma came down to the cemetery. She was real excited and handed Tom a paper. Tom asked her what it was, and she told him it was her marriage license and that she wanted him to be the first one to see it. He sent Ettie to town to get a dress that Thelma had on layaway to get married in. He also told her to pick up a pretty gown and some underclothes.

That Saturday they got married, and Thelma thought automatically that he would be there, but he told her he had to work, so Tom didn't go to the wedding. But when they came back to the house to leave, Ettie said he was in the backyard, repairing the chicken coop.

Thelma's feelings were hurt, and she asked her mother about it, and she said, "Well, Thelma, don't you know why he wasn't there? He knew that everyone else there would have dress clothes on and he wouldn't embarrass you by showing up with work clothes on."

It just broke Thelma's heart, but she pretended with him, that she thought he really had to work. But she always remembered her daddy not having enough money to buy himself a pair of dress pants and shirt, but he saw that she and Ettie both had a dress for the wedding and Thelma had a nice gown and underclothes.

Again, Tom's sidekick was married and left to start a life of her own. Ettie tried to tell Tom, that their kids were not their own to keep forever but a gift from God to raise and enjoy for a season. Then they would grow up and start their own life with their own husband or wife, having their own home and their own children. Tom told her, "Ettie, I know that, but it don't make it any easier."

Chapter 38

THEIR HOUSE WAS ALWAYS FULL of children and laughter; now how quiet and lonely the old house was. Very few people came by for food or help any more. With the war over, people had been able to get jobs. Tom and Ettie had grown old together. They had told him at work that he was going to have to retire. He had been having trouble with his heart. He had lied for years about his age, but now that social security had gone through and he had to fill out a complete history of his age and birth. He couldn't lie any more about it. So, one day, his boss for thirty-six years called him into the office and told him, "Tom, I think it's about time for you to retire." Tom didn't know what to say. He finally said, "When?" and his boss said, "Today." So Tom was out of a job for the first time in thirty-six years. His boss told him, "You will be able to draw your social security and your retirement from the city." Also, his boss volunteered to help him fill out the paperwork for it. For the first time he was out of work with nothing to do.

He finally started doing little jobs for rich widow women who wanted some extra work in keeping up their love ones' lots. It was all volunteer, and they just gave him a tip each time they got him to do something. It was on one of these times that our final story took place.

A widow woman came to the house to get Tom to go with her to show him where her husband was buried. She told him she was going to be gone for several weeks. That she had never left him before and she had made arrangements for the floral shop to put flowers on his grave each week. All she wanted Tom to do was check it each day and make sure they did. She wanted him to remove the old flowers and anything else to keep it nice while she was gone. In talking to her, Tom saw she kept looking at his hands. All of a sudden, she said, "Mr. Brisco, can I ask you a question?" Before he could say anything, she said, "I couldn't help but notice your old, rough, wrinkled, callused hands. Aren't you ashamed of them looking that way?"

Tom looked at his hands, then he said, "Let me tell you a story about these old rough, wrinkled, callused hands." And he told her this story. "With these old rough, wrinkled, callused hands, I raised five children to be grown. I taught them how to work hard for what they wanted, have respect for themself, to believe in God, and to love and respect their fellowman. Not one of them has ever been into any kind of trouble with the law. They have never stolen, cheated, or harmed any one. They have always worked for what they have, helped their neighbors, loved and respected God. I didn't have money to buy wood, but I borrowed one of the neighbor boy's little red wagon and with these old rough, wrinkled, callused hands, cut wood and hauled it to a sick man and his wife. With these same old rough, wrinkled callused hands, I built a fire for them, then took the little wagon and pulled it to town and went from grocery store to grocery store asking for help to get groceries for them. This wasn't the first time I did it, and not one store ever turned me down. When I asked them to help me, with people that were in need. With these old hands, I went by and got Ettie and we pulled the wagon over to their house. Ettie made soup, and we both fed them and then took turns staying with them day and night until they were well.

"We took in the sick and cared for them until they got well or died. We took in little babies that had lost one of their parents and cared for them until the surviving parent could take them back, and do you know, not one of them ever notice these old rough hands when I was caring for them. Not one of the little babies that I bathed, changed their diapers, and fed, or just sat and rocked at night when they were sick or just confused ever complained or refused to let me help them because of these old rough, wrinkled, callused hands. I never had one person that was in need to tell me, 'No Mr. Brisco, we won't take any help from you because your hands are so rough, callused, and chapped.'"

He went on to tell her, "During the flu episode, when people were dying on every hand, because they couldn't get whiskey to take for it, I risked a jail sentence. But with these old rough, callused, chapped hands, I made whiskey for the poor who couldn't get it or afford it. Where I was raised, whiskey was their main medicine. It was used for tooth ache, flu, cuts, and just about everything for humans and animals. It was considered a medicine, and they made their own. The man that raised me taught me how to make it, and the whiskey was as clear and pure as you could buy anywhere."

Tom told her, "When my family took the flu and the doctor came out, he asked me if we had plenty of whiskey. He had to know I was making it because the house reeked with the fumes. I didn't lie to him, but told him I do now. Then the doctor asked me if I had any to spare. I gave him a quart, and he told me to keep up the good work and he would see me tomorrow. But he was back that afternoon. He told me, 'Mr. Brisco, I know you are making whiskey. I smelled it way before I got to the door. I had it checked and it is as pure as any I have ever seen. I took it to the police station and got a permit for you to make it as long as we need it. That way you won't get in trouble. We need it desperately and can't get enough to fill our needs.' Back then they didn't have all these medicines that they have today. Whiskey was one of the best medicines they had to fight the flu. The doctor told me he had opened an account with a store in my name and to get what I needed to make it as long as it was needed."

Tom went on to tell her, "We shared our home, our food and our love with all that needed it." Tom looked down at his hands he turned the palms up. She was right. They were, just what she said they were—ruff, wrinkled, callused. And then he told her, "To answer your question, no, ma'am, I am not a bit ashamed of these old, rough, wrinkled, callused hands. In fact I am a little proud of them."

He went on to say, "Now let me ask you a question, I couldn't help but notice your smooth, pretty lily-white hands. Now tell me what have you ever done with your hands?"

She looked up with tears in her eyes and said, "You know, Mr. Brisco, you make me so ashamed of myself because I have never done anything with them but pamper myself. I have had plenty of money and time and I could have. But I was too selfish, but from now on, thanks to you, I will try to make my life count for the Lord." Then she thanked him for sharing his story with her.

A few months later, Ettie called all the kids and told them that their dad was in the hospital. He had a brain hemorrhage, and the doctor said there was not much hope for him. They had better come soon if they wanted to see him. But God wasn't quite ready for him. In spite of everything, he lived but did have some brain damage. He couldn't walk, and his mind wasn't as good as it was before. When Mama brought him home, Virgil and Lace moved in to help her take care of him.

He would have good days that he knew everything, and other days his personality would change and he would be a completely different person. The doctor said he couldn't help it. It was the pressure and frustration building up, and sooner or later he would have another attack. On days like that, he wasn't the same man or daddy that we had always had. His whole personality would change. It was like he was two different people.

Over a period of several years, he did have another one, and again the doctors said there was no hope for him. But again, Mama brought him home and again it did affect his memory until this time there were days when he didn't recognize his children or his grandchildren, but on his good days his memory would be all right.

A few months later, Tom had a heart attack and went home to be with the Lord. The day of the funeral, Tom's baby daughter slipped off and went to the funeral home. She asked the funeral director if she could go in for a little while just by herself. As she stood at the coffin and looked down at this old white-headed man who had spent his whole life helping others, she told him, "Good-bye, my daddy, and rest in peace."

About that time a man that they had known all their life came in and put his arm around her shoulders. Most everyone who knew Tom called him papa, so she said, "Jim, Papa is gone."

He told her this, and she said she would never forget it, "No, Papa will never be gone. He lives in too many people. All of us boys always knew who to turn to if any of us got in trouble, and he was always there for us. He never bawled us out but would tell us all, as he told me, 'Now, Jim, I don't want you to make a habit of this.' That he expected more than that out of me. He would always tell us, 'Now you have a second chance. Take it and make something better out of yourself.' For some reason, not very many of us ever let him down. We tried to do what he told us to."

I told him, "Jim, I didn't know you had ever been into any kind of trouble."

He said, "No, and no one else did, but Papa. I don't know where I would be today if it hadn't been for Papa."

We both stood there looking down into the coffin at this old man that had meant so much to us. His once auburn hair was now snow white, his face was old and wrinkled from spending so much time out in all the different kinds of weather, and, yes, his hands still showed the evidence of hard work and labor that he had done. Both of us thinking of what this old beloved man had meant to each of us. To Jim, the memories of times he had shared with "his" papa.

"As I said to those who knew and loved Tom, to them he was 'their' papa. I never called him papa. That name was for all of them. But he was more than that to me. He was always, my daddy, my hero, my friend.

"I couldn't help but believe that God looked down and saw this old tired worn-out man and reached down and took one of those old, rough, wrinkled, callused hands in His and said, 'Tom, my boy, I am so proud of you. You have used the talents I gave you well. You fought a good fight and all through the trials and hard times, and there was many, you have kept your faith. Now come, go home with Me to the eternal rest and a home that I have prepared for you in heaven.'"

About the Author

Thelma Inman grew up in Sherman, Texas, to a poor, hardworking family. They were taught to work hard. She started babysitting between nine and ten years old, working from five to midnight, receiving $1.50 a week.

She married Ira Inman in 1942. They were blessed with only two children, even though she wanted a large family. Many in their church call them mom and dad.

The author loves cooking, and in 1996, at the age of seventy-three, her granddaughter asked for copies of all her recipes. She started typing them all in her computer. It turned out to be a six-book set.

She and her husband love gardening and had a beautiful iris yard. They belonged to the Rainbow Iris Society and won quite a few ribbons each year in the shows from the thousands she raised.

Her hobbies are collecting recipes, angels, and has 170 cookie jars.

In 2014, at age ninety, Thelma didn't know why it was important to her to write the stories her dad told her, except she was the last of the five children. Her daughter kept telling her, "Mama, if you don't, who will?" Each time she sat down to the computer, she would pray, "Lord, if this is Your will, help me remember the stories," and each time a story would come to her. She finished her work in 2017.

The author and her husband, ninety-four and ninety-six, live in Sherman in an independent living facility.

CPSIA information can be obtained
at www.ICGtesting.com
Printed in the USA
BVHW070623291221
625049BV00001B/7